Cr
Gary L. M   *....ous book*

The Challenge of Bahá'u'lláh*

'What an amazing book — a book that really presents a challenge to the world, and is an absolute joy to read.'
Bahá'í Review Panel, UK

'Excellent! Should be read by every newly interested person.'
Marzieh Gail

'. . . a great deal of relatively unfamiliar material . . . presented in a readable fashion. The greatest value of the study . . . is the direct way in which it addresses the proof of Bahá'u'lláh's Revelation.'
J. Douglas Martin

'. . . a classic for this time in Bahá'í publishing . . .'
Dr David S. Ruhe

'. . . a marvellous opportunity to deepen and learn about Bahá-'u'lláh . . . reading this book could result in the awakening of a searching soul — the proofs are there.'
Bahá'í Review Panel, UK

*Also available from George Ronald, Publisher.

BY THE SAME AUTHOR

The Challenge of Bahá'u'lláh

He Cometh with Clouds

A Bahá'í View of Christ's Return

by Gary L. Matthews

George Ronald
Oxford

GEORGE RONALD, Publisher
46 High Street, Kidlington, Oxford OX5 2DN

Reprinted 2000

British Library Cataloguing in Publication Data
*A catalogue record for this book is available
from the British Library*

ISBN 0-85398-408-5

Typeset by ComputerCraft, Knoxville, Tennessee, USA
Cover design by Cheri & Gary Matthews
Printed in Great Britain by Redwood Books

Contents

TO MARZIEH GAIL
whose inner light never flickered

Acknowledgements and Notes

Seldom is any book truly the work of just one person. This one builds upon many essential contributions from valued friends and co-workers.

Heading this honour roll is my best friend and best adviser, Cheri Wallace Matthews. Without her active support, able assistance and honest feedback, this book could never have been begun, much less completed. It is fitting that its publication coincides with the tenth anniversary of our marriage.

Nor can words express my gratitude to my chief collaborators, Stephen Vaccaro of Norris, Tennessee, and Rebecca Smith of Lenoir City, Tennessee. These trusted friends have worked with me at every stage: through the initial planning, the research and organization, the composing of a draft manuscript, and seemingly endless stages of rewriting and polishing. Each has met with me for long sessions of brainstorming and problem-solving. Each has spent hours on the telephone. Each has provided line-by-line critiques of the manuscript as it evolved. Thanks to their participation, the book is much more than it might otherwise have been.

Equally pivotal has been the support of the staff at George Ronald, Publisher – particularly Wendi Momen, my editor, and Erica Leith, who manages the central office. Their expertise and shared vision have moved this project forward at a pace I would once have thought impossible.

Many other people have helped in important ways – some by reading the manuscript (or various portions of it), others by providing ideas, information, technical assistance, references or other forms of support. Some of these individuals are Kerry Carlson, John Adler, David Neidig, Steven J.

Wyandt, Michael Kafes, Charlie Jennison, Aniela Costello, Dee Lance, Brenda Beverly, David Ruhe, Margaret Ruhe, Norma Gimlin, Mark Piff, Jack McCants, Dann J. May, Charles Coffey, Kathy Bishop, Daniel Clement, Frankie Coley, Thom Thompson, Steve and Joan Hampton, David Hoffman, Linda Eugenis, Lou Meyer, William S. Hatcher, Vahid Alavian, Sam G. McClellan and Kenneth Kalantar.

Others have helped in ways that were less direct, but no less crucial:

My parents, Felix and Charmian Matthews, instilled in me from my youth a deep love for Christ, along with a conviction that the road to salvation is paved with tough questions that must be squarely faced and honestly answered.

My enthusiasm for study of the Second Coming reflects, in many ways, my admiration for the late Winston G. Evans Jr, the great Bahá'í travelling teacher who dedicated his life to raising public awareness of this issue. Winston's fearless devotion to Christ and the Bible, his warm respect for Christians of every theological leaning, and his commitment to unifying interfaith dialogue all combined to leave a deep impression upon those with whom he spoke. His words and example prompted much of the research detailed in these pages.

The particular idea for this book (and for my previous work, *The Challenge of Bahá'u'lláh*) I owe to a brief but wonderful essay entitled 'Will and Testament', by the late Marzieh Gail (*World Order* magazine, April 1940). It is to her that this volume is gratefully dedicated.

He Cometh with Clouds consists of thirteen chapters, plus a fairly long appendix dealing with questions which, though frequently asked, and though related in various ways to the topic, do not fit neatly within its main organizational structure.

Much of the historical data in Chapters 7 through 12 is adapted from *The Challenge of Bahá'u'lláh* (being updated, where necessary, to take note of recent developments). I have, however, used this material here in a radically different way and analyzed it from a completely different perspective. Whereas the earlier book interprets it in a framework that is primarily scientific and logical, this one takes an approach based explicitly and entirely on Christian scriptural premises. These distinct but complementary world-views, far from contradicting one another, seem here to support identical conclusions. I view this as compelling evidence for an underlying harmony between science and religion.

Bible verses are cited from the King James Version unless otherwise noted. In a few cases (for clarity's sake, or to compare different renderings), I also quote from the New International Version, the New English Bible or the Revised Standard Version. These instances are identified respectively as NIV, NEB or RSV.

Spelling Persian and Arabic names in English, which employs a radically different alphabet, can be confusing. I have tried to adhere strictly to the standardized system of spelling used and recommended by Shoghi Effendi, the Guardian of the Bahá'í Faith. Despite the conventions employed in this system (or perhaps because of them), place-names familiar to Western readers will for the most part remain instantly recognizable: 'Baghdad' becomes 'Baghdád', 'Shiraz' becomes 'Shíráz' and so forth. One minor wrinkle is that the capital of Persia is now generally spelled 'Teheran' or 'Tehran'; in Shoghi Effendi's standard system the name is transliterated as 'Tihrán'. After some hesitation, I opted for consistency by choosing the latter spelling.

The term 'billion' means one thing in American English, another in British English. To avoid this ambiguity, I have at certain points used the expression 'thousand million', which probably will sound awkward to readers from the United States. It was a case of sacrificing familiarity for precision.

Whenever I have felt it necessary to clarify terms used in quotations from other sources, I have used [brackets] to identify my insertions. Unless specified otherwise, however, all instances of *italics* or (parentheses) in quotations are those of the writer being quoted.

Contacting the Author

I want very much to know your reaction to this book. If you have comments or questions, please share them with me. If I do not have answers, I will do my best to find someone who does.

Letters may be addressed to me in care of the publisher, at the following address:

Gary L. Matthews
c/o George Ronald, Publisher
46 High Street
Kidlington, Oxford OX5 2DN
England

I can also be contacted by means of electronic mail: <Gary.L.Matthews@esper.com>.

Foreword

This book is a love letter to all those who love the Lord Christ and who cherish a belief in His Second Coming. As such, it assumes from the outset that its reader shares the author's belief in the divine authority of Christ and the inspiration of the Holy Bible.

My decision to begin from Christian premises is not meant to deter the reader who may, at this point, remain uncommitted to Christ. One of my goals has been to offer fresh and compelling reasons for making that very commitment. The message of this book is for every human being – for people of every religion, and people of no religion.

It is, however, to my Christian co-workers that the main appeal of this book is addressed. That appeal is summarized in the following passage from the Bahá'í sacred writings:

> Followers of the Gospel, behold the gates of heaven are flung open. He that had ascended unto it is now come. Give ear to His voice calling aloud over land and sea, announcing to all mankind the advent of this Revelation – a Revelation through the agency of which the Tongue of Grandeur is now proclaiming: 'Lo, the sacred pledge hath been fulfilled, for He, the Promised One, is come!' (WOB 104).

These majestic words are from the pen of Bahá'u'lláh, the nineteenth-century religious figure known to history as the founder of the Bahá'í Faith. With power and authority, Bahá'u'lláh proclaimed to the Christians of the world that He fulfils the Bible's sacred promises concerning the Return of Christ: 'Jesus, the Spirit of God . . . hath once more, in my person, been made manifest unto you' (G 101). To Pope Pius IX Bahá'u'lláh wrote:

O Pope! Rend the veils asunder. He who is the Lord of Lords is come overshadowed with clouds, and the decree hath been fulfilled by God, the Almighty, the Unrestrained . . . He, verily, hath again come down from Heaven even as He came down from it the first time . . . Beware lest any name debar thee from God . . . (PDC 31).

Many Christians, considering Bahá'u'lláh's claim for the first time, understandably find it difficult to accept that 'the Lord of Lords is come'. This book is an effort to address their concerns. It explores the relationship between Christ and Bahá'u'lláh in light of the Bible's teachings concerning the Second Coming. Bahá'u'lláh has written:

Happy is the man that pondereth in his heart that which hath been revealed in the Books of God, the Help in Peril, the Self-Subsisting. Meditate upon this, O ye beloved of God, and let your ears be attentive unto His Word, so that ye may, by His grace and mercy, drink your fill from the crystal waters of constancy, and become as steadfast and immovable as the mountain in His Cause (G 13).

PART ONE

That We May Open Unto Him

Therefore speak I to them in parables: because they seeing see not; and hearing they hear not, neither do they understand . . . But blessed are your eyes, for they see: and your ears, for they hear (Matt. 13:13-6).

And [be] ye yourselves like unto men that wait for their lord, when he will return from the wedding; that when he cometh and knocketh, they may open unto him immediately.

Blessed are those servants, whom the Lord when he cometh shall find watching . . . (Luke 12:36-7).

1

When He Cometh and Knocketh

Unto them that look for him shall he appear the second
time . . . (Heb. 9:28).

. . . that when he cometh and knocketh, they may open unto
him immediately (Luke 12:36).

No impending event has ever been hailed with keener
anticipation than the Second Coming of Christ. Nearly a
hundred generations of Christians have turned their faces
to the skies, eager to greet the Lord as He descends in power
and glory, seen by every eye. Millions have implored God
to hasten that Day when – as the scriptures foretell – 'the
heavens shall pass away with a great noise, and the elements
shall melt with fervent heat' (II Peter 3:10); the stars will fall
from heaven and the earth will move out of her place; the
dead will rise to stand before God and Christ in final judgement; and the saints will be 'caught up . . . in the clouds'
(I Thess. 4:17) to reign with their Lord over 'new heavens
and a new earth' (II Peter 3:13).

Those of us who take the Bible seriously have kept this
vision alive for twenty centuries, convinced that it represents
the last and only hope for a troubled world. This has naturally evoked scorn from sceptics who say such a scenario is
too far-fetched and fantastic to believe. Yet some of us have
learned, from personal experience as well as from scripture,
that the Almighty routinely performs feats every bit as fantastic as any described above – sometimes even more so. We
know that 'The Lord is not slack concerning his promise'

(II Peter 3:9); that He is both able and determined to fulfil every prophecy in His own good time.

As surely as we know that God is omnipotent and dependable, we also know that He often keeps His Word in surprising and completely unexpected ways. This knowledge comes, once again, both from Bible study and from experience. Who among us has never received an answer to prayer, or seen a scriptural promise materialize, in such a way as to challenge our preconceived notions? God seems to be a master of surprise endings. Often we find this a source of joy, wonder and heightened reverence. At other times, it may test our faith severely, stretching our capacity to believe. Either way, followers of Christ are intimately acquainted with this phenomenon as a normal and necessary part of spiritual growth.

The Bible is bursting at the seams with stories that illustrate this aspect of divine providence. One especially illuminating example is the manner in which Jesus Himself fulfilled the sacred prophecies of the Jewish people. The Old Testament is filled with promises of the Messiah. Many foreshadow the First Coming of Christ in Galilee two thousand years ago. Some anticipate His Second Coming, while others seem to involve both His first and second advents.

Ancient Hebrew scholars, of course, knew nothing of multiple visits by their Promised One. To them, the coming of the Messiah was a single spectacular event – one about which they had very definite ideas. The Jews of Jesus' time were familiar, for example, with Daniel's prophecy of 'one like the Son of Man' coming in 'the clouds of heaven' (Dan. 7:13). They knew from scripture that the Messiah would appear with power and glory as a conquering King, leading the hosts of heaven against armies of darkness. Though they may have differed as to details, there was one thing upon which all agreed: His advent would be impossible to overlook or ignore. On this point they left no room for discussion, no possibility for any alternative interpretation. Did not the Bible itself describe the Messiah's coming in plain terms?

'The glory of the Lord shall be revealed, and all flesh shall see it together' (Isa. 40:5).

When Christ appeared claiming to be the promised Messiah, He did not fit the mental image that scholars had built up from their study of prophecy. Aware of this discrepancy, people wondered how a humble carpenter from Nazareth could say seriously that He was the King of might and glory described in the Holy Book.

Christ might have replied (as do some of His modern followers) that the prophecies of an unmistakably glorious advent pertain not to His First Coming but only to His return at the time of the end. However, He said nothing of the sort. He took a far more radical tack. Despite appearances to the contrary, the prophecies – He taught – had *already been fulfilled!*

Christ and His disciples explained that the spectacular events foreshadowed in the Bible were not events of the distant future; they were events of the recent past. He had already descended from heaven. He had already come with power and great glory. He had already been seen by 'all flesh', and His gospel had already been preached to 'every creature'. Yet these long-awaited events – divine promises all – had occurred in so surprising and unexpected a manner that even those waiting for them had remained oblivious to their occurrence. Taken unawares, they had slept through the greatest event in history!

Here is some of what Christ and His Apostles had to say on this subject:

1) *Christ came down from heaven*: 'I came down from heaven', He says, 'not to do mine own will, but the will of him that sent me' (John 6:38). 'I am the living bread which came down from heaven . . .' (John 6:51). 'And no man hath ascended up to heaven, but he that came down from heaven, even the Son of Man which is in heaven' (John 3:13).

2) *Christ appeared with great power and glory*: 'All power', He says, 'is given unto me in heaven and in earth' (Matt. 28:18). 'We beheld his glory,' writes John, 'the glory as of the only begotten of the Father' (John 1:14). In the Garden of Gethsemane, Christ thanks God for giving Him 'power over all flesh' and prays that His followers be allowed to 'behold My glory, which Thou hast given Me: for Thou lovedst me before the foundation of the world' (John 17:1-2, 24). Taunted by the mob as He was being arrested and taken to trial, He reaffirmed His power: 'Thinkest thou that I cannot now pray to my Father, and he shall presently give me more than twelve legions of angels? But how then shall the scriptures be fulfilled, that thus it must be?' (Matt. 26:53-4).

3) *Christ was seen by, and His gospel was heard by, everyone*: The third chapter of Luke lists Isaiah's well-known prophecy – 'The glory of the Lord shall be revealed, and all flesh shall see it together' (Isa. 40:5) – among those fulfilled by Christ during the time of John the Baptist (Luke 3:4-6).* Paul states in his letter to the Colossians that the gospel of Christ was 'preached to every creature which is under heaven' (Col. 1:23). (We will discuss in a moment Paul's further comments on this puzzling claim and the sense in which he and Luke were entirely correct.)

The scribes and Pharisees hardly knew what to make of these statements. 'Is not this Jesus, the son of Joseph, whose father and mother we know?' they asked. 'How is it then that he saith, I came down from heaven?' (John 6:42). To His claims of 'glory' and 'power' they replied by pressing a crown of thorns upon His head and daring Him to save Himself from the cross. What of Luke's assertion that Christ was seen by 'all flesh'? What of Paul's teaching that His gospel was heard

---

*In the King James Version of the New Testament, Isaiah's words are translated (or perhaps paraphrased) by Luke as 'all flesh shall see the salvation of God'.

by 'every creature'? If their contemporaries deigned to dignify either of these (seemingly preposterous) statements with a reply, the Bible does not record it.

Yet if these listeners were baffled by Christ's claims, what are we ourselves to make of them two thousand years later? In what manner was Christ's coming from heaven with power and glory seen by 'all flesh' and heard by 'every creature'? And how is it that so spectacular an event was nonetheless overlooked by those blessed with the greatest opportunity to benefit from it? Why is it not universally acknowledged even today?

The answer, of course, is that while Christ's advent was spectacular in a spiritual sense (and sometimes in a physical sense as well), it was nothing like what the waiting masses expected. The Bible discloses three reasons for this confusion that led the people of ancient Palestine to reject their Messiah: 1) They confused 'seeing' with recognizing. 2) They insisted on a largely materialistic interpretation of prophecy. 3) They ignored large portions of Bible prophecy while concentrating narrowly on others. Let us look at each of these points.

1) They confused 'seeing' with recognizing.

Having concluded from prophecy that the coming of the Saviour would be visible and audible to everyone, the scribes and Pharisees made a fatal mistake. They took for granted that seeing the Lord in His glory (or hearing of His appearance) would automatically entail accepting Him. The former, they assumed, should include the latter, so that no effort of search would be needed on their part: no asking of questions; no remaining awake and watchful; no struggle to free themselves from possible prejudices or preconceptions they might have absorbed as part of their religious indoctrination.

From this naive assumption (which does not follow from any Bible prophecy), they made a further deduction also unsupported by scripture. They insisted that knowledge and recognition of the Messiah would be forced upon even those who did not want it. They would then be vindicated in the eyes of all the doubters and nay-sayers who had refused to take them seriously. This is a perfectly natural and reassuring feeling.

Christ, however, draws a sharp distinction between seeing and recognizing:

> Therefore speak I to them in parables: because they seeing see not; and hearing they hear not, neither do they understand. And in them is fulfilled the prophecy of Esaias [Isaiah], which saith, By hearing, ye shall hear, and shall not understand; and seeing, ye shall see, and shall not perceive; For this people's heart is waxed gross, and their ears are dull of hearing, and their eyes they have closed; lest at any time they should see with their eyes, and hear with their ears, and should understand with their heart . . . (Matt. 13:13-15).

Yet there remains a deep mystery. Although scripture clearly teaches that the Saviour's advent was seen by 'all flesh' and His Gospel heard by 'every creature', we know that even then there were people living on the opposite side of the earth. How may we explain those in North and South America, Africa, China and other places who never gazed upon His sacred body with outward eyes? For that matter, what of people who lived, relatively speaking, just a few miles down the road in Rome, or in a neighbouring province of Palestine, yet who never heard of Him with their physical ears? Paul acknowledges this paradox in his Epistle to the Romans, where he writes: 'how can they believe in the one of whom they have not heard? . . . But I ask: Did they not hear? Of course they did . . .' Despite every appearance to the contrary, he assures those who preach 'the word of Christ' that 'their voice has gone out into all the earth, their words to the ends of the world' (Rom. 10:14, 18 NIV). How may we reconcile these inspired teachings with the known facts of geography?

The Bahá'í Faith provides an illuminating answer. There are – Bahá'u'lláh, the founder of the Bahá'í Faith, teaches – two kinds of awareness: conscious and unconscious. When Christ appeared, all creatures were at least unconsciously aware of His presence and responded instinctively to His will. Depending on each individual's capacity, such awareness may have been strong or dim; the response may have been positive or negative; but no one remained unaffected. We read in the Bahá'í sacred writings:

> Thou hast written of a verse in the Gospels, asking if at the time of Christ all souls did hear His call. Know that faith is of two kinds. The first is objective faith that is expressed by the outer man, obedience of the limbs and senses. The other faith is subjective, and unconscious obedience to the will of God. There is no doubt that, in the day of . . . Christ, all contingent beings possessed subjective faith and had unconscious obedience to His Holiness Christ.
>
> For all parts of the creational world are of one whole. Christ the Manifestor reflecting the divine Sun represented the whole. All the parts are subordinate and obedient to the whole. The contingent beings are the branches of the tree of life while [Christ] is the root of that tree. The branches, leaves and fruit are dependent for their existence upon the root of the tree of life. This condition of unconscious obedience constitutes subjective faith. But the discerning faith that consists of true knowledge of God and the comprehension of divine words, of such faith there is very little in any age. That is why His Holiness Christ said to His followers, 'Many are called but few are chosen' (BWF 364).

Have we not all, at some time, learned some seemingly new truth, only to feel that we actually 'knew it all along' in some hidden corner of our mind? It is possible to know a thing (to 'see' it, in biblical terms) instinctively and unconsciously, without quite realizing that we have done so.

However we choose to think of this, the Bible's emphatic teaching that Christ was seen by 'all flesh' and heard by 'every creature' clearly implies some non-material concept of sight and hearing. Many other scriptures reinforce this insight. The Apostle John describes Christ as 'the true Light, which lighteth every man that cometh into the world', adding 'we beheld his glory' (John 1:9, 14). This obviously refers not to earthly sunlight, beheld by earthly eyes, but to that infinitely more powerful spiritual life-force He radiated. Christ's appearance on earth brought that Source of celestial light closer to humanity than ever before; it burst upon the relative darkness of the world with unprecedented brilliance and intensity. Although, as the Bible says, 'the darkness comprehended it not' (John 1:5), it is inconceivable that any living thing might fail to experience this divine outpouring on some deep level. How aptly did Jesus quote the words of Isaiah: 'By hearing, ye shall hear, and shall not understand; and seeing ye shall see, and shall not perceive' (Matt. 13:14).

This brings us to the second reason God's chosen people failed to recognize their Messiah:

2) They insisted on a strictly materialistic interpretation of prophecy.

The claims of Christ make sense only for those who read scripture with spiritual eyes and ears. Why? Because the Bible often uses concrete images and physical descriptions to convey spiritual truths – realities which in themselves are invisible and intangible. For example, when Christ said, 'Ye must be born again' (John 3:7), He did not mean – as Nicodemus suggested – that a man must 'enter the second time into his mother's womb' (John 3:4). He meant one must be 'born of the Spirit' rather than 'born of the flesh' (John 3:6). Through accepting Christ as Saviour and inviting Him, in a spirit of repentance, to take charge of one's life, one effectively becomes a new person. This second birth is unforgettably real to anyone who has truly experienced it – yet it is not a physical phenomenon. Likewise, when Christ says, 'I stand at the door, and knock: if any man hear my voice, and open the door, I will come in to him' (Rev. 3:20), He does not mean the door to anyone's house. He is referring to the 'door' of one's heart. God's Word provides thousands of examples of such figurative terminology.

The word 'heaven' also is used in scripture with various meanings, not all of them physical. Sometimes it refers not to the visible sky but to a spiritual condition of closeness to the invisible, omnipresent Creator. Christ's embodied spirit – the 'Word made Flesh' – was in itself the very presence of God on earth. In a very real sense, therefore, He carried heaven around with Him; it was wherever He had been, wherever He was going and wherever He happened to be: 'And no man hath ascended up to heaven, but he that came down from heaven, even the Son of man which is in heaven' (John 3:13). Since His body was born of Mary, and since Jesus was standing on earth when He stated that 'the Son of Man . . . is in heaven', He could only have been describing a spiritual heaven rather than a material one.

The scribes and Pharisees, however, would have none of it. Heaven to them meant the sky, nothing more. 'How is it then', they sneered, 'that he saith, I came down from heaven?' (John 6:42). Their heavenly Messiah was – according to the explicit text of the Bible – to be a king of power and glory; and to them the word 'king' meant a worldly king, nothing more. Christ's explanation that 'my kingdom is not of this world' (John 18:36) did not sit well with them. Power to them meant physical strength, nothing more. It meant power to slaughter enemies in battle, power to topple governments, power to annex neighbouring city-states, power to impose taxation. They could not accept the notion that a spiritual king wielding 'victorious power' (Luke 1:69 NEB) might use that power not for physical mayhem but to forgive sins and save souls. Glory to them meant material splendour, nothing more. It meant royal robes, a jewel-studded crown, ostentatious palaces, the first-century equivalent of ticker-tape parades, an army of slaves to do one's bidding – in short, it meant all the things Christ did not have and did not want. They could not understand that (as Paul was to write) 'the glory of the celestial is one, and the glory of the terrestrial is another' (I Cor. 15:40).

For despite its moral fervour and its devotion to holy scripture, the society in which Christ appeared was materialistic to its core. 'For where your treasure is, there will your heart be also' (Matt. 6:21), He warned its members. 'If I have told you earthly things, and ye believe not, how shall ye believe, if I tell you of heavenly things?' (John 3:12). Their fervent insistence on a material king, endowed by a material heaven with material power and material glory, demonstrated their heart-felt preference for fleeting earthly treasure over the eternal treasures of the spirit. One tragic result of such attachment to the material world (with its consequent insistence on material fulfilment of spiritual prophecy) is that its victims become largely deaf to the heavenly language of divine revelation. 'Why do you not understand my language?' asks Christ. 'It is because my revelation is beyond your grasp' (John 8:43 NEB). 'He who is from the earth belongs to the earth and uses earthly speech' (John 3:31 NEB). The Apostle Paul contrasts this 'earthly speech' with the specialized, figurative vocabulary of God's Word:

> . . . we speak of God's secret wisdom, a wisdom that has been hidden and that God destined for our glory before time began. None of the rulers of this age understood it, for if they had, they would not have crucified the Lord of glory . . .
> This is what we speak, not in words taught us by human wisdom but in words taught by the Spirit, expressing spiritual truths in spiritual words. The man without the spirit does not accept the things that come from the Spirit of God, for they are foolishness to him, and he cannot understand them, because they are spiritually discerned (I Cor. 2:7-8, 13-14 NIV).

However, the Old Testament contains many prophecies which, even if understood in a purely physical sense using

12

'earthly speech', could have alerted students of scripture to the possibility that they had painted a misleading picture of their coming Messiah. Why did they fail to benefit from these predictions? Because at this point they fell into a third trap:

3) They ignored large portions of Bible prophecy while concentrating narrowly on others.

Christian scholars have documented hundreds of Old Testament references to the first advent of Christ. These prophecies foreshadow many details of His earthly life and mission with uncanny accuracy. The fifth chapter of Micah identifies Bethlehem as the birthplace of the future 'ruler in Israel; whose goings forth have been from of old, from everlasting' (Micah 5:2). The ninth chapter of Daniel anticipates the time and duration of His mission, along with the fact that 'Messiah the Prince' would be 'cut off, but not for himself' (Dan. 9:24-7). (We will examine some of Daniel's time prophecies in Chapter 4.) Other scriptures depict the manner in which soldiers would gamble for His clothing at the crucifixion (Psalms 22:18), then pierce His side (Zech. 12:10) but decide at the last moment not to break His legs (Psalms 34:20). Isaiah foretells His suffering as one 'despised and rejected of men, a man of sorrows, and acquainted with grief . . . wounded for our transgressions . . . brought as a lamb to the slaughter . . . taken from prison and from judgement . . . cut off out of the land of the living; for the transgression of my people . . .' and the manner in which He would make 'his grave with the wicked' (Isa. 53:3-9).

Taken all together and in context, these and many other scriptures illustrate how the Old Testament describes the Messiah's mission from two radically different prophetic perspectives. On the one hand, He was to be a conquering 'Prince' and 'ruler' occupying a heavenly throne. On the other, He was to be – at the same time – a humble Servant suffering dire persecution under humiliating circumstances. Now if we assume (as did the scholars of Christ's time) that such prophetic terms as 'king', 'heaven', 'power', 'glory', 'seeing' and the like must be defined in their everyday, strictly physical senses, then we cannot reconcile these contrasting visions. Since we have two seemingly opposed sets of prophecies, we must – to be consistent – recognize that at least one set is using physical imagery to teach non-physical spiritual truths.

God, however, does not force us to be consistent. If we dislike the conclusion, we can simply ignore whichever prophecies happen to contradict our preconceived ideas. To anyone seeking earthly glory – to anyone who, as Christ expressed it, 'belongs to the earth and uses earthly speech' – this alternative will be powerfully tempting. Christ's countrymen wished for a Messiah whose military prowess would liberate them from the physical yoke of bondage to Rome. Many prophecies could be quoted out of context in such a way that, when misconstrued as 'earthly speech', they seemed to endorse this wish. The Israelites therefore focused all their attention upon only those scriptures that appealed to their love of physical drama and glamour. In so doing, they overlooked or ignored the much larger panorama of prophecy that could have balanced their outlook.

The Bible itself cautions us against this error of selective vision – against picking and choosing a few passages that seem at first glance to support our personal preferences, while tuning out the rest. Isaiah explains that in order to 'understand doctrine' one must study God's Word 'precept upon precept; line upon line', finding the truth 'here a little, and there a little' (Isa. 28:9-10). Only by reading the Bible as a whole, and considering everything it tells us on a given subject, can we see the big picture. Otherwise, the reality is likely to remain hidden from us: 'It is the glory of God to conceal a thing: but the honour of kings is to search out a matter' (Prov. 25:2).

Let us return to our theme: God's history of keeping His word in ways that defy conventional expectations. The first advent of Christ is far from the only biblical example. Among many others, there is the second coming of Elijah.

First-century Jews, as we noted earlier, interpreted all messianic prophecy as referring to a single advent; hence they knew nothing of the Second Coming of Christ. However, they were quite familiar with the idea of a second coming, for they were themselves anticipating the return or second advent of the Old Testament prophet Elijah. According to scripture, the reappearance of Elijah would precede and herald the mission of the Messiah: 'Behold, I will send you Elijah the prophet before the coming of the great and dreadful day of the Lord: And he shall turn the heart of the fathers to the children . . .' (Mal. 4:5-6). Interpreting the prophecies in the customary (i.e. materialistic) manner, the sages concluded that Elijah's second coming entailed his physical descent from the physical sky, with physical power and physical glory, seen by physical eyes.

When John the Baptist began preaching in the wilderness, claiming to be the Messiah's herald, it was natural to wonder whether this meant he was claiming to be Elijah. 'Art thou Elias [Elijah]?' the people asked him. 'And he saith, I am not. Art thou that prophet? And he answered, No' (John 1:21). The prophecy of Elijah's prior return was seized by enemies of Jesus in their efforts to prove He could not be the Messiah. This disturbed the disciples, who turned to their Master:

> And his disciples asked him, saying, Why then say the scribes that [Elijah] must first come? And Jesus answered and said unto them, [Elijah] truly shall first come, and restore all things. But I say unto you, That [Elijah] is come already, and they knew him not, but have done unto him whatsoever they listed. Likewise shall also the Son of man suffer of them. Then the disciples understood that he spake unto them of John the Baptist (Matt. 17:10-13).

What is happening here? John the Baptist states plainly that he is not Elijah; Christ says that he is. Are they contradicting each other? Surely not, for both were inspired of God, and God does not contradict Himself. What John meant was that he was not Elijah in the materialistic sense intended by his questioners. He was not Elijah in the flesh; he was, rather, a new individual with a new human identity and a new name. What Christ meant was that John the Baptist was a new embodiment of the power and authority wielded by the original Elijah. This 'second coming' was the return not of Elijah's human persona but of his true spiritual identity – the divine qualities that made him who and what he was. These prophetic attributes which constituted the 'real' Elijah were once again manifest in John the Baptist. That this was Christ's intended meaning is shown by the prophecy re-corded in Luke, spoken by an angel at the time of John's birth: '. . . he shall go before him in the spirit and power of [Elijah], to turn the hearts of the fathers to the children . . .' (Luke 1:17).

Once again God's promise was fulfilled to the letter – but not in the obvious physical manner wished for by the masses and their leaders. The prophecies had been delivered by God in that special 'language of revelation' to which Christ referred when He exclaimed: 'Why do you not understand my language? It is because my revelation is beyond your grasp' (John 8:43 NEB). This spiritual terminology makes divine prophecy incomprehensible to the 'natural man' who 'belongs to the earth and uses earthly speech' – he who, as Paul says, 'receiveth not the things of the Spirit of God, for they are foolishness unto him; neither can he know them, because they are spiritually discerned' (I Cor. 2:14).

A further prophecy linked in scripture to the coming of Elijah and Christ is that of Isaiah: 'Every valley shall be exalted, and every mountain and hill shall be made low; and the crooked shall be made straight, and the rough places plain' (Isa. 40:4). The third chapter of Luke's Gospel lists this among prophecies fulfilled in the days of John the

Baptist and Jesus. Construed as 'earthly speech', this fulfilment would mean that the visible landscape of Palestine (and
perhaps the entire planet) was physically levelled or
smoothed out, as by a divine steamroller. Yet visitors to the
Holy Land consistently find that its terrain remains as craggy
and uneven as ever. Does this mean God lied? Certainly not.
It means that the inward truth of the prophecy, as intended
by its divine revealer, concerned events of the invisible
spiritual plane – not those of the material earth. To the best
of my knowledge, this prophecy was never explicitly interpreted by the inspired writers of the New Testament, so I
cannot state with authority what it does mean. My personal
understanding is that it illustrates the levelling influence of
Christ's teaching: '. . . he that is greatest among you shall be
your servant. And whosoever shall exalt himself shall be
abased; and he that shall humble himself shall be exalted'
(Matt. 23:11-12). In other words, the 'world of humanity' has
its hills and valleys representing various high and low classes
– kings and servants, peasants and aristocrats – all of whom
are placed on an equal footing as brothers and sisters in
Christ.

There may well be other, equally reasonable or better
ways to explain this prophecy. This does not matter. The
point remains that the divine promise, whatever its meaning,
was indeed fulfilled – not in any crude outward sense recognizable to one who 'belongs to the earth and uses earthly
speech' but figuratively as a truth whose inspired inner
meaning is 'spiritually discerned'.

The Divine Design

How can we apply these lessons of history to our own understanding of Christ's Second Coming? Let us look into this
topic with new eyes, striving in the process 1) to recall the
biblical distinction between seeing and recognizing, 2) to set
aside the materialistic outlook of those who '[belong] to the
earth and [use] earthly speech' and 3) to judge individual
prophecies in light of the entire Bible.

While the Old Testament never explicitly spelled out the distinction between the First and Second Comings, it made many prophecies about the Messiah. Among these were that He would come 'with the clouds of heaven' (Dan. 7:13); that He would appear with great power and great glory; and that His glory and salvation would be seen by 'all flesh'. When Christ appeared in Palestine two thousand years ago, He and His Apostles announced that He had already fulfilled these divine predictions. They then made certain well-known prophecies regarding His Return in the last days:

> . . . then shall all the tribes of the earth mourn, and they shall see the Son of man coming in the clouds of heaven with power and great glory (Matt. 24:30).

> . . . this same Jesus, which is taken up from you into heaven, shall so come in like manner as ye have seen him go into heaven (Acts 1:11).

> . . . the Lord Himself shall descend from heaven with a shout, with the voice of the archangel, and with the trump of God . . . (I Thess. 4:16).

> Behold, he cometh with clouds, and every eye shall see him . . . (Rev. 1:7).

One startling thing about these and similar prophecies is that they repeat, almost word for word, the images and concepts of the Old Testament promises that Christ indicated He had already kept. He had already descended from heaven; He would again descend from heaven. He had already appeared with power and great glory; He would again appear with power and great glory. He had already been seen by 'all flesh' and heard by 'every creature'; He would in the future be seen by 'every eye'. We can represent the situation clearly with a simple table:

PROPHECIES ABOUT CHRIST:	
already fulfilled **in His First Coming**	*to be fulfilled* **in His Second Coming**
to come from heaven	to come from heaven
with power and glory	with power and glory
seen by 'all flesh' and heard by 'every creature'	seen by 'every eye'

What we see is that the divine promises to be kept by Christ in His second advent are identical to those He already fulfilled in the first. Is this design – this striking pattern of prophetic parallels – a meaningless coincidence? Or is God telling us something?

Christian scholars have traditionally interpreted the prophecies in one of two ways. Some read them in largely material terms as pointing to an outwardly miraculous public spectacle. Others find a purely symbolic spiritual meaning, such as the daily renewal of Christ's love in the heart of the believer. These traditional views represent opposite ends of the material/spiritual spectrum. However, the comparison described above suggests a third approach – a middle-of-the-road interpretation that combines the best elements of both the other two. Why not interpret the images of Christ's Second Coming in the same way He Himself interprets both a) the identical images of His First Coming and b) the second coming of Elijah? Could the Return not mean that Christ's spirit (rather than His physical body) is to once again 'descend' from the heaven of God's invisible presence, to 'dwell among us' as the 'Word made Flesh' in an outwardly new human temple? Cannot the 'glory' and 'power' of His advent be taken to mean the same spiritual glory and power with which He was invested in His first mission? Cannot being seen by 'every eye' refer to the same condition of unconscious dependence and obedience with which 'every creature' greeted Him two thousand years ago?

Bahá'ís believe this is indeed the intended meaning of the prophecies – that Christ in His Return will walk the earth as a man among men, 'seen' by all, yet consciously recognized at first only by a few. Which few? Those willing to free their hearts of prejudice and their minds of preconceived ideas. Such a view obviously clashes with traditional Christian theology (just as the truth of Christ's first appearance clashed with traditional Jewish theology). This fact, however, is simply one more parallel and not a valid argument against the Bahá'í position.

Before leaping to any conclusions, one way or another, let us continue our review of the biblical evidence.

Bible students considering this approach for the first time may well ask: What about the many other dramatic signs which the Bible associates with the coming of Christ? Does not the Bible say that the dead will be raised and that we all will stand before God in judgement? Does it not promise that Christ's followers will be caught up in the air with Him, that stars will fall from heaven, that the earth will 'reel to and fro like a drunkard' (Isa. 24:20), and so forth? Since these describe physical events, does it not make sense to assume that Christ's coming is likewise a physical event?

Perhaps – but do we know that these prophecies really describe physical events? Many Christian scholars have pointed out that such vivid images can easily be regarded as depicting inward truths rather than material phenomena. Consider, for example, the prediction that in the last days the earth will reel to and fro like a drunkard. As we have already seen, the Bible foretold that at the Messiah's first advent the earth would be levelled. The fact that this never happened in any purely physical sense suggests that the 'earth' in question is the world of humanity and that the levelling intended by the prophecy was the equalizing influence of Christian fellowship. Now if the 'earth' of the latter-day prophecy also means humanity, can we not truthfully say that this collective world of humanity is today reeling drunkenly in a spiritual stupor? And is this insight not of greater importance than any purely geophysical wobbling of the planet?

The crucial point is that we cannot justify a material interpretation of Christ's return simply by insisting on a material interpretation of some related prophecy. We could just as logically argue the reverse, that since the return is a spiritual reality the related prophecies must involve spiritual realities as well. In either case, however, we would be arguing in a circle by presupposing what we are trying to prove. The only valid approach is to turn to the Bible itself for further light on this question.

The Sealing of the Books

What the Bible explicitly says is that the end-time prophecies have hidden, coded meanings that are 'sealed' and 'closed up' until the time of the end. Only then, when their meaning is unsealed by Christ Himself, will either the masses or their spiritual leaders be able to understand the prophecies. After Daniel's preview of the Second Coming – a preview spanning the Great Tribulation, the raising of the dead, the final judgement and Daniel's vision of 'one like the Son of man [coming] with the clouds of heaven' – the prophet is told: 'But thou, O Daniel, shut up the words, and seal the book, even to the time of the end . . .' (Dan. 12:4). Daniel, upset by the fact that he 'understood not' the prophecies, persists in asking, 'O my Lord, what shall be the end of these things?' (Dan. 12:8). God replies:

> Go thy way, Daniel: for the words are closed up and sealed till the time of the end. Many shall be purified, and made white, and tried; but the wicked shall do wickedly: and none of the wicked shall understand, but the wise shall understand (Dan. 12:9-10).

Although the prophecies themselves are sealed, the meaning of 'sealing' is clear. Isaiah elaborates:

> For the Lord hath poured out upon you the spirit of deep sleep, and hath closed your eyes; the prophets and your rulers, the seers hath he covered.
>
> And the vision of all has become unto you like the words of a book that is sealed, which men deliver to one that is learned, saying, Read this, I pray thee; and he saith, I cannot; for it is sealed.
>
> And the book is delivered to him who is not learned, saying, Read this, I pray thee; and he saith, I am not learned (Isa. 29:10-12).

Isaiah adds that 'the wisdom of their wise men shall perish, and the understanding of their prudent men shall be hid' (Isa. 29:14). Like Daniel, he indicates that this lack of understanding will persist until the time of the end: 'And in that day shall the deaf hear the words of the book, and the eyes of the blind shall see out of obscurity, and out of darkness . . . and the poor among men shall rejoice in the Holy One of Israel' (Isa. 29:18-19).

The book of Revelation reiterates that no man will be 'found worthy to open and to read the book, neither to look thereon' until the day of Christ's return, when He – 'the Lion of the tribe of Judah, the Root of David' – will prevail to 'open the book, and to loose the seven seals thereof' (Rev. 5:4-5).

Since (as the Bible states) the prophecies surrounding Christ's return are not to be generally understood until after they are fulfilled, their traditional interpretation cannot possibly be correct. The most widely accepted view is based on the materialistic, everyday language of 'earthly speech' in which 'heaven' is presumed to mean the physical sky, 'grave' the physical earth and so forth. The very popularity of this interpretation demonstrates that it is not the 'closed' or 'sealed' meaning which 'the wise will understand' only in the last days.

But is there any independent scriptural evidence that the Second Coming of Christ will occur in an unexpected manner, perhaps to be overlooked at the outset by the masses of humanity? Indeed there is. The Bible emphatically declares that Christ will come 1) with a *new name*, 2) like a *thief* 3) for whom we must *watch* so 'that when he cometh and knocketh, [we] may open unto him immediately' (Luke 12:36). These 'surprise ending' prophecies are at least as numerous and insistent in the Bible as any which can be construed as suggesting a physically spectacular public arrival. Unlike the ones employing dramatic imagery, they typically are followed by such admonitions as, 'He that hath an ear, let him hear'. (This biblical emphasis is completely reversed in popular religious literature and discourse.) Here are some highlights:

The New Name

The book of Revelation makes this prophecy for the Messiah of the Second Coming:

> And I saw heaven opened, and behold a white horse; and he that sat upon him was called Faithful and True, and in righteousness he doth judge and make war. His eyes were as a flame of fire, and on his head were many crowns; and he had a name written, that no man knew, but he himself.
> And he was clothed with a vesture dipped in blood: and his name is called The Word of God (Rev. 19:11-13).

We learn from the opening verse of the Gospel of John that 'The Word of God' is a designation for the pre-existent Christ who existed 'in the beginning with God'. However, the very fact that this designation is well-known and widely used shows that it cannot be the secret name to which the previous verse alludes – the 'name written, that no man knew, but he himself'.

Just as the name of Christ is applied to His followers by the designation 'Christian', so will the Messiah's new name be applied to His latter-day followers:

Him that overcometh will I make a pillar in the temple of my God, and he shall go no more out: and I will write upon him the name of my God, and the name of the city of my God, which is new Jerusalem, which cometh down out of heaven from my God: and I will write upon him my new name (Rev. 3:12).

This name received by His adherents, like the new name of the returned Christ, will not be publicly known:

To him that overcometh will I give to eat of the hidden manna, and will give him a white stone, and in the stone a new name written, which no man knoweth saving he that receiveth it (Rev. 2:17).

Both of these latter references are accompanied by the injunction, 'He that hath an ear, let him hear'. Both also emphasize that in order to receive the new name, one must struggle to overcome obstacles. We may well ask ourselves: What obstacle requires more 'overcoming' than the prejudice we typically feel towards any new and unfamiliar name?

Watching for a Thief

Christ frequently likens His Second Coming to the visit of a thief in the night, cautioning us to remain vigilant and awake:

Watch therefore: for ye know not what hour your Lord doth come. But know this, that if the goodman of the house had known in what watch the thief would come, he would have watched, and would not have suffered his house to be broken up.

Therefore be ye also ready: for in such an hour as ye think not the Son of man cometh . . . The lord of that servant shall come in a day when he looketh not for him, and in an hour that he is not aware of (Matt. 24:42-4, 50).

The Apostle Paul says to the Thessalonians:

> For yourselves know perfectly that the day of the Lord so cometh as a thief in the night. For when they shall say, Peace and safety; then sudden destruction cometh upon them, as travail upon a woman with child; and they shall not escape. But ye, brethren, are not in darkness, that that day should overtake you as a thief (I Thess. 5:2-4).

St Peter echoes the same theme:

> But the day of the Lord will come as a thief in the night; in the which the heavens shall pass away with a great noise, and the elements shall melt with fervent heat, the earth also and the works that are therein shall be burned up . . . Nevertheless we, according to his promise, look for new heavens and a new earth, wherein dwelleth righteousness (II Peter 3:10, 13).

The thief-like Return is also a theme of the Book of Revelation: 'If therefore thou shalt not watch, I will come on thee as a thief, and thou shalt not know what hour I will come upon thee' (Rev. 3:3). 'Behold, I come as a thief. Blessed is he that watcheth, and keepeth his garments, lest he walk naked, and they see his shame' (Rev. 16:15).

We normally think of a thief as someone who comes secretly, stealthily, without fanfare. Of course, if that is what the expression means in this context, it is plainly irreconcilable with the notion that the Advent will be impossible to overlook. For this reason, many Christians argue that in this context the expression merely means Christ will come suddenly and unexpectedly. Well, a thief does strike in a sudden and unexpected manner – but to what purpose? He does so in order to come and go without being detected.

Besides, why should Christ instruct His followers to watch carefully for an event no one could possibly miss? This command to watch, so sternly and often repeated, underscores the obvious message of the thief metaphor: A thief's

25

entry goes unnoticed unless the householder remains awake and alert. Thus if we insist that 'thief' does not carry its usual connotation in these passages, we must take the next logical step and argue that 'watch' does not carry *its* usual connotation either.

There are many who do just that, saying that in this case the injunction to watch means simply 'Be prepared!' Yet prepared for what? For a Second Coming so intrusive that all will be compelled to recognize it instantly? If so, how may we explain this further warning from the Gospel of Luke:

> Let your loins be girded about, and your lights burning; And ye yourselves like unto men that wait for their lord, when he will return from the wedding; *that when he cometh and knocketh, they may open unto him immediately.*
>
> Blessed are those servants, whom the lord when he cometh shall find watching: verily I say unto you, that he shall gird himself, and make them to sit down to meat, and will come forth and serve them . . . Be ye therefore ready also: for the Son of man cometh at an hour when ye think not (Luke 12:35-40; emphasis added).

The imagery in this passage is identical to that of Revelation 3:20: 'I stand at the door and knock; if any man hear my voice, and open the door, I will come in to him, and will sup with him, and he with me.' Christians understand the latter verse as a reference to Christ's spiritual encounter with the unbeliever, who, having heard the gospel, must decide whether to invite the Saviour into his heart. Here, in Luke, Christ states plainly that His own followers will be in this same position at the time of His Return: We must keep our 'lights burning' so that 'when he cometh and knocketh, [we] may open unto him immediately'. If we choose to 'open unto him' (and the wording clearly implies choice), then and only then will He 'make [us] to sit down to meat, and will come forth and serve [us]'.

Apocalypse Now

The message of the Bahá'í Faith to the Christian world is urgent: 'the Lord of Lords is come overshadowed with clouds . . . [Christ] hath again come down from Heaven even as He came down from it the first time' (PDC 31). We are living in the very Day of God, the Day of Judgement, the Day of Christ's return. Having come as promised (like a 'thief' with a 'new name'), Christ once again is knocking at the doors of our hearts, calling us to 'open unto him immediately'.

Bahá'ís believe the new name of Christ is *Bahá'u'lláh* (pronounced 'bah-HAH-o-LAH'). They find abundant evidence to support this claim – evidence open to anyone who studies Bahá'u'lláh's life and teachings in light of the Bible. In Bahá'u'lláh, according to this view, we can discover the fulfilment of every Bible prophecy concerning the Second Coming and the Messiah of the latter days.

If this name seems strange at first, remember that the name 'Jesus' sounded equally strange to the Greeks and Romans of two thousand years ago. Bahá'u'lláh's name is an Arabic title meaning 'the Glory of God'. Like the name 'Jesus Christ', it is infinitely precious and beautiful and sacred to Bahá'ís. The name 'Bahá'í' itself signifies a follower of Bahá'u'lláh (just as the name 'Christian' signifies a follower of Christ). Bahá'ís regard this as the new name that the book of Revelation promises to those who overcome obstacles to follow Christ in the time of His return: 'Him that overcometh . . . I will write upon him my new name' (Rev. 3:12). A Bahá'í is any person who recognizes Bahá'u'lláh as the latter-day return of Christ's inner reality – the 'Word made Flesh' with a new name.

Bahá'u'lláh was born in 1817 in the biblical kingdom of Persia (known today as Iran). For His claims and His teachings He was banished from His homeland by the clergy and government of His own people. Throughout forty years of persecution, Bahá'u'lláh revealed the Word of God for this age of fulfilment, demonstrating at all times the same spiritual power and glory characteristic of Jesus. He left this world in 1892, returning to the invisible heaven from which He came. His sacred remains are enshrined across the Bay of Haifa from Mount Carmel, at 'Akká, now in the state of Israel, where He spent the last years of His earthly life.

Bahá'u'lláh writes:

> The Word which the Son concealed is made manifest. It hath been sent down in the form of the human temple in this day. Blessed be the Lord Who is the Father! He, verily, is come unto the nations in His most great majesty. Turn your faces towards Him, O concourse of the righteous! (PDC 32).

Although His name is new, as Christ promised it would be, Bahá'u'lláh is not a 'new Christ', or a 'substitute Christ' or a 'replacement Christ'. There is only one Christ, and He is 'the same yesterday, and to day, and for ever' (Heb. 13:8). Bahá'u'lláh is simply a new manifestation of the same spiritual Christ who said, 'Before Abraham was, I am' (John 8:58); who existed 'in the beginning with God' (John 1:2), and 'whose goings forth have been from of old, from everlasting' (Micah 5:2).

This being so, one does not 'give up' Christ in becoming a follower of Bahá'u'lláh. Far from it. A Bahá'í is someone who recognizes Christ in His Second Coming, obeying His command to 'open unto him' when He 'cometh and knocketh'. Bahá'ís view this as the meaning of the Day of Judgement – the biblical designation for this time of decision now facing every human being. Those who humbly seek the truth, free of pride and materialism, will recognize in Bahá'u'lláh the same divine Reality which descended from heaven two thousand years ago. Others will reject and oppose Him. Each soul is tested by the divine call, and every social institution is measured by the divine standard. We do, in effect, judge ourselves by our response to His message. (Chapter 4 will explore in more detail the Bahá'í understanding of 'judgement' in prophecy.)

Finally, let us note that Bahá'u'lláh asks no one to follow Him blindly. He asks only that we obey the Bible's injunction to 'test the spirits . . . whether they are of God' (I John 4:1, NIV, NEB), and to 'prove all things; hold fast that which is good' (I Thess. 5:21). Although Christ warned against false prophets, He gave the standard by which the true is distinguished from the false: 'By their fruits shall ye know them' (Matt. 7:20). Taking this as our standard, let us weigh Bahá'u'lláh's claim in the balance of the Bible.

Bahá'u'lláh sums up the situation in His appeal to Christians everywhere:

> O followers of the Son! Have ye shut out yourselves from Me by reason of My name? Wherefore ponder ye not in your hearts? Day and night ye have been calling upon your Lord, the Omnipotent, but when He came from the heaven of eternity in His great glory, ye turned aside from Him and remained sunk in heedlessness . . . We, verily, have come for your sakes, and have borne the misfortunes of the world for the sake of your salvation. Flee ye the One Who hath sacrificed His life that ye may be quickened? . . . He is come in the sheltering shadow of Testimony, invested with conclusive proof and evidence, and those who truly believe in Him regard His presence as the embodiment of the Kingdom of God. Blessed is the man who turneth towards Him, and woe betide such as deny or doubt Him (TB 9-12).

2

The Sword of the Spirit

For as the rain cometh down, and the snow from heaven, and returneth not thither, but watereth the earth, and maketh it bring forth and bud, that it may give seed to the sower, and bread to the eater; So shall my word be that goeth forth out of my mouth: it shall not return unto me void, but it shall accomplish that which I please, and it shall prosper in the thing whereto I sent it (Isa. 55:10-11).

And take the helmet of salvation, and the sword of the Spirit, which is the word of God (Eph. 6:17).

Before consenting to examine scriptural evidence for Bahá-'u'lláh, most Christians rightly insist on knowing two things: What is the Bahá'í attitude towards the Bible? and what is the Bahá'í attitude towards Christ? These are fair questions that deserve straight answers.

The preceding chapter makes clear my own belief in the divinity of Christ as the Son of God and in the inspiration of the Bible as the Word of God. These convictions are not merely mine but those of the entire worldwide Bahá'í community, for they are truths central to the writings of Bahá-'u'lláh Himself. Here is an authoritative summary of the Bahá'í view:

> As to the position of Christianity, let it be stated without any hesitation or equivocation that its divine origin is uncondi-tionally acknowledged, that the Sonship and Divinity of Christ are fearlessly asserted, that the divine inspiration of the Gospel is fully recognized . . . Such are the central, the

solid, the incontrovertible principles that constitute the bedrock of Bahá'í belief which the Faith of Bahá'u'lláh is proud to acknowledge, which its teachers proclaim, which its apologists defend, which its literature disseminates, which its summer schools expound, and which the rank and file of its followers attest by both word and deed (PDC 109-10).

While the Bahá'í Faith upholds the truth of the Bible as revealed scripture, it does not *necessarily* endorse any particular Bible interpretation advanced by theologians or church authorities. Nor, of course, does it automatically reject such interpretations. On many points of doctrine (such as the miracle of the virgin birth), Bahá'u'lláh's teachings are in complete accord with the most orthodox Christian creeds. But other Bahá'í views of the Bible may at first seem, to many people, new and surprising. Perhaps the most obvious example in this latter category is Bahá'u'lláh's claim to be the return of Christ, and the Bahá'í belief that the Bible supports His claim. Before presenting scriptural evidence for this view, I would like to outline my personal understanding of the common foundations of Christian and Bahá'í belief. Such an overview will span two chapters: this one, which affirms the authority of the Bible, and the next, which testifies to the Lordship of Christ.

Bahá'ís believe that God, having created man in His spiritual 'image and likeness', taught us His will through a succession of 'holy men' who 'spake as they were moved by the Holy Ghost' (II Peter 1:21). It is through this process of inspiration that the Bible came into being, even though it was revealed in stages, and through various writers, across a span of centuries. The divine authority of the Bible is therefore central to Bahá'í belief. Bahá'u'lláh writes that the books associated with Moses and Jesus are 'none other than the Word of God which is revealed in every age and dispensation' (KI 199). His teachings contain, among many others, these ringing endorsements: 'You must know the Old and the New Testaments as the Word of God' (PUP 201). 'Look at the Gospel of the Lord Christ and see how glorious it is!' (PT 48). A well-loved, widely quoted passage from Bahá'í scripture is this glowing tribute to the Bible:

> This book is the Holy Book of God, of celestial Inspiration. It is the Bible of Salvation, the noble Gospel. It is the mystery of the Kingdom and its light. It is the Divine Bounty, the sign of the guidance of God (AB 145).

Bahá'ís – like most Christians – regard the Bible's inspiration as a characteristic of the original words revealed by God, and not of any human transcript, translation or opinion based upon those words. This raises a question that has troubled many people (including some very staunch Christians). Even the most ancient available manuscripts of the Bible are handwritten copies, not the original documents. Can we be sure these copies faithfully convey the spiritual message of the originals? Bahá'u'lláh assures us that we can. In His native Persia, it was widely believed that the Bible had become 'corrupted' through alterations introduced by transcribers down through the centuries. Bahá'u'lláh denounces this belief as 'utter falsehood and sheer calumny', adding: 'Can a man who believeth in a book, and deemeth it to be inspired by God, mutilate it?' (KI 88, 86). With regard to Christian scripture, He writes:

> We have also heard a number of the foolish of the earth assert that the genuine text of the heavenly Gospel doth not exist amongst the Christians, that it hath ascended unto heaven. How grievously they have erred! How oblivious of the fact that such a statement imputeth the gravest injustice and tyranny to a gracious and loving Providence! How could God, when once the Day-star of the beauty of Jesus had disappeared from the sight of his people . . . cause His holy Book, His most great testimony amongst His creatures, to disappear also? (KI 89).

The knowledge that God has inspired the Bible, then guarded it against corruption, in no way lessens the need for scholarly research into its oldest and most reliable manuscripts. Nor does it guarantee that we will instantly understand the Bible's teaching on any particular topic. Bahá'ís believe that many incorrect ideas have crept into popular notions about scripture, to such an extent that these are mistakenly thought to be based on the sacred text itself. One goal of Bahá'í scholarship is to distinguish between such purely human notions and the actual intent of the Bible, 'rightly dividing the word of truth', as Paul expresses it (II Tim. 2:15). All believers in scripture are invited to join this quest through frank and loving consultation.

Literal or Symbolic?

Students of scripture are often asked: 'Do you interpret the Bible literally or symbolically?' In discussing this emotionally charged issue, it is important that we define our terms precisely and in some detail. Many people speak of scriptures as being 'literal' or 'symbolic' without realizing how differently others may interpret and react to the same words. Heated arguments sometimes result between Bible students who believe exactly (or almost exactly) the same things. Even where real differences exist, these can appear so magnified by semantic confusion that we overlook vast areas of common ground. With these words of caution, let me try to answer the question.

For many readers, 'taking the Bible literally' means taking it seriously as the Word of God – a living God whose intended meaning, in all that He reveals, is true. This orientation (whatever we choose to call it) is in complete harmony with Bahá'í teachings. While Bahá'ís may not endorse every specific church doctrine attributed to the Bible by its commentators, they share with traditional Christians an attitude of deep reverence for the scripture itself and bow to its divine authority. In this sense, Bahá'ís take the Bible very literally indeed.

34

Some believers describe their Bible interpretation as 'literal' to express their conviction that scripture says what it means and means what it says. Again, this is a position Bahá'ís embrace wholeheartedly, subject only to one condition: As the Bible itself teaches, we must consider all relevant passages, in context and in their entirety, to determine what the Bible actually does say on any given subject. Of course, most Christian literalists emphasize and insist upon this same condition. I would therefore say that in this sense, too, Bahá'ís take the Bible literally.

On the other hand, Bahá'ís do not believe we can discern God's intended meaning by interpreting everything He says in the physical language of the five senses. If this is what we mean – that is, if we define a 'literal' interpretation as one that is strictly materialistic – then neither Bahá'ís nor traditional Christians take the Bible literally.

This last point challenges a prevailing prejudice concerning Bible literalists. Literalism is often regarded (inaccurately, in my opinion) as an obsession with purely physical meanings and fulfilments. There is a notion afoot that literal-minded Christians arbitrarily force all scripture into the narrowest and most physical meaning consistent with its wording, regardless of context, of common sense, of clarification by related passages, or even of the writer's stated intent.

It would be amazing if this popular stereotype were true – but it is not. It paints a grossly distorted picture of many thoughtful and intelligent Bible students. Speaking from experience, I can report that my own family, friends and associates include a considerable number of devout Christians, whose views range from the strictly orthodox to the radically unconventional. During the past forty-plus years we have enjoyed countless hours discussing every biblical topic imaginable. As a writer and speaker I have also travelled in several countries, exchanging views in the process with Christians of many denominations and backgrounds. Whatever differing opinions we may have held, I have yet to meet any Christian who reads the Bible in an exclusively physical or materialistic sense. If this is the meaning of 'mindless literalism' (to use a derogatory expression one sometimes hears), then I do not know any mindless literalists.

By way of example, we already have discussed the Christian attitude towards two important Bible passages: 'I stand at the door and knock' (Rev. 3:20), and 'Ye must be born again' (John 3:7). All believers in the Bible (including those who interpret it literally) understand that in such passages God uses the language of the five physical senses to illustrate metaphysical phenomena – realities to which those senses have no access. Christ's physical knuckles do not rap on the physical door of anyone's house. Our physical bodies do not return to the physical wombs of our mothers. Why, then, does God express Himself primarily in concrete terms and images? Perhaps one reason is that purely abstract speech does not convey the overpowering reality He is expressing. Why do we nonetheless say we take these passages literally? To emphasize that reality. The spiritual Christ seeking access to our hearts is no mere imaginary friend, no mythical or illusory projection of a comforting father-fantasy. He is a living Presence of infinite power. The spiritual rebirth is no mere emotional outburst, nor is it simply a personal commitment similar to a New Year's resolution. It is a profound transformation of the soul's identity, mediated by the Holy Spirit. Individuals who have truly experienced these supernatural forces and processes know that they are real. For many, there is no satisfying way to express our conviction of that reality except by calling it literally true.

Consider these words of Christ:

> I am the true vine, and my Father is the husbandman. Every branch in me that beareth not fruit he taketh away: and every branch that beareth fruit, he purgeth it, that it may bring forth more fruit . . . I am the vine, ye are the branches: He that abideth in me, and I in him, the same bringeth forth much fruit: for without me ye can do nothing (John 15:1-5).

Christ obviously does not intend that we read this statement in any purely botanical sense. To understand it, we must allow figurative language as one of God's tools for communicating with us. So long as we focus on its intent, this passage neither means nor says that Christ was a climbing plant, with roots for feet, leafy tendrils for limbs and sap for blood. However, it speaks volumes about the relationship between Christ, His Father and His followers; and its intended meaning is literally true. No doubt the Saviour could have given us in its place a wordy dissertation on dependence, faithfulness, productivity, obligations, consequences and other abstractions. How dry and boring that would have been! Instead, He packs all these meanings (plus many, many more) into one rich analogy capable of lifting our spirits and stirring us to action. Every thoughtful Christian – literalist or otherwise – understands this principle, and anyone even modestly familiar with the Bible can quickly locate dozens of scriptures which employ a similar technique.

We see the same principle at work in the parables of Christ. A parable is a story that makes a point. In these cases it is the point of the story that is literally true – not necessarily the story itself, construed as bare history. In the parable of the Prodigal, Christ tells of a rebellious son who, after years of disobedience, returns in repentance to his father, receiving forgiveness and a royal welcome. It matters not at all whether Christ had in mind a particular human father; that is not the point of the story. The point – the timeless truth which down through the ages has transformed the lives of millions – is that we are all like that son, and God is like that father. Like any wise and loving parent, He is uncompromising with wrongdoing, but ready to forgive all who sincerely repent and return to Him. Christians who accept the Bible as literally true do not insist that Christ could have given the names, addresses and biological ages of the people in His narrative; of course they know better. 'Literally true' means in this case that divine forgiveness is a reality of Christian life-experience, and not – as cynics would have us believe – merely a fable designed to help us rationalize our shortcomings.

Bible prophecy is likewise recognized by literalists as being rich in physical imagery designed to convey metaphysical truths. Consider the prophetic promise 'Him that overcometh will I make a pillar in the temple of my God, and He shall go no more out' (Rev. 3:12). If 'literal' always meant 'purely physical', then believers who take the Bible literally would expect to be transformed into permanent stone columns and used by God to shore up a building of steel-reinforced concrete (or perhaps gold block or some other exotic structural substance). But of course no Christian, however literal-minded, believes anything of this sort. It is probably safe to say that all readers understand the expression 'pillar in the temple of my God' to mean 'supporter of God's church' (where 'church' is used to mean a body of believers rather than a physical building). We often use the word 'pillar' in just this way, as when we call someone a 'pillar of the community'. What of the prophecy that in the latter days, the nations 'shall beat their swords into plowshares, and their spears into pruninghooks' (Isa. 2:4)? No modern army, to my knowledge, still uses swords and spears. Does this mean the prophecy has become null and void? Hardly – and the last person to draw such a conclusion would be a thoughtful literalist. It makes far better sense to believe that 'swords' and 'spears' stand for military technology in general, and that 'plowshares' and 'pruninghooks' represent the various ways such technology can be turned to peaceful use. The image of 'swords into plowshares' is today widely used in just this way to signify the peaceful reorientation of war-related industries.

To be sure, we often find widely divergent schools of thought concerning whether or not a given scripture is figurative. Bahá'ís believe we need to approach all such issues in a spirit of tolerance and mutual respect. It may indeed be valuable to resolve such points of doctrine through reflection and dialogue. However, the thing that transcends them all in importance (and which alone can make possible their ultimate resolution) is our shared determination to serve Christ and to follow His truth wherever it may lead. So long as we fix our sights upon this unifying commitment, we can come together to investigate secondary issues with confidence that God Himself, in His own good time, will help us understand them.

In saying the Bible cannot always be understood materialistically I do not mean that the scriptures are devoid of information about material or physical phenomena. Christ said, 'If I have told you earthly things, and ye believe not, how shall ye believe, if I tell you of heavenly things?' (John 3:12). Obviously Christ and the Bible have a great deal to say about 'earthly things'. The point is that earthly things take second place to heavenly things and, usually, information about earthly things is included because of what it can teach us about heavenly things. No teaching of scripture is more literally true than the following: 'It is the spirit that quickeneth; the flesh profiteth nothing: The words that I speak unto you, they are spirit, and they are life' (John 6:63).

'But why call it a "literal" interpretation?' asked a Christian friend with whom I discussed the preceding examples. This young man – a knowledgeable student of the Bible, deeply devoted to Christ – was most uneasy with the conventional label. 'Look,' he told me, 'if taking the Bible literally means taking it seriously as the Word of God, then I'm a literalist. But lots of people think of a literal interpretation as one that emphasizes physical meaning to the exclusion of everything else – including all that God wants us to learn from the analogies, the parables, the prophecy codes and other figurative language He uses in scripture. If you acknowledge that at least some of the Bible is written in this way, why not say you interpret it symbolically rather than literally?'

This is a natural question; but there are grounds for caution with regard to the label proposed by my young friend. I prefer to use the term 'symbolic' sparingly – and then only in a context that emphasizes the reality of Bible truth. All concrete figures of speech are symbols, in that they point to something beyond the images they contain. If, therefore, we mean simply that some Bible verses convey their truths via figures of speech, we may call those passages symbolic even though we recognize them as literally inspired by God and accept His intended meaning as literally true. This is consistent with the strict dictionary definition of 'symbolic'. If only the word were always used in this technically correct manner! Unfortunately, it is not; and through persistent misuse it has gained as many negative and misleading connotations, for some people, as the word 'literal' has for others.

The problem is that the word 'symbolic' and its synonyms ('metaphorical', 'allegorical' and others generally identified with a 'non-literal' outlook) have been widely adopted by proponents of the belief that the Bible is an essentially human document, rather than a divine revelation in any factual sense. Having been largely monopolized by this school of thought, such terms have come to mean (for many who hear them) unreal, mythical, imaginary or illusory. As a result, when someone says, 'I don't take the Bible literally – I interpret it symbolically,' many listeners hear this as a denial of the Bible's inspiration. Not all people who say such things mean this; but enough do mean it to lend considerable weight to the assumption. This sceptical attitude contrasts sharply with the historic Christian view of the Bible as the authoritative statement of a personal God. Since Bahá'ís, like most Christians, take the latter position, it can be quite misleading to describe a Bahá'í interpretation of the Bible as 'symbolic' or 'non-literal' in any sweeping, all-inclusive sense. To do so may convey the impression that Bahá'ís endorse a humanistic philosophy with which, in fact, they strongly disagree.

Since the Bahá'í understanding of certain Bible passages differs from the conventional view, Christians unfamiliar with Bahá'u'lláh's teachings may at first tend to lump Bahá'ís with those who advocate 'symbolic' interpretation in order to discount the Bible's importance. The truth, however, is that Bahá'ís and Christian traditionalists are close and natural allies, bound together by belief in the reality of a personal God, in the unchallengeable authority of the Bible as His Word, in the superhuman greatness and eternal uniqueness of Christ, His Son, as the Lord and Saviour of humanity, in the miraculous reality of His birth and resurrection, and in the overshadowing importance of His Second Coming as the climactic event in history. Nowhere will any Christian find a deeper or more unshakable faith in these eternal verities than among the followers of Bahá'u'lláh.

'My Words Shall Not Pass Away'

Many Christians are troubled, however, by the fact that Bahá'ís also regard Bahá'u'lláh's teachings and writings as sacred scripture. Institutional Christianity has long taught that divine revelation ceased with the Bible. To consider any other literature in this same light may therefore appear inconsistent – if not downright blasphemous.

The belief that the Bible is God's 'last word' is so deeply etched in traditional church creeds that many people have come to regard it as a teaching of the Bible itself. Some even quote scripture to support this position. Bahá'ís, however, maintain that none of the passages thus quoted actually say divine revelation ended with the Bible. On the contrary, Bahá'ís believe the Bible clearly predicts that Christ, at the time of His return, is to reveal many new teachings and scriptures. Bahá'u'lláh's written teachings are seen as the fulfilment of these prophecies.

Let us examine, therefore, the passages traditionally taken to mean that the Bible is not only God's Word but His final and complete message for all time. Let us compare these with the prophecies Bahá'ís cite as support for their belief in continuing revelation.

'*Heaven and earth shall pass away, but my words shall not pass away*' (Matt. 24:35). People sometimes ask about this passage because; having heard that the Bahá'í Faith is a 'new religion', they mistakenly assume Bahá'ís wish somehow to 'do away with' the Bible or the words of Christ. As we already have seen, Bahá'u'lláh affirms the indispensability of the Bible as the revealed Word of God. Regarding the utterances of Jesus, Bahá'u'lláh has written 'whatsoever hath proceeded out of His blameless, His truth-speaking, trustworthy mouth can never be altered' (TB 14).

'*You shall not add to the word which I command you, nor take from it; that you may keep the commandments of the Lord your God which I command you*' (Deut. 4:2 RSV). This oft-cited verse prohibits unauthorized human tampering with the laws of God – the word 'which I command you'. But does such a prohibition apply to God Himself? Does it mean the Lord of Creation can never again reveal a new message of love and guidance through His divine emissary, or that He can never change His own ordinances? Clearly it means nothing of the sort. After all, this verse – from one of the five books associated with Moses – was revealed more than a thousand years before Christ appeared. Not only the New Testament but most books of the Old Testament were revealed by God centuries after He had put this prohibition into effect.

Despite such compelling logic, this very passage was cited by Christ's adversaries who insisted He had no right to modify the Sabbath, annul the Mosaic law of divorce or reveal new scriptures. In fact, Christ had every right to do these things, for the reason He Himself gave: 'I have spoken not of myself; but the Father which sent me, he gave me a commandment, what I should say, and what I should speak' (John 12:49). As the mouthpiece of God, His was the authority to keep the law of Moses or change it as needed. If – as Bahá'u'lláh claims – 'the Lord of Lords is come', then His word is also the Word of God and carries the same authority.

'For I testify unto every man that heareth the words of the prophecy of this book, If any man shall add unto these things, God shall add unto him the plagues that are written in this book: And if any man shall take away from the words of the book of this prophecy, God shall take away his part out of the book of life . . .' (Rev. 22:18-19). Here again, the text prohibits fallible human beings from altering God-breathed scripture – specifically, in this case, the Book of Revelation, one of the 66 books that make up the Bible. (The fact that the Book of Revelation speaks here of itself is clear from its references to 'the plagues that are written in this book' and 'the book of this prophecy'.) Bahá'ís would of course oppose any effort to revise either the Book of Revelation or any other book of the Bible. But we can hardly infer from this verse that God Himself has no right to reveal His will anew through the returned Christ.

'But though we, or an angel from heaven, preach any other gospel unto you than that which we have preached unto you, let him be accursed . . . For I neither received it of man, neither was I taught it, but by the revelation of Jesus Christ' (Gal. 1:8, 12). Again, this is not a ban on future revelation; it is a warning against teachings that are merely human in origin. The context shows that 'any other gospel' means any teaching that contradicts Christ's truth. In the verse immediately preceding this passage, Paul explains that he is referring to false teachers who 'trouble' the church with doctrines that 'pervert the gospel of Christ'. We know from I John 2:18-24, 4:1-3 and other Bible passages that during this period 'many antichrists' were abroad, denying the divinity and even the historicity of Christ. Paul's warning is of course one that every Christian must take seriously. But what possible bearing could it have on the question of whether God Himself might choose to speak again? Surely any message truly revealed by God, today or tomorrow, will be one in spirit with what He has spoken yesterday. (How to recognize authentic revelation is a separate – and of course critically important – issue, one we will explore in detail.)

All the books of the Bible manifest complete spiritual harmony one with another, though they were revealed centuries apart. Just as the New Testament builds upon the Old, the teachings of Bahá'u'lláh build upon those of Jesus. They are indivisible parts of one divine gospel – of what Bahá'u'lláh calls 'the changeless Faith of God, eternal in the past, eternal in the future' (G 136). The Bahá'í writings state that the Faith of Bahá'u'lláh 'can never, and in no aspect of its teachings, be at variance, much less conflict, with the purpose animating, or the authority invested in, the Faith of Jesus Christ' (WOB 185). Many prominent thinkers have recognized this underlying harmony. Dr George Washington Carver, for example, said: 'I am happy to know that the Christlike Gospel of good will is growing throughout the world. You hold in your organization the key that will settle all our difficulties . . .' (quoted in *Bahá'í World*, vol. 13, p. 826). Another outstanding Christian, Leo Tolstoy, called Bahá'u'lláh's precepts 'the highest and purest form of religious teaching' (quoted in *Bahá'í World*, vol. 13, p. 818). Queen Marie of Romania, a follower of Bahá'u'lláh and granddaughter of England's Queen Victoria, spoke for Bahá'ís everywhere when she wrote:

> I discovered in the Bahá'í teaching the real spirit of Christ so often denied and misunderstood: unity instead of strife, hope instead of condemnation, love instead of hate, and a great reassurance for all men (quoted in *Bahá'í World*, vol. 13, p. 806).

> It is Christ's message taken up anew, in the same words almost, but adapted to the thousand years and more difference that lies between the year one and today (quoted in *Bahá'í World*, vol. 13, p. 804).

A Voice Like Many Waters

But if the Bible does not actually preclude future revelation, does it specifically predict it? To Bahá'ís, the answer is 'yes'.

44

As we begin this inquiry, let us agree that every utterance of Christ – before or after His Second Coming – is the Word of God. Surely this principle is one that any Christian can embrace. Were we to insist that the Bible is 'all there ever will be' of the Word of God, would this not mean Christ can never again have anything to say to us – or to anyone else? Would we not be saying, in effect, that He can return only on condition that He remain eternally silent?

The Bible minces no words on this subject: 'Our God shall come,' declares the Psalmist, 'and shall not keep silence' (Psalms 50:3). The reference here is apparently to the Day of Judgement, for the text continues: 'He shall call to the heavens from above, and to the earth, that he may judge his people . . . And the heavens shall declare his righteousness: for God is judge himself' (Psalms 50:4-6). Bahá'ís, as explained previously, believe that the Day of Judgement is the day in which we now are living. Be that as it may, could any prophecy foretell more clearly a fresh outpouring of divine utterance and revelation in that day?

If any could, it might be Amos 1:2: 'The Lord will roar from Zion, and utter His voice from Jerusalem; and the habitations of the shepherds shall mourn, and the top of Carmel shall wither.' Then there is the vision of Ezekiel, in which 'the glory of the God of Israel came from the way of the east: and his voice was like a noise of many waters' (Eze. 43:2). And the testimony of Isaiah:

> And it shall come to pass in the last days, that the mountain of the Lord's house shall be established in the top of the mountains . . . and he will teach us of his ways . . . for out of Zion shall go forth the law, and the word of the Lord from Jerusalem. And He shall judge among the nations, and shall rebuke many people: and they shall beat their swords into plowshares, and their spears into pruninghooks . . . (Isa. 2:2-4).

This promise echoes the fourth chapter of Micah, where it is repeated almost word for word. Both passages emphasize that the 'word of the Lord' destined to 'go forth' in 'the last days' will include words of judgement and rebuke addressed to 'many people'. Is this not still another promise of latter-day revelation?

In his apocalyptic vision of the end time, St John describes the 'one like unto the Son of man' as having a 'voice as the sound of many waters', adding, 'out of his mouth went a sharp two-edged sword' (Rev. 1:13-16). The following chapter quotes Christ as saying: 'Repent; or else I will come unto thee quickly, and will fight against them with the sword of my mouth' (Rev. 2:16). In chapter 19 we read: 'And out of his mouth goeth a sharp sword, that with it he should smite the nations . . .' (Rev. 19:15). Is this sword a physical weapon? No, for according to Paul, 'the sword of the Spirit . . . is the word of God' (Eph. 6:17). Hebrews 4:12 declares 'the word of God is quick, and powerful, and sharper than any two-edged sword'. Evidently, then, the sword is the Word of God – a new revelation of cutting-edge truth destined to issue from the mouth of Christ in the time of the end.

As we discussed in Chapter 1, the Bible itself declares that its 'words are closed up and sealed till the time of the end' (Dan. 12:9), when they will be unsealed. No man, we are told, will be 'found worthy to open and to read the book, neither to look thereon' until the day of Christ's return, when He – 'the Lion of the tribe of Judah, the Root of David' – will prevail to 'open the book, and to loose the seven seals thereof' (Rev. 5:4-5). Since the Bible is not physically padlocked, we may infer that the prophecies are revealed in spiritual code to be understood only after Christ fulfils and explains them. Would not this explanation itself constitute a further revelation of God's word?

In these and countless other passages the Bible emphatically repudiates any claim to be the 'last and only' word of God. It assures us that the voice of God will never be silenced, and, in particular, that it will speak eloquently through Christ in the Day of His return.

3

The Image of the Invisible

[Christ] is the image of the invisible God, the firstborn of every creature: For by him were all things created, that are in heaven, and that are in earth . . . And he is before all things, and by him all things consist (Col. 1:15-17).

But we all, with open face beholding as in a glass the glory of the Lord, are changed into the same image from glory to glory, even as by the Spirit of the Lord (II Cor. 3:18).

In discussing Bahá'u'lláh's claim to be the return of Christ, we must emphasize a basic theological principle: *There is only one Christ.* Throughout eternity there has always been, and will ever be, only one Christ – unique, unchanging, indivisible, peerless and incomparable. His greatness and glory are infinitely beyond human comprehension, His importance impossible to exaggerate or over-emphasize.

This Christ-centred outlook is as fundamental to the Bahá'í Faith as to Christianity itself. However, the Bahá'í belief that Christ has returned 'like a thief' bearing a 'new name' sometimes invites confusion. It may be mistaken to mean there are multiple 'Christs', or that Bahá'u'lláh is some sort of replacement for or successor to Christ. This is not what Bahá'u'lláh says. On the contrary, He claims to be the *same* spiritual Christ who walked the hills of Galilee two thousand years ago, 'whose goings forth have been from of old, from eternity'(Micah 5:2), and who vowed to return with a new and different name. Bahá'u'lláh's fulfilment of Christ's prophecy need not blind us to their oneness as dawning-places of the same divine spirit. The Bahá'í writings explain:

Know that the return of Christ for a second time doth not mean what the people believe . . . He shall come with the Kingdom of God and His Power which hath surrounded the world. This dominion is in the world of hearts and spirits, and not in that of matter; for the material world is not comparable to a single wing of a fly, in the sight of the Lord, wert thou of those who know! Verily Christ came with His Kingdom from the beginning which hath no beginning, and will come with His Kingdom to the eternity of eternities, inasmuch as in this sense 'Christ' is an expression of the Divine Reality, the simple Essence and heavenly Entity, which hath no beginning nor ending (BNE 206-7).

Bahá'ís find ample support for this view in the Bible. Christ – according to the New Testament – is more than a name, more than a physical body, more than a human personality. The Christ of the Bible is a divine and spiritual Presence, eternally inseparable from God Himself. It follows that the name He chooses, the human temple He inhabits as the 'Word made flesh' – these are cosmetic superficialities which in no way change His inward spiritual identity. It is (Bahá'ís believe) in terms of this core Identity that Jesus and Bahá'u'lláh are one and the same Christ.

'A Quickening Spirit'

To understand how this can be, let us turn to the Bible. It is one thing to believe there is only one Christ; it is another to formulate a clear idea of how and why this is so. For example, is Christ's uniqueness a physical characteristic? An affirmative answer would rule Bahá'u'lláh's claim entirely out of order. The Bible tells us that when the pre-existent Word of God came 'down from heaven' (John 6:38), He 'was made flesh, and dwelt among us' (John 1:14). Did He, by taking human form, become forever trapped within the body He inhabited at that time? Can an all-powerful, ever-present spiritual Entity be limited in this way and thus unable to reappear later in a new and outwardly different human guise? Many people (perhaps without ever really expressing it in such terms) assume that this is precisely what happened.

Such an assumption (I will argue) contradicts not only the letter of the Bible but the glorious nature of Christ Himself. Unwittingly and by implication, it attributes human frailties and shortcomings to One who actually transcends them altogether. St Paul explains that 'the first man Adam was made a living soul; the last Adam [Christ] was made a quickening spirit' (I Cor. 15:45). Like the first Adam, we are living souls, confined while on this plane to earthly bodies. 'The first man', Paul continues, 'is of the earth, earthy: the second man is the Lord from heaven' (I Cor. 15:47). By describing that 'quickening spirit' which is Christ as 'the Lord from heaven', Paul places Christ in a sphere far above that of any mere 'living soul' subject to 'earthy' limitations. It follows that any religious dogma that confines Christ to purely human categories, that diminishes His power and glory or in any way compromises His universality, must be viewed with suspicion.

The thrust of this chapter is that Bahá'u'lláh and the Bible speak with one voice concerning the nature of Christ. (To a Bahá'í, this harmony betokens the fact that Christ and Bahá'u'lláh are themselves one.) Furthermore, Bahá'u'lláh's elucidations of the New Testament vastly expand our understanding of the greatness of Christ, His uniqueness and supreme authority. They do this by amplifying important biblical themes which, over the centuries, have become forgotten or neglected; by drawing attention to implications that were there all along but have been widely overlooked; and by reconciling scripture passages that on the surface may have seemed inconsistent or paradoxical. In short, Bahá'u'lláh glorifies Christ as no one has done before or since. The vision of Christ that He thus unfolds from the Bible is incomparably richer and more magnificent than any of those historically associated with denominational creeds. Let us now explore this vision.

The Mystery of Christ

A recurring Bible theme is the awe-inspiring mysteriousness of the nature and station of Christ. '. . . great beyond all question', writes Paul, 'is the mystery of our religion':

> He who was manifested in the body,
>> vindicated in the spirit,
>>> seen by angels,
> who was proclaimed among the nations,
>> believed in throughout the world,
>>> glorified in high heaven
>>> (I Tim. 3:16 NEB).

Paul's observation challenges us to recognize that however much we may understand about Christ, there always will be much more we do not. Early Christians strove to develop a theology which, while acknowledging this inherent mystery, would befittingly reflect what they did know of their Lord and Master.

In this endeavour they were fascinated by the fact that the Bible speaks of Christ in two different and, at first sight, seemingly contradictory ways. Some passages depict Christ as identical with God Himself. Others, while emphasizing His power and perfection as God's only begotten Son, depict Him just as clearly as distinct from, and subordinate to, God. Which view is correct? Since we believe the entire Bible, both must be correct – and therein lies the mystery. (One of the mysteries, at any rate.)

What are some of the specific scriptures that any comprehensive view of Christ must take into account?

'In the beginning was the Word, and the Word was with God, and the Word was God' (John 1:1). The 'Word' (from the Greek *logos*) is of course a biblical title for Christ. The closing phrase of this sentence – 'the Word was God' – is emphasized by Christians who insist that Christ was God Incarnate; that is, God in physical form. Christ says of His own position, 'I and my Father are one' (John 10:30). 'If ye had known me, ye should have known my Father also: and from henceforth ye know him, and have seen him . . . he that hath seen me hath seen the Father' (John 14:7, 10). God Himself, according to the author of Hebrews, states the case even more strongly: 'But unto the Son he saith, Thy throne, O God, is for ever and ever' (Heb. 1:8). The Old Testament name for Christ – Immanuel – means 'God with us'. Some theologians offer these and similar verses as proof that Christ is Himself God, there being no difference between them.

On the other hand, many Bible passages seem just as unmistakably to say that Christ is not God. 'My father', says Christ Himself, 'is greater than I' (John 14:28). 'The Son can do nothing of himself, but what he seeth the Father do' (John 5:19). 'I seek not mine own will, but the will of the Father which hath sent me' (John 5:30). In the Garden of Gethsemane Christ prayed: 'O my Father, if it be possible, let this cup pass from me: nevertheless not as I will, but as thou wilt' (Matt. 26:39). Is Christ praying to Himself in the latter passage? If so, why does He repeatedly speak of His own will as distinct from His Father's (even though He bows to God's Will)? Elsewhere He explicitly states that God has knowledge which Christ does not: 'But of that day and that hour knoweth no man, no, not the angels which are in heaven, neither the Son, but the Father' (Mark 13:32).

The paradox deepens when we consider the biblical meaning of 'seeing God'. On the one hand, Christ distinctly says, 'He that hath seen me hath seen the Father' (John 14:9). On the other, while standing in plain view of His disciples, He says of the Father: 'Ye have neither heard his voice at any time, nor seen his shape' (John 5:37). The Gospel of John assures us that 'No man hath seen God at any time; the only begotten Son, which is in the bosom of the Father, he hath declared him' (John 1:18). We find a similar thought in I John 4:20: 'for he that loveth not his brother whom he hath seen, how can he love God whom he hath not seen?'

How may we reconcile these seemingly contradictory assertions? In their efforts to solve this puzzle, church fathers articulated the doctrine now known as the Trinity. This means that God is a single Being comprising three aspects or Persons – Father, Son and Holy Spirit. The basis for the Trinity is I John 5:7: 'For there are three that bear record in heaven, the Father, the Word, and the Holy Ghost: and these three are one.' The meaning of this verse has been hotly debated for centuries. Some scholars maintain that 'these three are one' simply implies unity of purpose. Others insist that it connotes a literal, mathematical or even physical oneness. Contrary to a widely held belief, the Bible nowhere uses the expression 'God the Father, God the Son, and God the Holy Ghost', nor does the word 'trinity' itself appear in the Bible. As a result, some Christians reject the Trinity altogether. While it may be argued that a three-fold Deity is implied by various Bible teachings, the doctrine is fraught with ambiguity and conflicting interpretations.

Two of these interpretations are noteworthy because they illustrate opposite ends of the theological spectrum.

The first and perhaps best known version of the Trinity may be stated in these terms: 'Each of these three Persons – God the Father, God the Son, and God the Holy Spirit – is an individual, completely distinct from the other two; and each is God in every respect. And yet, since there is only one God, all three are one and the same God. This is a mystery to our human minds, since it is self-contradictory – but so what? Faith in an all-powerful Deity means believing He can do things that are logically impossible.'

This is a popular interpretation but one not universally accepted even by Christians who believe in the Trinity itself. The problem for many people is that such an approach, in its outright rejection of reason, seems contrary to the spirit of the Bible which strongly endorses our use of reason in seeking truth: 'Come now, and let us reason together, saith the Lord' (Isa. 1:18). '. . . be always ready to give an answer to every man that asketh you a reason of the hope that is in you . . .' (I Peter 3:15). Paul criticizes those who have 'lost the power to reason, and . . . cannot pass the tests of faith'. (II Timothy 3:8 NEB). He lists 'jealousy, quarrelling, slander, base suspicions, and endless wrangles' as 'all typical of men who have let their reasoning powers become atrophied and have lost grip on the truth' (I Timothy 6:4-5 NEB). Scripture counsels us to reject logical inconsistency: 'Turn a deaf ear to . . . the contradictions of so-called "knowledge" . . .' (I Timothy 6:20-1 NEB). Christ Himself, speaking with divine authority, often demonstrated His revealed truths by using rational arguments of the utmost subtlety and beauty.

At the opposite pole stands a second interpretation, which says, in effect: 'There is nothing irrational about the Trinity. The Father, Son and Holy Spirit are simply one God acting at different times in different capacities. He's like an actor playing three parts in one play. We all play different roles in our own lives; for example, a family man may be a father to his son, a son to his father, and a husband to his wife. A business executive may be a boss to her subordinates, a subordinate to her employer, and a colleague to her counterpart in a different department or company. In all these roles and capacities, one will be referred to in different ways, and by different names and titles. The Trinity is the same sort of thing.'

At first glance, this approach appears to remove all inconsistency from the teaching – yet many still find it unconvincing. It seems almost too reasonable, since it denies the mystery and the paradox as well as the outright contradiction. Moreover, it fails, on closer inspection, to address most of the issues raised by the scriptures quoted above. If the Son is merely the Father wearing a different hat, how can it be – as stated in Mark 13:32 – that God knows something Christ does not? How can Christ say, on the one hand, 'He that hath seen me hath seen the Father'; and on the other, 'Ye have neither heard his voice at any time, nor seen his shape'? How can the Son, in praying to the Father, say 'not as I will, but as thou wilt'? The more we stretch this explanation to cover all the bases it must cover, the thinner it becomes.

Many Christians are reluctant to move beyond traditional interpretations of the Trinity because they see no remaining choice except humanism – the view that Christ, though He may have been a spiritual giant like Paul or Isaiah, was 'merely human'. This cannot be correct. Christ clearly claimed for Himself a position far above that of mortal man. Since a purely humanistic concept contradicts the Bible, it is acceptable neither to Bahá'ís nor to traditional Christians.

There exists, however, a solution to this mystery which both makes sense and satisfies the soul. Such an answer is found in the Bahá'í view of the station of Christ and His relationship to God. Although Bahá'u'lláh's explanation is less well known than either of the two described above, it is completely consistent with, and supported by, the text of the New Testament. His exposition of this biblical theme is so simple and logical that a child can grasp it. At the same time, it fully preserves the mystery, the majesty and glory of Christ's position. Best of all, it encompasses the entirety of scripture, giving us a straightforward model by which we can integrate and reconcile all of the Bible's multifaceted teachings about God and Christ.

The Mirror Image of God

The Bible affirms the reality of one infinite, unknowable, transcendent God comparable in certain respects to the sun. A key similarity is that the astronomical sun, like God, is not directly accessible to human beings, nor can it physically descend to earth because it is inconceivably greater than the earth. Paul praises the Heavenly Father as 'dwelling in unapproachable light' where 'no man has ever seen or ever can see him' (I Tim. 6:16). However, Christ, in His spiritual nature, is 'the image of the invisible God' (Col. 1:15), 'the express image of his person' (Heb. 1:3). Turning to Him is equivalent to 'beholding as in a glass the glory of the Lord' (II Cor. 3:18) – to seeing God reflected in a perfect mirror.

These Bible verses, Bahá'u'lláh points out, hold the glittering key that unlocks the mystery of the Trinity. They enable us to express the relationship between Father, Son and Holy Spirit through a simple physical analogy:

1) God is like the sun — that is, the astronomical sun, inconceivably vast and unapproachable, its inner substance veiled by its own blazing glory.
2) Christ is like the sun's reflection, appearing with perfect fidelity in a polished and stainless mirror.
3) The Holy Spirit is like the sun's rays, which, having cast the reflection within the mirror, are shed by that same reflection over all who turn towards it.

God, the sun; Christ, its mirror image; the Holy Spirit, its rays. This illustration is, as the Bahá'í teachings state, 'so logical that it can easily be grasped by all minds willing to give it their consideration' (PT 26).

To think of Jesus Christ as a mirror reflecting the Divine Image is to confirm something Christians have long understood, namely that He has a dual nature – both human and divine. In strictly human terms, Christ is, according to the Bahá'í teachings, a 'Perfect Man' (SAQ 222) with a 'pure and stainless Soul' (G 66), created sinless and infallible. This human personality is in effect the mirror. We can think of Christ's physical body as the mirror's frame and His human soul as the polished glass or reflecting surface. In spiritual terms, however, Christ is infinitely more than a human body or even a human soul. His 'real' identity – the Divinity that makes Him who He is – is that of the mirror image of God shining with full intensity in and through His humanity.

For want of a better name, let us call this concept the 'Divine Reflection analogy'. It is so essential that I would like, before going further, to explore in detail its biblical justification. I will then show how it illuminates and harmonizes a number of Bible passages that many readers have found obscure.

'In the beginning, God . . .'

To understand Christ better, we must begin by considering what the Bible says about God.

It should not be necessary to emphasize the great truth that echoes like thunder through all the books of the Bible, namely that 'there is only one God' (Rom. 3:30 NIV). But since this point is crucial to an understanding of the Trinity, let us take it as our starting point. God is not a committee, or a colony creature, or a victim of multiple-personality disorder. He is alone in His absolute oneness. Unless we give due weight to this fundamental axiom we can never hope to arrive at a valid concept of the Trinity or any other doctrine. In His own words:

> I am the Lord, and there is none else, there is no God beside me . . . I am the Lord, and there is none else (Isa. 45:5-6).

> The first of all the commandments is, Hear, O Israel; The Lord our God is one Lord . . . (Mark 12:29)

> . . . there is none other God but one . . . to us there is but one God, the Father, of whom are all things, and we in him . . . (I Cor. 8:4, 6)

A further principle is that 'God is spirit, and his worshippers must worship in spirit and in truth' (John 4:24 NIV). It is surprising how many people – Christian and non-Christian – are under the impression that the Bible portrays God as a material being of flesh and blood. In fact, scripture draws a sharp distinction between physical and spiritual reality: 'That which is born of the flesh is flesh; and that which is born of the Spirit is spirit' (John 3:6). '. . . flesh and blood cannot inherit the kingdom of God . . .' (I Cor. 15:50). The Creator of matter is not Himself a creature of matter.

The Bible passage most often quoted to support the notion of a physical God is Genesis 1:26: 'And God said, Let us make man in our image, after our likeness . . .' Does this reference to the 'image' and 'likeness' of God mean He is visibly human in shape (and therefore material)? No, it does not. Since Paul speaks of the 'the image of the invisible God' (I Col. 1:15), we can hardly conclude that His image implies physical visibility. How, then, may we 'see' the image of God? Paul explains this in Romans 1:19-20. The most lucid translation is perhaps that of the New English Bible: 'For all that may be known of God by men lies plain before their eyes; indeed, God himself has disclosed it to them. His invisible attributes, that is to say his everlasting power and deity, have been visible, ever since the world began, to the eye of reason, in the things he has made.' The New International Version renders this same passage as follows: '. . .what may be known about God is plain to them, because God has made it plain to them. For since the creation of the world God's invisible qualities – his eternal power and divine nature – have been clearly seen, being understood from what has been made . . .'

How clearly Paul explains that 'all that may be known of God by men' is His 'invisible attributes' which are 'visible . . . to the eye of reason'. His 'eternal power and divine nature' are 'clearly seen' not with physical eyesight, but in the sense of 'being understood'. Apart from this, says Paul, 'No man has ever seen or ever can see him' (I Tim. 6:16 NEB). It follows that 'the image and likeness of God' in which we are created is not a physical but a spiritual likeness, a correspondence of 'invisible attributes'. In other words, by turning to God and obeying His Word we can increasingly manifest in our own lives His goodness, His love, His justice, His mercy, His forgiveness and other divine qualities.

The Bible does, of course, make countless references to 'the right hand of God', 'the finger of God', 'the eye of God', 'the mouth of the Lord' and so forth. A theological treatise I once read contained a hefty compilation of such verses, purporting to 'prove' in detail that God's 'anatomical structure' is physically human. It should be obvious, from the scriptures quoted above, that such colourful imagery is meant to express figuratively God's invisible power, omniscience, spiritual guidance and the like. It has no organic or biological significance. Isaiah devotes much of his fortieth chapter to mocking the notion that anyone could build an idol or statue which would in any way resemble God: 'To whom then will ye liken God?' he asks rhetorically. 'Or what likeness will ye compare unto him?' (Isa. 40:18). Paul charges those who insist on a material Deity with 'exchanging the splendour of immortal God for an image shaped like mortal man'; and he adds that those who do so 'have bartered away the true God for a false one, and have offered reverence and worship to created things instead of to the Creator . . .' (Rom. 1:19-25 NEB).

A further principle is that the Creator transcends His creation. 'Behold, heaven and the heaven of heavens cannot contain thee,' says Solomon in his dedication of the Temple at Jerusalem, 'how much less this house which I have built!' (II Chron. 6:18). Christian philosophers, such as St Thomas Aquinas, realized centuries ago that since space and time are characteristics of the material universe (itself a creation of God the Infinite Reality), God Himself must be in some sense outside of or beyond them. From a human standpoint, then, God can have no geographical location, no coordinates in three-dimensional space. He is both everywhere and nowhere. Surveying the universe from outside of time, He is not trapped in its flow (as we seem to be) and can see past, present and future as one. Although these ideas follow inevitably from the biblical description of God, they once seemed meaningless or nonsensical. This changed only with the onset of modern physics, when Einstein demonstrated mathematically the relative (and in some ways illusory) nature of space and time. Science today is abuzz with speculation about higher dimensions, parallel universes, branching space-time continuums and other novelties – many of them far more fantastic than the idea of a transcendent Supreme Being. However sceptical some of today's scientists may be about God, their theories now make room for Him in a way that nineteenth-century physics and cosmology never could.

Finally, the Bible makes it clear that we, as finite creations, can never completely encompass or comprehend the Infinite Creator. God in His fullness is therefore unknowable. 'Behold, God is great, and we know him not . . .' (Job 36:26). 'Touching the Almighty, we cannot find him out' (Job 37:23). 'There is no searching of his understanding' (Isa. 40:28). God Himself declares: 'For as the heavens are higher than the earth, so are my ways higher than your ways, and my thoughts higher than your thoughts' (Isa. 55:9). There is, of course, an important sense in which we can know God through Christ but this knowledge remains relative to our capacity. However much we may grow in our understanding of Him, we always have room to learn more. Our highest experience of human love, for example, is always a mere echo of that Absolute Reality concerning which the Bible says: 'God is love' (I John 4:8).

This, then, is the God of the Bible: an infinite, transcendent, unknowable Spirit, eternally single and indivisible. What does all this have to do with the nature of Christ? A lot! If we think of God in materialistic terms – visualizing Him, for example, merely as a super-evolved human being, or in any other way limiting His greatness – we inevitably will make the same mistake with regard to His Son. We cannot diminish one without diminishing the other, for there is an important sense in which Christ and God are identical. What that sense is, what the Bible says about it, and why it in no way contradicts the oneness of God, we will now explore.

The Sun of Righteousness

We said above that God is in some ways like the physical sun. Throughout the Bible we find passages that support this comparison: 'For the Lord God is a sun and shield . . .' (Psalms 84:11) 'And the city had no need of the sun, neither of the moon, to shine in it: for the glory of God did lighten it . . .' (Rev. 21:23). Malachi defines the 'great and dreadful day of the Lord' as the day when 'the Sun of righteousness [shall] arise, with healing in his wings . . .' (Mal. 4:5, 2). The book of Isaiah offers this wondrous comparison:

> Arise, shine; for thy light is come, and the glory of the Lord is risen upon thee. For, behold, the darkness shall cover the earth, and gross darkness the people: but the Lord shall arise upon thee . . . And the Gentiles shall come to thy light, and kings to the brightness of thy rising . . . The sun shall be no more thy light by day; neither for brightness shall the moon give light unto thee: but the Lord shall be unto thee an everlasting light, and thy God thy glory. Thy sun shall no more go down; neither shall thy moon withdraw itself: for the Lord shall be thine everlasting light, and the days of thy mourning shall be ended (Isa. 60:1-3, 19-20).

Speaking of the Heavenly Father, Paul says more specifically: 'He is King of kings and Lord of lords . . . dwelling in unapproachable light. No man has ever seen or ever can see him' (I Tim. 6:15-16 NEB). The reference here is to God's essence or inner nature which, like the sun's core, is masked by its own power and glory. This explains the many scriptures quoted above, which affirm that God is forever invisible and unknowable. Bahá'u'lláh comments:

> To every discerning and illumined heart it is evident that God, the unknowable Essence, the Divine Being, is immeasurably exalted beyond every human attribute such as corporeal existence, ascent and descent, egress and regress . . . He is, and hath ever been, veiled in the ancient eternity of His Essence, and will remain in His Reality everlastingly hidden from the sight of men (WOB 113).

If the Heavenly Father 'dwell[s] in unapproachable light' where 'no man . . . ever can see him', not so the divine Word or Logos: 'Christ', explains Paul, '. . . is the image of God' (II Cor. 4:4).

The Bible elsewhere describes Christ as 'being the brightness of [God's] glory, and the express image of his person, and upholding all things by the word of his power' (Heb. 1:3). The New International Version translates this passage as follows: 'The Son is the radiance of God's glory and the exact representation of his being, sustaining all things by his powerful word.'

The 'image of the invisible God', 'the exact representation of his being'. To Bahá'ís, these verses indicate that in spiritual terms Christ manifests His unknowable Father just as the sun's reflected image mirrors its inward nature. Obviously the divine 'image' is not a physical likeness visible to material eyes. It is an image consisting of (to repeat Paul's words) God's 'invisible attributes' which we discern with 'the eye of reason', 'beholding as in a glass the glory of God'. Christ's spiritual nature exhibits with full fidelity the glory of the Divine Essence – the sovereignty, wisdom, omnipotence, beauty, truth, goodness, justice, mercy and unnumbered other qualities of God. As the 'express image of [God's] person', He is the focal point of divine perfection, just as the sun's reflection is the focal point of its light.

If God is the sun's essence and Christ is the sun's mirror image, then the Holy Spirit is the sun's outpouring radiance – its heat and light: 'I will pour out my spirit upon all flesh' (Joel 2:28, Acts 2:17). It is the pre-existent power of God, the all-embracing energy through which He implements His will and communicates the knowledge of His attributes.

This Divine Reflection analogy reconciles many scriptures that otherwise would seem to contradict one another. As we saw before, the Bible in some passages says Christ is God but in others that He is not God. It states in some verses that to see Him is to see God but insists in others that no one can ever see God. These apparent contradictions vanish in light of the Bible teaching that God is a spiritual sun, reflected in the perfect mirror that is Christ. The Word – the 'image of the invisible God' – differs from the divine Essence in the same way the sun's reflection differs from its physical substance. Thus Christ could truthfully say, 'My father is greater than I.' Yet there is an important sense in which the sun's reflection *is* the sun. The Bahá'í sacred writings explain:

> Shouldst thou . . . turn thy gaze unto a Mirror, brilliant, stainless, and pure, wherein the divine Beauty is reflected, therein wilt thou find the Sun shining with Its rays, Its heat, Its disc, Its fair form all entire . . . This is the meaning of the Messiah's words, that the Father is in the Son. Dost thou not see that should a stainless mirror proclaim, 'Verily is the sun ashine within me, together with all its qualities, tokens and signs', such an utterance by such a mirror would be neither deceptive nor false? (SAB 42)

To learn the most from this (or any other) analogy, we must be aware not only of its strengths but of its limitations. The physical sun, however massive, is a finite object, confined to one distinct location. We can therefore see its image not only through a mirror but directly, by turning towards the sun itself. God is different in this respect. Although He is at all times with His creatures – in us, over us, through us – we cannot see God immanent and transcendent. We 'see' Him only through the divine reflection as it appears in the perfect mirror of the historical Christ-figure: 'No man hath seen God at any time; the only begotten son, which is in the bosom of the Father, he hath declared him' (John 1:18) – or 'made him known', as the expression is rendered in some Bible translations.

A further limitation of the solar model is this: The sun's physical reflection is a mere illusion, dependent for its continued existence on a material mirror. But the divine reflection, though it manifests itself in a human reflector, can also exist and operate independently. Being an inseparable aspect of God Himself, it is as real as anything in our experience – indeed, more real even than we are. Bahá'í scriptures emphasize this truth by using the expression 'Sun of Reality' as a title for this luminous, life-giving Christ-spirit.

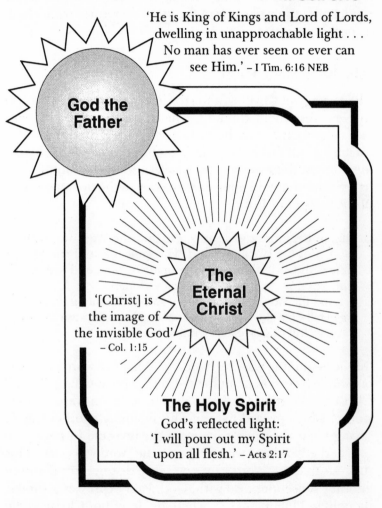

'Beholding as in a [mirror] the glory of God'
– II Cor. 3:18

'He is King of Kings and Lord of Lords, dwelling in unapproachable light . . . No man has ever seen or ever can see Him.' – I Tim. 6:16 NEB

God the Father

The Eternal Christ

'[Christ] is the image of the invisible God' – Col. 1:15

The Holy Spirit
God's reflected light: 'I will pour out my Spirit upon all flesh.' – Acts 2:17

Figure 1: The Trinity as presented in the Bible and in the Bahá'í teachings: God (the Divine Essence), Christ (the Divine Reflection), and the Holy Spirit (the Divine Radiance). In this analogy the mirror represents the human personality of Jesus.

The value of the sun-and-mirror analogy lies in its concreteness. It enables us easily to visualize a spiritual relationship that otherwise would be painfully abstract. Let us now look further into the Bible, seeking to discover how the same model may apply to some of the other scriptures with which it must harmonize.

'The Word Made Flesh'

The analogy of Christ as a mirror image of Divinity is central to New Testament thought, where it is (as we have seen) particularly explicit in the writings of Paul. What I find most exciting about this is the light it sheds on other Bible teachings. To test this assertion, let us take a specific example. Let us see how we might apply this analogy to the opening verses of the Gospel of John:

> In the beginning was the Word, and the Word was with God, and the Word was God. The same was in the beginning with God. All things were made by him, and without him was not any thing made that was made . . .
> And the Word was made flesh, and dwelt among us, (and we beheld his glory, the glory as of the only begotten of the Father,) full of grace and truth (John 1:1-3, 14).

'In the beginning was the Word . . .' What is a word? It is the outward expression of an inward reality or meaning. To call Christ the Word of God is to say He is the outward expression of God's inward nature. This is simply another way of saying He is the mirror image of the invisible Father.

'. . . the Word was with God, and the Word was God.' This suggests that the Word is in one sense distinct from, and in another sense identical with, God. Paul expresses a similar thought in Philippians 2:6, where he describes Christ as the One 'Who being in the form of God, thought it not robbery to be equal with God'. We already have seen how elegantly the Bible resolves this paradox by likening God to the sun and the Word to its reflection. The mirror image, being in the sun's exact form, is in one sense equal to and identical with the sun; in another sense, the two are distinct.

'The same was in the beginning with God.' The sun's image has existed as long as the sun itself has existed. Similarly, the Word – the 'image of the invisible God' – is co-eternal with the Father. The divine reflection has no beginning in time and will have no end.

'All things were made by him, and without him was not any thing made that was made . . .' This is one of many scriptures affirming that Christ, as the pre-existent Word, is the immediate creator of the cosmos. Paul, for example, explains that this 'image of the invisible God' is 'the firstborn of every creature: For by him were all things created, that are in heaven, and that are in earth . . . And he is before all things, and by him all things consist' (Col. 1:15-17). The sun's physical image is the 'firstborn' entity generated by its substance, and it is through that image that the sun floods the solar system with its light and power. As the divine reflection, Christ likewise is the 'firstborn of every creature', becoming thereby the agent through which God's creative power brings into being the material and spiritual universes. Bahá'u'lláh writes:

> . . . the irresistible Word of God . . . is the Cause of the entire creation, while all else besides His Word are but the creatures and effects thereof . . . Know thou, moreover, that the Word of God – exalted be His glory – is higher and far superior to that which the senses can perceive . . . It is God's all-pervasive grace, from which all grace doth emanate. It is an entity far removed above all that hath been and shall be . . . Verily, the Word of God is the cause which hath preceded the contingent world – a world which is adorned with the splendours of the Ancient of Days, yet is being renewed and regenerated at all times. Immeasurably exalted is the God of Wisdom Who hath raised this sublime structure (TB 140-1).

'And the Word was made flesh, and dwelt among us . . .' The physical sun does not leave the sky and descend to the earth; if it did so, it would destroy us all. Its image, however, can easily appear on earth. Likewise, God's unknowable infinite Essence, 'dwelling in unapproachable light' (I Tim. 6:16 NEB), does not approach or dwell within the physical universe; for 'the heaven and heaven of heavens cannot contain him' (II Chron. 2:6). It is the divine Word – the 'image of the invisible God', personified by that 'quickening spirit' called Christ – that takes human form to dwell among us.

'. . . and we beheld his glory . . .' How does the sun 'descend' to earth? By appearing in a mirror. Paul explains that seeing God in Christ means 'beholding as in a glass the glory of the Lord' (II Cor. 3:18). The 'glass' to which he refers is of course a looking-glass or mirror. The mirror in which the 'image of the invisible God' came to be reflected was the human personality of Jesus of Nazareth.

'. . . the glory as of the only begotten of the Father . . .' The Bible teaches that Christ was conceived of a virgin through the power of the Holy Spirit. Because of this, we tend to assume that His miraculous conception is what makes Him the only begotten Son of God. Such an assumption, however, raises an obvious question: As the pre-existent Word or Logos, was He not already the Son of God before coming to earth via the womb of His mother, Mary?

The only possible answer, in my opinion, is 'yes'. Christ was the Son of God from all eternity. Paul clearly says so when he calls Christ the 'firstborn of every creature' (Col. 1:15). We can easily understand this through the Bible's analogy of Christ as the image or reflection of God. The sun's image is 'born' (directly generated) from the sun through its radiance or energy field; and it is the 'only begotten' child or offspring born in this direct way – all other effects are indirect and mediated. Christ, in much the same way, was 'born' of God prior to the creation of heaven and earth, certainly long before His physical birth in a human body just two thousand years ago.

Does this understanding in any way lessen the importance of the virgin birth? Of course not. It magnifies that importance by enabling us to see its underlying spiritual meaning. The virgin birth is not the cause of Christ's being the Son of God; it is the result. It is an outward and indeed physical token of an inward truth. The pre-existent 'quickening spirit' we call Christ is at all times the only begotten Son – the reflection or 'express image' – of His invisible heavenly Father.

These are just a few examples of the many ways in which the Divine Reflection analogy illumines, harmonizes and derives from various Bible passages. Let us now shift our focus to consider a Bahá'í view of three other important theological issues: the atonement, the resurrection and the ascension of Christ.

The Atonement

One cornerstone of Christianity is the atonement – the fact that Christ sacrificed His life as a ransom for the sins of the world. The Bahá'í Faith categorically affirms this wonderful truth, which can be understood on many levels.

The atonement revolves around that best-beloved Gospel verse: 'For God so loved the world, that he gave his only begotten Son, that whosoever believeth in him should not perish, but have everlasting life' (John 3:16). Why is this necessary? For one thing, we cannot directly see God. Even when we feel His spirit moving in our hearts, we are impure channels. Burdened with sin and imperfection, we cannot infallibly distinguish the voice of God from that of our own desires and wishful thinking. That is why the divine Word must manifest itself in human form. When we turn towards the 'Word made flesh' we are (to repeat once more Paul's exquisite words) 'beholding as in a glass the glory of the Lord'. We see the 'image' of God reflected in a human mirror. Through the divine reflection personified we hear the actual words of God. We observe His behaviour under varied and challenging circumstances. We gradually learn, through His words and deeds, as much as we can grasp of His character. His sacrificial love draws us into a personal relationship with Himself. Without this divine outreach, our access to God would be forever blocked by our own flaws and limitations.

By following Christ's teachings, and – more importantly – by opening our hearts to the cleansing power of His Holy Spirit, we become increasingly freed from material attachments and from the demands of our own sinful natures. Paul describes this process of spiritual rebirth as one in which we are 'changed into his likeness from one degree of glory to another; for this comes from the Lord who is the Spirit' (II Cor. 3:18 RSV). In other words, little by little we become more Christ-like.

But our liberation from sin comes at a price – a price paid not by ourselves but by the divine Word of God. To promulgate His teachings which could free us from sin, and to impart the celestial power by which we could translate those teachings into action, Christ had to oppose ruthless, entrenched religious and political vested interests. Accepting this burden meant certain persecution, humiliation, torture and crucifixion – a consequence He willingly faced in order to complete His mission of redemption. On this pragmatic level we can view the atonement as meaning Christ did what had to be done – regardless of cost – to reconcile imperfect humanity to its perfect Creator.

His sacrifice means even more in the light of Jewish religious history. Under Old Testament law, worshippers sought access to God through a complex system of ritual sacrifice that involved the shedding of animal blood. These sacrifices, repeated year after year, prefigured and pointed forward to the ultimate sacrifice by Christ of Himself. As the pure and spotless 'Lamb of God' Christ shed His blood in a one-time act of atonement sufficient to fulfil and satisfy forever the demands of Jewish law. In the words of the prophet Daniel, He 'cause[d] the sacrifice and the oblation [offering] to cease' (Dan. 9:27), rendering further animal sacrifice unnecessary. He thus brought the Jewish dispensation to its befitting climax, opening in its place the Christian era in which humankind could seek God not through legalistic ritual but through faith, sincere repentance and a personal relationship.

Bahá'u'lláh makes clear, moreover, that there are still deeper mysteries in the atonement – mysteries that can never be reduced to merely pragmatic or historical explanations:

> Know thou that when the Son of Man yielded up His breath to God, the whole creation wept with a great weeping. By sacrificing Himself, however, a fresh capacity was infused into all created things. Its evidences, as witnessed in all the peoples of the earth, are now manifest before thee. The deepest wisdom which the sages have uttered, the profoundest learning which any mind hath unfolded, the arts which the ablest hands have produced, the influence exerted by the most potent of rulers, are but manifestations of the quickening power released by His transcendent, His all-pervasive, and resplendent Spirit . . . He it is Who purified the world (G 85-6).

The Resurrection

A second cornerstone of Christianity is Christ's resurrection after three days in the tomb. The miracle of the resurrection is – like the atonement – a truth which Bahá'ís affirm with complete conviction. It constitutes incontrovertible proof of Christ's immortality and of His unfailing redemptive power.

Since the resurrection is a divine mystery, it is neither possible nor important for us to understand precisely how it occurred. We can, however, glean important insights from the various Gospel accounts. These suggest that the risen Christ appeared to His disciples in what some Christian scholars call a 'glorified' body. Such a form apparently is one He can manifest as He chooses, through either our physical or spiritual senses. New Testament writers consistently emphasize the extraordinary nature of His post-resurrection presence:

The Gospels relate that Christ was crucified and buried; that His tomb was examined three days later and found empty; and that shortly thereafter He appeared, alive and well, to His disciples and certain other followers who saw Him, touched Him, shared food with Him and heard Him declare: '. . . it is I myself: handle me, and see; for a spirit hath not flesh and bones, as ye see me have' (Luke 24:39). Curiously, even His closest associates failed to recognize Him during these encounters except when Christ Himself somehow permitted them to do so. To two of His companions He appeared 'in another form' (Mark 16:12), though the Bible does not specify what that form was. He came and went mysteriously, unhindered by obstacles such as walls and locked doors. Stephen, the first Christian martyr, on his way to death by stoning, 'looked up stedfastly into heaven, and saw the glory of God, and Jesus standing on the right hand of God . . .' (Acts 7:55). Stephen's experience clearly was a vision, since apparently none of those around him saw what he saw. Saul of Tarsus, one of Christianity's deadliest persecutors, became the inspired Apostle Paul, its greatest missionary, after an encounter he describes as the last sighting of the resurrected Jesus: 'And last of all he was seen of me . . .' (I Cor. 15:8). What Saul saw on this occasion was not a human form but a blinding light, which left him 'three days without sight' (Acts 9:9); he heard a voice say, 'Saul, Saul, why persecutest thou me?' (Acts 9:4); while 'the men who journeyed with him stood speechless, hearing a voice, but seeing no man' (Acts 9:7).

These Bible accounts depict the resurrection as a reality with both physical and spiritual ramifications. By thus proving His own immortality, Christ triumphantly vindicated His offer of eternal life to all who would accept His salvation. This raises, however, a crucial question: Is the immortality which the resurrection demonstrates a physical or a spiritual immortality?

One tempting answer might be: 'Christ appeared to His disciples in physical form. It follows that His immortality, and the immortality granted to His followers, must also be physical. It means we will live forever on this earth in material bodies.' Before leaping to such a conclusion, however, let us explore a different possibility. Could we not interpret the resurrection's outward manifestations (like those of the virgin birth) as visible signs of an invisible reality? The virgin birth, as we discussed earlier, was the physical expression of a metaphysical truth – of the fact that the pre-existent Word had lived as the 'firstborn of every creature' and the 'only begotten of the Father' 'from of old, from everlasting' (Micah 5:2). Since this first episode of Christ's earthly life testifies to His spiritual immortality in the past, might we regard its last episode – His resurrection – as similarly testifying to His spiritual immortality in the future?

Bahá'ís believe the Bible supports this latter view. It teaches that the resurrection, in all its earthly and heavenly aspects (for there were both), was God's way of demonstrating Christ's *spiritual* immortality, and, by extension, His power to confer eternal *spiritual* life on those who follow Him. By 'spiritual immortality' and 'eternal spiritual life', I mean a life in which the physical body as we know it plays no part. Let us consider Paul's explanation:

> But someone may ask, 'How are the dead raised? With what kind of body will they come?' How foolish! What you sow does not come to life unless it dies. When you sow, you do not plant the body that will be, but just a seed, perhaps of wheat or of something else. But God gives it a body as he has determined, and to each kind of seed he gives its own body . . . There also are heavenly bodies and there are earthly bodies; but the splendour of the heavenly bodies is one kind, and the splendour of the earthly bodies is another. The sun has one kind of splendour, the moon another, and the stars another; and star differs from star in splendour.

So will it be with the resurrection of the dead. The body that is sown is perishable, it is raised imperishable . . . it is sown a natural body, it is raised a spiritual body.

If there is a natural body, there is also a spiritual body. So it is written: 'The first man Adam became a living being'; the last Adam, a life-giving spirit . . . The first man was of the dust of the earth, the second man from heaven. As was the earthly man, so are those who are of the earth; and as is the man from heaven, so also are those who are of heaven. And just as we have borne the likeness of the earthly man, so shall we bear the likeness of the man from heaven.

I declare to you, brothers, that flesh and blood cannot inherit the kingdom of God, nor does the perishable inherit the imperishable (I Cor. 15:35-50 NIV).

Paul's commentary, of course, raises new questions even as it answers old ones. The crucial point here is that 'children of the resurrection' who inhabit 'that world' (Luke 20:34-5) live on in a form utterly different from the material bodies with which we are familiar as 'children of this world' (Luke 20:36). The difference, Paul says, between the 'body that is sown' (buried in the ground) and the 'body that will be' is at least as vast as the difference between an ungerminated grain of wheat and the ripened sheaf that rises from it. The 'heavenly body' of the resurrection is no longer a 'natural', 'perishable', 'flesh and blood' body made from the 'dust of the earth' but an indestructible 'spiritual body' in 'the likeness of the man from heaven'.

This last point is particularly significant. Far from making Him an exception to this the rule, Paul cites Christ ('the man from heaven') as its chief example and illustration. He thereby implies that Christ, at an appropriate time and in some manner God chose not to reveal, traded His earthly body for a more befitting celestial form – one with greatly enhanced powers.

Since the Bible does not say when this exchange took place, the realization that it did occur need not conflict with

Christ's statement that He appeared to His disciples with 'flesh and bone'. We may find, however, that it clashes at first with our own deeply ingrained habits of thought. While confined to this earthly plane, we experience reality mostly through our five bodily senses. This predisposes us to think of 'spirit' as less than matter – as something illusory, uncertain, ephemeral. Solid matter, in contrast, appears reassuringly stable and powerful. Given such conditioning, we recoil from the idea that the Lord Christ might be 'reduced' to 'mere' spirit.

The Bible shows, however, that this all-too-human way of looking at things is misleading. God is spirit; and the glorious reality of Christ also is a 'quickening spirit'. It is the latter who – as the mediator of God's power – creates both the physical and spiritual universes, 'sustaining all things by His powerful word'. This was true at the dawn of creation, and it is still true; the resurrection changed nothing in this respect. All that exists – oceans and mountains, heaven and hell, whatever lies between – does so at His command. Our own material existence, our very flesh and bone, are expressions of that primal Will. If His all-embracing power were withheld for less than a nanosecond, we would vanish.

An omnipotent Being of this order surely can reveal Himself to us in whatever way best suits His purpose: either through our spiritual faculties, or – just as easily – through our physical senses, in a form we would register as visible, audible and tangible. Yet doing so would not make Him less intrinsically spiritual; it would not confine Him to the earthly plane or require that He maintain an earthly form at all times. The divine Source of both matter and spirit must be something more than either (as we ordinarily think of them). He cannot be 'merely' anything.

It is in terms of this 'something more' that we must seek the real intent of Christ's statement concerning 'flesh and bones'. When the risen Lord visited His disciples, they were 'affrighted', thinking they had seen 'a spirit'. The expression so translated in the King James Version means, in this context, that they thought they had seen a ghost. (Both the New International Version and New English Bible make this explicit.) Ghosts, then as now, were thought of as flimsy things, not altogether real – evil omens, perhaps, or figments of a troubled imagination. Christ assured His disciples that He was absolutely real and alive, that He was the same Christ He always had been: 'A ghost does not have flesh and bones, as you see I have' (Luke 24:39 NIV). This statement does not deny Christ's essential nature as that transcendent 'Lord who is the Spirit' (II Cor. 3:18 RSV, NIV). It simply demonstrates (among other things) that One who can manifest worlds and galaxies with but a thought can also manifest to our senses a palpable image of His human form – without limiting Himself to that form.

If I were asked, 'Does Christ have a physical body today?' my answer would be, 'Only when He wants one.' The Bible makes it quite clear, however, that He normally would have no reason to want one. Paul and his contemporaries clearly thought of 'being with Christ' as a spiritual experience: 'whilst we are at home in the body, we are absent from the Lord,' the Apostle explains, adding that Christians should therefore be 'willing rather to be absent from the body, and present with the Lord' (II Cor. 5:6, 8). Since Paul tells us that 'flesh and blood cannot inherit the kingdom of God', and Christ is the appointed Heir of that Kingdom as well as of 'all things' (Heb. 1:2), it follows that flesh and blood is a liability He no longer needs. The author of Hebrews confirms this by referring in the past tense to Christ's earthly life as 'the days of his flesh' (Heb. 5:7). Such a reference can only mean that by the time this verse was revealed, He was no longer in the flesh anywhere, either on earth or in heaven.

If we take these Bible verses at face value (as Bahá'ís do), then it is logical to ask what Christ did with His earthly body once it had served His purpose. This, however, is a question the Bible seems not to answer. It does not say whether the

risen Saviour abandoned His original body, destroyed it or
(as suggested by the theologians mentioned above) transformed and glorified it. Does this make any difference? We
know that the timeless Word of God, with or without a
material body, is all-powerful, ever-present and eternally
alive. This is the glorious and undeniable reality of the
resurrection.

'Why Stand Ye Gazing Up?'

Another issue is the nature of Christ's ascension to heaven,
which Bahá'ís also accept and affirm. This event is described
in the first chapter of Acts and discussed in several other
parts of the New Testament. Some Christians see the ascension as proof that Christ's physical body still exists beyond
the clouds, preparing to 're-enter' the earth's atmosphere
like an orbiting rocket. Others believe He ascended physically but then changed to a non-corporeal state. Still others
(including most Bahá'ís) view the ascension itself as a transition occurring on the invisible spiritual plane. Close inspection will show why the Bible narrative lends itself to such a
wide range of interpretations.

Acts records that to His disciples Christ 'shewed himself
alive after his passion by many infallible proofs, being seen
of them forty days, and speaking of the things pertaining to
the kingdom of God' (Acts 1:3). Promising them the power
of the Holy Spirit, He charged them to 'be witnesses unto me
. . . unto the uttermost part of the earth' (Acts 1:8). The
account continues:

> And when he had spoken these things, while they beheld,
> he was taken up; and a cloud received him out of their
> sight.
>   And while they looked stedfastly toward heaven as he
> went up, behold, two men stood by them in white apparel;
> Which also said, Ye men of Galilee, why stand ye gazing up
> into heaven? this same Jesus, which is taken up from you

into heaven, shall so come in like manner as ye have seen him go into heaven (Acts 1:9-11).

The last verse, which states that 'this same Jesus' will return 'in like manner as ye have seen him go', is sometimes cited as proof that the Second Coming will take place in the visible sky. I see no basis for such an inference. Christ Himself describes His spiritual appearance in the womb using the language of physical descent ('I came down from heaven'). Here His future advent is also described as a physical descent (or – which is the same thing – as an ascent in reverse). We know that the Bible often uses physical symbols and events to prefigure spiritual realities. Thus, even if Christ's body did rise physically into the sky, this reference to His coming 'in like manner' could easily foreshadow a new advent precisely like the old. Bahá'u'lláh states that this is indeed the case: 'He, verily, hath again come down from Heaven even as He came down from it the first time' (PDC 31).

However, the above-quoted passage from Acts does not say that Christ rose physically into the sky. It says He was 'taken up . . . into heaven', which is not necessarily the same thing. We already know from the Bible that 'heaven' does not always mean the sky. The materialistic interpretation suffers in this case from a serious flaw: It offers no reasonable explanation for the odd question posed by the two (presumably angelic) beings described as men 'in white apparel'.

The question is straightforward: 'Why stand ye gazing up into heaven?' (Acts 1:11). Why, indeed – or rather, why not? If a materialistic view of the ascension is correct, this question makes little sense. Let us put ourselves in the place of Christ's disciples. Watching in stunned awe, we have just seen our Redeemer leave the ground and float into the sky, suspended by an unseen force, gradually appearing smaller and smaller and finally vanishing in mist. How should we behave in such extraordinary circumstances? What constitutes a normal human reaction? Well, I know what I would do: I would stare up after Him, struggling to keep Him in sight as long as

possible. Even if I could ignore the perfectly natural aston-
ishment any sane person would feel under such circumstances, I could not ignore the wrenching realization that this
would probably be my last glimpse (in this earthly lifetime)
of my beloved Lord and Master. Knowing that much, I would
fight all the angels of heaven and all the demons of hell for
that last, sweet, lingering look. Nor do I believe that any
Christian on earth would do otherwise.

However, the sharp question – 'Why stand ye gazing up
into heaven?' – strongly suggests that 'gazing up' was in this
instance inappropriate. Let us therefore consider a less
conventional explanation: Christ's post-resurrection presence among His disciples lasted for forty days, until 'a cloud
received him out of their sight' (Acts 1:9), meaning they
suddenly sensed He no longer was among them. The cloud
in this case represents the confusion, uncertainty and dismay
that the disciples must have felt.* While they sought to
penetrate the cloud (i.e. to understand Christ's mysterious
departure), the Saviour Himself was being invisibly 'taken
up' to the same spiritual heaven from which His immortal
reality had 'descended' into His mother's womb. The disciples, even at this late date, still suffered from their human
tendency to misinterpret His 'language of revelation' as
'earthly speech'. Having heard Him speak often of His
ascension, they scanned the skies for some clue to His disappearance. The angels then chided them for their failure to
grasp the inner reality: 'Ye men of Galilee, why stand ye
gazing up into heaven? this same Jesus, which is taken up
from you into heaven, shall so come in like manner as ye
have seen him go into heaven' (Acts 1:11). The meaning, in
this context, is not that Christ will return physically from the
sky. It is that His Second Coming will take place under the
same 'cloudy' circumstances as His departure – a cloud, that
is, of confusion, ambiguity and mystery.

*The term 'cloud' is often used in the Bible to denote mystery and
confusion. See Chapter 4 for Bahá'u'lláh's comments on this usage.

Christ Himself had already hinted that His ascension would test the spiritual insight of many believers. When the disciples, clinging to their material frames of reference, struggled with His statement that He 'came down from heaven', Christ replied: 'Doth this offend you? What and if ye see the Son of man ascend up where he was before? It is the spirit that quickeneth; the flesh profiteth nothing . . .' (John 6:61-3). We know that 'where he was before' was not the visible sky, for His body was born of Mary. It was His innermost reality that was 'with God' and that 'was God' in the domain Bahá'u'lláh calls the 'Paradise of the Placeless'. The ascension (as Christ's words imply) was the return of His spirit to its heavenly home beyond space and time.

Further evidence for a non-material ascension comes from these words of Christ: 'And no man hath ascended up to heaven, but he that came down from heaven, even the Son of Man which is in heaven' (John 3:13). This verse shows that heavenly ascent and descent are parallel actions, either of which Christ can undertake without leaving heaven at all. We can understand this easily in terms of the Divine Reflection analogy. When the sun shines in a mirror its image has in one sense 'descended' from the sky – yet both the sun and its image, in another sense, remain in the sky. When the mirror ceases to reflect the sun, the image 'ascends' to the sky, not as a bird or an airplane would ascend but simply in the sense that we now must turn to the sky in order to continue seeing it. When the divine Word (the 'image of the invisible') appeared in its earthly mirror (the human temple of Jesus), this constituted its true descent from the heaven of God's presence. When the Word ceased to shine in that same physical lamp, this constituted its true ascension. Whether this inward reality had an outward, visible counterpart is of no importance: 'It is the spirit that quickeneth; the flesh profiteth nothing' (John 6:63).

Reflections

To review our main points: The physical sun, placed before a mirror, has three aspects – the sun itself, its reflection and its rays. This material 'trinity' closely parallels the Bible's three aspects of God – the Father, the Word and the Holy Spirit:

1) The Father is the Divine Essence, 'dwelling in unapproachable light' where 'no man has ever seen or ever can see him'.
2) The Word is the Divine Reflection, the 'image of the invisible', 'the exact representation of his being', eternally manifesting 'all that may be known of God' to 'the eye of reason' in the form of God's 'invisible attributes'.
3) The Holy Spirit is the Divine Energy, the radiance of God's power, glory and creativity, of which God says: 'I will pour out my spirit upon all flesh.'

The pre-existent Word – that 'quickening spirit' called Christ – is the 'only begotten Son of God' in the sense of being the only entity directly generated from God's hidden essence. As the 'firstborn of every creature', it is the agency through which God's power brings into existence all other created things. The greatness of the Word is infinitely beyond human comprehension. We may think of the Word in philosophical terms as a metaphysical principle or universal life-force; but such abstractions hardly begin to tell the story. Both the Bible and Bahá'í sacred writings depict the Word in moving personal terms as a more-than-human Entity of sublime goodness, all-encompassing knowledge and wisdom, tender compassion and irresistible power. He is, in Bahá'u'lláh's memorable phrase, 'the supreme embodiment of all that is lovable' (GBP 119).

Christ's spiritual nature is therefore a divine reality distinct from, and immeasurably superior to, His human nature. Many Christian theologians have emphasized this distinction between the 'divine Christ' (the eternal Word He personified) and the 'human Christ' (the earthly personality within which the Word became resplendent). Others make the same point by differentiating the 'metaphysical Jesus' from the 'historical Jesus'. Such a distinction is clear from the very titles 'Christ' and 'Messiah', both of which mean (in Greek and Hebrew respectively) 'the Anointed One'. The Son of Man was simultaneously the Son of God in the sense that He was 'anointed' with the pre-existent Word or Logos born of God's essence. As a human being, the Galilean carpenter was the earthly vehicle for a heavenly and super-human Spirit.

These considerations answer the question posed at the outset of this chapter. According to the Bible, Christ's absolute uniqueness lies in His spiritual nature as the pre-existent Word. This nature is not a physical characteristic – certainly not in any sense that might trap Him for all time within a particular earthly body or that would prevent Him from reappearing in an outwardly different form with a new human identity. The sun's image may appear in a new mirror, yet both the sun and its image remain unchanged. Likewise, the Word of God, the 'image of the invisible' sun-like Father, can manifest itself within a new human mirror – yet that spiritual image remains one and indivisible. It is this timeless, divine Reality to which Christ referred when He told His contemporaries: 'Before Abraham was, I am.' Since the 'I am' that was speaking on that occasion could hardly have included the material body of Jesus, why must we assume He included His material body when He promised: 'I shall come again'?

As we saw in Chapter 1, Old Testament prophets foretold that the Messiah would come from heaven with power and great glory, seen by all flesh. From a spiritual perspective, Christ's first advent fulfilled all of these promises – a fact that Christ and His Apostles emphasize throughout the New Testament. In strictly human terms, however, He appeared like a thief with a new and unfamiliar name, recognized only by a chosen few. As we have learned, the conditions prophesied for the Second Coming are identical to those fulfilled in the First: Christ promised to come from heaven with power and great glory, seen by every eye, while appearing like a thief with a new name. Moreover, the Bible plainly states that the latter-day prophecies (like those for the Messiah's earlier visitation) are written with a 'sealed' or coded meaning not to be found in any purely material interpretation. Do not such astonishing parallels suggest that Christ, as the divine Logos or 'quickening spirit', might reappear in the same manner as before – on earth, that is, with an outwardly new human persona?

Millions of devoted believers in the Bible now accept Bahá'u'lláh as the intended fulfilment of these divine prophecies. Bahá'u'lláh challenges every individual to ascertain whether or not He represents the promised return of Christ for whom the world's Christians are waiting: 'He, verily, hath again come down from Heaven even as He came down from it the first time. Beware that thou dispute not with Him even as the Pharisees disputed with Him without a clear token or proof' (PDC 31). Bahá'u'lláh obviously does not claim to possess the same physical body or the same human personality as the historical Jesus. What He claims to be is a new mirror reflecting the same divine sun – the 'Word made flesh' in a new human temple with a new name. As such, Bahá'u'lláh (if His claim is true) manifests the spiritually pre-existent Christ 'whose goings forth have been from of old, from eternity'.

'None Other Name'

Some Christians hesitate because of uncertainty as to how we can reconcile Bahá'u'lláh's claim with various Bible passages. Such questions are of course important and necessary. In every case with which I am familiar, the answers become clear from the Bible itself once we understand Bahá'u'lláh's position. A few examples:

'I am the way, the truth, and the life: no man cometh unto the Father, but by me' (John 14:6). The voice speaking in this passage is that of the same 'quickening spirit' who said 'Before Abraham was, I am.' Both passages refer to Christ's station as the timeless Word of God. Neither refers to the temporal personality within which and through which 'the Word was made flesh'. Just as we know the sun's inward nature solely through its outward image, it is only through the Word – the 'image of the invisible God' – that we can know anything of God or receive His spiritual gifts. Even though the divine image reflected in the mirror of Jesus reappears in the mirror of Bahá'u'lláh, it remains the same pre-existent Word, the same quickening Christ-spirit or Logos. Wherever it appears, this luminous reality is 'the way, the truth, and the life' through which alone we may approach the Father.

'Jesus Christ [is] the same yesterday, and to day and for ever' (Heb. 13:7). Again, this essential truth has nothing to do with the physical body of Jesus. That body, having been conceived through the power of the Holy Spirit, developed in the womb of Mary, was born, then matured and aged quite normally. Since His human temple plainly is not 'the same' at all times, this passage can only be a reference to the divine nature of Christ which Bahá'ís believe has reappeared in Bahá'u'lláh.

'There is none other name under heaven given among men, whereby we must be saved' (Acts 4:12). This well-known verse in no way contradicts Christ's related prophecy of the 'new name' through which He and His followers are to be known in the day of His Return. Whenever that 'quickening spirit' takes human form, He adopts and is known by a human name. Any such name becomes – within that historical context – the 'only name' through which we can obey the Voice of God for that particular day. This in no way restricts Christ's right to take, at any time, any name and human identity He pleases. It means we must turn to Him whenever and wherever He

appears, accepting the name He has chosen – for no other name will do.

We can also understand this passage in terms of Revelation 19:13. After speaking of the new and secret name which the returned Messiah, in His human station, will bear, the scripture continues 'and his name is called The Word of God'. The reference here is not to the personal label but to the descriptive title designating Christ's 'real' identity as the Divine Logos. Throughout eternity there is only one Logos. This pre-existent 'quickening spirit', whenever it appears, is always called 'The Word of God'. No other name, referring to any other reality, can save us, for it is only through the Logos that we can approach God. Though outwardly different as individuals, both Jesus and Bahá'u'lláh personified this same Logos or divine reflection; and both were therefore known as 'The Word of God'. From this standpoint they may be, in Bahá'u'lláh's words, 'regarded as . . . the same person' (WOB 115); and they share this unique name distinctive of the historical Christ-figure.

It is true that anyone claiming to embody the return of Christ must satisfy some very strict conditions. Discussing the signs of His Second Coming, Jesus says:

> For many shall come in my name, saying, I am Christ; and shall deceive many . . . Then if any man shall say unto you, Lo, here is Christ, or there; believe it not. For there shall arise false Christs, and false prophets, and shall shew great signs and wonders; insomuch that, if it were possible, they shall deceive the very elect . . . Wherefore, if they shall say unto you, Behold, he is in the desert; go not forth: behold, he is in the secret chambers; believe it not. For as the lightning cometh out of the east, and shineth even unto the west; so shall also the coming of the Son of man be (Matt. 24:5, 23-7).

This statement is part of Christ's discourse on the Mount of

Olives, a sermon containing many of His most significant prophecies concerning the Return. Bahá'u'lláh Himself discusses some of these prophecies in His *Book of Certitude*. A detailed Bahá'í perspective on the entire Olivet Discourse is found in *The Prophecies of Jesus* by Bible scholar Michael Sours. We have space here for only a few personal observations:

1) First and foremost, this passage (as I understand it) warns us against purported Messiahs who take the actual name of Christ. The translation in which this meaning comes across most clearly is perhaps that of the New English Bible, which reads: '. . . many shall come claiming my name, saying "I am the Messiah".' Using different words, therefore, this verse restates and reinforces the other prophecies in which Christ promises to come with a 'new name'. Although Bahá'u'lláh claims to be a new human temple for the everlasting Logos, He at no time used or was known by the names 'Christ', 'Jesus' or any variations of these.

2) Christ also denounces impostors who 'shall shew great signs and wonders' – that is, who support their claims by displaying apparently miraculous powers. Bahá'u'lláh does not do this. Bahá'ís certainly recognize that the pre-existent Word, even in human form, is omnipotent and thus capable of performing miracles. But Bahá'u'lláh has emphasized that such feats constitute evidence only for those who actually see them and that seldom if ever are they sufficient even then. Bahá'ís are therefore forbidden to cite reported miracles as proofs of Bahá'u'lláh's validity. As we shall see, the proofs of Bahá'u'lláh's claims are based upon logical and intuitive criteria, and, in particular, on the fact that He meets the standards set forth in the Bible for the genuineness of His claims.

3) Christ states that He will not be hidden in 'secret chambers' or a 'desert'. 'For as the lightning cometh out of the east, and shineth even unto the west; so shall also the coming of the Son of man be.' These comments are widely interpreted as supporting the traditional view that Christ will

appear in the sky. Bahá'ís, however, tend to read them as allusions to the startling openness of Bahá'u'lláh's public proclamation and to the lightning-like speed with which knowledge of His Faith spread from the East to the West. His enemies (including the all-powerful kings of Persia and Turkey) tried vainly to suppress all knowledge of His Cause and to cut Him off from the world, first through successive banishments, then by confining Him to the Turkish prison-fortress of 'Akká (now part of Israel). These efforts notwith-standing, Bahá'u'lláh publicly proclaimed His mission to the governments and peoples of the world, burst free of the restrictions with which He was shackled, and attained a degree of influence almost unheard-of for a prisoner. His constant interactions with individuals from every walk of life – scholars, statesmen, religious leaders and ordinary people – are a matter of public record.

In the middle and late 1800s the dramatic birth of the Cause in the Middle East captured the attention of European historians such as Comte de Gobineau, A. L. M. Nicolas, Edward Granville Browne and others, who spared no effort to collect and disseminate first-hand information about its origins. During the opening decade of the twentieth century, Bahá'í communities, significant both in size and number, sprang up in Europe and America. Bahá'u'lláh's eldest son, 'Abdu'l-Bahá, travelled through Europe and America in 1911-13 to promote His father's teachings. His journeys generated sensational press coverage, which tracked His every move from coast to coast. North American Bahá'ís subsequently took a leading role in establishing the adminis-trative structure of the Faith throughout the world. Anticipat-ing these developments, Bahá'u'lláh had written: 'In the East the light of His Revelation hath broken; in the West have appeared the signs of His dominion' (TB 13).

The upshot is that less than a century after the passing of its Founder, the Faith of Bahá'u'lláh had become – after Christianity itself – the world's most widespread religion. Successive issues of the *Encyclopedia Britannica* and the *World*

Christian Encyclopedia, in statistics compiled by leading scholars, list the Bahá'í Faith as second only to Christianity in the number of countries where it has established a 'significant following'. This geographical extension is even more startling when we consider that the Faith still is relatively small among other world religions. Its spread has been accomplished through the sustained and systematic dispersion of Bahá'í 'pioneers', intent on carrying the glad-tidings of Bahá'u'lláh throughout the globe. Michael Sours comments:

> The words 'like lightning' suggest the open visibility of Bahá'u'lláh's proclamation, its startling nature, and the speed of its development. It is a sudden bright light amidst a storm, carrying a forceful message (Sours, *Prophecies of Jesus* 100).

Finally, some Christians hesitate to consider Bahá'u'lláh because they have been taught that a sinister individual known as 'the Antichrist' will arise in the last days to persecute the Church. 'Couldn't Bahá'u'lláh be the Antichrist?' they ask. 'And if this is even remotely possible, should we not play it safe by acting on the assumption that He is?'

The answer is found in those passages of scripture where the term 'antichrist' occurs. The word occurs five times in three passages – three, and no more:

> Little children, it is the last time: and as ye have heard that antichrist shall come, even now are there many antichrists; whereby we know that it is the last time. They went out from us, but they were not of us . . . Who is a liar but he that denieth that Jesus is the Christ? He is antichrist, that denieth the Father and the Son. Whosoever denieth the Son, the same hath not the Father: but he that acknowledgeth the Son hath the Father also (I John 2:18-23).

> Beloved, believe not every spirit, but try the spirits whether they are of God: because many false prophets are gone out into the world. Hereby know ye the Spirit of God: Every

spirit that confesseth that Jesus Christ is come in the flesh is of God: And every spirit that confesseth not that Jesus Christ is come in the flesh is not of God: and this is that spirit of antichrist, whereof ye have heard that it should come; and even now already is it in the world (I John 4:1-3).

For many deceivers are entered into the world, who confess not that Jesus Christ is come in the flesh. This is a deceiver and an antichrist (II John 7).

This is a complete list of scriptural references to the term 'antichrist'. As we can see, the Bible speaks of 'many antichrists', 'many false prophets', 'many deceivers . . . who confess not that Jesus Christ is come in the flesh'; and it emphasizes that such persons have troubled the church since its beginning. Nowhere does scripture apply the term 'antichrist' to one specific individual or institution. The Bible defines the term to mean anyone who denies the reality of Christ's divine position as the 'Word made flesh'. Bahá'u'lláh, on the contrary, affirms this reality, defending all of Christ's claims and testifying to the truth of all that the Bible teaches about Him. Throughout Bahá'u'lláh's writings and teachings we find such moving tributes as these:

We testify that when He [Christ] came into the world, He shed the splendour of His glory upon all created things . . . Through Him, the unchaste and wayward were healed. Through His power, born of Almighty God, the eyes of the blind were opened, and the soul of the sinner sanctified . . . We bear witness that through the power of the Word of God every leper was cleansed, every sickness was healed, every human infirmity was banished (G 85-6).

. . . whatsoever hath proceeded out of His blameless, His truth-speaking, trustworthy mouth, can never be altered (TB 14).

See how many conquering kings there have been, how many statesmen and princes, powerful organizers, all of whom have disappeared, whereas the breezes of Christ are still blowing; His light is still shining; His melody is still resounding; His standard is still waving; His armies are still fighting; His heavenly voice is still sweetly melodious; His clouds are still showering gems; His lightning is still flashing; His reflection is still clear and brilliant; His splendour is still radiating and luminous; and it is the same with those souls who are under His protection and are shining with His light (SAQ 152-3).

The position of Christ was that of absolute perfection; He made His divine perfections shine like the sun upon all believing souls, and the bounties of the light shone and radiated in the reality of men (SAQ 121).

So Christ – may my spirit be sacrificed to Him! – was the manifestation of these words, 'He doeth whatsoever He willeth,' but the disciples were not partakers of this condition; for as they were under the shadow of Christ, they could not deviate from His command and will (SAQ 174). In the Gospel it is said, 'In the beginning was the Word, and the Word was with God.' Then it is evident and clear that Christ . . . from all eternity has always been, and will be, in the exaltation of sanctification (SAQ 153).

These are but a few of the many, many passages from Bahá'í scripture praising and glorifying Christ. We already have cited other examples and in future chapters we will quote from still others. The more deeply we delve into Bahá'u'lláh's teachings, the more they confirm and strengthen our finding that Bahá'u'lláh is passionately 'pro-Christ', not the opposite.

The Bible's guidance with regard to 'antichrists' is clear. The fact that 'many false prophets are gone out into the world' in no way excuses us from investigating. Our mandate is rather to 'try the spirits whether they are of God'. This book is an invitation to every earnest Christian to do exactly that – to 'test everything', as Paul advises in I Thessalonians 5:21 (RSV), and 'hold fast what is good'.

4

A More Sure Word of Prophecy

> We have also a more sure word of prophecy; whereunto ye
> do well that ye take heed, as unto a light that shineth in a
> dark place, until the day dawn, and the day star arise in
> your hearts (II Peter 1:19).

It may be useful, at this point, to illustrate some of the principles of scripture interpretation mentioned in Chapter 2. What better way than to survey the Bible's prophecies about the coming of the Lord in the 'last days'?

It is, of course, important to indicate how the prophecies can reasonably be applied to Bahá'u'lláh; but it is one thing to offer such an interpretation and quite another to prove that it is correct. I do not believe that any interpretation of Bible prophecy can by itself prove or disprove Bahá'u'lláh's authenticity. Any such interpretation advanced by a Bahá'í, no matter how plausible or convincing, can be matched by an equally plausible and convincing interpretation by a different reader who does not accept Bahá'u'lláh. The reverse is also true.

This being so, I do not insist that anyone accept at once the explanations of Bible prophecy I am about to offer. It is possible to understand a Bahá'í perspective without necessarily agreeing with it; and all I ask, at this point, is such understanding. The next chapter will explore other biblical criteria – criteria not based on messianic prophecy – by which we can test Bahá'u'lláh's claim. It is these additional criteria which, I will argue, establish the validity of Bahá'u'lláh's claim (and by extension the rightness of His prophetic interpretation).

For the time being, then, while setting aside questions of proof, let us see how a Bahá'í might view the prophecies. Since a comprehensive commentary on end-time prophecy is beyond the scope of this book, I will present a somewhat simplified outline.

The Day of God

The Bible depicts human history as moving toward a stupendous climax referred to as the 'day of the Lord', the 'time of the end' or – often – simply as 'that day'. This finale, though characterized at the outset by cataclysmic tribulation, is to usher in a millennium of peace and divine justice. In Bible prophecy, the high point of this drama is the Second Coming of Christ destined to establish, in visible worldwide form, the Kingdom of God on earth.

The coming of the Kingdom is extolled in promise, prophecy and prayer: 'Thy kingdom come, thy will be done, in earth as it is in heaven' (Matt. 6:10). It is a time of world peace: 'and they shall beat their swords into plowshares, and their spears into pruninghooks: nation shall not lift up sword against nation, neither shall they learn war any more' (Isa. 2:4). It is a time of secure and universal prosperity: 'But they shall sit every man under his vine and under his fig tree; and none shall make them afraid . . .' (Micah 4:4). True spirituality will reign: '. . . the earth shall be full of the knowledge of the Lord, as the waters cover the sea' (Isa. 11:9). 'For all people will walk every one in the name of his god, and we will walk in the name of the Lord our God for ever and ever' (Micah 4:5).

The Holy Land is assigned a pre-eminent role in God's government:

And it shall come to pass in the last days, that the mountain of the Lord's house shall be established in the top of the mountains . . . for out of Zion shall go forth the law, and the word of the Lord from Jerusalem (Isa. 2:3).

God's dominion will be world-embracing: 'all nations shall flow unto it' (Isa. 2:2). The divine kingdom will command the allegiance not only of the world's peoples but their political institutions: 'And the nations of them which are saved shall walk in the light of it: and the kings of the earth do bring their glory and honour into it' (Rev. 21:24).

Such expressions as 'day of the Lord' and 'end of the world' have given rise to images of an earth demolished within a twenty-four-hour day (to be replaced, presumably, by the 'new heavens and a new earth' of which the scriptures also speak – II Peter 3:13). Bahá'ís believe that the word 'day', in this context, refers to an age or dispensation. This is in keeping with the statement of Peter that 'one day is with the Lord as a thousand years, and a thousand years as one day' (II Peter 3:8). As many Christian scholars have noted, the biblical expression 'end of the world' is more accurately translated 'end of the age'. It refers (Bahá'ís believe) to a time of transition between the present, largely man-made order of things, and the divine system destined to replace it. The 'end of the world' means the end of civilization as we know it, while the 'new heavens' and 'new earth' refer to a new and higher civilization governed by God Himself.

The Bible makes it clear that warfare and desolation will prevail until the second coming of Christ, who alone can institute real peace and unity. Recognizing this principle, some Christians are deeply suspicious of any movement towards what they regard as a 'man-made' peace. Any such peace (the reasoning goes) would be artificial and unstable, as well as subject to manipulation by satanic forces.

Bahá'ís agree that real peace is possible only through the return of Christ. However, they believe this return has already occurred with the reappearance of His 'spirit and power' in Bahá'u'lláh. This return – according to Bahá'u'lláh Himself – has set in motion vast historical forces that already are ushering in the Kingdom of God on earth. This fulfil-ment of prophecy, though far from instantaneous, is well under way. It is occurring in stages that will in time lead to the unification of the world and the consequent abolition of war. These developments will lay the foundation for humanity's spiritual education and upliftment – a process which, over a span of centuries, will bring into being a World Commonwealth dedicated to God and energized by obedience to His Law. The Bahá'í teachings describe this future civilization as one 'with a fullness of life such as the world has never seen nor can as yet conceive' (PDC 123).

The Day of Resurrection

The biblical term 'day' has a further significance to Bahá'ís. Bahá'u'lláh taught that the appearance on earth of that 'quickening spirit' called Christ is like the rising of the sun. His presence floods the world with the rays of the Holy Spirit. This radiance increases slowly in intensity, both while He walks the earth and, later, after His ascension to Heaven. Just as the material sun awakens the physical earth, stirring all things to new life, so does the dawning Sun of the Logos gradually energize the world of humanity. And just as the natural sun affects even dark corners of the material world, giving warmth and life to creatures that never have seen the sun itself, so does the 'Light of the World' exert its influence even among those who outwardly have never heard of it.

The advent of the historical Christ-figure is therefore a divine springtime for the entire world. New ideas, new discoveries and a new passion for advancement – inspired either directly or indirectly by the Messiah's revelation – permeate all of human society. This happened two thousand years ago with the advent of Jesus, and it is happening today with the advent of Bahá'u'lláh. How aptly does the Bible speak of Christ's return as 'the regeneration when the Son of man shall sit in the throne of His glory' (Matt. 19:28), in the day when 'the times of refreshing shall come from the presence of the Lord' (Acts 3:19).

If this revitalizing impulse so strongly stirs even those unaware of its heavenly Source, how much more true must this be of those who recognize and turn towards it. A principal effect of the Lord's advent is a widespread rebirth of faith, resulting in a community of believers – and later, a great civilization – based on His revealed laws and teachings. Bahá'u'lláh explains that this renewal of spiritual life is one meaning of the biblical 'Day of Resurrection':

> By the terms 'life' and 'death', spoken of in the scriptures, is intended the life of faith and the death of unbelief . . . In every age and century, the purpose of the Prophets of God and their chosen ones hath been no other but to affirm the spiritual significance of the terms 'life', 'resurrection', and 'judgement' . . . But oh! how strange and pitiful! Behold, all the people are imprisoned within the tomb of self, and lie buried beneath the nethermost depths of worldly desire! Wert thou to attain to but a dewdrop of the crystal waters of divine knowledge, thou wouldst readily realize that true life is not the life of the flesh but the life of the spirit. For the life of the flesh is common to both men and animals, whereas the life of the spirit is possessed only by the pure in heart who have quaffed from the ocean of faith and partaken of the fruit of certitude. This life knoweth no death, and this existence is crowned by immortality . . . If by 'life' be meant this earthly life, it is evident that death must needs overtake it (KI 114, 120-1).

Resurrection, then, is the birth of the individual to spiritual life. This 'second birth' comes about through the influence of the Holy Spirit, shining from the focal point of the personified Christ. The grave from which one arises is the grave of ignorance and heedlessness of God.

In both the Bible and Bahá'í scriptures there is another usage of 'resurrection' having to do with afterlife – the continuing growth and development of the soul after physical death. However, the Great Resurrection of the Last Day (as Bahá'ís interpret the Bible) means the collective spiritualization of humanity through the coming of Bahá'u'lláh.

The Day of Judgement

The analogy of Christ's arrival as a divine springtime is apt in yet another way. Springtime in the natural world is not only a time of growth and renewal. It also is a 'day of judgement' for whatever is dead and decaying. Ice melts. Frozen ground shifts. Powerful winds blow. Dead branches, loosened by fresh growth, crash to the ground. Spring storms and floods lash the earth, cleansing it of all that is not prepared to greet the new dawn.

The spiritual Day of Resurrection is a Day of Judgement in a similar sense. It is a day of intense turmoil, one in which light battles darkness, life battles death, growth battles stagnation, change battles immobility. As with the natural springtime, new life stirs almost imperceptibly at first, gathering strength so slowly that many fail to notice until it bursts into bloom. Ancient customs, having once served a useful purpose, no longer are appropriate and must be set aside. Powerful institutions, once vibrant with vision and purpose, have become corrupt defenders of a status quo that must be abandoned. Principles that once marked the cutting edge of social and spiritual progress now bring up its rear and must be superseded by new and still higher principles.

In this upheaval it is God's new revelation that sets the standard – that determines what will stand and what will fall. Ideas that conform to the spirit of the new day will flourish. Those that do not will die – some with barely a whimper, others after a cataclysmic struggle. Institutions and individuals are 'judged' by their response to the divine revelation, and they benefit or suffer accordingly.

The Bible describes this process in the following words:

> . . . so shall it be in the end of this world. The Son of man shall send forth his angels, and they shall gather out of his kingdom all things that offend, and them which do iniquity; And shall cast them into a furnace of fire: there shall be wailing and gnashing of teeth. Then shall the righteous shine forth as the sun in the kingdom of their Father (Matt. 13:40-3).

A common response to the Bahá'í interpretation is this: 'But how is it possible to be judged and not know it?' Such objections result from thinking of judgement in material terms (as taking place, for example, in a large courtroom). In reality, says Bahá'u'lláh, 'the peoples of the world are judged by their countenance. By it, their misbelief, their faith, and their iniquity are all made manifest' (KI 173). In a sense, then, we judge ourselves by our attitude towards the new dawn. We may demonstrate our willingness to investigate its Source with an open mind and heart. Or we may show our readiness to ignore it – perhaps even attack it – simply because it is strange and unfamiliar. St Paul describes divine judgement in these terms:

> . . . He that judgeth me is the Lord. Therefore judge nothing before the time, until the Lord come, who both will bring to light the hidden things of darkness, and will make manifest the counsels of the hearts . . . (I Cor. 4:4-5).

How are the counsels of the hearts made manifest? Through our own reaction to the divine utterance:

> For the word of God is quick, and powerful, and sharper than any two-edged sword, piercing even to the dividing asunder of soul and spirit, and of the joints and marrow, and is a discerner of the thoughts and intents of the heart (Heb. 4:12).

Coming in the Clouds

A recurring theme of prophecy is that of the 'clouds' associated with Christ's descent from heaven:

> . . . and they shall see the Son of man coming in the clouds of heaven with power and great glory. And he shall send his angels with a great sound of a trumpet . . . (Matt. 24:30-1).

This prophecy, too, we can understand through the now-familiar Bible analogy of Christ as the image of the sun-like God. A cloud is anything that obscures the sun's image and hinders us from recognizing its glory. It conceals the coming of the Lord: 'He bowed the heavens and came down . . . He made darkness his secret place; his pavilion round about him were dark waters and thick clouds . . .' (Psalms 18:9-11). Bahá'u'lláh comments:

> By the term 'clouds' is meant those things that are contrary to the ways and desires of men . . . These 'clouds' signify, in one sense, the annulment of laws, the abrogation of former Dispensations, the repeal of rituals and customs current amongst men, the exalting of the illiterate faithful above the learned opposers of the Faith. In another sense, they mean the appearance of that immortal Beauty in the image of mortal man, with such human limitations as eating and drinking, poverty and riches, glory and abasement, sleeping and waking, and such other things as cast doubt in the minds of men, and cause them to turn away. All such veils are symbolically referred to as 'clouds' . . .
>
> Even as the clouds prevent the eyes of men from beholding the sun, so do these things hinder the souls of men from recognizing the light of the divine Luminary. To this beareth witness that which hath proceeded out of the mouth of the unbelievers as revealed in the sacred Book . . . How, they wondered, could such a person be sent down from God, assert His ascendancy over all the peoples and kindreds of the earth, and claim Himself to be the goal of all creation . . . and yet be subject to such trivial things?
>
> . . . The All-Glorious hath decreed these very things, that are contrary to the desires of men, to be the touchstone and standard whereby He proveth His servants, that the just may be known from the wicked, and the faithful distinguished from the infidel . . .
>
> And now, concerning His words: 'And He shall send His angels . . .' By 'angels' is meant those who, reinforced by the power of the spirit, have consumed, with the fire of the love of God, all human traits and limitations, and have clothed themselves with the attributes of the most exalted Beings and of the Cherubim . . .

As the adherents of Jesus have never understood the hidden meaning of these words, and as the signs which they and the leaders of their Faith have expected have failed to appear, they . . . have thus deprived themselves of the outpourings of God's holy grace, and of the wonders of His divine utterance. Such is their low estate in this, the Day of Resurrection! They have even failed to perceive that were the signs of the Manifestation of God in every age to appear in the visible realm in accordance with the text of established traditions, none could possibly deny or turn away, nor would the blessed be distinguished from the miserable, and the transgressor from the God-fearing. Judge fairly: Were the prophecies recorded in the Gospel to be literally fulfilled; were Jesus, Son of Mary, accompanied by angels, to descend from the visible heaven upon the clouds; who would dare to disbelieve, who would dare to reject the truth, and wax disdainful? Nay, such consternation would immediately seize all the dwellers of the earth that no soul would be able to utter a word, much less to reject or accept the truth (KI 71-81).

The Elijah Paradigm

In the Revelation of St John, the promised Redeemer is sometimes described as 'one like unto the Son of man' (Rev. 1:13, 14:14) – not the same person, but one with the same divine attributes. We have already discussed Christ's teaching that the Second Coming of Elijah was fulfilled in John the Baptist. Though the two were distinct personalities (with different bodies and, presumably, different souls), John appeared 'in the spirit and power of Elijah' and therefore embodied his spiritual return. For Bahá'ís this episode prefigures the return of Christ Himself and illustrates its manner. Bahá'u'lláh comments:

. . . [Jesus], the Revealer of the unseen Beauty, addressing one day His disciples, referred unto His passing, and, kindling in their hearts the fire of bereavement, said unto them: 'I go away and come again unto you.' And in another

97

place He said: 'I go and another will come Who will tell you all that I have not told you, and will fulfil all that I have said.' Both these sayings have but one meaning . . . (KI 20).

The 'one meaning' to which Bahá'u'lláh refers is the reappearance of the divine image – Christ's 'quickening spirit' – in another human mirror through the reflected light of the Holy Spirit. This interpretation sheds new light on Christ's familiar words:

> I have yet many things to say unto you, but ye cannot bear them now. Howbeit when he, the Spirit of truth, is come, he will guide you into all truth: for he shall not speak of himself; but whatsoever he shall hear, that shall he speak: and he will shew you things to come (John 16:12-13).

Christians typically understand this prophecy as fulfilled completely by the descent of the Holy Spirit on the Church at Pentecost (Acts 2:1-4). Applying the 'Elijah paradigm', however, Bahá'ís read it as a prediction of Christ's own Second Coming. The Bahá'í teachings say:

> Now consider carefully that from these words, 'for He shall not speak of Himself; but whatsoever He shall hear, that shall He speak', it is clear that the Spirit of truth is embodied in a Man Who has individuality, Who has ears to hear and a tongue to speak. In the same way the name 'Spirit of God' is used in relation to Christ, as you speak of a light, meaning both the light and the lamp (SAQ 109).

The more customary Pentecost interpretation is necessary if we assume that divine revelation ended with the Bible. However, as we have seen, the Bible itself makes no such claim and in fact explicitly predicts future revelation. Bahá'ís, therefore, take the words 'He will guide you into all truth' as foreshadowing a vastly expanded revelation from One who would explain the 'many things' Christ said His disciples could not 'bear' at the time. Writing long after the Pentecost visitation, Paul makes a strikingly similar prediction:

For we know in part, and we prophesy in part. But when that which is perfect is come, then that which is in part shall be done away (I Cor. 13:9-10).

If Paul, through whose inspired words much of the New Testament was recorded and who is considered by many to be the greatest Apostle, did not claim a complete understanding of Christian truth, how can it be argued that such knowledge was fully revealed at Pentecost? Both Christ and Paul foresaw a fuller and vastly more complete revelation at the time of the end – a revelation which, Bahá'ís believe, has been delivered by Christ through the manifestation of His 'quickening spirit' in Bahá'u'lláh.

The Branch

In the Old Testament we find several prophecies about a figure called the Branch.

> . . . for, behold, I will bring forth my servant the Branch . . .
> In that day, saith the Lord of hosts, shall ye call every man his neighbour under the vine and under the fig tree (Zech. 3:8, 10).

The Branch is rightly interpreted by Christians as a title of Christ; and most of the events described in connection with His ministry are those the Bible associates with His Second Coming. For this reason, Bahá'ís regard them as prophecies of Christ's spiritual return in the person of Bahá'u'lláh. The most detailed prophecy of the Branch is from the eleventh chapter of Isaiah:

> And there shall come forth a rod out of the stem of Jesse, and a Branch shall grow out of his roots: And the spirit of the Lord shall rest upon him, the spirit of wisdom and understanding, the spirit of counsel and might, the spirit of knowledge and of the fear of the Lord; And shall make him of quick understanding in the fear of the Lord: and he

99

shall not judge after the sight of his eyes, neither reprove after the hearing of his ears: But with righteousness shall he judge the poor, and reprove with equity for the meek of the earth: and he shall smite the earth with the rod of his mouth, and with the breath of his lips shall he slay the wicked. And righteousness shall be the girdle of his loins, and faithfulness the girdle of his reins. The wolf also shall dwell with the lamb, and the leopard shall lie down with the kid; and the calf and the young lion and the fatling together; and a little child shall lead them. And the cow and the bear shall feed; their young ones shall lie down together: and the lion shall eat straw like the ox. And the sucking child shall play on the hole of the asp, and the weaned child shall put his hand on the cockatrice' den. They shall not hurt nor destroy in all my holy mountain: for the earth shall be full of the knowledge of the Lord, as the waters cover the sea.

And in that day there shall be a root of Jesse, which shall stand for an ensign of the people; to it shall the Gentiles seek: and his rest shall be glorious (Isa. 11:1-10).

A recurring theme of this and other prophecies of the Branch is that He is to be a descendant of Jesse. This was true of Bahá'u'lláh, whose family traced its lineage not only from Jesse but from Abraham, the 'Father of the Faithful', as well as from ancient Persian royalty. The animals mentioned in the prophecy – wolf and lamb, lion and calf, etc. – signify for Bahá'ís the various warring nations coming together to beat swords into plowshares and learn war no more. (The use of animals to symbolize kingdoms and nations in prophecy is exemplified by the Bible's own interpretation of similar imagery in Daniel and Revelation.)

A particularly significant event associated with the Branch is the return of the Jewish people to the Holy Land. Various Old Testament prophets warned the children of Israel that they would be scattered throughout the world until the coming of the Messiah, when God, ending their long desolation, would restore them to their ancestral homeland.

Isaiah's prophecy of the Branch, quoted above, continues in this vein:

> And in that day there shall be a root of Jesse, which shall stand for an ensign of the people ... and it shall come to pass in that day, that the Lord shall set his hand again the second time to recover the remnant of his people, which shall be left . . . And he shall set up an ensign for the nations, and shall assemble the outcasts of Israel, and gather together the dispersed of Judah from the four corners of the earth (Isa. 11:10-12).

Concerning these and other prophecies of the Branch, the Bahá'í sacred writings comment as follows:

> One of the great events which is to occur in the Day of the manifestation of that Incomparable Branch is the hoisting of the Standard of God among all nations. By this is meant that all nations and kindreds will be gathered together under the shadow of this Divine Banner, which is no other than the Lordly Branch itself, and will become a single nation. Religious and sectarian antagonism, the hostility of races and peoples, and differences among nations, will be eliminated . . . Universal peace and concord will be realized between all the nations, and that Incomparable Branch will gather together all Israel, signifying that in this cycle Israel will be gathered in the Holy Land, and that the Jewish people who are scattered to the East and West, South and North, will be assembled together.
>
> Now see: these events did not take place in the Christian cycle, for the nations did not come under the One Standard which is the Divine Branch. But in this cycle of the Lord of Hosts all the nations and peoples will enter under the shadow of this Flag. In the same way, Israel, scattered all over the world, was not reassembled in the Holy Land in the Christian cycle; but in the beginning of the cycle of Bahá'u'lláh this divine promise, as is clearly stated in all the Books of the Prophets, has begun to be manifest. You can see that from all the parts of the world tribes of Jews are

coming to the Holy Land; they live in villages and lands which they make their own, and day by day they are increasing to such an extent that all Palestine will become their home (SAQ 65-6).

Here is one of Jeremiah's prophecies of the Branch:

> Behold, the days come, saith the Lord, that I will perform that good thing which I have promised unto the house of Israel and to the house of Judah.
>
> In those days, and at that time, will I cause the Branch of righteousness to grow up unto David; and he shall execute judgement and righteousness in the land. In those days shall Judah be saved, and Jerusalem shall dwell safely: and this is the name wherewith she shall be called, The Lord our righteousness (Jer. 33:14-16).

Note the repetition and emphasis of these three consecutive verses: 'Behold, the days come . . .' 'In those days, and at that time . . .' 'In those days . . .' The pattern here shows clearly that all three verses refer to the same 'days'. The Branch must therefore 'grow up unto David' in the same general period when 'Jerusalem shall dwell safely'. This statement echoes an earlier passage in which Jeremiah not only gives the same prophecy almost word for word but states exactly what he means by dwelling safely:

> Behold, the days come, saith the Lord, that I will raise unto David a righteous Branch, and a King shall reign and prosper, and shall execute judgement and justice in the earth. In his days shall Judah be saved, and Israel shall dwell safely: and this is his name whereby he shall be called, The Lord Our Righteousness. Therefore, behold, the days come, saith the Lord, that they shall no more say, The Lord liveth, which brought up the children of Israel out of the land of Egypt; But, the Lord liveth, which brought up and which led the seed of the house of Israel out of the north country, and from all the countries whither I had driven them; and they shall dwell in their own land (Jer. 23:5-8).

Here Jeremiah plainly defines the promise that 'Israel shall dwell safely' as referring to the day when the children of Israel 'shall dwell in their own land', after God has 'led the seed of the house of Israel out of the north country, and from all countries whither I had driven them'. It is in this day (according to Jeremiah's previously quoted words) that the Branch must 'grow up unto David'. As we already have seen, Israel did not 'dwell safely' during the Messiah's first advent. Christ Himself predicted the utter destruction of Jerusalem – a tragedy that materialized within seventy years, when Titus razed the city and the temple site. Israel was at that time dispersed, not regathered.

For many centuries hence Jews were largely or completely barred from the Holy Land, which remained in the hands of Gentiles. This banishment continued until 1844, when the Edict of Toleration opened the door to their return. They began doing so at once, and have continued, in ever-increasing numbers, until the present day. The formation in 1948 of the State of Israel added momentum to a vast relocation that began more than a century earlier.

This flood of immigration began in the lifetime of Bahá'u'lláh, who walked this earth from 1817 to 1892, and who, by government decree, was exiled to the Holy Land in 1868 as a prisoner of the Turks. The restoration of Israel to Jews thus synchronized with the coming of the One regarded by Bahá'ís as embodying the spiritual Return of Christ. From this perspective, every detail of Jeremiah's prophecy was literally fulfilled.

'When Shall These Things Be?'

One of the most remarkable predictions in the Bible is that of the 'abomination of desolation, spoken of by Daniel the prophet'. This prophecy, which clearly pinpoints the year 1844, is cited by Christ in answer to His disciples' question as to the time of His Second Coming. The Faith of Bahá'u'lláh dates from 1844 when His mission (as explained in the next chapter of this book) was proclaimed to the world by His Herald, a young man known as 'the Gate'.

In the 24th chapter of Matthew the disciples ask Christ: '. . . what will be the signal for your coming and the end of the age?' One of Christ's answers is that the end will come 'when you see "the abomination of desolation", of which the prophet Daniel spoke' (Matt. 24:3, 15 NEB). He emphasizes the importance of this sign by adding parenthetically: 'Let the reader understand.' His reference is to the abomination or 'transgression of desolation' described in the eighth chapter of the book of Daniel.

This chapter describes a vision in which Daniel hears a saint ask: 'How long shall be the vision concerning the daily sacrifice, and the transgression [abomination] of desolation? . . .' Another saint replies: 'Unto two thousand and three hundred days; then shall the sanctuary be cleansed.' The angel Gabriel then tells Daniel: 'Understand, O son of man: for at the time of the end shall be the vision' (Dan. 8:13-14, 17). The 'cleansing of the sanctuary' seems to represent the purification of God's religion in the last days, after a 2300-day period of 'desolation' during which it is profaned by sacrilegious transgressions or 'abominations'. From Christ's comment, it becomes clear that the 2300 days are to close with His own return at the 'end of the age'.

This raises two questions: 1) What is meant by a 'day' in this prophecy? 2) What is the starting point of the 2300 days?

Regarding the first question, Bible scholars are well-nigh unanimous in insisting that a 'day' in Bible prophecy represents a year. The Bible itself says, 'I have appointed thee each day for a year' (Eze. 4:6) and 'even forty days, each day for a year' (Num. 14:34). Throughout the Bible, one can find specific predictions which were fulfilled if – but only if – we interpret them using the 'day for a year' formula.* Such usage is clearly indicated in this instance by Gabriel's further comment that Daniel's vision 'concerns the distant future' (Dan. 8:26 NIV). If interpreted simply as twenty-four-hour days, the 2300 days would amount to barely six and a half years. The 2300 days, then, equal 2300 years.

But what is the commencement of this 2300-year period (which is to terminate in the Second Coming of Christ)? Gabriel, having been commanded to make Daniel understand the vision, does explain many particulars, but omits this crucial detail – the starting date. Daniel therefore reports that 'I was astonished at the vision, but none understood it' (Dan. 8:27).

As the next chapter, the ninth, opens, Daniel seeks insight into the meaning of his vision: 'So I turned to the Lord God, and pleaded with him in prayer and petition, in fasting, and in sackcloth and ashes' (Dan. 9:3 NIV). His prayer is answered, for the command to Gabriel remains in force: 'make this man to understand the vision' (Dan. 8:16). Obeying this mandate, the angel returns to Daniel in chapter 9, saying, 'Daniel, I have now come to give you insight and understanding. As soon as you began to pray, an answer was given, which I have come to tell you, for you are highly esteemed. Therefore, consider the message and understand the vision . . .' (Dan. 9:22-3 NIV). Since the main thing yet to be explained involves the starting point for the vision, Gabriel turns to this topic:

> Seventy weeks are determined upon thy people and upon thy holy city . . . Know therefore and understand, that from the going forth of the commandment to restore and to build Jerusalem unto the Messiah the Prince shall be seven weeks, and threescore and two [sixty-two] weeks: the street shall be built again, and the wall, even in troublous times.

*For more information see *I Shall Come Again* by Hushidar Motlagh and *Thief in the Night* by William Sears.

And after threescore and two weeks shall Messiah be cut off, but not for Himself: and the people of the prince that shall come shall destroy the city and the sanctuary . . . And he shall confirm the covenant with many for one week: and in the midst of the week He shall cause the sacrifice and the oblation [offering] to cease . . . (Dan. 9:24-7).

By explaining that the Messiah 'shall cause the sacrifice and the [offering] to cease', Gabriel clearly links this prophecy to the opening of the 2300-year timeline with its 'vision concerning the daily sacrifice'. Two points of translation can help us grasp this crucial passage:

First, in keeping with the 'day for a year' reckoning mentioned above, almost all Bible scholars concur that the 'weeks' in this passage (literally 'sevens' in the original Hebrew) actually refer to intervals of seven years, rather than seven twenty-four-hour days. This consensus is reflected, for example, in the Revised Standard Version, which translates the opening expression as 'seventy weeks of years'.

Second, the angel came for the express purpose of explaining to Daniel the point he had failed to understand in his earlier vision – the commencement of the 2300 years (which terminate at the 'time of the end' when Christ, as we learn from Matthew 24, is to return). After telling Daniel to 'understand the matter, and consider the vision', Gabriel's first words are 'Seventy weeks are determined upon thy people and upon thy holy city'. The Hebrew word translated in the King James Version as 'determined' is '*chathak*', which literally means 'cut off' or 'marked off'.

Seventy weeks, then, representing 490 years (70 x 7 = 490), are cut off from some longer period. They constitute a subset pertaining especially to the Jewish people. But from what are the 490 years marked off? There can be but one answer: Since the 2300-year period of desolation is the only other interval under consideration, it clearly is the period from which the 490 years are cut off. The shorter period being part of the longer, the two must begin together. This correlation is the key that enables us to decipher the starting date.

The 'seventy weeks of years' are stated by Gabriel to commence with 'the going forth of the commandment to restore and to build Jerusalem', the Hebrew holy city that had previously been levelled by conquering armies. If the date of this decree can be ascertained, then the starting point of the 2300-year timeline will be known – as will (by implication) its all-important ending date. This fateful culmination marks the 'end of the age' when Christ, by His Second Coming, is to cleanse the holy sanctuary and establish God's Kingdom on earth.

The Bible describes four edicts, by three Persians kings, any one of which might conceivably be the decree to which Gabriel refers.* However, the first two were strictly verbal and partial and were never implemented while the fourth was a confirmation and extension of the third. It was this third decree that resulted in the actual rebuilding of Jerusalem, complete with street and wall, as the prophecy stipulates. Most Christian scholars therefore believe the relevant decree is the third: the formal written commandment 'to restore and to build Jerusalem' issued in 457 BC by King Artaxerxes (Ezra 7:12-26).

How can we test whether 457 BC is indeed the correct starting point? By referring to the other predictions made by Gabriel in connection with the 'seventy weeks'. If – but only if – we use this date as our point of reference, all the prophecies concerning 'Messiah the Prince' (Christ in His first advent) are fulfilled to the letter.

The angel's prophecy describes the opening seventy weeks (490 prophetic years) of the 2300-year interval as pertaining especially to the Jews. He then expresses the seventy-week

---

*These decrees, identified by their respective issuers, dates and biblical references, are as follows: Cyrus, 536 BC, recorded in Ezra 1; Darius, 519 BC, recorded in Ezra 6; Artaxerxes, 457 BC, recorded in Ezra 7; and Artaxerxes, 444 BC, recorded in Nehemiah 2.

period as seven weeks, sixty-two weeks and one week (7 + 62 + 1 = 70). These periods are associated with the following events:

1) *Seven weeks (forty-nine prophetic years)*: During this first interval 'the street shall be built again, and the wall, even in troublous times'. The rebuilding of Jerusalem did indeed span exactly forty-nine turbulent years, dating from 457 BC.

2) *Sixty-two weeks (434 prophetic years)*: The 434 years commence with the completion of the rebuilding of Jerusalem, and extend 'unto the Messiah the Prince'. This interval (49 + 434 = 483 years) brings us to 27 AD, well into the lifetime of Christ. (The date is 27 rather than 26 because we must add a year to compensate for the fact that there is no 'year zero'.)

3) *One week (seven prophetic years)*: These remaining seven years (49 + 434 + 7 = 490) bring us to 34 AD, the year when Christ was crucified (according to standard chronology). His sacrificial martyrdom 'caused the sacrifice and the oblation to cease' by rendering the traditional Jewish offering obsolete. (Although Christ is believed to have been 33 years old when martyred, not all historians agree as to the year of His birth; thus, He could have been crucified as early as six years before 34 AD. However, this in no way affects the accuracy of Gabriel's prophecy, which requires only that His self-sacrifice be 'after' the sixty-two weeks and 'in the midst' of the last week, or seven-year period.)

The prophecy makes one last point: that after the cutting off of the Messiah, 'the people of the prince that shall come shall destroy the city and the sanctuary'. This occurred in 70 AD when the Roman general Titus, son of the Emperor Vespasian, once more demolished Jerusalem and the Temple in the course of crushing a Jewish rebellion. Thus was each detail of the prophecy fulfilled, to the last word. (It is note-

Daniel's Prophecy of '2300 Days' (years)

'I have appointed thee each day for a year' – Eze. 4:6

Figure 2: The prophetic timeline associated with Daniel's vision covering the first and second Advents of the Messiah. This prophecy – terminating in the year 1844 – was pointed to by Christ as holding the key to the time of His return.

worthy that Christ Himself also predicted this destruction in Luke 19:43-4 and Matthew 24:2.)

Taking 457 BC as the starting point of the 2300 years, we find that 2300 minus 457 equals 1843. As noted above, however, we must add a year to make up for the lack of any 'year zero' in the Gregorian calendar. Thus 2300 years from 457 BC bring us precisely to 1844 AD.

The only logical way to deny that 1844 represents the culmination of the 2300-year cycle is to deny that 457 BC is its starting point. If we do this, however, we must also deny that the latter date is the starting point of the 490-year interval that encompasses the various prophecies about the Messiah's first advent. We cannot do this without throwing these latter prophecies out of sync with known historical facts. Small wonder the Bahá'í teachings state that 'there could be no clearer prophecy for a manifestation than this' (SAQ 42).

During the opening years of the nineteenth century, dozens of Bible scholars, working independently, calculated from these and related prophecies that Christ would return in 1843 or 1844. (Those who favoured 1843 generally did so because they overlooked the need to allow for the missing 'year zero'.) The best known of these was William Miller, whose 'Millerite' movement was the precursor of today's Seventh-Day Adventist church. A tide of millennial anticipation swept the Christian world, reaching its crescendo in 1844. When the skies did not open as expected and Christ's nail-scarred body did not descend upon a visible cloud, 1844 became known to many Christians as 'the Year of the Great Disappointment'. Of course, to those who recognize the fulfilment of Christ's return in Bahá'u'lláh, the events of 1844 are cause not for disappointment but for jubilation and rejoicing.

Summary

As noted above, I do not insist that any of these prophecies 'prove' the correctness of the Bahá'í outlook, for they can all be interpreted in other ways. Christian commentators have themselves debated their meaning for centuries and no doubt will continue to do so. It is well-nigh impossible, within the context of prophecy alone, to demonstrate decisively which view is correct. My point is simply that the Bahá'í Faith offers a coherent, consistent and reasonable way of looking at the prophecies. This interpretation upholds the integrity of the Bible and opens the door to a consideration of Bahá'u'lláh's claim on the basis of other scriptural criteria.

Once we accept that 'heaven', 'clouds', 'angels', 'eyes' and similar terms may refer as easily to spiritual as to physical realities, we are free to take literally the promise of a new name, of His thief-like advent, and of the need to 'watch' so that 'when he cometh and knocketh, [we] may open unto Him immediately'. We can then glimpse the urgency of the Gospel admonition to 'try the spirits, whether they are of God', to 'test everything, and hold onto the good'.

5

Who is this King of Glory?

Lift up your heads, O ye gates; even lift them up, ye everlasting doors; and the King of glory shall come in. Who is
this King of glory? The Lord of hosts, he is the King of
glory (Psalms 24:9-10).

This book has heretofore given relatively little information
about Bahá'u'lláh. Instead I have sought to provide, from the
Bible itself, essential background information that a Christian reader must have in order to evaluate Bahá'u'lláh fairly.

Many volumes have been written on the history and
teachings of the Bahá'í Faith. This book is not one of them.
What we will do, in the chapters that lie ahead, is explore the
proofs of Bahá'u'lláh's mission from the standpoint of Christian holy scripture. It is hardly possible, however, to consider
such proofs without at least a cursory understanding of the
Faith's historical development and basic principles.

This chapter therefore presents a brief – very brief –
outline of Bahá'í history and teachings. Any reader already
familiar with this information is welcome to skip to the next
chapter, which will take up the all-important question of
scriptural standards: How (according to the Bible) may we
test Bahá'u'lláh's authenticity? Only then will we be in a
position to sift the evidence which, in the light of God's
Word, may enable us to render a fair and accurate verdict.

The Historical Background

Light always shines brightest when surrounded by darkness.
Christ, who could easily have manifested Himself in some

113

flourishing centre of Greek or Roman culture, chose instead the downtrodden realm of Palestine. The Bahá'í Faith, like Christianity itself, was born in a land regarded throughout most of the world as backward and insignificant. Persia (today called Iran) was in biblical times the heart of a fabulous empire. By the mid-nineteenth century, however, it had entirely lost its ancient glory and sunk to the depths of ignominy. A reactionary monarchy held absolute sway over a largely superstitious and apathetic populace. Government and people alike were subject, in turn, to the pervasive influence of a fanatical Muslim priesthood. The prevailing religion was the Shí'ih sect of Islam. It was a closed – one might say locked – society, hostile to all progressive ideas and particularly those of the 'satanic' West.

It was from this dark corner that the Bahá'í Faith, like 'lightning from the East', burst upon the world scene in 1844.

The Gate of the Dawn

Bahá'u'lláh, like Christ, had a Herald and Forerunner. The herald of Jesus was John the Baptist who, as the spiritual return of Elijah, cried in the wilderness: 'Prepare ye the way of the Lord, make his paths straight' (Matt. 3:3). The herald of Bahá'u'lláh was Siyyid 'Alí-Muhammad (1819-50), a native of the Persian city of Shíráz. (Shíráz is the principal city of southern Persia, a province formerly known as Elam and referred to in the Old Testament by God Himself as the place where 'I will set my throne' in the last days – Jer. 49:38.) On 23 May 1844, this twenty-five-year-old merchant declared that He was a Messenger from God, sent to proclaim the imminent appearance of the Promised One foretold in the Bible and indeed in the holy books of all religions. He took the title of the Báb, meaning 'Gate'.

John the Baptist, though he showed great reverence towards Jesus, never explicitly identified the Messiah of whom he said: 'He it is, who coming after me is preferred before me, whose shoe's latchet I am not worthy to unloose' (John 1:27). The Báb showed similar reverence towards Bahá'u'lláh but likewise refrained from naming the promised Redeemer, praising Him instead with such veiled statements as these: 'I Myself am, verily, but a ring upon the hand of Him Whom God shall make manifest' (GPB 30). 'Of all the tributes I have paid to Him Who is to come after Me, the greatest is this, My written confession, that no words of Mine can adequately describe Him, nor can any reference to Him in My Book, the Bayán, do justice to His Cause' (TB 77-8).

The Báb's teaching convulsed all of Persia, evoking violent resistance from both government and clergy. He was arrested, tortured, imprisoned and eventually slain by firing squad in Tabríz on 9 July 1850. (The Persians have never forgotten that the first volley of shots, from 750 rifles, failed to touch or harm him, though it shredded the ropes by which He was bound.*) More than twenty thousand of His followers, like the early Christian martyrs, joyously went to their deaths when authorities tried to exterminate His Faith with a gruesome – but ultimately futile – campaign of terror and torture.

The riddled remains of the Báb were dumped on the ground outside the city's moat, in the hope they would be eaten by wild animals. His disciples, however, rescued His body surreptitiously from careless guards and moved it to a safe hiding place. Today, surrounded by magnificent gardens, it rests in a golden-domed shrine on Mount Carmel, at Haifa, Israel.

---

*This amazing incident, which took place before ten thousand eyewitnesses, is attested by European historians and foreign diplomats who investigated its particulars. For example, Sir Justin Sheil, Queen Victoria's minister in Ṭihrán, confirms it in a letter of 22 July 1850 to Lord Palmerston. See document F.O. 60/153/88 in the Foreign Office archives at the Public Records Office in London.

The King of Glory

No biographical sketch, concentrating as it must on dry facts and figures, can capture the real essence even of an ordinary individual – how much less that of 'One like unto the Son of man'! Consider, for example, the absurdity of trying either to grasp or to convey an adequate impression of Christ in just a few paragraphs. Bahá'u'lláh's Herald, the Báb, having written volumes in praise of 'Him whom God shall make manifest', despaired of describing Him adequately. The more we study the earthly life of Bahá'u'lláh (1817-92), the more we share this sense of helplessness to encompass Him.

Recognizing this problem, I must emphasize that the capsule summary below is intended only to introduce the historical context of Bahá'u'lláh's message – not the man behind the message. It omits virtually all of the important incidents and episodes that might help us better appreciate His stupendous station. Many of these accounts I am saving for later chapters, where we can explore them (however inadequately) in greater detail, as part of the evidence bearing on the validity of His claim.

Mírzá Ḥusayn-'Alí, later known as Bahá'u'lláh ('the Glory of God'), came from one of the oldest and most distinguished noble families of Ṭihrán, Persia's capital city. In outward circumstances, the lives of Jesus and Bahá'u'lláh differed considerably. Jesus was the son of a humble carpenter; Bahá'u'lláh was born to wealth and privilege. Jesus never married; Bahá'u'lláh was a family man with children. Jesus was crucified at the age of thirty-three; Bahá'u'lláh left this world as a prisoner at the age of seventy-five. The similarities, however, run deep. Bahá'u'lláh, like Jesus, was a child prodigy, astonishing even the wisest scholars with His inborn knowledge and wisdom. Like Jesus, He was without formal schooling. Like Jesus, He shunned political affairs (though He might easily have followed His father, Mírzá Buzurg, into high government office). Like Jesus, He earned a reputation for unsurpassed moral integrity, compassion and courage, as well as for the magnetic attraction of His personality and the serene authority with which He spoke. Before embarking upon His spiritual mission, He devoted His time (and His inherited fortune) to humanitarian service, becoming known as the 'Father of the Poor'. Just as Jesus espoused the cause of John the Baptist (calling John 'a prophet and more than a prophet'), so did Bahá'u'lláh in 1844 spring fearlessly to the aid of the Báb and His message.

The result was inevitable: Being the foremost defender of the Bábí community (as it then was called), Bahá'u'lláh became a prime target for the persecution that followed the Báb's martyrdom. In 1852 He was arrested, chained, beaten, imprisoned, tortured, stripped of His wealth and marked for death. At the last moment, however, the royal authorities, fearing awkward repercussions, decided instead to deport Him and His family to Baghdád, Iraq. (Iraq at that time was part of the Turkish Empire, also known as the Ottoman Empire.)

For a while the government and clergy felt they had extinguished the Faith of the Báb. Their relief was short-lived, however, as the movement revived under Bahá'u'lláh's leadership. Seeking to remove Him even farther from their borders, Persia prevailed upon the Ottoman government to banish Him again. Bahá'u'lláh and His family were therefore 'invited' to Constantinople, capital of the Turkish Empire, where authorities assumed they could more easily watch and control His activities.

On the eve of this transfer, in April 1863, Bahá'u'lláh declared to His companions that He was the promised Redeemer and Christ-figure whose coming it had been the Báb's mission to announce. Almost all Bábís eventually accepted this claim, thereafter becoming known as Bahá'ís.

Bahá'u'lláh's removal to the Ottoman capital, far from silencing Him, had the opposite effect. A cosmopolitan trade-centre, Constantinople was a frequent stopover for visiting Persians and other travellers, who carried His teach-

ings far and wide. Leaders of thought residing in Constantinople itself began falling under the spell of His mysterious
spiritual attraction. Though He and His followers shunned
political pursuits, Bahá'u'lláh's growing prestige soon
alarmed Turkish officials, already under pressure from the
government of Persia to send Him still farther away. Once
again He was uprooted and banished, this time to distant
Adrianople – the Turkish equivalent of Siberia. This latest
countermeasure, however, proved simply another exercise
in futility, its chief result being to amplify Bahá'u'lláh's
message and fan the flames of His Cause. In 1868 His dis-
mayed adversaries reacted by locking Him and His retinue
in the remote Turkish fortress-prison of 'Akká (now a city
in Israel, though at that time within the Ottoman Empire).
This punishment was equivalent to a death sentence, conditions in 'Akká being so foul and inhumane that the hardiest
prisoner seldom survived more than a year. Many of
Bahá'u'lláh's companions, including His beloved youngest
son, Mírzá Mihdí, did perish in the prison. He Himself was
strictly confined within the fortress walls for no less than nine
years.

It is hard to imagine, in hindsight, any other development
that could more forcefully have demonstrated the magic of
Bahá'u'lláh's influence. 'Akká quickly became a centre of
pilgrimage for thousands whose lives He had touched, and
who yearned, at whatever cost, to share His incarceration.
Breaking into the prison (rather than out) became their
consuming obsession, as countless travellers devoted vast
quantities of time, treasure and ingenuity to attaining His
presence. Few succeeded, the vast majority having to content
themselves with a glimpse of His hand from His cell window,
barely visible above the city walls. So preoccupied at times
were the guards with keeping out these pilgrims, continually
seeking access to Bahá'u'lláh, that many of His fellow-in-
mates paradoxically found themselves able to wander in and
out of the prison more or less at will.

Despite lifelong persecution, Bahá'u'lláh continually

guided His movement to new victories and augmented His vast collection of writings. From Adrianople and 'Akká He proclaimed His mission in letters to the kings and rulers of the world, urging them to compose their differences and create a global federation to secure a just and lasting peace. 'Had they hearkened unto Me,' He later wrote, 'they would have beheld the earth another earth' (PDC 6). Nevertheless, He vowed that God would ensure victory for the Bahá'í Cause, with or without assistance from any king.

His harsh confinement eventually was relaxed as Bahá'u'lláh's Christ-like character won the admiration of His gaolers. Towards the end of His life, though still nominally a prisoner, He was allowed to move about as He pleased, continue His writing, and meet with the many pilgrims and visiting dignitaries who sought His presence.

When He left this world on 29 May 1892, the news reached the Turkish government in a cable opening with the words 'the Sun of Bahá has set'. His earthly remains are interred near 'Akká in a shrine at Bahjí (Delight), across the Bay of Haifa from Mount Carmel.

The Covenant of Bahá'u'lláh

Before leaving this earth Christ passed the mantle of His own authority to His closest disciples ('Whatsoever ye shall bind on earth shall be bound in heaven; and whatsoever ye shall loose on earth shall be loosed in heaven' – Matt. 18:18), emphasizing particularly the station of Peter ('thou art Peter, and upon this rock I will build my church' – Matt. 16:18). Upon these specially empowered believers He bestowed the Great Commission: 'Go ye therefore, and teach all nations, baptizing them in the name of the Father, and of the Son, and of the Holy Ghost: Teaching them to observe all things whatsoever I have commanded you . . .' (Matt. 28:19-20).

In somewhat the same way Bahá'u'lláh established a 'covenant' providing for the guidance and expansion of His Faith after His departure. His instructions, written and sealed with His own hand, leave no doubt concerning His intentions in this all-important question of succession. In His Most Holy Book He created a supreme elected body, the Universal House of Justice, to teach and administer His Cause throughout the world and to pass judgement on any questions of Bahá'í law not specifically addressed in His own writings.* He also appointed His eldest son, 'Abbás Effendi (1844-1921), as head and interpreter of the Faith.

'Abbás Effendi was born 23 May 1844 – the night of the Báb's declaration. From the age of eight He shared the bitter persecution that rained upon Bahá'u'lláh. As He grew to manhood, His selfless life of service and sacrifice earned Him universal recognition as His father's ablest assistant and spokesman. Known to Bahá'ís everywhere as 'the Master', He preferred the title 'Abdu'l-Bahá, meaning 'the Servant of Bahá' or 'Servant of the Glory'. His designation as head of the Cause had the effect of making His word equal in authority (though not, of course, in rank) to Bahá'u'lláh's own.

While still a prisoner in 1898, 'Abdu'l-Bahá greeted the first Western Bahá'í pilgrims to 'Akká. After His release in 1908 He undertook a series of teaching trips comparable, in many ways, to the amazing missionary journeys of St Paul. These travels brought Him in 1911-13 to Europe and America, where He expounded Bahá'u'lláh's message before large audiences in churches, auditoriums and private homes, drew extensive press coverage and met with many leaders of thought.

Returning to Palestine, 'Abdu'l-Bahá began to implement the Administrative Order envisioned in the writings of Bahá'u'lláh and designed a long-range teaching plan to establish the Bahá'í Faith throughout the earth. He received a knighthood from the British Crown for His relief work during World War I.

*Headquartered in Haifa, Israel, the Universal House of Justice was first elected in 1963.

When 'Abdu'l-Bahá died in 1921 His will designated His grandson, Shoghi Effendi, 'Guardian' of the Bahá'í Cause and (like Himself) the authorized interpreter of its teachings. Shoghi Effendi worked tirelessly toward the establishment of the Universal House of Justice, passing away in 1957 a mere six years before its first election. He also produced masterful translations of the Bahá'í sacred writings, wrote extensively on the administration, history and goals of the Faith, and launched the successive teaching campaigns planned by 'Abdu'l-Bahá. Under his guidance, Bahá'ís painstakingly erected throughout the globe the institutions designed by Bahá'u'lláh to be the earthly framework for God's Kingdom. Local and national Bahá'í affairs are administered by a network of Spiritual Assemblies, each consisting of nine believers elected without regard to gender, race, class or other social or economic distinction, and functioning under the laws of Bahá'u'lláh and the overall direction of the Universal House of Justice. (Bahá'u'lláh stated that this House of Justice – the Faith's only all-male agency – is guided by God and protected from error in its rulings.) Elections are by secret ballot, with no campaigns or nominations; and the religion has no clergy, paid or otherwise. Financial support is accepted only from declared believers, all contributions being strictly voluntary and confidential.

As part of their global teaching effort, Bahá'ís have sought consistently to disperse throughout the world. As a result, though there are as yet relatively few large concentrations of Bahá'ís, the Faith has already become the second most widely-spread religion on earth, with a significant following in more countries than any other except Christianity. (The Encyclopedia Britannica yearbook, in successive editions beginning with 1988, lists Christianity as the first with 254 countries, the Bahá'í Faith second with 205 and Islam third with 172.) Moreover, the Faith exhibits extraordinary cultural and ethnic diversity and rapidly accelerating growth. Its broadly based unity has made it an effective champion of such causes as international peace, women's rights, social and economic development, environmental conservation, and literacy training.

Bahá'u'lláh's Teachings

The writings of Bahá'u'lláh comprise books, treatises, commentaries, prayers and meditations – many in the form of personal letters (generally known as 'Tablets'). So prolific was He that these writings, if compiled, would fill more than one hundred volumes. They touch on literally thousands of issues, ancient and modern, disclosing in the process a comprehensive blueprint for a unified world society. No summary can do more than hint at so vast a panorama of truths.

Bahá'u'lláh's fundamental teaching is that all human beings are children of one God who, through successive revelations of His will, has patiently guided humanity towards spiritual and social maturity. Having passed through infancy and adolescence, humanity is now coming of age. Its collective life is undergoing a profound transformation, akin to that of a caterpillar turning into a butterfly. This metamorphosis will in time produce a divine civilization, the very 'kingdom of God on earth' foretold in the Lord's Prayer.

This pivotal concept – planetary unification as the fruit of humanity's dawning maturity – is the principle Bahá'ís call the 'oneness of humankind'. All Bahá'u'lláh's social teachings revolve around the oneness of humankind, as spokes revolve around the hub of a wheel. To implement this overriding goal, Bahá'u'lláh calls for widespread application of many secondary principles. In summarizing some of these, Shoghi Effendi has stated that the Bahá'í Faith:

1) Upholds the unity of God
2) Recognizes the unity of His Prophets
3) Inculcates the principle of the oneness and wholeness of the entire human race

4) Proclaims the necessity and the inevitability of the unification of mankind
5) Asserts that (this unification) is gradually approaching
6) Claims that nothing short of the transmuting spirit of God, working through His chosen Mouthpiece in this day, can ultimately succeed in bringing (this unification) about
7) Enjoins upon its followers the primary duty of an unfettered search after truth
8) Condemns all manner of prejudice and superstition
9) Declares the purpose of religion to be the promotion of amity and concord
10) Proclaims (religion's) essential harmony with science
11) Recognizes (religion) as the foremost agency for the pacification and the orderly progress of human society
12) Unequivocally maintains the principle of equal rights, opportunities, and privileges for men and women
13) Insists on compulsory education
14) Eliminates extremes of poverty and wealth
15) Abolishes the institution of the priesthood
16) Prohibits slavery, asceticism, mendicancy (begging) and monasticism
17) Prescribes monogamy
18) Discourages divorce
19) Emphasizes the necessity of strict obedience to one's government
20) Exalts any work performed in the spirit of service to the level of worship
21) Urges either the creation or selection of an auxiliary international language
22) Delineates the outlines of those institutions that must establish and perpetuate the general peace of mankind

While these themes aptly capture the spirit of the Bahá'í Faith, they in no way exhaust its teachings. The writings of Bahá'u'lláh set forth detailed laws and ordinances covering marriage and divorce, burial and inheritance, prayer and fasting, personal conduct and others matters; create a revolutionary new type of administrative order, designed to implement His laws and principles throughout the world and serve as a pattern for future society; and provide vast amounts of never-before-revealed information concerning God's purpose for humankind, the nature of life after death and how to prepare for it, and countless other topics.

Bahá'u'lláh's teachings emphasize, moreover, that 'ideas and principles are helpless without a divine power to put them into effect' (PUP 250). The principal purpose of His coming is not to bring new teachings (important though these are) but to provide such a power. Chapter 4 discussed, among other things, the Bahá'í belief that this divine agency is the Holy Spirit, radiating from the focal point of the personified Christ-figure in His reappearance and flooding the world with divine energy. The Bahá'í sacred writings explain:

> The effulgence of God's splendrous mercy hath enveloped the peoples and kindreds of the earth, and the whole world is bathed in its shining glory . . . The day will soon come when the light of Divine unity will have so permeated the East and West that no man dare any longer ignore it (WOB 111).

> Now in the world of being the Hand of divine power hath firmly laid the foundations of this all-highest bounty and this wondrous gift. Whatsoever is latent in the innermost of this holy cycle shall gradually appear and be made manifest, for now is but the beginning of its growth and the dayspring of the revelation of its signs. Ere the close of this century and of this age, it shall be made clear and evident how wondrous was that springtide and how heavenly was that gift! (WOB 111).

Christ expresses a similar idea:

Whereunto shall we liken the kingdom of God? or with what comparison shall we compare it? It is like a grain of mustard seed, which, when it is sown in the earth, is less than all the seeds that be in the earth: But when it is sown, it groweth up, and becometh greater than all herbs, and shooteth out great branches, so that the fowls of the air may lodge under the shadow of it (Mark 4:30-2).

Bahá'ís believe that as the spiritual impulse generated by Bahá'u'lláh gradually permeates society, it will attract ever-increasing numbers to rally around Him and recognize His divine authority. Sooner or later this impulse must culminate in the birth of a new social order based on His revealed laws and teachings. Such a process, according to Bahá'u'lláh, not only guarantees the eventual emergence of a world commonwealth based on His social principles but also the continued growth and development of that commonwealth under the influence of future Prophets*. He indicates, however, that while this divinely ordained process is both irresistible and inevitable, it is not automatic. The social transformation it entails may be relatively quick and benign; it may be exceedingly long and painful; or it may fall somewhere between these extremes. How easily humanity navigates the transition will be determined primarily by our readiness as individuals to investigate and accept Bahá'u'lláh's divine mandate. Our response also determines whether, and to what extent, we as individuals benefit spiritually from the new revelation.

Our expectations concerning the feasibility of Bahá'u'lláh's social reforms will depend greatly on whether we accept the reality of this mysterious animating power – the power of the Holy Spirit from which (Bahá'ís believe) the teachings derive their force. Most of Bahá'u'lláh's principles by now command widespread acceptance as desirable goals.

---

*The first of these, He says, will appear only after the passage of one thousand or more years from the time of His own revelation.

Many people still question, however, whether such goals can ever be translated into practice. It should be clear that if the Bahá'í programme is truly a divine revelation, its aims are attainable because 'the power of the Kingdom of God will aid and assist in their realization' (SAB 32).

Be that as it may, we can investigate Bahá'u'lláh's claim and ascertain whether it is true or false, without first accepting the reality of this spiritual power. Nor is it necessary that we embrace in advance all of Bahá'u'lláh's teachings. Not only is a healthy scepticism quite natural; it is, when channelled wisely, a useful investigative tool. What is essential, at this point, is that we reserve judgement until all the evidence is in.

But what evidence might that be? What facts and findings are relevant to our investigation of Bahá'u'lláh's veracity? For light on these all-important questions, let us turn once again to the Bible.

6

How Shall We Know the Word?

Produce your cause, saith the Lord; bring forth your strong reasons . . . that we may consider them . . . (Isa. 41:21-2).

. . . test the spirits to see whether they are from God, because many false prophets have gone out into the world. This is how you can recognize the spirit of God . . . (I John 4:1-2 NIV).

As we prepare to explore questions of proof and evidence, it may be helpful to glance back over the ground already covered.

The Bible (as we noted in our first chapter) demonstrates that although God always keeps His promise, He typically does so in ways that defy the expectations of the waiting masses and their leaders. Such has been His way in the past and such (we have every reason to believe) it remains, now and forever. In particular, the Bible states that the events surrounding Christ's return have been foretold in 'sealed' prophecies – that is, prophecies not to be generally understood until after their fulfilment, when He Himself unveils their inner meaning.

Among these predictions are that He will 1) descend from heaven, 2) with power and glory, 3) and be seen by every eye. Yet He also warns repeatedly that He will come 4) with a 'new name' and 5) like a 'thief' for whom 6) we must 'watch' so that 'when He cometh and knocketh, [we] may open unto him immediately'. These latter prophecies – unlike the first three – are often reinforced by the admonition 'He that hath an ear, let him hear'. This Bible emphasis is completely reversed in popular religious thought, which paints a starkly materialistic picture of the Second Coming as an event impossible for anyone to overlook.

How might Christ fulfil the first three prophecies while appearing with a new name in a thief-like manner one might easily overlook? According to the Bible, He could do so simply by coming as He came two thousand years ago. His spiritual presence, that is, could once more come 'down from heaven' to dwell on earth in a human frame, born of a human mother, growing to maturity with a new name and an outwardly different human persona. Christ Himself explains that His first advent was just such a visitation from His Heavenly Father, and that the spiritual 'power and glory' He then manifested is the only kind with any real worth in the sight of God. Moreover, the New Testament points out that Christ, even at that time, was spiritually 'seen' by 'all flesh', and that His gospel was 'preached to every creature which is under heaven' – even though most were not consciously aware of His presence. Christ points out in this connection that it is possible to 'see' without recognizing, to 'hear' without understanding.

The public in Christ's time pictured the second coming of Elijah very much as it now pictures the Second Coming of Christ. Christ explained, however, that the prophecies of Elijah's return were fulfilled in John the Baptist – a new individual who nevertheless embodied the 'spirit and power' of the original Elijah. In light of the other parallels, we may reasonably interpret Elijah's return as a possible model or prototype for that of Christ Himself in the 'time of the end'.

Within this context, we discussed briefly the claim of Bahá'u'lláh that He fulfils the prophecies of Christ's latter-day return: 'Jesus, the Spirit of God . . . hath once more, in My person, been made manifest unto you' (G 101). 'He Who is the Lord of Lords is come overshadowed with clouds, and the decree hath been fulfilled by God . . . He, verily, hath again come down from Heaven even as He came down from it the first time' (PB 83).

However, we postponed any detailed discussion of Bahá-'u'lláh because most Christians insist – rightly, in my view – on first knowing more about His stance on the Bible and on Christ. The second chapter therefore explored a Bahá'í view of the Bible, showing that its divine authority as the Word of God lies at the very heart and foundation of Bahá'u'lláh's teaching. The third chapter likewise explored a Bahá'í view of Christ, showing that Bahá'u'lláh testifies to Christ's son-ship, lordship and divinity as the 'Word made flesh' and the 'only begotten of the Father'. We learned that Bahá'u'lláh not only glorifies Christ but explains and illumines many biblical mysteries which, in the past, have caused dissension among Christ's devoted followers.

The fourth chapter offered a brief Bahá'í overview of the many dramatic events portrayed in the Bible as surrounding the Second Coming of Christ and the emergence of the divine Kingdom. The fifth sketched an outline of the history and teachings of Bahá'u'lláh's Faith, limiting itself to names, events and concepts bound to arise in any discussion of Bahá'í proofs.

Our path to this point has been somewhat long and has involved several side trips. These have been necessary, for without such background information it may be difficult to resolve our core issue. At last, however, we are in a position to consider that most challenging question of questions: *How can we find out whether Bahá'u'lláh's claim is true?*

Let there be no mistake on one point: Bahá'u'lláh, be He true or false, asks no one to accept Him blindly on His own say-so. Echoing the biblical injunction to 'prove all things, and hold fast that which is good', He invites seekers to 'consider His clear evidence' (PB 99) and to 'gaze, with an open and unbiased mind, on the signs of His Revelation, the proofs of His Mission, and the tokens of His glory' (PB 111). '. . . the evidences of His effulgent glory', He writes, 'are now actually manifest. It behoveth you to ascertain whether or not such a light hath appeared' (G 103).

Bahá'u'lláh further makes it clear that for Christians, the Bible is the all-sufficient standard of judgement. It is to the Bible's verdict that He appeals, to the Bible's rules of evidence that He confidently submits:

> In mine hand I carry the testimony of God, your Lord and the Lord of your sires of old. Weigh it with the just Balance that ye possess, the Balance of the testimony of the Prophets and Messengers of God. If ye find it to be established in truth, if ye believe it to be of God, beware, then, lest ye cavil at it, and render your works vain . . . (G 281).

> Read ye the Evangel [the Gospel of Christ] and yet refuse to acknowledge the All-Glorious Lord? This indeed beseemeth you not, O concourse of learned men! (PDC 103).

With this sanction, let us turn to the Bible for light on how to resolve this crucial question of Bahá'u'lláh's true station.

However we may interpret the Bible, one point stands out: Prophecy clearly foreshadows a figure who, in the 'last days', will reveal the Word of God (see Chapter 4.) If we can identify and validate that individual, and if He, speaking with divine authority, claims to be the Return of Christ, then we are obliged by simple logic to accept Him as such. Let us therefore set aside debates over whether such a figure should appear in the sky with the name 'Jesus' or on the ground with a new name. Instead, let us step back and ask the broader question: What – according to the Bible – are the signs and tokens of divine authority? By what scriptural standards can we distinguish one genuine revealer of God's Word from a host of impostors and deceivers?

Here, of course, we must come to grips with the unsettling possibility of fraud. The Bible warns that 'many false prophets are gone out into the world' (I John 4:1); that there have been, and continue to be, 'many antichrists' (I John 2:18).

We also know that many who claim to speak in God's name do so by flashing forged credentials: 'For there shall arise false Christs, and false prophets, and shall shew great signs and wonders; insomuch that, if it were possible, they shall deceive the very elect' (Matt. 24:24). These impostors will appear in 'sheep's clothing, but inwardly they are ravening wolves' (Matt. 7:15). Paul explains that 'Satan himself is transformed into an angel of light', and his ministers likewise (II Cor. 11:14-15). Bahá'u'lláh echoes these warnings: 'Watch over yourselves, for the Evil One is lying in wait, ready to entrap you. Gird yourselves against his wicked devices . . .' (G 94).

One all-too-common response to such cautionary statements is this: 'Well, I know how to avoid being deceived – I just won't investigate! Whenever someone claims to be the Messiah, I will turn away and pay no attention. That way, I can never be taken in by a false prophet.' This policy, of course, is precisely the one followed two thousand years ago by most people hearing for the first time of the Lord Christ. Every one of these same people, as a result, denied Him and became thereby a party to the Saviour's eventual crucifixion. For fear of being deceived, they deceived themselves and lost everything.

Small wonder then that the Bible, if we heed its wisdom, steers us clear of this self-destructive impulse to turn a blind eye and a deaf ear. While acknowledging the confusion which bogus Messiahs generate, its counsel is ever the same: Watch! Listen! Investigate! 'Try the spirits, whether they are of God: because many false prophets are gone out into the world' (I John 4:1). Many – but not necessarily all. Surely if all were to be false, the Lord would not waste our precious time with this command to test and investigate.

If the bad news is that false prophets abound, the good news is this: Counterfeit Christs – like counterfeit currency – can be exposed if we carefully examine the evidence. The Bible assures us that this is so and provides detailed guidance on how we may distinguish the true from the false.

Any discussion of scriptural credentials for divine authority must begin with these words of Christ:

> Beware of false prophets, which come to you in sheep's clothing, but inwardly they are ravening wolves. Ye shall know them by their fruits. Do men gather grapes of thorns, or figs of thistles?
>
> Even so every good tree bringeth forth good fruit; but a corrupt tree bringeth forth evil fruit. A good tree cannot bring forth evil fruit, neither can a corrupt tree bring forth good fruit. Every tree that bringeth not forth good fruit is hewn down, and cast into the fire. Wherefore by their fruits ye shall know them (Matt. 7:15-20).

There we have the standard: 'Ye shall know them by their fruits.' This statement is of course very broad – intentionally so, it seems to me. Christ does not, in this particular passage, define what He means by 'fruits'. He neither specifies which fruits are most relevant to a prophet's authenticity, nor tells us how to evaluate them as good or evil. Why not? Perhaps because these 'fruits' are defined and enumerated in other passages of the Bible, to which He wants us to turn for details. Christ is not trying to relieve us of the need to do our homework. Just the same, by expressing the standard here in the broadest possible terms, He calls to our attention some all-important points we might miss if we plunged immediately into the minutia of sifting evidence.

First among these points is that we can indeed tell the difference between one who speaks with divine authority and one who does not. He says we 'shall know them' – not that we will be unable to know. This promise by Christ deprives us of any excuse we might otherwise have for refusing to investigate. We cannot evade responsibility by saying that although Bahá'u'lláh might or might not be a false prophet, we have no way of finding out. Christ assures us that we *will know* – if we examine the evidence.

A second point is that we must decide. Christ's instructions leave no middle ground: 'Either make the tree good, and his fruit good; or else make the tree corrupt, and his fruit corrupt: for the tree is known by his fruit' (Matt. 12:33). We may think of this in terms of the popular argument spelled out by C. S. Lewis in *Mere Christianity*: When a man claims divine powers and perfection, he leaves us only three choices: 1) He may be a lunatic, a victim of delusions on the level of someone claiming seriously to be a 'poached egg'; 2) he may be a conniving liar, seeking to deceive us, and driven by motives that are selfish or even satanic; 3) his claim may be true. There are no other logical possibilities. It makes no sense to sidestep the issue by saying, 'Perhaps he was simply a great moral teacher – nothing more'; or 'Perhaps he was simply an inspired prophet like Isaiah – nothing more.' The magnitude of his claim removes these condescending objections from consideration. That claim must be one of these three: a monstrous mistake, a monstrous fraud, or the truth. There is no in-between position. Moreover, the sheer gravity of the claim requires some response. If, as Lewis rightly insists, this argument applies to Christ, then does it not apply with equal force to Bahá'u'lláh?

A third point is that the evidence by which we must decide is the purported prophet's accomplishments – the results of his life and teachings. Although Christ leaves us to search the scriptures for more concrete guidance on how to proceed, the context clearly shows that by fruits He means results. My dictionary defines 'fruit' in this sense as 'the result, product or consequence of any action: as, *Prosperity is the fruit of planning*'. We use the expression this way today and it was used so in Christ's time as well. (This, as we shall see, is clear from a number of related Bible verses.)

It is not surprising, then, that in every passage where the Bible spells out how we are to recognize the Voice of God, its focus is on results. The Bible insists that there are certain fruits or achievements that can come *only* from One who reveals the authentic Word of God through the breath of the Holy Spirit. These tokens of prophetic authenticity cannot

– according to the Bible – be successfully faked, forged, mimicked or replicated by any deceiver or false prophet. Such attempts may be made but they are bound to fail if we ourselves faithfully apply the divine standard.

Before turning to these biblically sanctioned criteria, I would like to comment on two other tests which, though frequently proposed, are woefully inadequate. These potentially misleading tests are 1) miracles and 2) ancient messianic prophecy.

Miracles

We may feel strongly tempted to demand that God's emissary prove His position by performing miracles. As a Bahá'í, I believe that both Jesus and Bahá'u'lláh did indeed perform miracles, for both were embodiments of that all-powerful Word by whom 'all things were made'. Many mysterious feats are attributed to both figures and we are free to make of such accounts what we will. Bahá'u'lláh, however, cautions us not to offer these as evidence of His Faith's validity:

> We beseech Our loved ones not to . . . allow references to what they have regarded as miracles and prodigies to debase Our rank and station, or to mar the purity and sanctity of Our name (ESW 33).

There are several reasons for this policy. First, miracles are a proof – if at all – only for those who actually experience them. The rest of us must decide, in each case, whether it is easier to believe that a miracle actually happened or simply that the witnesses are unreliable. The more impressive the alleged miracle, the easier it becomes to doubt its reality.

Even when we recognize a miracle as genuine we may reasonably question its source. Christ tells us that 'false Christs and false prophets' will use 'great signs and wonders' to 'deceive', if possible, 'the very elect'. The Book of Revelation describes a satanic 'beast' destined to seduce people away from God's truth by performing astounding miracles. In light of such warnings, how can we take seriously anyone who brandishes miracles as a supposed proof of divine authenticity?

When doubters demanded of Christ a reason to accept Him, He could easily have overwhelmed them with a dazzling show of supernatural might. Instead, He simply referred them to the Old Testament: 'Search the scriptures . . . they are they which testify of me . . . had ye believed Moses, ye would have believed me, for he wrote of me' (John 5:39, 46). Moses and the prophets after Him did indeed write of a coming Saviour to be recognized – they indicated – by certain definite signs. Miracles, as we shall see, were not among the signs they specified. Christ knew that anyone unwilling to follow Him on the basis of the established scriptural standards would never do so because of miracles: 'If they hear not Moses and the prophets, neither will they be persuaded, though one rose from the dead' (Luke 16:31).

The Bible demonstrates that Christ was correct: '. . . though he had done so many miracles before them [the people], yet they believed not on him' (John 12:37). When He healed a group of lepers and only one paused even to thank Him, He wryly observed: 'Were there not ten cleansed? but where are the nine? There are not found that returned to give glory to God, save this stranger' (Luke 17:17-18).

Small wonder, then, that Christ played down the importance of His own miracles. He thus instructed the beneficiary of another healing: 'See thou tell no man . . .' (Matt. 8:4). When sceptics demanded that He put on a show for them, He replied: 'An evil and adulterous generation seeketh after a sign; and there shall no sign be given to it, but the sign of the prophet Jonas. For as Jonas was three days and three nights in the whale's belly; so shall the Son of man be three days and three nights in the heart of the earth' (Matt. 12:39-40). When Christ, true to His word, rose after His three-day disappearance into the tomb, He showed Himself alive almost exclusively to persons who already believed in Him. (The lone exception was Saul of Tarsus, who, as the Apostle Paul, was destined to become His greatest missionary.) Thus none of the miracle-seeking cynics ever saw the 'sign' they sought.

Even for those who sincerely believed and followed Christ, miracles were seldom sufficient. 'Ye seek me,' He says, 'not because ye saw the miracles, but because ye did eat of the loaves, and were filled' (John 6:26). Christ cannot be speaking here of the bread He had recently multiplied in the famous 'miracle of the loaves and fishes'. If this were His meaning, He would be contradicting Himself, for He plainly states that it is 'not because ye saw the miracles'. He goes on to identify the 'loaves' to which He refers:

> Labour not for the meat which perisheth, but for that meat which endureth unto everlasting life . . . my Father giveth you the true bread from heaven. For the bread of God is he which cometh down from heaven, and giveth life unto the world . . . I am the bread of life: he that cometh to me shall never hunger; and he that believeth on me shall never thirst (John 6:27, 32-5).

Christ, in other words, asks that we believe in Him not because of His miracles but because He nourishes our souls with spiritual food. The trouble with an over-emphasis on material miracles is that it can make us forget this greatest miracle of all: Christ's power to awaken the spiritually dead to a new and eternal spiritual life. This, after all, is the mission of a 'quickening spirit'. Physical feats are purely incidental. Bahá'u'lláh has explained:

> . . . the Cause of God is not a theatrical display that is presented every hour, of which some new diversion may be asked for every day. If it were thus, the Cause of God would become mere child's play (SAQ 29).

The point, once more, is not that the omnipotent 'Lord who is the Spirit' is unable to perform miracles. Of course He can do so, whether He appears as Jesus or as Bahá'u'lláh. The point is that He wishes to be recognized, not for physical showmanship, but for His infinitely greater accomplishments in the world of hearts and souls. An early Bahá'í, apparently unaware of Bahá'u'lláh's distaste for such tales, compiled a book from eyewitness accounts of His reputed miracles. The Bahá'í proudly showed the book to Bahá'u'lláh, who – recognizing the man's sincerity – thanked him for his service but promptly destroyed the only manuscript. Bahá'u'lláh emphasizes that He does not want His religion spread through such unworthy means:

> Whoso hath in bygone ages asked Us to produce the signs of God, hath, no sooner We revealed them to him, repudiated God's truth. The people, however, have, for the most part, remained heedless. They whose eyes are illumined with the light of understanding will perceive the sweet savours of the All-Merciful, and will embrace His truth. These are they who are truly sincere (G 132).

Ancient Prophecy

Since the widespread foreknowledge of Christ's return is based upon Bible prophecies, anyone claiming to fulfil these prophecies must be able to explain them in a clear and coherent manner. I have devoted many pages to showing why Bahá'ís believe Bahá'u'lláh has done just that. Nevertheless, Bahá'u'lláh does not base His claim primarily upon ancient prophecy; nor do I believe that the mere plausibility of His interpretation constitutes proof of His authenticity. Prophecy is one piece of a much larger puzzle. While the piece must fit, it cannot by itself show the whole picture. Bahá'u'lláh writes:

> Although We did not intend to make mention of the tradi-
> tions of a bygone age, yet, because of Our love for thee, We
> will cite a few which are applicable to Our argument. We do
> not feel their necessity, however, inasmuch as the things We
> have already mentioned suffice the world and all that is
> therein (KI 237).

The Bible's messianic prophecies serve two functions. On the
one hand, by creating an expectation of Christ's return, they
motivate many people to search for Him. On the other, they
test our spiritual discernment. They do this, as we noted
previously, by virtue of being written in 'sealed' language –
images deliberately coded so as to be understood only after
their fulfilment, when the promised Redeemer 'unseals'
them. If we cling to a materialistic outlook, we will see no
reason to take Him seriously. Only by reading with spiritual
vision are we able to consider His claim and investigate
further. The prophecies thus act as a sieve, by which God
tests and separates us in the Day of Judgement.

This very fact, however, limits their usefulness as evidence.
If the Bible's predictions of Christ's return are open to
various interpretations, then we cannot cite Bahá'u'lláh's
interpretation as 'proof' that He fulfils them. This would be
circular reasoning – assuming in advance what we wish to
prove. However convincingly we may expound a 'sealed'
prophecy, a different reader, starting from different premises, always will be able to advance what for him or her will
be an equally convincing alternative interpretation.

Much the same situation prevailed at Christ's First Coming. Though the Old Testament is filled with predictions of
the Messiah, few people recognized Christ primarily on that
basis. Indeed, most of those who followed Him did so in spite
of – not because of – the prophecies. Only in hindsight were
Jewish converts to Christianity able to reread the messianic
descriptions by Moses, Isaiah, Jeremiah and others and say,
'Oh, *that's* what they meant! Now I understand.' It should not
surprise us to find the same pattern repeated in the time of
Bahá'u'lláh.

Bahá'í scholars, analyzing the Bible's latter-day prophecies within a Bahá'í framework, have found them rich with hints and clues to Bahá'u'lláh's identity. There are prophecies that seem to indicate the time and place of His appearance, the duration of His ministry, and various events and locations associated with His life. These have been enumerated in several books, of which the best known is *Thief in the Night* by William Sears. Many thoughtful students have found this prophetic tapestry quite impressive and have, as a result, accepted Bahá'u'lláh. While this strikes me as an entirely valid response, it entails subjective judgements that two equally reasonable people may well make differently. We have no reason to expect that everyone should find the Bahá'í interpretation convincing (any more than Jewish scholars find the Christian interpretation of Old Testament prophecy convincing).

The problem of subjectivity will, of course, somewhat remain no matter how we proceed. Whenever we evaluate evidence we make value judgements. But this is a matter of degree. The interpretation of ancient prophecy is an unusually subjective enterprise, offering extraordinarily wide scope for differing opinions. There are other Bible-based ways to test the credibility of anyone who claims to be the Messiah. Some of these alternatives involve criteria which, when compared with ancient prophecy, are relatively concrete, measurable and objective – hence less subject to the whims of personal interpretation.

BIBLE GUIDELINES

When we turn to these truly biblical guidelines we find that they can be grouped under three broad headings – three 'fruits' of the Holy Spirit by which we 'shall know' the truth about anyone claiming to speak in the Lord's name. These are 1) His own prophetic foreknowledge, 2) His glorification of Christ and 3) His success in manifesting divine virtues.

The first item warrants comment: It may seem odd that, having just discounted prophecy as a criterion of divine authority, I now list prophecy as our first such criterion! What is happening here? The answer is that we are dealing with two distinctly different prophetic categories. The test we previously discussed (and found to be doubtful) is whether Bahá'u'lláh's advent matches our interpretation of coded prophecies revealed centuries ago in the Bible. This new criterion (to which the Bible itself attaches immense importance) is whether Bahá'u'lláh makes easily understood prophecies *of His own* which are then fulfilled through events outside His control. The issue is not whether the Bible correctly foretells the future (of course it does), but whether Bahá'u'lláh does so. Let us see what scripture tells us in this regard.

'He will shew you things to come'

There are certain things only God can do, certain accomplishments possible only by divine power. One of these is the foretelling of future events:

> Remember the former things of old: for I am God, and there is none else; I am God, and there is none like me, declaring the end from the beginning, and from ancient times the things that are not yet done, saying, My counsel shall stand, and I shall do all my pleasure: Calling a ravenous bird from the east, the man that executeth my counsel from a far country: yea, I have spoken it, I will also bring it to pass; I have purposed it, I will also do it (Isa. 46:9-11).

In this exquisite scripture God states categorically that 'there is none like me, declaring the end from the beginning, and from ancient times the things that are not yet done'. This is, if we think about it, perfectly logical: Time itself is God's creation, and it is only natural that He should be able to see beyond it. Moreover, as the passage above indicates, God is able not only to see the future but to control it: 'I have spoken it, I will also bring it to pass.' Thus God's prophecies come true not merely because His vision transcends time but because, when necessary, He intervenes in history to fulfil them.

Prophecy is a prerogative God has reserved to Himself, for He clearly announces that 'there is none like me' in this respect. Prophetic foreknowledge, then, is a clear sign which no one – unaided by God – can replicate. God has chosen not to share this power with any false prophet, satanic deceiver or bogus messiah. Indeed, He taunts all such impostors, daring them to step forward and demonstrate this ability which is His and His alone:

> Produce your cause, saith the Lord; bring forth your strong reasons, saith the King of Jacob. Let them bring them forth, and shew us what shall happen: let them shew the former things, what they be, that we may consider them, and know the latter end of them; or declare us things for to come. Shew the things that are to come hereafter, that we may know that ye are gods: yea, do good, or do evil, that we may be dismayed, and behold it together. Behold, ye are of nothing, and your work of nought: an abomination is he that chooseth you (Isa. 41:21-4).

There is nothing ambiguous about this divine challenge. No one can meet it except one who truly reveals the Word of God through the gift of the Holy Spirit – that 'Spirit of Truth' of which the Bible says 'he will shew you things to come' (John 16:13). A false prophet will always give himself away, either by evading the challenge or – if he is foolhardy enough to accept it – by failing its test. God has established this as an ironclad rule by which we are to judge the authenticity of anyone claiming to speak in His name:

> And if thou say in thine heart, How shall we know the word which the Lord hath not spoken? When a prophet speaketh in the name of the Lord, if the thing follow not, nor come

to pass, that is the thing which the Lord hath not spoken, but the prophet hath spoken it presumptuously: thou shalt not be afraid of him (Deut. 18:21-2).

Prophecy, then, is indeed a crucial test of divine authority. But the test – as set forth in these scriptures – is not whether the purported prophet conforms to our understanding of prophecies revealed centuries ago in deliberately cryptic language. The biblical test is whether he himself, in his own time and in plain language, accurately predicts events that have not yet happened. What counts most heavily is not prophecy from the past, but prophecy of the future; not whether he supposedly fulfils traditional expectations but whether he successfully anticipates 'things to come'.

One of the ways in which Jesus Christ demonstrated His own authenticity was through this very fruit of the Spirit: 'behold, I have foretold you all things' (Mark 13:23). He predicted not only His own crucifixion and His resurrection after three days but such details as His betrayal by a trusted disciple and Peter's triple denial ('Before the cock crow twice, thou shalt deny me thrice' – Mark 14:30). He described, in graphic detail, the impending destruction of Jerusalem by Titus in 70 AD:

> For the days shall come upon thee, that thine enemies shall cast a trench about thee, and compass thee round, and keep thee in on every side, And shall lay thee even with the ground, and thy children within thee; and they shall not leave in thee one stone upon another, because thou knewest not the time of thy visitation (Luke 19:43-4).

In addition, Christ anticipated many of the tribulations His Church would face; and He foresaw, centuries in advance, that His gospel would be preached throughout the world. Surely we would expect similar foresight on the part of that towering figure identified in Revelation as 'One like unto the Son of Man'.

According to the Bible, anyone representing himself as the voice of God must pass this scriptural test. Such a requirement becomes, for obvious reasons, doubly crucial if he claims in addition to be the return of the Lord Christ Himself. Any pretender who fails to produce this divine fruit is exposed as false. If, on the other hand, he discloses a clear, sweeping and precisely accurate prophetic vision of the future; if in so doing he specifies a wealth of details and events no human being could reasonably have anticipated; if he demonstrates this power again and again, never lapsing into error; then we must at some point concede his claim as genuine and his authority as divine. To do otherwise would be to set aside the Bible's explicit guidance.

To benefit from this biblical standard we must apply it in a severe and even ruthless manner. We must bar the door to every possibility of trickery. For example, if a self-proclaimed 'prophet' reveals only a handful of predictions (even spectacularly successful ones), we are entitled to write them off as lucky guesses. We must disqualify anyone who speaks mostly in vague generalities such as 'economic fluctuations', 'new discoveries' and the like; anyone can do that. We have no use for prognostications so open-ended that nothing could ever disprove them; for example, 'Someday there will be a cure for cancer.' Equally worthless are 'predictions' of trends or events which the forecaster might have extrapolated from data already available to him. Bygone prophets may have spoken mostly in 'sealed' codes and symbols but our latter-day candidate has no such luxury. In measuring him, we will give credence only to prophecies revealed in clear and unambiguous language; prophecies documented, circulated and understood well in advance of the events they portray.

Most of all, we must determine how willing our prospective messiah is to 'go out on a limb'. Does he commit himself, publicly and in advance, to testable predictions of such seeming improbability that they maximize our opportunity to expose him as a fraud? Does he do this not just once but over and over again, until there remains no reasonable doubt as to the reality of his foreknowledge? Only a claimant who can confidently run this remorseless gauntlet deserves our consideration.

Bahá'u'lláh is such a claimant.

Repeatedly throughout His ministry, Bahá'u'lláh – like Christ – made weighty and daring predictions. All, so far as I can discover, have withstood the test of time. To substantiate this assertion, I have chosen from His teachings the thirty specific prophecies I deem most important. Beginning with the next chapter, I will document each one and compare it with subsequent events, showing how each has been completely and unambiguously fulfilled. This review will span Chapters 7 and 8. Following that, in Chapter 9, I will review an additional half dozen or so Bahá'í prophecies that relate to on-going developments taking place in the world today. All of these seem already to be in various stages of partial fulfilment, while daily headlines testify to their accelerating unfoldment. Most, when first publicized, seemed so incredible that no informed observer could have taken them seriously. Any or all could have turned out differently in such a way as to discredit Bahá'u'lláh. Yet not one of His predictions (whether cited here or not) has proved wrong. Each was borne out by events which fell into place with clockwork precision, usually in spectacular ways and sometimes at the last possible moment.

Nor is there anything random about Bahá'u'lláh's prophecies. Placed against the background of His spiritual and humanitarian teachings, they form a distinct pattern, showing that He correctly anticipated the most important historical events, the most revolutionary scientific discoveries and the most significant social upheavals of the past hundred and thirty years. One could spend months in a good library studying historical summaries and compiling a concise outline of seminal developments since, say, the year 1870.

Yet one would fail – even with hindsight – to improve on the outline sketched in Bahá'u'lláh's teachings before any of these things had happened.

Is prophetic foresight really one of the 'fruits' Christ had in mind when He said: 'By their fruits ye shall know them'? The inference seems reasonable since the 'fruits' are the signs by which we 'shall know' divine authority, and the Bible identifies this distinctive gift of the Spirit as such a sign. Classification, however, is by its nature somewhat arbitrary. If we prefer to think of this criterion under a different heading we are free to do so. The point remains that we have here a measurable, objective and undeniably scriptural standard for recognizing the Word of God.

One further question may be expressed as follows: 'There have been many great seers who made inspired predictions: Isaiah, Daniel and others – maybe even Nostradamus. Yet they were not Christ. Even if Bahá'u'lláh could reveal the future, how does that prove He is the return of Christ?' Part of the answer is that these other individuals do not claim to be the return of Christ whereas Bahá'u'lláh does. Such a claim (as the previously mentioned C. S. Lewis argument demonstrates) leaves no middle ground. It is possible to be divinely inspired without being oneself divine and it certainly is possible to claim divinity without being either inspired or divine. But it is *not* possible, through genuine divine inspiration, to claim divinity unless one is genuinely divine. If we find that Bahá'u'lláh is truly 'of God', and if, speaking with God's authority, He assures us that He is the return of Christ, then that is who He is. Prophetic foreknowledge is important not for its entertainment value but because – according to God's Word – it is a completely reliable and objective test of divine authority. Having empowered us, through such a criterion, to recognize His divine envoy, God holds us accountable for our response: '. . . whosoever will not hearken unto my words which he shall speak in my name, I will require it of him' (Deut. 18:19).

145

'He shall glorify Me'

Speaking again of that 'Spirit of Truth' who 'shall not speak of himself; but whatsoever he shall hear, that shall he speak', Christ says: 'He shall glorify me: for he shall receive of mine, and shall shew it unto you' (John 16:13-14). It is logical to expect that anyone who reveals the Word of God through the gift of the Holy Spirit should manifest this sign. Paul elaborates this principle:

> Now concerning spiritual gifts, brethren, I would not have you ignorant . . . Wherefore I give you to understand, that no man speaking by the Spirit of God calleth Jesus accursed: and that no man can say that Jesus is the Lord, but by the Holy Ghost (I Cor. 12:1-3).

Paul's context shows that he is speaking particularly of those who demonstrate extraordinary spiritual powers or 'gifts'. The Apostle John expresses a similar thought:

> Beloved, believe not every spirit, but try the spirits whether they are of God: because many false prophets are gone out into the world. Hereby know ye the Spirit of God: Every spirit that confesseth that Jesus Christ is come in the flesh is of God: And every spirit that confesseth not that Jesus Christ is come in the flesh is not of God: and this is that spirit of antichrist, whereof ye have heard that it should come; and even now already is it in the world (I John 4:1-3).

> . . . even now are there many antichrists . . . Who is a liar but he that denieth that Jesus is the Christ? He is antichrist, that denieth the Father and the Son. Whosoever denieth the Son, the same hath not the Father: but he that acknowledgeth the Son hath the Father also (I John 2:18, 22-3).

Paul and John, as I understand them, are not speaking of ordinary people in everyday circumstances. Both apostles recognize that an insincere individual, feigning love for

Christ, may say all the right things so convincingly as to fool others and perhaps even himself. The point seems to be that no malevolent supernatural power, manifesting itself through a false prophet while posing as the voice of God, can do this. Miraculous abilities (even if genuine) are in themselves no proof of prophetic authenticity, for we still must discern whether they are divine or demonic. The Bible provides us here with a practical way to make this decision. If a purported prophet demonstrates power and influence that clearly is more than human in character, we can test its source by observing his stand on Christ. Does he testify that 'Jesus is the Lord'? Does he confess that Jesus Christ came 'in the flesh' as the divine Messiah, the Son of the living God? If so, then his demonstrated spiritual gifts must be of divine origin, for no satanic agency can makes such assertions: '. . . no man can say that Jesus is the Lord, but by the Holy Ghost .' 'Every spirit that confesseth that Jesus Christ is come in the flesh is of God . . .' '. . . he that acknowledgeth the Son hath the Father also.'

This criterion carries an implied condition. To 'say' that Jesus is Lord and to 'confess' His divine station as the Christ is more than a matter of mouthing words. It involves both speech and behaviour – the living of a life that testifies to His truth. Actions, as we say, 'speak louder than words', for they reveal what is in our hearts. Christ Himself, in explaining that true and false prophets may be differentiated 'by their fruits', cautions: 'Not every one that saith unto me, Lord, Lord, shall enter into the kingdom of heaven; but he that doeth the will of my Father which is in heaven' (Matt. 7:21).

To be considered authentic, then, anyone claiming divine authority must do more than display superhuman power and insight. He also must glorify Christ both in word and deed. The Bible clearly teaches that this sign – like prophetic foreknowledge – is one that no satanic spirit can manifest. By examining the evidence in light of this scriptural principle, we can readily expose any counterfeit Messiah.

We may interpret this criterion in any reasonable way we

like and apply it as strictly as we wish. However we may do so, it reveals Bahá'u'lláh as One whose spiritual gifts are the genuine fruit of the Holy Spirit. 'Say, this is the One', He states, referring to Himself, 'Who hath glorified the Son and hath exalted His Cause' (TB 12). He repeatedly extols Christ as Lord, using such expressions as 'Lord of all being' (ESW 100) and 'Lord of the visible and invisible' (G 57). Throughout Bahá'u'lláh's written and spoken teachings, Jesus Christ is referred to by such titles as 'the Lord Christ', 'His Holiness Jesus Christ', 'Jesus, the Spirit of God' and similar titles of praise. As we saw in Chapter 2, Christ's divine position as the Son of God and the 'Word made flesh' is fully upheld in the Bahá'í teachings, where it is both defended and elucidated.

What remains to be shown – and what I will explain in a future chapter – is that Bahá'u'lláh glorified Christ by deed as well as by word. He did so by living a life of sacrificial devotion to God, upholding the teachings of Christ and the Bible even in the face of agonizing persecution. This testimony of His life provides proof not only of His unquestionable sincerity, but – from a biblical perspective – of the divine origin of His demonstrated prophetic powers.

'The wisdom that is from above'

The Bible lists, in addition, a number of other fruits by which we can test whether Bahá'u'lláh is truly 'of God'. These may be grouped under the single broad heading of 'spiritual attributes' or 'divine virtues':

> But the fruit of the Spirit is love, joy, peace, longsuffering, gentleness, goodness, faith, meekness, temperance . . . (Gal. 5:22-3).

> But the wisdom that is from above is first pure, then peaceable, gentle, and easy to be entreated, full of mercy and good fruits, without partiality, and without hypocrisy. And the fruit of righteousness is sown in peace of them that make peace (James 3:17-18).

(For the fruit of the Spirit is in all goodness and righteousness and truth;) Proving what is acceptable unto the Lord (Eph. 5:9-10).

The Bible contains many similar references to spiritual 'fruits'; these are simply examples. From these three passages alone, however, we can compile an extensive list of admirable spiritual qualities. These include love, joy, peace, longsuffering, gentleness, goodness, faith, meekness, temperance, purity, mercy, impartiality, sincerity and others – in short, 'all goodness and righteousness and truth'. Such fruit of the Spirit characterizes 'the wisdom that is from above'. It springs forth, that is, from the Word of God uttered with divine authority through inspiration of the Holy Spirit. A true Revealer of that Word will, by flawlessly manifesting these divine attributes in His own life and words, cause them to flourish also among those who turn to Him. 'By their fruits ye shall know them.'

Why is this particular fruit – the manifestation of spiritual qualities – of such overriding importance? Because without it other standards such as prophecy, or even the recognition of Christ's Lordship, would be meaningless. As Paul so eloquently put it:

If I speak in the tongues of men and of angels, but have not love, I am only a resounding gong or a clanging cymbal. If I have the gift of prophecy and can fathom all mysteries and all knowledge, and if I have a faith that can move mountains, but have not love, I am nothing (I Cor. 13:1-2 NIV).

A crucial implication of these guidelines is that we can, in fact, recognize genuine love, genuine joy, genuine peace and the like. Christ's promise – 'By their fruits ye shall know them' – means at the very least that we will be able correctly to identify the fruits. Does this involve value judgements? Of course it does. But this in no way implies that we cannot make such judgements with confidence, or that 'it's only a matter of opinion'. Christ says we will *know*. We will know, that is, if we investigate with an open mind and an open heart.

This investigation, more than any other, is one that each individual must make for himself or herself. I can do no more than present my own findings. The historical record, however, could hardly be more clear: Even Bahá'u'lláh's bitterest enemies testified to the Christ-like perfection of His character, to the nobility of His actions and to the airtight consistency of His words and deeds. Hardened sceptics – people of rank and capacity, accustomed to dealing on an equal footing with notables of every description – often found themselves bowing spontaneously in His presence, so profoundly moved were they by His luminous spirituality. Nowhere are His personal qualities more evident than in their uplifting impact on the lives of those who followed Him. More than a century after His ascension the accelerating spread of His influence and its efficacy in breaking down age-long barriers of strife and prejudice appear among the most amazing phenomena of the modern world. Bahá-'u'lláh's own life is an open book; and any inquirer can learn, through direct experience, His continuing impact on the inner lives and organized activities of those who belong to the worldwide community He called into being.

Reflections

We have discussed three scriptural standards by which to recognize the voice of divine authority – 1) prophetic foreknowledge, 2) glorification of Christ, and 3) the manifesting of spiritual attributes. These are the primary tests set forth in the Bible, the main avenues through which we are to investigate and discover the truth about anyone claiming to reveal the Will of God – the 'wisdom that is from above'.

In any case where the results of these three tests clash, we would be obliged to set aside such a claim as doubtful. Where Bahá'u'lláh is concerned, however, all three yardsticks produce the same measurement; and all three testify in harmony to the truth of His claim. I do not ask any reader to accept this statement without further probing. The purpose of this book is to set forth what I see as the relevant facts and to encourage each inquirer to verify those facts through independent research.

We will examine this evidence beginning with the fulfilment of Bahá'u'lláh's own prophecies, showing how He demonstrated His predictive abilities repeatedly in the most amazing fashion. Such foresight (I will argue) is precisely the sort which the Bible identifies as possible only through God's power. With these facts in hand we will explore further the manner in which Bahá'u'lláh glorified Christ and manifested Christ-like attributes. The Bible teaches that it is impossible for anyone claiming divine authority to pass all three of these tests unless his spiritual gifts are of God. If Bahá'u'lláh does so – and the facts, I believe, will show that He does indeed – then we have the clearest possible biblical warrant for accepting that 'the Lord of Lords is come'.

PART TWO

By Their Fruits We Shall Know

. . . prepare to meet thy God, O Israel. For lo, he that
formeth the mountains, and createth the wind, and
declareth unto man what is his thought, that maketh the
morning darkness, and treadeth upon the high places of
the earth, The Lord, The God of hosts, is his name (Amos
4:12-3).

Seek ye the Lord while he may be found, call upon him
while he is near . . . For ye shall go out with joy, and be led
forth with peace: the mountains and the hills shall break
forth before you into singing, and all the trees of the field
shall clap their hands (Isa. 55:6, 12).

Beware of false prophets . . . Every tree that bringeth not
forth good fruit is hewn down, and cast into the fire. Wherefore by their fruits ye shall know them (Matt. 7:15-20).

7

Prophetic Fruits:
Historical Events

> The prophecy came not in old time by the will of man; but
> holy men of God spake as they were moved by the Holy
> Ghost (II Peter 1:21).

The fulfilment of Bahá'u'lláh's prophecies is a particularly
crucial biblical test because, as we have learned, it addresses
two questions at once: whether He possessed 'spiritual gifts'
in the form of supernatural inspiration, and whether those
gifts and that inspiration were 'of God'. This chapter will
begin to explore evidence bearing on this issue.

Foreknowledge is of course a divine attribute: 'Known
unto God are all his works from the beginning of the world'
(Acts 15:18). Such power comes only from God, who assures
us that 'there is none like me, declaring the end from the
beginning, and from ancient times the things that are not
yet done . . .' (Isa. 46:9-10). God challenges all who claim
to speak in His name to vindicate themselves by demonstrating this uniquely reserved ability (Isa. 41:21-4). Repeatedly
He reminds us that no pretender can meet this challenge –
no human trickster, no false prophet, no satanic deceiver.
We previously examined several scriptures that emphasize
this principle, and there are more:

> Who hath declared from the beginning that we may know?
> and beforetime, that we may say, He is righteous? yea, there
> is none that sheweth, yea, there is none that declareth . . .
> (Isa. 41:26).

> I am the Lord: that is my name: and my glory will I not give
> to another . . . Behold, the former things are come to pass,
> and new things do I declare: before they spring forth I tell
> you of them (Isa. 42:8-9).

The spiritual implication is plain: False prophecy is the
telltale sign of a false prophet. God promises that we will
'know the word which the Lord hath not spoken' by the fact
that 'when a prophet speaketh in the name of the Lord, if
the thing follow not, nor come to pass, that is the thing which
the Lord hath not spoken' (Deut. 18:21-2). Genuine predictive power comes from God and God alone.

It follows that even one demonstrably wrong prediction
would convict Bahá'u'lláh of imposture. However, the situation becomes more complex if we find we cannot tie Him at
once to a mistaken forecast. We should then be obliged to
probe more deeply. Did He perhaps shy away from making
predictions at all? Do His predictions – however impressive
individually – number only a handful? Are they expressed
in ambiguous or overly broad language? How widely were
they circulated and understood in advance of the events to
which they refer? How well documented are His predictions
and any purported fulfilments?

These are not frivolous questions. Insofar as they help us
discern who Bahá'u'lláh really is, they are of spiritual life-
and-death importance. We can tolerate no nonsense in this
regard, overlook no lapses, make no allowances. A divine
claim such as Bahá'u'lláh's does not qualify for 'benefit of the
doubt'. It is not enough that He establish merely a 'good
record' for prognostication, or even a spectacular record. A
less-than-perfect score would be, for purposes of our inquiry,
a score of less than zero.

Instead of shrinking from so rigorous an examination (as
one would expect of a fraudulent Messiah), Bahá'u'lláh
welcomes and indeed invites it. Foremost among the 'clearest
proofs' which He says 'attest the truth of His Cause' is the
fact that 'the prophecies He, in an unmistakable language,
hath made have been fulfilled' (G 58). He writes:

. . . We have laid bare the divine mysteries and in most explicit language foretold future events, that neither the doubts of the faithless, nor the denials of the froward, nor the whisperings of the heedless may keep back the seekers after truth from the Source of the light of the One true God (TB 241).

. . . most of the things which have come to pass on this earth have been announced and prophesied by the Most Sublime Pen . . . All that hath been sent down hath and will come to pass, word for word, upon earth. No possibility is left for anyone either to turn aside or protest (ESW 148, 150).

In this inquiry we must consider not only the prophecies written or spoken by Bahá'u'lláh Himself, but those of His Forerunner, the Báb, and His Successor, 'Abdu'l-Bahá. The Báb was more than simply a Herald of Bahá'u'lláh. He claimed to be – and was recognized by Bahá'u'lláh as – the bearer in His own right of independent divine revelation. 'Abdu'l-Bahá was not a direct revealer of God's words in the same sense. He was, however, appointed by Bahá'u'lláh as the authorized Interpreter of Bahá'í teachings, which He was empowered to elaborate at will with unerring divine protection. By investing the Báb and 'Abdu'l-Bahá with such authority, Bahá'u'lláh implicitly embraced their teachings and prophecies as His own – increasing both His own burden and our opportunity to test His validity. Most of the predictions cited below are from Bahá'u'lláh's own words, while a few are from the Báb or 'Abdu'l-Bahá. All, however, are Bahá'u'lláh's either directly or indirectly, since all bear His endorsement.

What are the developments that have, in Bahá'u'lláh's words, 'come to pass on this earth' after being 'announced and prophesied by the Most Sublime Pen'? Those of which I am aware, and which I discuss in the following pages, include:

1) The fall from power of the French Emperor Napoleon III and the consequent loss of his empire.

2) The defeat of Germany in two bloody wars, resulting in the 'lamentations of Berlin'.

3) The success and stability of Queen Victoria's reign.

4) The dismissal of 'Álí Páshá, prime minister of Turkey.

5) The overthrow and murder of Sulṭán 'Abdu'l-'Azíz of Turkey.

6) The breakup of the Ottoman Empire, leading to the extinction of the 'outward splendour' of its capital, Constantinople.

7) The downfall of Náṣiri'd-Dín Sháh, the Persian monarch.

8) The advent of constitutional government in Persia.

9) A massive (albeit temporary) decline in the fortunes of monarchy throughout the world.

10) A worldwide erosion of ecclesiastical authority.

11) The collapse of the Muslim Caliphate.

12) The spread of communism, the 'Movement of the Left', and its rise to world power.

13) The catastrophic decline of that same movement, triggered by the collapse of its egalitarian economy.

14) The rise of Israel as a Jewish homeland.

15) The persecution of Jews on the European continent (the Nazi holocaust).

16) America's violent racial struggles.

17) Bahá'u'lláh's release from the prison of 'Akká and the pitching of His tent on Mount Carmel.

18) The seizure and desecration of Bahá'u'lláh's House in Baghdád.

19) The failure of all attempts to create schism within the Bahá'í Faith.

20) The explosive acceleration of scientific and technological progress.

21) The development of nuclear weapons.

22) The achievement of transmutation of elements, the age-old alchemist's dream.

23) Dire peril for all humanity as a result of that achievement.

24) The discovery that complex elements evolve in nature from simpler ones.

25) The recognition of planets as a necessary by-product of star formation.

26) Space travel.

27) The realization that some forms of cancer are communicable.

28) Failure to find evidence for a 'missing link' between man and ape.

29) The non-existence of a mechanical ether (the supposed light-carrying substance posited by classical physics), and its redefinition as an abstract reality.

30) The breakdown of mechanical models (literal images) as a basis for understanding the physical world.

I will now sketch the salient facts concerning these prophecies, describing when and how each one was made and the circumstances by which each was fulfilled. For each prophecy there is a two-tier explanation: first, an 'abstract' or capsule summary, distilling the bare highlights; and second, a 'background' narrative exploring these and related points in more depth while giving needed reference citations. This dual approach is designed to encourage each reader to study the particulars without losing sight of the larger pattern of prediction and fulfilment.

TABLETS TO THE KINGS

Before examining individual prophecies, let us look at their common historical context.

Shortly before reaching the prison-city of 'Akká in 1868, and continuing for several years thereafter, Bahá'u'lláh, in words of supreme majesty, announced the inception of the long-awaited Kingdom of God on Earth. To the world's reigning monarchs He addressed a series of letters (also known as 'Tablets'), setting forth His claims and the highlights of God's plan whereby the nations could fulfil the vision of Isaiah: 'They shall beat their swords into plowshares, and their spears into pruninghooks . . . neither shall they learn war any more' (Isa. 2:4). Bahá'u'lláh addressed similar letters collectively to these same rulers and heads of state, as well as to leaders of religion, various segments of society, and humanity in general.

In these Tablets Bahá'u'lláh declared that human society was about to be revolutionized by the birth of a divine and world-embracing civilization. 'The whole earth', He exclaimed, 'is now in a state of pregnancy. The day is approaching when it will have yielded its noblest fruits, when from it will have sprung forth the loftiest trees, the most enchanting blossoms, the most heavenly blessings' (PDC 5). This mighty transformation, He said, would come about through historical forces which God had irreversibly set in motion and which the kings could resist or ignore only at their own peril. He advised them to 'have mercy on yourselves and on those beneath you' (PDC 23) by joining forces to 'summon the nations unto God' (PDC 55).

Every birth, however glorious its outcome, is a potentially grueling ordeal preceded by sharp labour pains. The birth of a new civilization is no exception. Bahá'u'lláh indicated to the kings that their response would largely determine the difficulty of the coming transition. He outlined three possible choices: 1) They could investigate His claim, acknowledge Him as the promised Inaugurator of God's kingdom, and establish in His lifetime what He called the 'Most Great Peace' – that earthly paradise in which 'the earth shall be filled with the knowledge of the Lord, as the waters cover the sea' (Isa. 11:9). 2) Rejecting His claim, the kings might still establish at once the 'Lesser Peace', a strictly political plan to abolish war through a worldwide system of representative self-government. Although this stopgap measure would not in itself heal the deeper spiritual maladies afflicting humanity, it would make such healing possible by paving the way for the long-range establishment of the Most Great Peace. 3) They could reject both the proposals outlined above. In that case God, working through the ordinary masses, would in His own time still bring about both the Lesser and the Most Great Peace. The immediate result, however, would be 'convulsions and chaos' (PDC 116) on a scale hitherto unimaginable.

Within this broad context, Bahá'u'lláh offered specific advice to individual rulers and, in so doing, made a number of detailed prophecies. The most important of these letters were compiled in a book entitled *Súriy-i-Haykal* (Discourse of the Temple), published in 1869 in Bombay and later reprinted several times. Many of the prophecies I will cite appeared in that book; all were published and widely circulated in advance of the events to which they refer.

Napoleon III

PROPHECY 1: *The fall from power of the French Emperor Napoleon III and the consequent loss of his empire.*

ABSTRACT: *Bahá'u'lláh warned Napoleon III, emperor of France, that 'thy kingdom shall be thrown into confusion, and thine empire shall pass from thine hands . . . Commotions shall seize all the people in that land . . . We see abasement hastening after thee . . .' This dire prediction, defying conventional wisdom, came true within a year of its publication, as a result of the Franco-Prussian War of 1870. Napoleon's empire did indeed 'pass from' his hands; he himself was taken prisoner and exiled to England, where he died in 'abasement' two years later.*

BACKGROUND: Emperor Napoleon III of France, nephew of the more famous Napoleon I, was the most powerful and brilliant Western monarch of his day. His dream was to walk in the footsteps of his imperial uncle and complete his interrupted campaign of conquest. Upon receiving the first of two letters from Bahá'u'lláh he reportedly cast it aside, saying, 'If this man is God, I am two Gods!' (PDC 51).

Bahá'u'lláh's second letter is the one published in the *Súriy-i-Haykal*. After rebuking the emperor for his insincerity and lust for war, Bahá'u'lláh wrote:

> For what thou hast done, thy kingdom shall be thrown into confusion, and thine empire shall pass from thine hands, as a punishment for that which thou hast wrought. Then wilt thou know how thou hast plainly erred. Commotions shall seize all the people in that land, unless thou arisest to help this Cause, and followest Him Who is the Spirit of God [Jesus] in this, the straight Path. Hath thy pomp made thee proud? By My Life! It shall not endure; nay, it shall soon pass away, unless thou holdest fast by this firm Cord. We see abasement hastening after thee, while thou art of the heedless . . . (PDC 30).

'Abdu'l-Bahá recalls: 'The text of this warning reached the whole of Persia . . . and as this *Súriy-i-Haykal* was circulated in Persia and India and was in the hands of all believers, they were waiting to see what would come to pass' (SAQ 33). Napoleon, then at the height of his power, went to war in 1870 with Germany, believing he could easily take Berlin. Although, as 'Abdu'l-Bahá notes, 'no one at that time expected the victory of Germany' (SAQ 33), the French army was defeated that year at Saarbruck, Weissenburg and Metz, then finally in crushing catastrophe at Sedan. The breakup and surrender of Napoleon's forces constituted 'the greatest capitulation hitherto recorded in modern history' (PDC 52). Napoleon himself was carried prisoner to Germany and perished miserably in England two years later.

Germany

PROPHECY 2: *The defeat of Germany in two bloody wars, resulting in the 'lamentations of Berlin'.*

ABSTRACT: *To Napoleon's jubilant conqueror, Kaiser William I of Germany, Bahá'u'lláh then disclosed that country's grim future. He foresaw the 'banks of the Rhine . . . covered with gore, inasmuch as the swords of retribution were drawn against you . . . And we hear the lamentations of Berlin, though she be today in conspicuous glory'. He added ominously that Germany would have 'another turn' at bloody defeat. Interpreting this and other prophecies of His father, 'Abdu'l-Bahá stated in 1912 that the imminent struggle would 'set aflame the whole of Europe' and that 'By 1917 kingdoms will fall and cataclysms will rock the earth'. After this part of the prediction materialized in World War I (1914-18), He wrote that the 'vanquished Powers' would 'rekindle the flame of war' and that the inevitable next conflict would be 'fiercer than the last'. World War II handed Germany its second and still greater loss, while both defeats brought retributive sanctions resulting in decades of agonizing 'lamentations' for Berlin.*

BACKGROUND: While shouts of victory were still echoing throughout Germany, Bahá'u'lláh warned its rulers not to tread the same path of aggression the French Emperor had followed to his doom. In His book of laws, the Kitáb-i-Aqdas (Most Holy Book), composed around 1873, Bahá'u'lláh addressed these words to Germany's Kaiser William I:

> O King of Berlin! . . . Do thou remember the one whose power transcended thy power [Napoleon III], and whose station excelled thy station. Where is he? Whither are gone the things he possessed? Take warning, and be not of them that are fast asleep. He it was who cast the Tablet of God behind him, when We made known unto him what the hosts of tyranny had caused Us to suffer. Wherefore, disgrace assailed him from all sides, and he went down to dust in great loss. Think deeply, O King, concerning him, and

concerning them who, like unto thee, have conquered cities and ruled over men. The All-Merciful brought them down from their palaces to their graves. Be warned, be of them who reflect (PDC 36-7).

Bahá'u'lláh then painted this amazing word-picture of a Germany broken and bleeding in the wake of two successive armed conflicts:

> O banks of the Rhine! We have seen you covered with gore, inasmuch as the swords of retribution were drawn against you; and you shall have another turn. And we hear the lamentations of Berlin, though she be today in conspicuous glory (PDC 37).

During His Western tour in 1912, 'Abdu'l-Bahá, citing this and other prophecies of Bahá'u'lláh, warned that a 'universal European war' was both imminent and inevitable. His predictions were widely reported at the time in the American, Canadian and European press, as were His appeals for a multinational peace process based on His father's principles. Returning to His home in the Holy Land, 'Abdu'l-Bahá prepared for the coming upheaval by stockpiling food and medical supplies. Haifa, as the world centre of the growing Bahá'í movement, was by now a site of pilgrimage for large numbers of believers from East and West. About six months before the outbreak of hostilities, 'Abdu'l-Bahá imposed a moratorium on new pilgrimages and began sending away pilgrims already at Haifa. The timing of these phased departures was such that by the end of July 1914 no visitors remained. The wisdom of His actions became apparent when, in the opening days of August, World War I suddenly erupted, stunning the world and incidentally exposing Haifa and the Holy Land to grave hardships and danger.

While touring California in 1912, 'Abdu'l-Bahá reportedly said the impending struggle would 'set aflame the whole of Europe', wreaking unprecedented havoc: 'By 1917 kingdoms will fall and cataclysms will rock the earth' (BNE 65).* Subsequent events fully justified these projections. However, German victories during this period, and especially during its last great push in the spring of 1918, were so imposing that Bahá'u'lláh's vision of Germany in defeat was widely ridiculed throughout Persia by enemies of the Bahá'í Faith. Only with the sudden, unexpected breakup of the German juggernaut did the truth of the prophecy become clear. Then the banks of the Rhine were, indeed, 'covered with gore' as the 'swords of retribution' were drawn against the nation.

Germany's national nightmare was, however, only beginning. Further disclosing the implications of His father's words, 'Abdu'l-Bahá wrote in January 1920: 'The Balkans will remain discontented. Its restlessness will increase. The vanquished Powers will continue to agitate. They will resort to every measure that may rekindle the flame of war' (WOB 30). He still more explicitly stated that 'another war, fiercer than the last, will assuredly break out' (WOB 46). This came to pass with the rise of Hitler's Third Reich and the onset of World War II – although, as before, the German campaigns were at first so successful they seemed more apt to discredit than to confirm Bahá'u'lláh's vision. The Allied victory seemed, until the very end of the war, anything but a foregone conclusion.

And still, events continued to unfold the meaning of the prophecy. The 'lamentations of Berlin', as predicted by Bahá'u'lláh, replaced the 'conspicuous glory' it had enjoyed in His day. After the first war, that once-great city was tortured by the terms of a treaty monstrous in its severity; after the second, it was carved into zones controlled by the Eastern and Western blocs. The infamous Berlin Wall, erected in 1961, became a concrete symbol of the tragedy and agony that for more than forty years continued to wrack the city.

*These comments (from notes taken by Mrs Corinne True, a prominent American Bahá'í of the period) were published in *The North Shore Review*, Chicago, 26 September 1914.

The wall stood until November 1989, when it was opened for the first time, and more than two million jubilant persons poured through it in a single day. Less than a year later, Germany was once again one nation, though still troubled by many difficulties.

Queen Victoria

PROPHECY 3: *The success and stability of Queen Victoria's reign.*

ABSTRACT: *Whereas the French and German rulers had been widely perceived as unstoppable, the reign of England's Queen Victoria was generally viewed as precarious and uncertain. Bahá'u'lláh again challenged the pundits: He informed the Queen that God had smiled upon her just and humanitarian policies and that, as a result, 'the foundations of the edifice of thine affairs will be strengthened, and the hearts of all that are beneath thy shadow, whether high or low, will be tranquillized'. Britain did indeed prosper under her administration, which lasted until 1901, fully justifying Bahá'u'lláh's bright forecast.*

BACKGROUND: Bahá'u'lláh's message to Great Britain's Queen Victoria – unlike those He addressed to Napoleon III and Kaiser William I – was optimistic. Like them, however, it defied conventional wisdom. Queen Victoria's position seemed precarious at the time; she was in poor health and out of favour because she had taken a German consort. Bahá'u'lláh promised her that God would strengthen her administration as a reward for her just and humanitarian actions. He particularly commended two policies of her government: its enforcement of recently enacted laws prohibiting the slave trade, and its action in extending and broadening voting rights throughout the island kingdom. (The Representation of the People Act of 1867, for example, almost doubled the English electorate; and corresponding acts for Scotland and Ireland the following year achieved similar results.)

'O Queen in London!' wrote Bahá'u'lláh:

> Incline thine ear unto the voice of thy Lord, the Lord of all mankind . . . He, in truth, hath come into the world in His most great glory, and all that hath been mentioned in the Gospel hath been fulfilled . . . We have been informed that thou hast forbidden the trading in slaves, both men and women. This, verily, is what God hath enjoined in this wondrous Revelation. God hath, truly, destined a reward for thee, because of this . . . We have also heard that thou hast entrusted the reins of counsel into the hands of the representatives of the people. Thou, indeed, hast done well, for thereby the foundations of the edifice of thine affairs will be strengthened, and the hearts of all that are beneath thy shadow, whether high or low, will be tranquillized (PDC 35-6).

Of all the rulers invited by Bahá'u'lláh to investigate and help His Cause, only Queen Victoria offered so much as a courteous reply. 'If this is of God', she reportedly commented, 'it will endure; if not, it can do no harm' (PDC 65). Just as Bahá'u'lláh had foreseen, her government was 'strengthened' and Britain prospered under her administration. Her reign lasted until 1901, and of all the dynasties whose incumbents Bahá'u'lláh addressed, only hers remains.*

---

*Queen Victoria's granddaughter, Queen Marie of Romania, became a devoted and outspoken follower of Bahá'u'lláh. Her belief in His divine authority, which she proclaimed frequently in the press, raised so many eyebrows among her royal peers that she wrote: 'Some of those of my caste wonder at and disapprove my courage to step forward pronouncing words not habitual for Crowned Heads to pronounce, but I advance by an inner urge I cannot resist' (*Appreciations of the Bahá'í Faith*, p. 9).

The Crown of Turkey

PROPHECY 4: *The dismissal of 'Álí Páshá as prime minister of Turkey.*

PROPHECY 5: *The overthrow and murder of Sulṭán 'Abdu'l-'Azíz of Turkey.*

ABSTRACT: *In a Tablet revealed and circulated around 1870 Bahá'u'lláh foretold that God would soon 'dismiss' 'Álí Páshá, the entrenched and vastly powerful prime minister of Ottoman Turkey, then 'lay hold on' Sulṭán 'Abdu'l-'Azíz, the tyrannical 'Chief who ruleth the land'. The Arabic expression 'lay hold on' is a figure of speech implying violent and untimely death – a meaning rendered especially portentous by Bahá'u'lláh's added warning to the sulṭán himself that he stood in grave danger of betrayal by faithless subordinates. So impossible did these prophecies sound at the time that they were publicized by Bahá'u'lláh's adversaries in an attempt to discredit Him. A few years later, however, the abrupt dismissal of 'Álí Páshá, followed by an 1876 palace coup resulting in the overthrow and subsequent assassination of 'Abdu'l-'Azíz, fulfilled the prophecies to the last word.*

BACKGROUND: Turkey's Sulṭán 'Abdu'l-'Azíz ruled the Ottoman Empire to which Bahá'u'lláh was banished in 1853 and in which He spent the remaining forty years of His earthly life. The Turkish government at first left Bahá'u'lláh in peace but slowly came to regard Him as a potential source of political unrest. Responding to this fear, and to strong pressure from Persian authorities, the sulṭán subjected Bahá'u'lláh, His family and companions to three further banishments, ending with their confinement in the fortress-prison of 'Akká. A considerable number of women and small children – obviously innocent of any crimes against the state – were among the victims of this brutal repression.

As these successive blows fell, Bahá'u'lláh sent several strongly-worded protests to the sulṭán, directly and through various ministers of government. He condemned the injustice and cruelty of the orders; appealed without success for a ten-minute hearing to answer the charges against Him; denied that He ever had sought, or ever would seek, to undermine imperial authority; pointed out that His teachings require loyal obedience to established governments; and counselled the sulṭán to act with justice towards all his subjects. He also made some striking prophecies.

Two key players in this drama were the sulṭán's top-ranking subordinates: 'Álí Páshá, the Turkish prime minister, and Fu'ád Páshá, minister of foreign affairs. These powerful men did much to engineer the policy of suppression to which 'Abdu'l-'Azíz gave his kingly sanction. During His exile in Adrianople Bahá'u'lláh addressed to 'Álí Páshá a Tablet called the *Súriy-i-Ra'ís*, stating that the prime minister soon would find himself in 'manifest loss' (GPB 74). In 1868, shortly after arriving at 'Akká, He repeated this prophecy in a second letter to 'Álí Páshá and further reproved the entire Ottoman government:

> Soon will He [God] seize you in His wrathful anger, and sedition will be stirred up in your midst, and your dominions will be disrupted. Then will ye bewail and lament, and will find none to help or succor you . . . Be expectant . . . for the wrath of God is ready to overtake you. Erelong will ye behold that which hath been sent down from the Pen of My command (PDC 61).

Shortly thereafter, in a widely circulated Tablet called the *Lawḥ-i-Fu'ád*, Bahá'u'lláh again forecast the prime minister's downfall. This time, however, He expanded the prophecy to include Sulṭán 'Abdu'l-'Azíz as well. Commenting on the premature death in 1869 of Fu'ád Páshá, the Tablet stated: 'Soon will We dismiss the one ['Álí Páshá] who was like unto him, and will lay hold on their Chief ['Abdu'l-'Azíz] who ruleth the land, and I, verily, am the Almighty, the All-Compelling' (PDC 62).

So preposterous did this prophecy seem that a distinguished scholar and cleric, Mírzá Abu'l-Faḍl, seized upon it as a chance to discredit Bahá'u'lláh. He pointed out that the expression 'lay hold on' is a figure of speech which, in the Tablet's original language, signifies violent and untimely death as a result of divine justice. Thus Bahá'u'lláh was saying clearly that the sulṭán would be unexpectedly killed. Finding this unthinkable, Mírzá Abu'l-Faḍl declared that for him, the fulfilment or non-fulfilment of this one prophecy would constitute a decisive test of the so-called revelation's authenticity. To dramatize his certainty that the prophecy would fail, he vowed to join the ranks of Bahá'u'lláh's followers should the sulṭán's doom occur as predicted.

Further insight into Bahá'u'lláh's meaning came from yet another Tablet, in which Bahá'u'lláh warned the sulṭán to guard himself against betrayal by faithless subordinates:

> He that acteth treacherously towards God will, also, act treacherously towards his king . . . Take heed that thou resign not the reins of the affairs of thy state into the hands of others, and repose not thy confidence in ministers unworthy of thy trust . . . Avoid them, and preserve strict guard over thyself, lest their devices and mischief hurt thee (G 232-3).

A few years after Bahá'u'lláh's banishment to 'Akká, 'Álí Páshá was fired from his post as prime minister. Stripped of all power, he sank into oblivion. The first stage of the prophecy was thus fulfilled. The second stage came to pass in 1876 when a palace conspiracy abruptly deposed Sulṭán 'Abdu'l-'Azíz and led, four days later, to his murder. The monarch was thus betrayed and assassinated by the very subordinates against whom Bahá'u'lláh had warned him.

In some ideal world, perhaps, Mírzá Abu'l-Faḍl might have calmly considered this outcome as an intriguing demonstration of Bahá'u'lláh's prophetic power. In this real one, he did nothing of the sort. The unexpected fulfilment so angered and frightened him that when Bahá'ís reminded him of his pledge, he became incoherent. Nevertheless, the episode cracked his smugness and impelled him, for the first time, to consider seriously Bahá'u'lláh's claim. After thorough and prayerful investigation, he became convinced of its truth. Forfeiting his high position – he had headed one of Ṭihrán's leading religious universities – he embarked on a life of poverty and sometimes imprisonment in order to teach Bahá'u'lláh's message. His book *The Bahá'í Proofs* (a product of outstanding Bible scholarship) and a lengthy visit to America did much to introduce the Faith to Christian audiences during the early 1900s.*

The Ottoman Empire

PROPHECY 6: *The breakup of the Ottoman Empire, leading to the extinction of the 'outward splendour' of its capital, Constantinople.*

ABSTRACT: *Bahá'u'lláh also turned His prophetic spotlight from the Ottoman rulers to the Turkish Empire itself: 'Soon', He told them, '. . . sedition will be stirred up in your midst, and your dominions will be disrupted . . . Be expectant . . . Erelong will ye behold that which hath been sent down from the Pen of My command' (PDC 61). He described a series of nightmarish disasters 'ready to overtake' the empire and drive it to its knees. During the course of these catastrophes, He wrote, Adrianople would 'pass out of the hands of the king'; the 'outward splendour' of the imperial capital, Constantinople, would 'perish' (PDC 61-2); and conditions would 'wax so grievous, that the very sands on the desolate hills will moan, and the trees on the mountain will weep, and blood will flow out of all things' (PDC 61). These dire predictions were more than justified by a seemingly endless succession of invasions, wars,*

---

*For Mírzá Abu'l-Faḍl's own detailed account of this episode, see Taherzadeh, *Revelation of Bahá'u'lláh*, vol. 3, pp. 97-104.

epidemics, famines, massacres and revolutions in which nine-tenths of the Turkish army died or deserted and a quarter of the populace perished. Adrianople was occupied by Russian troops. The once-vast Turkish empire was shrivelled into a tiny Asiatic republic, while its capital, Constantinople, was abandoned by its conquerors and indeed stripped of its 'outward splendour'.

BACKGROUND: In one of the above-quoted letters, Bahá'u'lláh warned Turkish authorities that 'your dominions will be disrupted'. Those dominions, at the time, extended from the centre of Hungary to the Persian Gulf and the Sudan, and from the Caspian Sea to Oran in Africa. Bahá'u'lláh also made specific prophecies about Adrianople and Constantinople (the latter being the capital of the empire). In the first of His two letters to 'Álí Páshá, He wrote:

> The day is approaching when the Land of Mystery [Adrianople], and what is beside it shall be changed, and shall pass out of the hands of the king, and commotions shall appear, and the voice of lamentation shall be raised, and the evidences of mischief shall be revealed on all sides, and confusion shall be spread by reason of that which hath befallen these captives at the hands of the hosts of oppression. The course of things shall be altered, and conditions shall wax so grievous, that the very sands on the desolate hills will moan, and the trees on the mountain will weep, and blood will flow out of all things. Then wilt thou behold the people in sore distress (PDC 61).

In the Kitáb-i-Aqdas, revealed shortly after His banishment from Adrianople to 'Akká, Bahá'u'lláh addressed the seat of Turkish power:

> O Spot [Constantinople] that art situate on the shores of the two seas! The throne of tyranny hath, verily, been stablished upon thee, and the flame of hatred hath been kindled

within thy bosom . . . Thou art indeed filled with manifest pride. Hath thine outward splendour made thee vainglorious? By Him Who is the Lord of mankind! It shall soon perish, and thy daughters, and thy widows, and all the kindreds that dwell within thee shall lament. Thus informeth thee, the All-Knowing, the All-Wise (PDC 61-2).

If these prophecies sounded perhaps melodramatic when Bahá'u'lláh wrote them, they did not long remain that way. History soon made them appear almost as masterpieces of understatement. Uprisings in Crete and the Balkans were followed by the War of 1877-8, in which at least eleven million people were liberated from Turkish misrule. Russian troops occupied Adrianople, fulfilling the prediction that it would 'pass out of the hands of the king'. Serbia, Montenegro and Romania proclaimed their independence; Bulgaria became a self-governing tributary state; Cyprus and Egypt were occupied; the French assumed a protectorate over Tunis; Eastern Rumelia was ceded to Bulgaria; thousands of Armenians lost their lives in a series of massacres; Bosnia and Herzegovina were lost to Austria; and universal hatred for the government precipitated the Young Turks' Revolution. Military reverses in World War I further weakened the empire; the Arabian provinces revolted; nine-tenths of the Turkish army died or deserted; and a fourth of the whole population perished from war, disease, famine and massacre. Muḥammad VI, the last sulṭán, was deposed, ending the centuries-old dynasty to which he and 'Abdu'l-'Azíz had belonged. The once-vast Turkish empire was shrivelled into a tiny Asiatic republic, while its capital, Constantinople, was abandoned by its conquerors and shorn of its 'outward splendour'.

Náṣiri'd-Dín Sháh

PROPHECY 7: *The downfall of Náṣiri'd-Dín Sháh, the Persian monarch.*

ABSTRACT: *Náṣiri'd-Dín Sháh, ruler of Bahá'u'lláh's native Persia, was a callous dictator to whom policies of genocide and blood-curdling torture seemed second nature. Bahá'u'lláh wrote of him and others like him: 'God hath not blinked . . . at the tyranny of the oppressor. More particularly in this Revelation He hath visited each and every tyrant with His vengeance.' He added that Náṣiri'd-Dín, being the 'Prince of Oppressors', was therefore destined to become an 'object-lesson for the world'. This stroke fell on 1 May 1896, the eve of his fiftieth anniversary Jubilee, when Náṣiri'd-Dín died at the hand of a terrorist hired by a political adversary (who also was, incidentally, a prominent persecutor of the Bahá'í Faith). Since the shooting occurred while the sháh was away from the capital, his ministers – desperate to suppress the news – propped up his corpse in the royal carriage during the return trip, hoping that the watching public would assume all was well.*

BACKGROUND: Bahá'u'lláh's longest Tablet to any single sovereign was addressed to the ruler of His native land, Náṣiri'd-Dín, sháh of Persia. In it Bahá'u'lláh assured the sháh of His loyalty, offered His aid and appealed for a fair inquiry into His claim. A significant passage reads:

> Would that the world-adorning wish of His Majesty might decree that this Servant be brought face to face with the divines of the age, and produce proofs and testimonies in the presence of His Majesty the Sháh! This Servant is ready, and taketh hope in God, that such a gathering may be convened in order that the truth of the matter may be made clear and manifest before His Majesty the Sháh. It is then for thee to command, and I stand ready before the throne of thy sovereignty. Decide, then, for Me or against Me (PDC 45).

The <u>sh</u>áh responded to this eminently reasonable request by torturing to death the courier who had delivered it. By his order this young man, a seventeen-year-old Bahá'í named Badí', was chained to the rack, branded for three days with red-hot bricks, and otherwise tormented in an effort to extract information or a denial of faith. Badí', calm and steadfast, was photographed under torture. Unable to crush his spirit, his frustrated persecutors finally crushed his head.

Such atrocities were the norm, rather than the exception, under the rule of a king whose hands were already stained with the blood of the Báb and twenty thousand Bábí martyrs. Of such rulers Bahá'u'lláh vowed: 'God hath not blinked, nor will He ever blink His eyes at the tyranny of the oppressor. More particularly in this Revelation hath He visited each and every tyrant with His vengeance' (GPB 224). Denouncing Náṣiri'd-Dín <u>Sh</u>áh as the 'Prince of Oppressors' (GPB 225), Bahá'u'lláh wrote that the Persian monarch would be made 'an object-lesson for the world' (PDC 225).

Náṣiri'd-Dín survived until 1896, outliving Bahá'u'lláh by four years; his reign lasted nearly half a century.* To celebrate the fiftieth anniversary of that reign, Persia prepared the most elaborate festival in its history. Prisoners were to be released without condition. Peasants were to be exempt from taxation for two years. The <u>sh</u>áh planned to inaugurate a new era, declare himself the 'Majestic Father of all Persians', and renounce his prerogatives as despot. So jubilant was the country's mood that authorities even 'decided, for the time being, to discontinue persecuting the [Bahá'ís] and other infidels' (PDC 68).

One doubts that Náṣiri'd-Dín, watching the exuberant preparations for his Jubilee, gave a moment's thought to the

---

*Náṣiri'd-Dín ascended the throne in 1848, somewhat less than 50 years earlier by the Gregorian solar calendar. Islamic lunar years, however, are slightly shorter; and 1896 was the fiftieth year of his reign by this reckoning.

humiliating end forecast for him by Bahá'u'lláh. At this late date in his career, with everything going his way, he appeared invincible and triumphant. On 1 May 1896 – the eve of his grand celebration – he visited the shrine of a former sháh. During that visit he died by an assassin's bullet. In a ghoulish after-twist, his ministers drove his body back to the capital propped up in the royal carriage, placing it on display in such a manner as to hide the truth from the massed onlookers.

Bahá'ís were initially blamed for the crime. A number were executed in retaliation, including the famous Bahá'í poet Varqá and his twelve-year-old son, Rúḥu'lláh, both of whom were outstanding teachers of the Faith. The accusation was dropped, however, after the assassin, Mírzá Riḍá, turned out to be a Pan-Islamic terrorist and a follower of Siyyid Jamálu'd-Dín-i-Afghání, himself a well-known enemy of the Bahá'í Cause.*

---

*If Bahá'u'lláh had wished to connive at the overthrow of Náṣiri'd-Dín, He had had an obvious opening some years before, courtesy of Prince Ẓillu's-Sulṭán, who was the sháh's eldest son but could not (because his mother was a commoner) legally accede to the throne. Ẓillu's-Sulṭán had sent an emissary to Bahá'u'lláh offering protection for Persia's Bahá'ís in return for their help in murdering his two brothers and seizing the throne from his father. Bahá'u'lláh had emphatically rejected the plea, making it clear that the Bahá'í Faith was strictly non-political and could not be toyed with. As governor of provinces constituting almost half of Persia, Ẓillu's-Sulṭán had responded by unleashing yet another bloody campaign of terror against the Bahá'ís. (See Kazem Kazemzadeh, 'Varqá and Rúḥu'lláh: Deathless in Martyrdom', *World Order* magazine, Winter 1974-5, p. 32.)

The Persian Constitution

PROPHECY 8: *The advent of constitutional government in Persia.*

ABSTRACT: *Bahá'u'lláh had also predicted, in the early 1870s, that the 'reins of power' in Persia would soon 'fall into the hands of the people'. No political analyst of His time could have taken such a prophecy seriously, since age-old Persian culture and tradition required that its sovereign wield godlike power, unhampered by constitutional constraints or public participation. However, the murder of Náṣiri'd-Dín S͟háh signalled the start of a movement to curb the powers of the monarchy. This movement, slowly gathering steam, plunged the country into a Constitutional Revolution spanning 1906 to 1911. After a bitter and at times violent struggle, the monarchy was forced to concede much of its authority to the new parliament. Although the Peacock Throne remained in place until Persia's Islamic Revolution of 1979, its occupants never again enjoyed the unfettered prerogatives of Náṣiri'd-Dín and his predecessors.*

BACKGROUND: Around 1873 Bahá'u'lláh, in the Kitáb-i-Aqdas, addressed these words to His native Persia: 'Ere long will the state of affairs within thee be changed, and the reins of power fall into the hands of the people' (G 111).

The assassination of Náṣiri'd-Dín S͟háh was the first rumble of the revolution alluded to in this passage. Support for a constitution restricting the monarch's power grew so strong after his death that the next king, Muẓaffari'd-Dín S͟háh, had little choice but to sign the document in 1906, shortly before his death. The next occupants of the throne, however, refused to honour its provisions, and Persia remained embroiled in its Constitutional Revolution from 1906 to 1911. Muḥammad-'Alí S͟háh, who succeeded Muẓaffari'd-Dín, was so hostile to the constitution that he bombarded the parliament's meeting-place with the members inside; whereupon insurgents deposed him. His successor,

the boy-king Aḥmad S͟háh, behaved so irresponsibly that
parliament not only deposed him but abolished, in the
process, the Qájár dynasty to which he and his predecessors
had belonged (see PDC 68-70).

In a talk delivered on 11 July 1909, 'Abdu'l-Bahá said:

> The revolution now rampant in Persia was foretold by
> [Bahá'u'lláh] forty years ago . . . in the Book of Laws [Kitáb-
> i-Aqdas]. And this prophecy was made when Ṭihrán was in
> the utmost quietude and the government of Náṣiri'd-Dín
> S͟háh was well established (*Diary of Juliet Thompson* 100).

The new state of affairs did not, of course, guarantee Persia's
future stability. 'Abdu'l-Bahá wrote (also in July 1909) that
unless union was effected between the opposing sides, foreign powers would step in and divide the country (*Diary of
Juliet Thompson* 26). This happened when Persia, weakened
by the long struggle, later was divided into spheres of influence: Russia took the north, Great Britain the south.

Although Bahá'u'lláh had foreseen the emergence of
constitutional government in Persia, He did not allow Bahá'ís
to take part in the agitation that brought it about. This was
in keeping with His policy of prohibiting Bahá'í involvement
in political movements – movements that, whatever their
merits, would inevitably compromise the Faith's universality
and hamper its all-important mission of achieving world
spiritual unity. One secondary benefit of the policy, in this
case, was that no one could fairly accuse the Bahá'ís of
having promoted the constitution in order to fulfil Bahá-
'u'lláh's prophecy.

The operative word here, of course, is 'fairly'. As 'Abdu'l-
Bahá explains:

> This prophecy, so clearly and evidently stated, printed and
> published, is well-known among the people. Therefore,
> when the Constitution was granted in Persia, the mullás who
> took the Royalist side proclaimed from the pulpit that

'whosoever accepted the Constitution had necessarily accepted the Bahá'í Religion, because the Head of this Religion, His Holiness Bahá'u'lláh, had prophesied this in His Book and the Bahá'ís are agitators and promoters of Constitutionalism. They have brought about the Constitution in order to fulfil the prophecy made by their Chief. Therefore, beware, beware lest ye accept it!' (*Diary of Juliet Thompson* 101).

GENERAL PROPHECIES

When His claims and His peace proposals both went unheeded, Bahá'u'lláh reiterated His warning of dire consequences. 'The winds of despair are, alas, blowing from every direction,' He wrote, 'and the strife that divides and afflicts the human race is daily increasing. The signs of impending convulsions and chaos can now be discerned, inasmuch as the prevailing order appears to be lamentably defective' (PDC 116).

He pointed out that those with the most to lose from the coming upheaval were the very ones whose negligence had brought it about: namely, the world's secular and religious leaders. He stated that God, holding them accountable for their conduct, would strip them of influence: 'From two ranks amongst men power hath been seized: kings and ecclesiastics' (PDC 71).

Let us now look more closely at Bahá'u'lláh's statements concerning each of these groups.

Monarchy

PROPHECY 9: *A massive (albeit temporary) decline in the fortunes of monarchy throughout the world.*

ABSTRACT: *In His general letters to the kings of East and West, Bahá'u'lláh warned that if they ignored His advice, a resistless 'Divine chastisement' would overwhelm them. Absolute monarchy*

– the standard and time-honoured mode of government during Bahá'u'lláh's lifetime – has since been transformed by a rising tide of calamities into the quaint relic of a bygone age.

BACKGROUND: The prophecy quoted above echoes a warning from the *Súriy-i-Múluk* (Discourse of Kings), one of Bahá-'u'lláh's earliest proclamations, addressed to the entire company of monarchs of East and West:

> If ye pay no heed unto the counsels which, in peerless and unequivocal language, We have revealed in this Tablet, Divine chastisement shall assail you from every direction, and the sentence of His justice shall be pronounced against you. On that day ye shall have no power to resist Him, and shall recognize your own impotence (PDC 23).

Looking beyond the individual rulers whose fates Bahá'u'lláh announced, what can we say about the fortunes of royalty in general?

In Bahá'u'lláh's lifetime much of humankind – especially in Europe and Asia – lived within vast empires, ruled by absolute, all-powerful sovereigns who strode the earth with seven-league boots. Although monarchy had never been the safest of occupations for an individual, the institution itself seemed invulnerable.

Within a few decades after Bahá'u'lláh voiced His prophecy, that illusion of security had vanished. A whirlwind of change, roaring into every region of the earth, was not only toppling thrones but systematically digging up their foundations. By 1944 (the end of the first Bahá'í century), it had dissolved the Ottoman, Napoleonic, German, Austrian and Russian empires; swept away the Qájár dynasty in Persia; converted the Chinese empire and the Spanish and Portuguese monarchies into republics; exiled the crowned heads of Holland, Norway, Greece, Yugoslavia and Albania, and stripped of power the kings of Denmark, Belgium, Bulgaria, Romania and Italy. Losing none of its fury, this 'relentless revolutionizing process', as Shoghi Effendi calls it (PDC 49), has continued to the present day. Among its more recent and colourful effects are the transformation of the ancient Japanese empire into a republic and the toppling of the centuries-old Peacock Throne in Persia.

Today, the great powers are governed by legislatures or central bodies; their chief executives are either elected or appointed; and monarchy on the grand scale no longer exists. The British Crown, which once ruled the world's largest empire, is today purely ceremonial and facing troubled times. The few remaining thrones are small in scale and limited in power.

Having said all this, it is necessary to explain that Bahá'ís believe the current decline in the fortunes of royalty is only temporary. Bahá'u'lláh states that 'just kings' will arise in the future who, placing the welfare of their subjects ahead of their own, will restore the prestige of monarchy (PDC 71-4). 'Although a republican form of government profiteth all the peoples of the world,' He writes, 'yet the majesty of kingship is one of the signs of God. We do not wish that the countries of the world should remain deprived thereof. If the sagacious combine the two forms into one, great will be their reward in the presence of God' (TB 28).

Ecclesiasticism

PROPHECY 10: *A worldwide erosion of ecclesiastical authority.*

PROPHECY 11: *The collapse of the Muslim Caliphate.*

ABSTRACT: *Bahá'u'lláh predicted a dramatic loss of power by ecclesiastical institutions. Within this context He specifically arraigned the Catholic Papacy and the Muslim Caliphate, the two agencies that had, for centuries, combined both kingly and ecclesiastical powers.*

BACKGROUND: Bahá'u'lláh in predicting the eclipse of royal authority, also stated that 'power hath been seized' from ecclesiastics. Elsewhere He thus addressed the world's religious leaders:

> O concourse of divines! Ye shall not henceforward behold yourselves possessed of any power, inasmuch as We have seized it from you, and destined it for such as have believed in God, the One, the All-Powerful, the Almighty, the Unconstrained (PDC 81).

The ensuing fate of established religious institutions has been as spectacular and catastrophic as that of the world's secular rulers. Let us consider first the two agencies which, in Bahá'u'lláh's time, had for centuries wielded both spiritual and temporal power – the Papacy and the Caliphate.

Bahá'u'lláh's Tablets to the Kings included one to Pope Pius IX, containing the following words:

> O Pope! Rend the veils asunder. He Who is the Lord of Lords is come overshadowed with clouds, and the decree hath been fulfilled by God, the Almighty, the Unrestrained . . . He, verily, hath again come down from Heaven even as He came down from it the first time . . . Beware lest any name debar thee from God . . . Dwellest thou in palaces whilst He Who is the King of Revelation liveth in the most desolate of abodes? Leave them unto such as desire them, and set thy face with joy and delight towards the Kingdom . . . The Word which the Son concealed is made manifest. It hath been sent down in the form of the human temple in this day. Blessed be the Lord Who is the Father! He, verily, is come unto the nations in His most great majesty (PDC 31-2).

The once-vast temporal power of the Papacy had shrunk considerably before Bahá'u'lláh's letter, but it still embraced the Kingdom of Italy. Bahá'u'lláh commanded the Pope to renounce this remaining power voluntarily: 'Abandon thy kingdom unto the kings . . .' (PDC 32). Had he done so, the ageing pontiff would have spared himself the humiliating loss of freedom, dignity and prestige that followed the seizure of his kingdom in 1870 by King Victor Emmanuel. By ignoring the advice of the Prisoner of 'Akká, Pope Pius IX became the Prisoner of the Vatican.*

Even more spectacular was the collapse of the Caliphate, which both the Báb and Bahá'u'lláh had clearly foreshadowed in their writings.

Islam is divided into two main branches, Sunní and Shí'ih, corresponding in some ways to the division of Christianity into Catholic and Protestant branches. The Caliph, as spiritual head of the much larger Sunní branch, was a Muslim counterpart to the Catholic Pope. Though representing different offices, the Muslim Caliphate and the Turkish Sultanate traditionally were vested in the same person. This gave the Caliph enormous temporal power, while his spiritual jurisdiction extended far beyond the Ottoman Empire and embraced the vast majority of Muslims throughout the world.

This religious monarchy dated back to 632 AD, when Islam split into two camps over the issue of leadership. At that time the Caliphate was accepted by the majority of Muslims, who became known as Sunnís. A minority, later called Shí'ihs, followed a rival institution called the Imamate. Its third and most distinguished representative was Imám Ḥusayn, who – along with many others – lost his life in the 260-year war of succession which ensued. Ḥusayn, whose name is virtually synonymous in Persian literature with the Imamate itself, is the best-beloved of all Shí'ih martyrs.

Given this context (with which His Middle Eastern contemporaries were of course familiar), the Báb clearly referred to the Caliphate when He wrote: 'Erelong We will, in very truth, torment such as waged war against Ḥusayn, in the

---

*It is noteworthy that 1870 was also the year in which the Pope first proclaimed the new dogma of Papal Infallibility.

Land of the Euphrates, with the most afflictive torment, and the most dire and exemplary punishment' (GPB 231). Nor was this divine chastisement to consist simply of some mystical or metaphysical judgement, confined to an unseen future realm of existence. It would operate, the Báb wrote, both 'in the world to come' (i.e. in the afterlife) and on this earthly plane, after the coming of Bahá'u'lláh.

Bahá'u'lláh reaffirmed this prophecy. Referring to the all-powerful Caliphate as the 'mighty throne' of Islam, He described its collapse as a foregone conclusion: 'By your deeds', He wrote to the Muslim clergy, 'the exalted station of the people hath been abased, the standard of Islám hath been reversed, and its mighty throne hath fallen' (GPB 231).

When the Sultanate was abolished after World War I, the Caliphate did not at once die with it. The former sulṭán, Muḥammad VI, retained for a time his spiritual title, occupying an 'anomalous and precarious position' (GPB 228). The government of the new Turkish republic, however, was unhappy with this awkward situation; it reacted in March 1924 by proclaiming the abolition of the Caliphate and formally dissociating itself from that institution. The ex-Caliph fled to Europe. This development shattered the unity of the Sunní world, which had not been in the least consulted. A Congress of the Caliphate was convened in Cairo in 1926 to restore the institution; it dissolved in disagreement.

The collapse of the Caliphate brought in its wake the formal secularization of the Turkish republic and a drastic loss of power by the Sunní clergy. Sunní canonical law was replaced by a civil code; its religious orders were suppressed, its hierarchy disbanded and its ecclesiastical institutions disendowed.

The Shí'ih clergy in Persia experienced a parallel decline. The royal government, although formally affiliated with the religious hierarchy, began systematically breaking its strangle hold on every aspect of Persian life and culture. Priests whose every whim had once been law soon found themselves subject to civil authority. Time-honoured religious institutions fell into ruin, while Western customs and dress were introduced over the clergy's objections. Throughout most of this century one humiliating catastrophe after another battered the <u>Sh</u>í'ih order. The Islamic Revolution of 1979 has, for the present, restored a small measure of the vast power the clergy once enjoyed. Even so, the long-term consequences of that revolution remain far from clear.

After the demise of the Pope's temporal sovereignty, many other Christian establishments found themselves on a slippery slope. France, Spain, Russia and other countries divested themselves of their state religions; the breakup of the Austro-Hungarian empire deprived the Catholic Church of its strongest political and financial backer; the spread of communism brought with it efforts to eradicate all religious influence from the life of the masses; a rising nationalism in many lands undermined Christianity or, more insidiously, found ways to manipulate it for its own ends. Throughout most of this century, a growing crisis of confidence in organized religion has steadily eroded the moral authority of Christian leaders. During the 1980s a wave of scandals involving financial and sexual misconduct destroyed the ministries of some of Christendom's most popular evangelists.

Bahá'u'lláh's sombre forecast for ecclesiastical institutions should never be misconstrued as a blanket condemnation of individual leaders, much less of the whole Christian community. He writes:

Respect ye the divines amongst you, they whose acts conform to the knowledge they possess, who observe the statutes of God, and decree the things God hath decreed in the Book. Know ye that they are the lamps of guidance betwixt earth and heaven. They that have no consideration for the position and merit of the divines amongst them have, verily, altered the bounty of God vouchsafed unto them (PDC 111).

Why have once-flourishing hierarchies sustained so sudden and dramatic a reversal of fortune? Two reasons stand out:

First, Bahá'u'lláh says the institution of priesthood is approaching the end of its usefulness. In bygone ages, when education was confined to a chosen few, it was necessary that there be spiritual guides trained to interpret religion to the masses. Today, with literacy and information access rapidly becoming universal, that need is gone; yet the structures and habits of the past remain. There is now a new moral imperative – the independent investigation of truth. God is calling each human being to assume full responsibility for his or her own spiritual destiny, to explore divine reality without relying unduly on any other person. There is therefore no clergy in the Bahá'í Faith, nor will there ever be.

Second, despite its admitted contributions, ecclesiasticism has throughout history led the opposition to every new revelation sent by God. The priests of Pharaoh opposed Moses; the Jewish scribes and Pharisees likewise opposed Jesus. Islamic religious leaders subjected Bahá'u'lláh to forty years of hellish persecution, caused the brutal deaths of twenty thousand early believers, and still persecute Bahá'ís to this day. Christian officialdom has, with notable exceptions, turned a deaf ear to the call of Bahá'u'lláh. Time alone will tell how its spokesmen respond once they absorb the full impact of His claim and understand its magnitude.

Although the wane of ecclesiasticism is hardly to be mourned, Bahá'ís view with deep concern the backlash that too often follows – specifically, declining public interest in spiritual verities and the behavioural precepts of religion. Bahá'u'lláh has said that religion is 'verily the chief instrument for the establishment of order in the world, and of tranquillity amongst its peoples . . . The greater the decline of religion, the more grievous the waywardness of the ungodly' (PDC 113). Fortunately, there are many signs that this trend may have run its course and that growing masses are heeding the words of Jesus: 'Blessed are they which do hunger and thirst after righteousness: for they shall be filled' (Matt. 5:6).

The Movement of the Left

PROPHECY 12: *The spread of communism, the 'Movement of the Left', and its rise to world power.*

PROPHECY 13: *The catastrophic decline of that same movement, triggered by the collapse of its egalitarian economy.*

ABSTRACT: *Communism is denounced in the Bahá'í teachings as one of three 'false gods' at whose altars nations in this century have worshipped. (The other two are racialism and nationalism.) Shortly after the Bolshevik Revolution of 1917 'Abdu'l-Bahá, speaking of 'Movements, newly-born and worldwide in their range', stated: 'The Movement of the Left will acquire great importance. Its influence will spread.' Leftist ideology, embodied in a variety of communist and socialist uprisings, did indeed gain worldwide momentum hardly any of 'Abdu'l-Bahá's contemporaries could have visualized. The resulting Cold War polarized and paralyzed the world for decades, holding every human being hostage to a hair-trigger nuclear standoff. Nevertheless, the basic economic premise of communism was denounced in the Bahá'í teachings as certain to 'end in disorderliness, in chaos, in disorganization of the means of existence, and in universal disappointment', destroying the order of the community. The truth of this prophecy became evident in the late 1980s and early 1990s as the worldwide collapse of communism reduced its mighty empire to a wasteland of splintered and squabbling republics.*

BACKGROUND: Shortly after World War I, 'Abdu'l-Bahá wrote:

> The ills from which the world now suffers will multiply; the gloom which envelops it will deepen . . . Movements, newly-born and worldwide in their range, will exert their utmost effort for the advancement of their designs. The Movement of the Left will acquire great importance. Its influence will spread (WOB 30).

The 'Movement of the Left' was that of communism and socialism, which had gained power in Russia through the Bolshevik Revolution of 1917. The multiplying ills and deepening gloom of the post-war world did occasion the lightning-like spread of leftist ideology foreseen by 'Abdu'l-Bahá. From its beginning in the Soviet Union, the movement led to the emergence of communist governments in Eastern Europe, China and many other countries of Asia and Africa, as well as Western outposts such as Cuba and Nicaragua. Far beyond the borders of these countries leftist sentiments evoked fervent support and equally fervent opposition. Containing communism became the major preoccupation of non-communist countries, raising emotions on both sides to fever pitch during the so-called Cold War.

Inspired by the teachings of Karl Marx, communism derived much of its appeal from its passionate commitment to the dream of a 'classless society'. The term refers to a society in which private property is abolished and the means and fruits of production are owned equally ('in common') by all citizens. Wealth is to be distributed according to the classic Marxist dictum 'From each according to his ability; to each according to his needs'. Since human beings have more or less the same needs (except in cases of sickness, disability and the like), this translates in practice into a policy of forcibly equalizing wages and standards of living.

Such levelling policies, supported by an ethic of radical egalitarianism, have been a marked feature of communist societies throughout the world. Through public education and political indoctrination, these societies systematically fostered a climate of deep hostility, on the part of both regulatory agencies and the public, towards anyone who profited or prospered as a result of private initiative. The unintended result, in every case, was to suppress innovation, productivity and service without noticeably discouraging greed or exploitation by those occupying positions of power.

To predict the expansion of communism (or any other

movement) is not, of course, to endorse it. The Bahá'í writings name communism as one of three 'false gods' worshipped by twentieth-century nations – the other two are racialism and nationalism (PDC 113). Although the Bahá'í Faith proposes to limit gross extremes of wealth and poverty, it upholds the right to private property and opposes, as both unjust and impractical, any scheme to enforce strict economic equality.* Around 1905, long before the communist revolution in Russia, 'Abdu'l-Bahá said: '. . . absolute equality in fortunes, honours, commerce, agriculture, industry would end in disorderliness, in chaos, in disorganization of the means of existence, and in universal disappointment: the order of the community would be quite destroyed' (SAQ 274).

These accumulating disasters – the fruits of a seventy-year experiment in artificially engineered economic equality – finally swamped the communist bloc in the late 1980s. The world watched in awe as every word of 'Abdu'l-Bahá's chilling prediction came true. The breakdown triggered revolution, social turmoil and massive political and economic restructuring. As the 1990s dawned, most of Eastern Europe left the communist fold. The Soviet communist party, desperate to survive, voluntarily relinquished its monopoly on political power and tinkered with market reforms. Not to be placated by half-measures, the disgruntled republics proclaimed the dissolution of the once-mighty Soviet Union and the birth of a new Commonwealth of Independent States. Elsewhere in Asia, communist regimes reacted in various

---

*Bahá'u'lláh does not prescribe a fixed or complete system of economics. However, He does state that economics must be based squarely on spiritual principles; and He indicates in general terms what some of those principles are. For two excellent discussions, see William S. Hatcher, 'Economics and Moral Values', *World Order* magazine, Winter 1974-5, pp. 14-27; and Gregory C. Dahl, 'Economics and the Bahá'í Teachings', *World Order* magazine, Fall 1975, pp. 19-40.

ways to growing dissatisfaction – some reintroducing profit incentives, some tightening central control.

It would be premature to speculate on the short-term outcome of these cataclysmic upheavals. However, one thing seems certain: Marxism, in its extreme form, is no longer taken seriously by the masses it once promised to liberate. Seldom in history has any movement experienced such a meteoric rise and fall.

The Jews: Homeland and Holocaust

PROPHECY 14: *The rise of Israel as a Jewish homeland.*

PROPHECY 15: *The persecution of Jews on the European continent (the Nazi Holocaust).*

ABSTRACT: *Both Bahá'u'lláh and 'Abdu'l-Bahá clearly anticipated the fulfilment, in our own time, of Old Testament promises concerning the regathering of Jews in the Holy Land. These expectations have been largely vindicated by the establishment and continuing consolidation of the State of Israel. The Bahá'í outlook was tempered, however, by a dire warning. Decades before the Nazi Holocaust 'Abdu'l-Bahá pleaded with Jewish audiences to guard against a renewed outbreak of savage persecution on the European continent.*

BACKGROUND: Christians who study Bible prophecy are well aware that the return of Jews to the Holy Land is a sign of Christ's Second Coming. Less well known is the fact that this return began in 1844 – the very year the Bahá'í Faith was born. The Edict of Toleration, signed that year in Constantinople, abolished with one stroke the Muslim stranglehold by which Hebrew people had for centuries been barred from their ancestral homeland.

Both Bahá'u'lláh and 'Abdu'l-Bahá referred frequently to the future growth and consolidation of the Jewish community in the Holy Land. In a talk delivered around 1905 (and first published in 1908), 'Abdu'l-Bahá said:

. . . in this cycle Israel will be gathered in the Holy Land, and . . . the Jewish people who are scattered to the East and West, South and North, will be assembled together . . . You can see that from all parts of the world tribes of Jews are coming to the Holy Land; they live in villages and lands which they make their own, and day by day they are increasing to such an extent that all Palestine will become their home (SAQ 65-6).

At that time, of course, the 'return' was little more than a slowly increasing trickle. When 'Abdu'l-Bahá spoke, few people could have visualized the momentum this process would gain, much less the creation in 1948 of the State of Israel or the strategic importance it would acquire. This process has been greatly accelerated in recent years through the lifting of travel restrictions on Jews in the former Soviet Union, who began emigrating to Israel in vast numbers.

If Bahá'í prophecy disclosed a bright future for the Jews of Palestine, not so for those of Europe. During His Western tour, 'Abdu'l-Bahá lovingly urged Jewish audiences to accept Jesus Christ, first for the spiritual benefit of embracing divine truth but also because such recognition, by building bridges of friendship with Christians, could mitigate the unjust oppression that otherwise would befall their race. '. . . you must not think that this is ended,' He said, referring to past persecutions. 'The time may come when in Europe itself they will arise against the Jews' (PUP 414). However unpopular His advice may have been in 1912, its wisdom was demonstrated thirty years later during the Holocaust when six million Jews perished in Nazi concentration camps.

America's Racial Upheavals

PROPHECY 16: *America's violent racial struggles.*

ABSTRACT: *Long before most Americans recognized either the injustice or the danger of their country's 'race problem', the Bahá'í teachings sounded a trumpet-call for action to bridge black-white differences. 'Abdu'l-Bahá plainly stated in 1912 that without a prompt change of heart, America would lose credibility and moral authority throughout the globe, eventually finding its own streets red with blood. Most white Americans of that era would have found such warnings extravagant, if not incomprehensible. Yet they have since been justified by decades of racial strife, bloodshed and polarization.*

BACKGROUND: God, says St Paul, 'hath made of one blood all nations of men for to dwell on all the face of the earth. . .' (Acts 17:26). America's urgent need to swallow this principle was a favourite theme of 'Abdu'l-Bahá as He crisscrossed the country in 1912, speaking to audiences black and white. He told His astonished listeners that if they resolved this major spiritual issue, the race problem, America's influence would as a result become decisive in the building of God's Kingdom. '. . . gather together these two races,' He said, '. . . and put such love into their hearts that they shall not only unite but even intermarry. Be sure that the result of this will abolish differences and disputes between black and white. Moreover, by the Will of God, may it be so. This is a great service to humanity' (BWF 359).

The intense and sometimes bloody racial struggles which lay ahead for America were as clear to 'Abdu'l-Bahá in 1912 as if they had already occurred.

'This question of the union of the white and the black is very important,' He warned during His American tour, 'for if it is not realized, erelong great difficulties will arise, and harmful results will follow' (ADJ 33). In a 1912 letter to a Chicago Bahá'í, He wrote, 'If this matter remaineth without change, enmity will be increased day by day, and the final result will be hardship and may end in bloodshed.' Until racial prejudice could be overcome, He added, 'the realm of humanity will not find rest. Nay, rather, discord and bloodshed will be increased day by day, and the foundation of the prosperity of man will be destroyed' (letter to Antoinette Crump Cone, *Star of the West*, vol. 22, 24 June 1921, p. 121).

From the vantage point of the 1990s, such observations may seem obvious. To white America in 1912 they seemed unthinkable. However, the resurgence of the Ku Klux Klan in 1915 and economic dislocations after World War I soon raised racial tensions to new levels. These came to a head in the 'Red Summer' of 1919, a year when twenty-five race riots occurred in various cities (see Morrison, *To Move the World*, pp. 129-30).

'Abdu'l-Bahá Himself interpreted these outbreaks as merely the first signs of a greater struggle. 'Now is the time', He said in 1920, 'for Americans to take up this matter and unite both the white and the coloured races. Otherwise, hasten ye towards destruction! Hasten ye towards devastation!' (*Star of the West*, vol. 22, 24 June 1921, p. 121). Shoghi Effendi, recalling these and many similar words, wrote in 1954 of 'the supreme, the inescapable and urgent duty – so repeatedly and graphically represented and stressed by 'Abdu'l-Bahá in His arraignment of the basic weaknesses in the social fabric of the nation – of remedying, while there is yet time, through a revolutionary change in the concept and attitude of the average white American toward his Negro fellow citizen, a situation which, if allowed to drift, will, in the words of 'Abdu'l-Bahá, cause the streets of American cities to run with blood . . .' (CF 126).

The racial upheavals of the 1960s, as American blacks intensified their demands for long-overdue economic and social justice, fully vindicated 'Abdu'l-Bahá's predictions. In race riots between 1965 and 1969, according to *The New York Times* of 26 February 1978, about 250 persons were killed, 12,000 were injured and 83,000 were arrested. During one summer about forty cities were ablaze and at least one, Detroit, was occupied by federal troops (*World Order*, Summer 1979, p. 2). Bloodshed would have been far worse but for the success of the Rev Martin Luther King in steering the civil rights movement into nonviolent channels.

Ironically, Rev King's own assassination triggered open racial warfare in some of America's largest cities, as blacks and whites alike reacted with despair, frustration and pent-up rage.

In the spring of 1992, four white police officers were acquitted by an all-white jury of the video-taped beating of Rodney King, a Los Angeles motorist, after a high-speed chase. Five days of rioting followed, leaving about sixty persons dead, many more injured, and seven thousand arrested on riot-related charges. Violence spread to cities as far away as Atlanta, Las Vegas, San Francisco, Miami and Seattle. The verdict and its grim aftermath demonstrated that the uneasy truce of the past two decades had merely masked the symptoms of racism, without curing the disease.

In forecasting such events more than fifty years earlier, 'Abdu'l-Bahá called attention to a broader and critically important dimension of the conflict. He stated that if American whites and blacks would join in true fellowship, their unity would so enhance the nation's international influence as to provide 'an assurance of the world's peace' (ADJ 33). Otherwise, racial strife would gravely weaken America from within at a time when its very existence was already imperilled from without. Failure to act in time, He said, could easily lead to 'the destruction of America' (*Star of the West*, vol. 22, 24 June 1921, p. 120). Shoghi Effendi echoed His words in the 1954 letter quoted above, stating that the American nation had 'dangerously underestimated' the crisis into which it was heading. True to these warnings, the racial clashes of the late sixties peaked during the darkest days of the Cold War, at a time when America's survival turned on a highly unstable nuclear standoff with its enemies.

America, as we now know, survived the crisis of the moment. Both the Cold War and the formal system of racial segregation that prompted the civil rights movement are today relics of the dead past. Discrimination, though still widespread, now is at least illegal; and politicians may no longer with impunity voice openly racist sentiments. However, as recent events have shown, these cosmetic signs of progress do not necessarily indicate the 'revolutionary change' in attitude which 'Abdu'l-Bahá prescribed as the only permanent cure for America's racial maladies. So long as racism remains a significant part of the American psyche, one must wonder when the last chapter in this tragic drama will have been written.

BAHÁ'U'LLÁH AND HIS FAITH

Bahá'u'lláh and 'Abdu'l-Bahá predicted a number of remarkable developments involving the Bahá'í Faith itself. Several of these are described below.

Bahá'u'lláh's Release from Prison

PROPHECY 17: *Bahá'u'lláh's release from the prison of 'Akká and the pitching of His tent on Mount Carmel.*

ABSTRACT: *En route to the maximum-security penal colony of 'Akká, Bahá'u'lláh – sentenced to life without appeal or parole – confidently promised that He would leave the prison, pitch His tent on Mount Carmel and transform His sufferings into 'the outpourings of a supreme mercy'. Against all odds, and through circumstances so miraculous as to defy belief, He did precisely that.*

BACKGROUND: Bahá'u'lláh's enemies, Sulṭán 'Abdu'l-'Azíz and Náṣiri'd-Dín S̲h̲áh, had every reason to believe He would quickly perish in the fortified prison-city of 'Akká. So foul and pestilential was its climate that a proverb declared, 'If a bird flies over 'Akká, it dies!' Its cruel conditions seemed certain to ensure Bahá'u'lláh's early death, and the sulṭán's decree made it clear that His incarceration was to be perpetual. Bahá'u'lláh entered the prison already broken in health, devoid of material resources and surrounded by an army of ruthless spies and gaolers determined to carry out His sentence. His writings from this period show that He understood, all too well, how many heartbreaking tragedies and paralyzing sufferings faced Him during the years ahead.

Yet the ink was scarcely dry on His sentence when Bahá'u'lláh assured His royal captors that He, not they, would ultimately prevail. Soon after arriving at 'Akká in 1868 He wrote to Náṣiri'd-Dín Sháh: 'No doubt is there whatever that these tribulations will be followed by the outpourings of a supreme mercy, and these dire adversities be succeeded by an overflowing prosperity' (PDC 42). During the darkest days of His imprisonment He wrote to His friends: 'Fear not. These doors shall be opened. My tent shall be pitched on Mount Carmel, and the utmost joy shall be realized' (AB 39).

Bahá'u'lláh's confinement was enforced with strict severity for many years and He endured indescribable agony. Little by little, however, His shackles began to crumble. Bahá'u'lláh's innocence and integrity slowly were recognized by the region's entire population, once fiercely antagonistic; the benevolent spirit of His teachings gradually won the admiration of high and low alike; and hostile officials were one by one replaced or dismissed. 'Akká eventually had a new governor, the 'sagacious and humane' Aḥmad Big Tawfíq, who became such an admirer of the exiles that he sent his son to 'Abdu'l-Bahá for instruction and enlightenment. Increasing numbers of scholars and dignitaries sought audience with the prisoner of 'Akká and testified to His greatness. The Turkish government, disturbed by reports of the increasing respect being shown to Bahá'u'lláh, occasionally dispatched to the prison-city unfriendly officials, armed with dictatorial authority and orders to reverse the situation. Even these men, finding no one to cooperate with their plans, proved helpless to check the tide of events now flowing in Bahá'u'lláh's favour.

Throughout this period Bahá'u'lláh made no effort to obtain His own release; rather, He repeatedly refused to leave the prison even when opportunities were presented.

No less a personage than the governor of 'Akká offered Him His freedom; He politely declined, insisting He was still a prisoner. Eventually, however, the drastic edict of the sulṭán had become a dead letter. The muftí of 'Akká – head of the Muslim religious community – kneeled at Bahá'u'lláh's feet and begged Him to leave the city walls for a comfortable home in the country. 'Who has the power to make you a prisoner?' the muftí asked. 'You have kept yourself in prison.' He pleaded for an entire hour with Bahá'u'lláh, who finally agreed to leave.

Bahá'u'lláh spent His remaining years in the countryside, whose beauty He had always loved, devoting His time to His writing and the education of His followers. 'The rulers of Palestine', says 'Abdu'l-Bahá, 'envied His influence and power. Governors and mutiṣarrifs, generals and local officials, would humbly request the honour of attaining His presence – a request to which He seldom acceded' (GPB 193).

As a result of these incredible events, Bahá'u'lláh was able, in His latter years, to travel several times to Haifa. There, as He had long ago prophesied, He pitched His tent on Mount Carmel. During one of these journeys He pointed out to 'Abdu'l-Bahá the spot where the Shrine of the Báb was to be erected. During another, He revealed the gloriously beautiful Tablet of Carmel – the charter for the future establishment on that mountain of the world spiritual and administrative centre of His Faith.

The House of Bahá'u'lláh

PROPHECY 18: *The seizure and desecration of the House of Bahá'u'lláh in Baghdád.*

ABSTRACT: *Bahá'u'lláh foretold that the house He occupied while living in Baghdád (and which He later ordained as a centre of pilgrimage for Bahá'ís) would one day be 'abased' by enemies of the*

197

Faith, that the 'veil of [its] sanctity' would be 'rent asunder' by them in such manner as to 'cause tears to flow from every discerning eye'. Around the time of 'Abdu'l-Bahá's passing, Shí'ih Muslims in Baghdád – seemingly intent on vindicating Bahá'u'lláh's prediction – occupied the building, expelled its Bahá'í owners and defied a later high court ruling unanimously denouncing the seizure as illegal. Although Bahá'ís are certain they will one day regain their rightful property, they have now been barred from this sacred and historic site for more than seventy years.

BACKGROUND: The house that Bahá'u'lláh occupied during His exile in Baghdád was designated by Him, in His Book of Laws, as a centre of pilgrimage for Bahá'ís. He Himself acquired title to the residence, which remained in unbroken and undisputed possession of the Bahá'í community after His departure from Baghdád.

Bahá'u'lláh, however, wrote of it: 'Grieve not, O House of God, if the veil of thy sanctity be rent asunder by the infidels' (G 114). 'Verily, it shall be so abased in the days to come as to cause tears to flow from every discerning eye. Thus have We unfolded to thee things hidden beyond the veil . . .' (G 115).

Around the time of 'Abdu'l-Bahá's passing, the Shí'ih Muslim community of Baghdád, which had no conceivable claim to the property, seized it and expelled the Bahá'ís. After a succession of legal battles, Iraq's Court of Appeals ruled in favour of the Muslims. Bahá'ís appealed to the League of Nations, which at the time exercised control over Iraq. The Council of the League – the world's highest tribunal – ruled unanimously in favour of the Bahá'ís, concluding that both the seizure and the subsequent appeals court verdict had been motivated by religious passion.

There followed many years of delays, protests and evasions. Bahá'ís, as a result, have never regained possession of the property. Their sole consolation is the further prophecy of Bahá'u'lláh regarding His house:

In the fullness of time, the Lord shall, by the power of truth, exalt it in the eyes of all men. He shall cause it to become the Standard of His Kingdom, the Shrine round which will circle the concourse of the faithful. Thus hath spoken the Lord, thy God, ere the day of lamentation arriveth (G 115).

Bahá'í Unity

PROPHECY 19: *The failure of all attempts to create schism within the Bahá'í Faith.*

ABSTRACT: *Almost every world faith has repeatedly divided and subdivided into sects, denominations, factions and splinter groups, all competing for the allegiance of believers. Bahá'u'lláh took steps to protect the Bahá'í Faith from this divisive tendency; and He promised that it would, as a result, remain both administratively and spiritually unified for all time. The strength of this amazing prophecy has been tested, time and again, by cunning internal enemies eager to advance their own agendas. Not one of the off-shoots they have devised, however ingeniously, has ever flourished or attracted a significant following. Meanwhile, Bahá'u'lláh's Cause, structured as He Himself intended, has spread throughout the earth, becoming (according to non-Bahá'í authorities) the most widespread religion after Christianity and in all likelihood the most diverse organized body on the planet.*

BACKGROUND: Fragmentation into sects is so universal a phenomenon of religion that historians tend to regard it as natural and inescapable. No outside observer, therefore, during the Bahá'í Faith's infancy, could have imagined that it would spread throughout the world while resisting every attempt to create schism within its own ranks.

Bahá'u'lláh predicted precisely this development – a development that is (so far as I know) unique and unprecedented in the annals of religion. If the Bahá'í Cause had no other claim to world attention, its fulfilment of this remarkable prophecy should suffice.

The point obviously is crucial, since the Bahá'í Faith claims to be the divinely chosen instrument destined to usher in the worldwide Kingdom of God on earth. Such a purpose clearly requires that its own unity remain intact. To preserve this unity, Bahá'u'lláh appointed 'Abdu'l-Bahá as His successor and created in the Bahá'í administrative order a centre of authority (the Universal House of Justice) to which all Bahá'ís must turn. These protective provisions are known as the Covenant. Because it incorporates this unifying Covenant, Bahá'u'lláh called His Revelation 'the Day which shall never be followed by night', the 'Springtime which autumn will never overtake' (GPB 99) and said of its administrative order: 'The Hand of Omnipotence hath established His Revelation upon an unassailable, an enduring foundation. Storms of human strife are powerless to undermine its basis, nor will men's fanciful theories succeed in damaging its structure' (WOB 109). 'Abdu'l-Bahá characterized efforts to disrupt Bahá'í unity as 'no more than the foam of the ocean', adding, 'this froth of the ocean shall not endure and shall soon disappear and vanish, while on the other hand the ocean of the Covenant shall eternally surge and roar' (MUHJ 42). Shoghi Effendi wrote that the Bahá'í Administrative Order 'must and will, in a manner unparalleled in any previous religion, safeguard from schism the Faith from which it has sprung' (GPB 326); and he stated: '. . . this priceless gem of Divine Revelation, now still in its embryonic state, shall evolve within the shell of His Law, and shall forge ahead, undivided and unimpaired, till it embraces the whole of mankind' (WOB 23).

It is impossible, of course, to place a final stamp of fulfilment on any prophecy indicating something will 'never' happen. The most one can say is that it has not happened yet. Nevertheless, the Bahá'í Faith has emerged 'undivided and unimpaired' from numerous attempts, by powerful internal enemies, to create rifts in its membership. Not one of these attempts has ever flourished or gained a significant following.

The first such effort came from Bahá'u'lláh's younger half-brother, Mírzá Yaḥyá. When Bahá'u'lláh announced Himself as the Promised One foretold by the Báb, and was accepted as such by most Bábís, Yaḥyá became extremely jealous. He countered with a similar claim, which he sought to advance by theft, poison, slander and forgery. Though he inflicted terrible suffering on Bahá'u'lláh, he failed in the end to divide the religion. His 'Azalí' splinter group faded away and Yaḥyá himself died in obscurity.

'Abdu'l-Bahá faced similar attacks on His leadership, including one by Muḥammad-'Alí, His own half-brother, and another by Ibráhím Khayr'u'lláh, a Syrian who at His direction had introduced the Faith to America. Shoghi Effendi, who next headed the Bahá'í Cause as its duly appointed Guardian, had to block attempts by 'Abdu'l-Bahá's former assistant, Ahmad Sohrab, to establish offshoots called the 'New History Society' and the 'Caravan of East and West'. After Shoghi Effendi's death, a prominent Bahá'í teacher named Charles Mason Remey tried to establish himself as Guardian, in clear violation of 'Abdu'l-Baha's Will and Testament.

Each of these men was energetic, resourceful, ambitious for leadership and well placed to seize it. Moreover, each seemed for a brief time to have succeeded. Each one, however, watched in bewilderment as his following vanished like smoke, while the unity of the Bahá'í Faith (as Bahá'u'lláh had promised) remained inviolate.

8

Prophetic Fruits:
Scientific Discoveries

If I have told you earthly things, and ye believe not, how
shall ye believe, if I tell you of heavenly things? (John 3:12).

. . . ye can discern the face of the sky and of the earth; but
how is it that ye do not discern this time? (Luke 12:56).

Up to now we have examined Bahá'í prophecies that forecast
world trends and historical events. Let us now consider
prophecies that anticipated scientific developments, either
by making specific predictions or by stating previously
undiscovered facts.

We must exercise caution in assessing the scientific implications of divine revelation. As we discussed previously, many
scriptures are written in figurative language and to insist on
a physical interpretation of such passages may be unwarranted. On the other hand, the Bahá'í teachings explain that
physical reality is itself a metaphor of the spiritual world: '. . .
the outward is the expression of the inward; the earth is the
mirror of the Kingdom . . .' (SAQ 283). Consequently, many
revealed truths carry both an inward, spiritual meaning
and an outward, literal one, 'and neither their outward
preventeth their inward, nor doth their inward prevent their
outward meaning' (TAB 608).

It follows that we cannot necessarily dismiss a given statement of scripture as 'purely spiritual' in meaning simply
because that statement happens to contradict a current
scientific theory. Bahá'ís believe that a correct understanding

of true science and true religion will always show their underlying harmony. However, scholars of any given science
occasionally misread the facts of nature, just as theologians
sometimes misunderstand the Word of God. Scientists revise
their pronouncements daily and the findings of one age are
always superseded by those of the next.

Bahá'u'lláh writes:

> Weigh not the Book of God with such standards and sci-
> ences as are current amongst you, for the Book itself is the
> unerring balance established amongst men. In this most
> perfect balance whatsoever the peoples and kindreds of the
> earth possess must be weighed . . . (G 198).

Still, if Bahá'u'lláh's revelation is genuine, time should bring
an ever-growing realization of the correspondence between
His teachings and scientific reality. Let us consider whether
such has been the case.

The Knowledge Explosion

PROPHECY 20: *The explosive acceleration of scientific and technological progress.*

ABSTRACT: *Bahá'u'lláh appeared in a world where technical progress, though uneven, had always been relatively slow. Genera-tions before Him had lived and died knowing that their great-grandchildren would be born into a world little more advanced than their own. The prophecies of Bahá'u'lláh made it clear that that world had ended; that in the new heavens and new earth of His revelation, scientific knowledge and invention would dart forward with jackrabbit speed. Beginning at once, He said, humanity would 'behold things of which ye have never heard before' including 'the knowledge of the most marvellous sciences' – hitherto unimaginable discoveries that would shrink the globe to a veritable village. These advances (though exposing humankind to catastrophic danger) would provide a material framework for the infinitely more glorious spiritual revolution to follow, a revolution destined to usher in the millennial paradise promised in scriptures of old.*

BACKGROUND: Bahá'u'lláh stated that humankind was entering an age of unprecedented scientific and technical advancement, when new discoveries would gradually increase from a trickle to a tidal wave.

'A new life is, in this age, stirring within all the peoples of the earth,' He wrote, 'and yet none hath discovered its cause, or perceived its motive' (WOB 202). He identified its source as the 'fertilizing winds' (PDC 46) of the Holy Spirit, released anew into the world through His revelation:

> Every word that proceedeth out of the mouth of God is endowed with such potency as can instil new life into every human frame . . . Through the mere revelation of the word 'Fashioner', issuing forth from His lips and proclaiming His attribute to mankind, such power is released as can generate, through successive ages, all the manifold arts which the hands of man can produce . . . All the wondrous achievements ye now witness are the direct consequences of the Revelation of this Name. In the days to come, ye will, verily, behold things of which ye have never heard before . . . every created thing will, according to its capacity and limitations, be invested with the power to unfold the knowledge of the most marvellous sciences, and will be empowered to manifest them in the course of time at the bidding of Him Who is the Almighty, the All-Knowing (G 141-2).

Thus the revelation of God's Word, according to Bahá'u'lláh, has always been accompanied by an upsurge of invention and discovery. (See Chapter 4 for a fuller explanation of this creative principle.) He indicated that this newest divine outpouring, being immeasurably greater in scope and intensity than those of the past, would stimulate a correspondingly greater burst of progress. He wrote in the *Súriy-i-Haykal* that God would soon raise up scientists of great calibre who would bring about technological achievements so marvellous that no one could yet imagine them (paraphrased by Taherzadeh, *Revelation of Bahá'u'lláh*, vol. 3, p. 137). To suggest the immensity of the coming knowledge revolution, Bahá'u'lláh likened knowledge to twenty-seven letters, of which only two had been disclosed prior to the Báb's appearance. Now, He said, humanity was about to receive the remaining twenty-five (WOB 125).

'The heights which, through the most gracious favour of God, mortal man can attain in this Day, are as yet unrevealed to his sight,' He wrote. 'This is the Day of which it hath been said: "O my son! verily God will bring everything to light though it were but the weight of a grain of mustard seed, and hidden in a rock, or in the heavens or in the earth . . ."' (WOB 107).

Until about the first third of the nineteenth century (well into the lifetimes of the Báb and Bahá'u'lláh) human progress was fairly steady. Such progress could be shown on a graph as a line with a gentle upward slope, punctuated by occasional spurts and squiggles, but with an overall orientation more horizontal than vertical. As the century continued, however, the knowledge revolution foretold by Bahá'u'lláh kicked in, imperceptibly at first but with rapidly gathering momentum, sharply tilting the angle of the line until it became more vertical than horizontal. A restless new spirit of adventure and discovery came into science, literature, music, art, education, medicine, invention and all other departments of human life, producing unprecedented advances. This process is still roaring forward with ever-increasing speed and force. Today, the sum of all human knowledge doubles every few years – just how rapidly, no one can really say. (I have read estimates ranging from ten years to six months). As a result, far more progress has been achieved in technology since Bahá'u'lláh made His prediction than in all previous recorded history.

It may seem obvious, in hindsight, that nineteenth-century knowledge was about to reach critical mass and leap forward explosively. ('Any event, once it has occurred, can be made to appear inevitable by a competent historian,' says Lee Simonson.) However, the impending knowledge revolution was anything but obvious at the time. Many thoughtful observers believed, on the contrary, that civilization was near its apex and that science and technology were reaching their limits. In 1844 philosopher Auguste Comte cited the composition of stars as an example of information forever beyond human reach. Long after the flood of new discoveries had begun, experts tended to misread it as just another brief spasm of progress destined to run its course, or even as the final flowering of human research and creativity. The celebrated theorist A. A. Michelson said in 1894 that future science would consist only of 'adding a few decimal places to results already obtained' (Cooper, *Meaning and Structure of Physics* 431) Max Born, one of the world's top physicists, in 1929 expressed the same pessimistic idea: 'Physics, as we know it, will be over in six months' (quoted in Hawking, *Brief History of Time* 156).*

No serious scholar or scientist would make such unguarded comments today. What has become clear is that the knowledge explosion, impressive though it has been, is barely begun – indeed, it appears certain to continue indefinitely and exponentially unless we first destroy ourselves with its fruits.

Bahá'u'lláh understood that these material advances would come before mankind had acquired the spiritual maturity to use them wisely. He wrote:

> The civilization, so often vaunted by the learned exponents of arts and sciences, will, if allowed to overleap the bounds of moderation, bring great evil upon men . . . If carried to excess, civilization will prove as prolific a source of evil as

---

*Both Michelson and Born, we should note in fairness, came to rue the day they had said such rash things; and both made pioneering contributions to the very revolution in physics that turned their own statements into quaint anachronisms.

it had been of goodness when kept within the restraints of moderation . . . The day is approaching when its flame will devour the cities . . . (G 342-3).

Bahá'u'lláh indicated that science would not only give us the means to unify our planet but would, by unleashing the threat of mass destruction, make it imperative that we do so. Only then would humanity be prepared for a planetary religious renaissance, fuelled by the same divine impulse as the one driving physical science.

ATOMIC MANDATE

The coming dawn of the Atomic Age was writ large in the prophecies of Bahá'u'lláh and 'Abdu'l-Bahá.

Nuclear Terror

PROPHECY 21: *The development of nuclear weapons.*

ABSTRACT: *Shortly before His ascension in 1892, Bahá'u'lláh warned that the arms race, if not halted, could lead to 'strange and astonishing' weapons of unthinkable horror: 'These things are capable of changing the whole atmosphere of the earth and their contamination would prove lethal.' These measured words must have sounded, to His generation, like the ravings of a madman. 'Abdu'l-Bahá in 1911 advised a Japanese diplomat to pray that this 'stupendous force, as yet, happily, undiscovered by man . . . be not discovered until spiritual civilization shall dominate the human mind'. In the hands of unredeemed men, He added, 'this power would be able to destroy the whole earth'. The 1945 atomic bombing of Hiroshima and Nagasaki announced to the world that Bahá'u'lláh and His successor knew whereof they spoke.*

BACKGROUND: In a Tablet entitled *Words of Paradise* (written shortly before His ascension in 1892), Bahá'u'lláh noted the rush by Western civilization to develop ever more deadly weapons of war. Explaining the urgency of His call for world peace, He declared:

> Strange and astonishing things exist in the earth but they are hidden from the minds and the understanding of men. These things are capable of changing the whole atmosphere of the earth and their contamination would prove lethal (TB 69).

This reference to 'strange and astonishing things' aptly describes the twin processes of fission and fusion by which we obtain nuclear energy. The reality of such a power was again affirmed in 1911 by 'Abdu'l-Bahá:

> There is in existence a stupendous force, as yet, happily, undiscovered by man. Let us supplicate God, the Beloved, that this force be not discovered by science until spiritual civilization shall dominate the human mind. In the hands of men of lower material nature, this power would be able to destroy the whole earth (CH 184).

'Abdu'l-Bahá spoke these portentous words to the Japanese ambassador to Spain, Viscount Arawaka, for whose country the warning carried grave implications. An ironic coincidence? If so, it was not the only one. In 1920 'Abdu'l-Bahá wrote to a group of young students in Tokyo: 'In Japan the divine proclamation will be heard as a formidable explosion . . .' (*Japan will Turn Ablaze* 30).* A quarter of a century later, the Japanese cities of Hiroshima and Nagasaki were vaporized in the first wartime use of atomic bombs. Today the world's nuclear arsenals contain enough firepower not only to destroy humanity many times over but to alter climate and atmosphere so drastically as to render the planet uninhabitable.

---

*I am aware of no other explosion metaphor in the Bahá'í writings.

Copper into Gold

PROPHECY 22: *The achievement of transmutation of elements, the age-old alchemist's dream.*

PROPHECY 23: *Dire peril for all humanity as a result of that achievement.*

ABSTRACT: *Western scientists of Bahá'u'lláh's day believed that transmutation – the changing of one chemical element into another – was theoretically impossible. Bahá'u'lláh explained that they were mistaken. He wrote that copper (for example) can become gold or vice versa: 'Every mineral can be made to acquire the density, form and substance of each and every other mineral.' Only decades later did physicists realize that elemental atoms are not, as they once thought, the smallest irreducible building blocks of matter. Atoms are composed of still smaller particles that can be separated and recombined, the result being that any element can indeed change into any other. Unfortunately, transmutation (as Bahá'u'lláh also foresaw) is far from an unmixed blessing. It has opened the door to global holocaust by virtue of its link with nuclear explosive technology.*

BACKGROUND: The discovery of nuclear energy shed new light on an old question: Is it possible to transmute base metals into gold? Ancient alchemists eagerly sought the secret of this transmutation; by Bahá'u'lláh's time, however, scientists had long since concluded that such a feat was altogether impossible. No element (they believed) could ever be changed into any other element.

Their belief was firmly grounded in experience. Centuries of experimentation, research and trial and error had convinced chemists that certain substances could not be broken down into two or more simpler ones or built up from two or more simpler ones. These fundamental substances were called elements (to distinguish them from compounds, which could be broken down into, or built up from, other substances). Both compounds and elements were regarded as being composed of basic units or building blocks called atoms. Why do elements resist change? The natural interpretation was that atoms differ from one element to another but are all alike for any given element. Thus a compound such as water (composed of hydrogen and oxygen) could be broken down into its component elements merely by separating its hydrogen atoms from its oxygen atoms. But oxygen, being an element, could not be broken down into simpler substances by any conceivable reshuffling of its identical atoms.

Atoms were postulated by the ancient Greeks but their existence (though widely accepted) was never definitely verified until 1905 – thirteen years after the passing of Bahá'u'lláh. During His lifetime it was thought that atoms, if they existed, were the smallest particles of matter, indivisible and impenetrable. This notion implied that no element could ever be changed into another, since this would mean altering the supposedly immutable atoms.

Bahá'u'lláh, as far back as the early 1860s, challenged this assumption. He wrote on several occasions that the alchemists' age-old dream – that of changing copper into gold – was entirely possible,* although copper and gold are both elements. When this statement was cited by His detractors as proof of His ignorance, Bahá'u'lláh wrote:

> Consider the doubts which they . . . have instilled into the hearts of the people of this land. 'Is it ever possible,' they ask, 'for copper to be transmuted into gold?' Say, Yes, by my Lord, it is possible. Its secret, however, lieth hidden in

---

*Bahá'u'lláh wrote extensively on the subject of alchemy. He discouraged His followers from practising the physical aspects of this branch of learning, encouraging them to turn to the spiritual implications of transformation. He regarded traditional alchemy, which was an odd mixture of pseudo-science and superstition with occasional insights or lucky guesses, as 'vain and discarded learnings' and 'mere pretension' (KI 186, 189).

Our Knowledge . . . That copper can be turned into gold
is in itself sufficient proof that gold can, in like manner, be
transmuted into copper . . . Every mineral can be made to
acquire the density, form and substance of each and every
other mineral (G 197-8).

Elsewhere Bahá'u'lláh wrote that transmutation of elements
would become a reality, and that its achievement would be
one of the signs of the coming of age of the human race. He
further prophesied that after its discovery a great calamity
would threaten the world unless humankind came under the
shelter of the Cause of God (quoted in Taherzadeh, *Revelation of Bahá'u'lláh,* vol. 2, p. 268).

This latter prophecy seemed somewhat puzzling. Transmutation might or might not be possible, but one thing had
always seemed self-evident: If it were possible, it would be
an unadulterated boon for humanity. The power to change
copper into gold, or any element into any other, would bring
boundless wealth. Human beings would be able to manufac-
ture all manner of previously expensive commodities – food,
medicine, industrial raw materials – cheaply and in limitless
quantities. Wondrous new inventions and spellbinding discoveries would herald a golden age of material well-being.
Such visions had fired the imaginations of alchemists for
thousands of years.

Transmutation of elements was finally achieved, and its
age-old secret unlocked, early in this century. But – as
Bahá'u'lláh had foreseen – there was a catch. Changing one
element into another is associated with the release of nuclear
energy. The two phenomena (transmutation of elements and
nuclear energy) are twin aspects of a single process; they are
flip sides of the same coin.

Most of an atom's energy is frozen within its nucleus
(hence the term 'nuclear'). A portion of this energy can be
freed by either fission (the splitting of an atom's nucleus into
two lighter nuclei) or fusion (the combining of two or more
nuclei into a larger nucleus). This release of energy by

splitting or combining atomic nuclei produces new atoms with new sizes and weights, thus changing one element into another. The blast of a hydrogen bomb is the result of transmuting hydrogen into helium through fusion. This same process of hydrogen-to-helium fusion powers the sun and all the stars (which, of course, are also suns). In a conventional atomic power plant the fission of uranium atoms produces a variety of lighter elements, while some of the unsplit uranium atoms change into plutonium by absorbing extra neutrons. Transmutation of elements also occurs through the natural process of radioactive decay, whereby uranium, thorium and a number of other unstable elements gradually change into the lighter element lead.

There is, then, a striking connection between Bahá'u'lláh's prediction of success in transmuting elements and His separate prediction (detailed in the preceding section) of a force capable of poisoning the whole earth's atmosphere. Both prophecies pointed to the same discovery: nuclear power. No less astonishing than either prophecy taken singly, however, was the fact that Bahá'u'lláh Himself clearly saw the connection between them – a connection no human being of His generation should have known. The ancient alchemist's dream, as He and He alone foresaw, represents not an unmixed blessing but a dangerous instrument. Used unwisely, it has brought humankind to the brink of nuclear holocaust.

Although various elements have been transmuted in bombs and reactors, as well as in laboratory experiments, most transmutations are too complex and expensive to be practical, given current technology. The changing of copper into gold still falls within this category. Modern atomic science, however, has definitely proved Bahá'u'lláh right in saying such reactions are possible. It is now clear, moreover, that transmutations of equal and even greater complexity occur continually in stars. This point, which relates to yet another Bahá'í scientific prophecy, is considered in the next section.

The Evolution of Elements

PROPHECY 24: *The discovery that complex elements evolve in nature from simpler ones.*

ABSTRACT: *The Bahá'í teachings state that 'in the beginning matter was one', giving rise to elements which became differentiated only 'after a very long time' into their present complex forms. This teaching seemed, at the time, irreconcilable with known facts; but its truth became apparent by the middle of the twentieth century. Physicists now realize that all matter begins as hydrogen gas which, collecting slowly in suns and stars, cooks under enormous pressure for thousands of millions of years. The resulting nuclear reactions combine the original atoms of hydrogen into heavier and ever-more-complex elements. These elements eventually render the star unstable, triggering (if it is sufficiently massive) a 'supernova' explosion which welds vast quantities of starstuff into still heavier elements and flings them into space as gas. The constant repetition of this process throughout the universe provides the raw material for suns and planets such as our own.*

BACKGROUND: Since there are well over one hundred elements, with atoms of widely varying sizes and weights, it is natural to wonder how such diversity came about. If we assume (as scientists did until well into this century) that atoms are unchanging, there seem to be only two possibilities. One is that this diversity always existed; the other is that it came into being all at once (whether naturally or by divine creation) in the remote past.

'Abdu'l-Bahá endorsed a third possibility, found in the book *Some Answered Questions*. This remarkable work is a collection of table talks He delivered in 'Akká from 1904 to 1906 in answer to questions put to Him by Laura Clifford Barney. The answers were written down in Persian as He spoke. 'Abdu'l-Bahá later reviewed these notes for accuracy, 'sometimes changing a word or a line with His reed pen', then signed them (SAQ xv). The talks were translated into

214

English by Miss Barney and were first published in 1908.

According to 'Abdu'l-Bahá, the various elements all began as a single form of matter, arriving at their present-day condition by passing through intermediate stages:

> . . . it is evident that in the beginning matter was one, and that one matter appeared in different aspects in each element. Thus various forms were produced, and these various aspects as they were produced became permanent, and each element was specialized. But this permanence was not definite, and did not attain realization and perfect existence until after a very long time (SAQ 181).

The detailed verification of this teaching is one of the most amazing stories of modern science. It began in 1929 with the seemingly unrelated discovery, by astronomer Edwin Hubble, that all observable galaxies appear to be moving away from each other at a rate proportional to their distance. (In other words, the farther apart they already are, the faster the distance between them grows.) This led to the conclusion that we live in an expanding universe which must once have been compressed into an infinitesimally small region. Several converging lines of evidence now suggest that our cosmos erupted from such a point of origin, fifteen to eighteen thousand million years ago, in a primordial explosion whimsically dubbed the 'Big Bang'.

Many Bible-oriented scientists have drawn attention to remarkable parallels between the Big Bang hypothesis and the account of divine creation in Genesis. The details are of course shrouded in mystery. Some cosmologists postulate an 'oscillating universe', where each expansion is followed by a contraction leading to yet another explosion. Others believe we live in a 'space-time continuum' that is one of many, each with its own Big Bang, and each hidden from, and existing independently of, the others. Some interpretations are so subtle and complex that they can be described only by higher mathematics. Whichever version is correct, few cosmologists doubt that the Big Bang itself must somehow have occurred.

The Big Bang model clearly ruled out any possibility that the complex elements we see today always existed in their present forms. Any atoms that might have appeared within such a conflagration would have been instantly ripped apart by its titanic pressure. Nor could those elements have appeared all at once in its aftermath, as a direct result of the explosion's heat and force. Calculations indicated that the fireball, powerful as it was, would have expanded and cooled too quickly to sustain the intricate interactions needed to produce any but the simplest elements. Where and how, then, did the elements arise? After decades of detective work, based on studies of nuclear reactions and spectroscopic analysis of stars, astrophysicists worked out what must have happened. The last few pieces of the puzzle fell into place as recently as 1957. Here is a summary (grossly over-simplified) of the process as currently understood:

The early universe was a boiling cauldron of raw energy, too hot for matter to exist in any form. Its density exceeded that of rock; its temperature reached thousands of millions of degrees. As this hellish proto-matter expanded and cooled it condensed into a shower of subatomic particles, which arranged themselves by mutual attraction into atoms of hydrogen, the simplest element. The rapidly falling temperature had time to fuse about a fifth of this hydrogen into helium (the next simplest element), along with traces of lithium and beryllium, before it dropped too low to sustain further nuclear transmutations.

All of this happened within a few minutes. The next several thousand million years passed uneventfully, as hydrogen/helium clouds billowed through the darkness, thinning here, thickening there. (Space is not a perfect vacuum; even today, it is still suffused with remnants of this primordial gas.) Denser clouds, collapsing in upon themselves under their own weight, eventually built up enough internal pressure to blaze into the fusion furnaces visible to us as stars.

A young star obtains most of its energy from the fusion of hydrogen into helium. As the star ages and contracts, however, it becomes a simmering pressure-cooker wherein a variety of more complex fusion reactions occur. These reactions gradually breed all of the lighter elements (carbon, oxygen and the like), which sort themselves by weight into layers around the star's core. This phase of the process normally occupies thousands of millions of years.

The heaviest element so produced is iron, which forms the gaseous inner layer and renders the star unstable. If the star is sufficiently massive, this instability causes its core to collapse suddenly, sending an inconceivably loud clang or gong upward through the surrounding layers. This sonic boom – the most powerful shock wave known to science – destroys the star in a supernova explosion characterized by intense heat, pressure and an abundance of free neutrons. The nuclei of atoms caught in this 'neutron flux' tend rapidly to absorb neutrons, about half of which change into protons through beta particle emission. Since the number of protons is what gives an atom its chemical identity, this process causes it to evolve quickly, becoming, at each step, a new and slightly heavier element.

Thus an atom entering the supernova blast as iron may, within a split-second, change from iron to cobalt to nickel to copper, its nucleus gaining weight with each promotion. Additional steps up the ladder of increasingly heavy elements can bring it to the state of gold or, further, to that of lead, cadmium or any heavier element. Indeed, any lower element may evolve into any higher one, typically within the blink of an eye. A dying star, then, is the ultimate alchemist's crucible: It is here that base metals are literally transmuted into gold, lead, uranium and all other elements heavier than iron, then blown into space as gas to mingle with the hydrogen and helium already there. When latter-day stars and planets condense from the interstellar mist, they inherit some of the elements born in earlier stars. Our own sun, a relatively new star, and our own planet, the earth, are among the heavenly bodies nourished from this cosmic cornucopia. Stellar alchemy has furnished the raw material for virtually everything we see around us (including our own bodies). As Carl Sagan puts it, 'We are starstuff.'

Current theory, as indicated above, holds that the hydrogen/helium mixture that forms the raw material for this process emerged from the Big Bang itself. However, the discovery that more complex elements are forged in stars, reaching their permanent specialized forms only after aeons of evolution, in no way depends on the correctness of the Big Bang model, for that discovery has since been confirmed by many independent observations. Thus, even should the Big Bang theory be later modified or abandoned, the basic picture of elemental evolution will remain. When this picture came into focus in 1957 it was precisely as 'Abdu'l-Bahá had described it more than half a century earlier.

These facts also confirm something Bahá'u'lláh wrote in 1862: namely, that copper can change into gold in as little as a single instant. In His *Book of Certitude*, He uses the following analogy to illustrate the profound effect of divine revelation upon the human soul:

> For instance, consider the substance of copper. Were it to be protected in its own mine from becoming solidified, it would, within the space of seventy years, attain to the state of gold . . . Be that as it may, the real elixir will, in one instant, cause the substance of copper to attain the state of gold, and will traverse the seventy-year stages in a single moment (KI 157).

As many readers have pointed out, this passage is a metaphorical description of spiritual rebirth; and as such its primary implications are those that concern human life and character. However, we cannot discount it as a 'purely symbolic' image possessing no literal or physical significance. Bahá'u'lláh is drawing a parallel between a spiritual reality and a material fact. Thus Shoghi Effendi, in a letter written by his secretary on his behalf, comments as follows: 'We as Bahá'ís must assume that, as He [Bahá'u'lláh] had access to all knowledge, He was referring to a definite physical condition which theoretically might exist' (LOG 478).

But how can copper 'in its own mine' be prevented from becoming solidified – much less change to gold? One doubts that Bahá'u'lláh was referring to any mine on earth, for copper ore in a terrestrial mine always is solid. One might, of course, maintain molten or gaseous copper indefinitely in a metallurgical laboratory; but such an environment hardly constitutes a mine in any recognizable sense.

But the situation changes if we suppose that by copper's 'own mine' Bahá'u'lláh means an exploding star. Copper is born in the fireworks of a supernova. In this atomic furnace – its true place of origin, from which every atom of copper on earth ultimately derives – it can never solidify. Moreover, any copper that appears in the explosion will tend, as the nuclear reaction progresses, to gain neutrons and protons until it becomes gold (or some even heavier element). In this scenario, copper's stellar birthplace may be regarded as its mine, and the supernova's neutron flux as the 'elixir' which, literally in a flash, accomplishes the transmutation.

This admittedly speculative interpretation does raise one question: If Bahá'u'lláh was alluding to a supernova explosion, and if (as currently understood) such explosions last only a few moments, why does He describe the transmutation as occurring 'within the space' of seventy years? While it is true – in a strictly literal sense – that any event of less than seventy years' duration transpires 'within' that period, reason suggests the seventy-year reference may have some more specific meaning. Two possible answers come to mind.

The first is that there may be some as-yet-unknown condition in which copper's transition to gold would occur more slowly than in the supernovae we can observe. In fact, simply by virtue of knowing that the transition can and does occur rapidly, we also know that a slower version is at least theoretically possible (in the sense that it would violate no laws of physics). Of the infinite possible varieties of nuclear interactions, only a vanishingly small percentage have as yet been studied or even postulated.

The second answer (suggested by Charles Coffey) is that Bahá'u'lláh may have described the process as occurring 'within the space of seventy years' simply to strengthen the intended analogy between elemental transmutation and human spiritual development. Seventy years is the traditional human lifespan of 'threescore years and ten'. By expressing the duration in these literally accurate terms (while noting its actual quickness in the statement that follows), Bahá'u'lláh may be emphasizing that although human character can and sometimes does change rapidly, this process of refinement typically involves lifelong struggle.

Bahá'u'lláh's statement on the transmutation of copper to gold 'in its own mine' is one that has puzzled generations of readers. These tentative observations are offered in the hope of spurring further study and research. We may well have as much to learn of Bahá'u'lláh's intended meaning as astrophysicists have to learn about atomic genesis. As a result of modern discoveries, however, we can state one conclusion with reasonable assurance: What we do know of His meaning is entirely consistent with what we now know about the evolution of elements.

THE SKY IS NOT THE LIMIT

The Space Age, like the Atomic Age, figures prominently in Bahá'í prophecy.

Stars and Planets

PROPHECY 25: *The recognition of planets as a necessary by-product of star formation.*

ABSTRACT: *Another scientific mystery in Bahá'u'lláh's day was whether stars other than our own sun have planets. Bahá'u'lláh Himself was very explicit: 'Every fixed star', He wrote, 'hath its own planets . . .' (The traditional term 'fixed star' refers to self-luminous stellar bodies like our own sun, in contrast to planets that once were called 'wandering stars'.) Throughout most of our present century astronomers insisted that planets cannot occur naturally but only as a result of some freak catastrophe such as a near-collision between stars. Not until the early 1970s did new mathematical models show that the rotation of a star necessarily spins off a disk of matter, forming rings that coalesce into orbiting bodies. According to current knowledge, then, every normal star will at some point sire planets as part of its natural life-cycle.*

BACKGROUND: Stars come in a rainbow of colours and are grouped into galaxies with a delightful assortment of shapes. Our sun, a fairly typical yellow star, is part of the Milky Way, an equally typical spiral galaxy. There are at least a hundred thousand million stars in the Milky Way galaxy alone and a similar number of galaxies in the observable universe. It seems certain the 'observable' universe is itself a flyspeck in the larger cosmos.

Since our sun and galaxy are so ordinary, it is natural to wonder whether the same is true of our planet, the earth. Bahá'u'lláh wrote that 'every fixed star hath its own planets',* whose age and number the 'learned men' of His generation had 'failed' to 'consider' (G 163).

It has been clear, since fairly early in this century, that both the age and size of the physical universe are millions

---

*The term 'fixed star' is of ancient origin. It refers to any of those celestial bodies that do not, over the course of a human lifespan, visibly change position relative to one another. The expression was created to differentiate such bodies from 'wandering stars', which travel across the sky following paths similar to those of the sun and moon. We now know, of course, that 'fixed stars' are self-luminous suns like our sun, while 'wandering stars' are planets like our earth.

of times greater than was generally believed in Bahá'u'lláh's lifetime. Regarding the existence of planets around other stars, however, there has been no such agreement. Astronomers have long known that stars, like blazing raindrops, condense from the thin mist of hydrogen and other gases pervading the near-vacuum of space; but until recently they had no evidence indicating that this process could explain the formation of planets circling those stars.

Lacking such evidence, many theorists turned to the idea that the earth, and our solar system's other planets such as Mars, Venus, Jupiter and so forth, are the result of a near collision between the sun and another star (or some other large celestial body). According to this model, the gravitational tides produced by such an upheaval pulled blobs of molten matter away from the sun; these fell into orbit, hardening into worlds as they cooled. Since close encounters between stars seldom occur, this hypothesis suggested that planets like ours are extremely rare in the cosmos.

A less catastrophic model had been formulated by Kant and Laplace in the eighteenth and early nineteenth centuries. They conjectured that planets were spun off by the rotating sun as it condensed. Powerful arguments, however, weighed against this notion, which was therefore rejected by a majority of astronomers. By 1946 the case against the Kant-Laplace 'spin-off' model seemed so airtight that astrophysicist George Gamow, in his classic *The Birth and Death of the Sun*, could sum up the scientific consensus as follows: 'In view of our present knowledge this attractive and simple hypothesis [the spin-off model] will not stand up to serious criticism.' 'It seems, therefore, necessary to assume . . . that the rotational momentum was put into the system of planets from the outside and to consider the formation of the planets as due to an encounter of our Sun with some other stellar body of comparable size.' 'Thus we should be forced to the conclusion that planetary systems are very rare phenomena, and that our Sun must be extremely lucky to have one' (Gamow, *Birth and Death* 200-4).

This consensus prevailed until the 1970s when newly-developed mathematical models prompted astrophysicists to revive (in a more sophisticated form) the Kant-Laplace hypothesis. They now believe that the condensation of a rotating star does bring into being around it a 'dusty disk' of gas, ice, rock and other leftover debris. Larger particles, sweeping through the disk, collect smaller ones, forming ever-more-massive chunks that soon begin to attract one another through mutual gravitation. These chunks, arranged into bands like the rings of Saturn, eventually smash together to form still larger objects (see Ferris, *Coming of Age* 167).

Although the current body of knowledge, as summed up by Carl Sagan, does not constitute 'definitive evidence', it 'strongly suggests that stars like our own Sun frequently, if not invariably, are accompanied by planets' (*Parade* magazine, 9 June 1996, p. 10). These may range in size from tiny proto-worlds called 'planetesimals' to 'superplanets' far more massive than Jupiter, the largest object circling our own sun. The new model interprets planetary bodies as a natural and probably inevitable by-product of stellar dynamics. Far from being the mutant offspring of a freak accident, they are the normal children of any normal star – as inseparable a part of the star's life-cycle as its heat and light.*

The worth of any theory depends less on its elegance and plausibility than on whether its predictions are upheld by evidence. Support for the current concept came initially from an infrared orbiting telescope, which detected cold disks of matter around Vega and other young, bright stars. During the latter half of the eighties, astronomers found tantalizing

---

*Certain stars – specifically, binary stars of intermediate separation – orbit one another in ways that apparently would render them unable to maintain normal planets. In such cases, however, each star might in some broad sense be considered a planet in relation to the other. Of course, a system of planets may at any stage of its evolution be destroyed by some violent celestial event such as a supernova explosion or stellar collision.

indications of actual planets around a dozen or more nearby stars (Carl Sagan, *Parade* magazine, 30 April 1989, p. 16).

October 1995 brought positive identification of an 'extra-solar' planet (i.e., one circling a star other than our own sun). The newly discovered world is associated with the star 51 Pegasi (in the constellation Pegasus), a scant 42 light-years from Earth. Two more planets – one belonging to 70 Virginis (in the constellation Virgo), the other to 47 Ursae Majoris (in the Big Dipper or Ursa Major) – were announced in January 1996. Yet another has since been found orbiting the star 55 Cancri in the constellation Cancer the Crab. All were identified by telltale wobbles in the stars' movements.

Astronomers are, of course, rightly reluctant to generalize on the basis of a few proven planets and an incomplete mathematical model. Much more research would be needed to establish conclusively Bahá'u'lláh's statement that 'every fixed star' has 'its own planets'. (Nor is there even universal agreement as to how large or small an object must be in order to constitute a planet.) Nevertheless, His position – long considered untenable – now is at least provisionally confirmed. Since on-going research is yielding new evidence at a rapid rate, the interested reader would do well to consult a current science periodical for the latest developments in this fast-breaking news story.

Railroads to Heaven

PROPHECY 26: *Space travel.*

ABSTRACT: *The Bahá'í teachings specifically predict space travel and describe some of its characteristics and future accomplishments. Speaking in Paris in 1913, 'Abdu'l-Bahá stated that the time had come to direct efforts towards reaching other planets. Elsewhere He envisioned vehicles travelling with 'the rapidity of rising lightning' from the earth to the heavens and even 'from the globe of the earth to the globe of the sun'. Today's reusable shuttle, the solar probe Ulysses and other space ventures have fulfilled every word of these predictions.*

BACKGROUND: With the age of aviation barely under way, 'Abdu'l-Bahá recognized – more clearly than many of today's political leaders – the need for an organized programme of space exploration. Speaking in Paris on 19 February 1913, He urged that efforts be directed towards reaching other planets. Such an undertaking, He indicated, was a natural extension of scientific and technological strides already being made (AB 377).

In one of His letters He also referred to space travel, describing it in graphic terms. In this letter He cautioned Bahá'ís against being distracted by the glitter of the space programme (or any other spectacular undertakings) from the more tedious but infinitely more vital task of spreading Bahá'u'lláh's teachings:

> I know, verily, that the universal, never ending, eternal, bright and divine establishments are only the diffusing of the breaths of God, and the spreading of the instructions of God, and all that are beside these, though they be the reigning over all regions of the earth, or the construction of railroads from the earth to the heavens, or means of transportation with the rapidity of rising lightning from the globe of the earth to the globe of the sun, all are but mortal, perishing, demolishing and disadvantageous, in comparison with the divine establishments (TAB 32).

If we wished to describe today's reusable space shuttle in images familiar to 'Abdu'l-Bahá's early-twentieth-century readers, we could hardly do better than to call it a railroad from earth to heaven. Nor could we more clearly express the awesome speed attained by modern spacecraft than by likening it to the 'rapidity of rising lightning'. Perhaps the most remarkable aspect of this passage is its reference to transportation 'from the globe of the earth to the globe of the sun'. Even this development – one completely inconceivable to 'Abdu'l-Bahá's contemporaries – became reality in October 1990 with the launching of the European-built Ulysses solar probe from the American space shuttle Discovery. After a Jupiter flyby, the robot spacecraft made in mid-1994 a close sweep of the sun's 'south pole', followed in mid-1995 by a similar pass over its 'north pole', sending back, at each stage, large amounts of data.

Ulysses is, of course, unlikely to be the end of the story. Arthur C. Clarke, writing in *Profiles of the Future*, suggests that prospective advances in plasma physics could someday make it possible to generate an impenetrable 'force field' (that old science-fiction standby) capable of withstanding direct contact with solar fires. 'When we possess it,' he writes, 'we may have a key not only to the interior of the Earth, but even, perhaps, to the interior of the Sun' (Clarke, *Profiles of the Future* 121).

GENERAL PROPHECIES

Transmission of Cancer

PROPHECY 27: *The realization that some forms of cancer are communicable.*

ABSTRACT: *'Abdu'l-Bahá counted cancer among 'bodily diseases' which (in at least some forms and to some extent) are communicable among human beings. This statement, when published in 1921, defied established medical opinion. In recent years, however, new evidence has linked some cancers of the reproductive system to human papilloma virus, an infection authorities believe can be sexually transmitted. (This is not true of most – much less all – malignancies; and none, so far as we now know, are spread by casual contact.)*

BACKGROUND: 'Abdu'l-Bahá wrote that 'bodily diseases like consumption and cancer are contagious'* in the same manner as other infections against which 'safe and healthy persons' must guard themselves (LOG 183). This was obviously true of consumption (tuberculosis) – but what of cancer?

In this regard the statement, when published in 1921, was diametrically opposed to established medical opinion. Evidence against it seemed solid; the sole supporting clue – at best ambiguous – had been the discovery in 1908 and 1911 of certain 'virus-induced tumours' in chickens. These were commonly discounted as 'a biological curiosity, either not true cancers or perhaps a peculiarity of the avian species (Dulbecco and Ginsberg, *Virology* 335). In any case, 'Abdu'l-Bahá had made His comment on cancer in a discussion of human diseases, both spiritual and physical, to which this finding had no obvious relevance.

The possibility that it might have a less-than-obvious relevance loomed larger after researchers found similar tumours in rabbits (1932), frogs (1934) and mice (1936). These infectious cancers had long been overlooked because they tend to spread in ways that mask their true nature. They may, for example, be transmitted through a virus in the mother's milk or placenta, appearing to be hereditary. Many such viruses cease to display infective activity as soon as they have induced cancer, making their role extremely difficult to recognize. These findings fanned suspicion that similar tumour-producing viruses might be able to spread from human being to human being.

No responsible authority has ever suggested that all, or even most, forms of cancer are communicable, much less that they spread through casual contact. Most malignant tumours clearly are induced by exposure to chemicals,

---

*The Persian word for 'contagious' embraces all the shades of meaning represented by the English words 'contagious', 'infectious' and 'communicable'. It can therefore connote mild, infrequent infectivity as well as dramatic and obvious contagion.

radiation or similar environmental agents; by hereditary and genetic factors; or by combinations of such causes. Nevertheless, the infectious origin of some human cancers is now considered 'almost certain' and 'the evidence grows stronger with each passing month' (Robbins and Kumar, *Basic Pathology* 205, 207). Cervical cancer, for example, is linked in clinical studies to the human papilloma virus. On the basis of such studies, many authorities now believe that if a man is sexually involved with a number of women, one of whom has cervical cancer, he can become a carrier for the virus and thus transmit the disease from the infected partner to the healthy ones (Cotran, Kumar and Robbins, *Robbins Pathologic Basis of Disease* 1142). A different infection, Epstein-Barr virus, is implicated in the African form of Burkitt's lymphoma and in nasopharyngeal cancer (Robbins and Kumar, *Basic Pathology* 207). Various other human cancers are under indictment for possible contagion and definitive answers seem imminent.

With regard to cancer communicability, then, the situation resembles that of planets in other star systems: Current knowledge strongly supports the statement of the Bahá'í writings, although researchers have yet to dot the last 'i' and cross the last 't'. Again, the reader is urged to consult an up-to-the-minute scientific journal or other authoritative source for the latest findings.

The Missing 'Missing Link'

PROPHECY 28: *Failure to find evidence for a 'missing link' between man and ape.*

ABSTRACT: *'Abdu'l-Bahá stated flatly in 1912 that no anthropologist or palaeontologist would ever unearth fossil proof for the so-called 'missing link' – the purported common ancestor between human beings and modern apes. His statement, though debunked for decades by sceptics, has held up to more than eighty years of intense archeological scrutiny. The only skeletal specimen ever seriously touted as likely to overturn it was the notorious 'Piltdown Man', announced the very year 'Abdu'l-Bahá made His prediction. More than forty years later, Piltdown Man was exposed as a clever hoax.*

BACKGROUND: A particularly remarkable Bahá'í prophecy concerns palaeontology, the study of fossils. To place this in its proper context, we first must digress to explore briefly the topic of creation and biological evolution.

Theories about evolution have sparked angry religious debate ever since the publication in 1859 of Charles Darwin's *The Origin of Species*. Such arguments have fostered the unfortunate impression that evolution is one topic where science and religion can never meet. This attitude, though far from universal, is taken for granted by many outspoken people in both the religious and scientific communities. One result is that isolated comments about evolution tend to be quickly tagged as representing one 'side' or the other. The Bahá'í position on this subject (as on so many others) is one that does not fit neatly into any of these stereotyped categories.

First, Bahá'ís believe that the account of creation recorded in Genesis is indeed divinely inspired, and therefore true in every detail. The sense in which those details are true naturally depends on what God meant by the various terms He used in reporting them. Many conservative Christian scholars have pointed out, for example, that the seven days of creation need not be understood as twenty-four-hour chronological days. In the original Hebrew of Genesis the word for 'day' (*yôm*, used without a definite article) suggests sequence rather than duration. Thus it apparently means a further creative stage of indeterminate length in an orderly and systematic process.*

*For an in-depth Christian analysis of the linguistic and textual issues here, see pp. 55-63 of the *Encyclopedia of Bible Difficulties* by Gleason (continued...)

Second, everything in creation changes continually according to laws ordained and kept in force by God. Nor is there anything remote about God: He is not a 'deistic' Creator who, having set in motion the universe as we might wind up a watch, retires to watch it run itself. His hand is at work in every 'natural' process, and His loving providence continually overshadows all things. To a Bahá'í, then, there is no conflict between divine creation and what we might call 'theistic evolution'.

Thus Bahá'u'lláh strongly supports the biologist who finds for life a history stretching back through long but orderly stages of development. However, His teachings reject certain assumptions normally associated with this view. For one thing, Bahá'ís – unlike materialists – see nothing 'blind' about evolution. From start to finish, the process represents a gradual but resistless working out of God's purpose. Even though each step, viewed individually, may appear automatic or even random, the process as a whole is one of deliberate design. More importantly, Bahá'ís reject the idea that man differs only in degree from other primates such as chimpanzees and gorillas. Of all creatures, only man, according to Bahá'u'lláh's teachings, has an immortal soul (SAQ 143-4) and only man has the capacities for abstract thought and spiritual development that are innate properties of that soul (SAQ 185-90). This fundamental component of human nature is a divine gift rather than a product of biological evolution or an inheritance from animal ancestors. This – and not any question of chronology – is the intended point of the Genesis creation report.

Darwinism, the prevailing evolutionary model, is sometimes described as the belief that 'man is descended from a

---

*(...continued)
L. Archer Jr, professor of Old Testament and Semitic studies at Trinity Evangelical Divinity School. An expert in the original languages and manuscripts of the Bible, Dr Archer is well known as a proponent of scriptural inerrancy.

monkey'. This description is at best imprecise. Neither Darwin nor his successors ever thought man evolved from animals identical to present-day apes; what they do say, however, is that both species evolved from an earlier, ape-like creature more primitive than either. Men and monkeys are therefore seen as relatively close cousins, sharing a common ancestor from whom they are thought to have diverged several million years ago. This hypothetical common ancestor is designated the 'missing link'. (The term 'missing link' is sometimes loosely applied to any more primitive form of early man, such as Neanderthal. In its original sense, however, it refers strictly to a creature who was both early ape and early man.)

According to 'Abdu'l-Bahá, modern evolutionists are mistaken in teaching that 'man's descent is from the animal' (SAQ 177). Man, He explains, 'was always a distinct species, a man, not an animal' (SAQ 184). If we assume that the ancestor of any modern animal was itself an animal, this statement appears difficult to reconcile with the belief that men and apes share a common ancestor. One may argue, however, that the apparent contradiction is simply one of semantics: Perhaps 'Abdu'l-Bahá is merely dating man's beginning as a distinct species from the soul's first appearance, to emphasize that we do not derive our higher spiritual nature from our animal forebears. Further research – both on His intended meaning and on the biological relationships at issue – may someday settle this issue.

One thing, however, is indisputable: 'Abdu'l-Bahá predicted, at the very least, that fossil remains of the alleged missing link would remain forever undiscovered. 'Between man and the ape,' He told an audience at Leland Stanford University in 1912,

> there is one link missing, and to the present time scientists have not been able to discover it . . . The lost link of Darwinian theory is itself a proof that man is not an animal. How is it possible to have all the links present and that

important link absent? Its absence is an indication that man has never been an animal. It will never be found (PUP 358-9).

Scientists, before and since, have sought fossil evidence for the missing link with all the fervour of Arthurian knights seeking the Holy Grail. In 1912 – ironically, the very year 'Abdu'l-Bahá made His prediction – their quest turned up Piltdown Man, an ape-like creature whose skeletal fragments showed both human and simian traits. The popular and scientific press trumpeted that the missing link was missing no longer. This conclusion reigned as scientific gospel until 1953 when researchers discovered that Piltdown Man actually was a link in a somewhat different sense of the word. Some prankster, it turned out, had joined a human jawbone to a chimpanzee cranium, then treated the construct chemically to make it appear fossilized. Piltdown Man quietly disappeared from the textbooks through whose pages he had shambled for two generations.

Many legitimate fossil specimens of early man have been found. None, however, has qualified to fill the position of missing link vacated in disgrace by Piltdown Man. Until recently, the oldest primate fossil considered ancestral to humanity was 'Lucy', a member of the erect-walking species *Australopithecus*. Lucy, whose bones were found in 1974 in Ethiopia, is thought to have lived about three million years ago. She could not, however, have been a common ancestor to human beings and modern apes. 'Lucy's ancestors must have left the trees and risen from four limbs onto two well before her time, probably at the very beginning of human evolution,' writes C. Owen Lovejoy in *Scientific American*. 'If upright walking was well established by the time of *Australopithecus*, its advent could date back as far as the earliest hominids, whose lineage probably diverged from other primates some eight or 10 million years ago' (C. Owen Lovejoy, 'Evolution of Human Walking', *Scientific American*, November 1988, pp. 89, 82). Such a chronology would place the true missing link at least five to seven million years before Lucy.

This timetable, however, is currently under fire. New genetic studies in molecular biology suggest to many authorities that apes and human beings were a single species as recently as six million years ago. The latest skeletal discoveries point to two species even more primitive and ape-like than Lucy. The most ancient, *Ardipithecus ramidus*, is dated as 4.4 million years old. (Like Lucy, it was unearthed in Ethiopia.) Confirmation of these estimates might narrow the gap to just over one and a half million years.

Having come this far, many palaeontologists feel they are within striking distance of uncovering the missing link. Others, remembering false dawns and frustrated hopes of past excavations, remain deeply sceptical. The *Los Angeles Times*, in an article dated 17 August 1995, enumerates some of the issues left unresolved by the discovery of *ramidus*:

> Could the new species be the ancestors not of modern human beings, but of the great apes of contemporary Africa? Could the fossil fragments exhumed from several sites be the mixed bones of more than one species? Do the three early hominid species now identified lie in the same lineage? Or are they just distant relatives? Peter Andrews, an expert on early apes and human origins at the Natural History Museum in London sums it up this way, 'It seems to me that this fossil raises more questions than it answers.'

Positive identification of any missing link will require more than filling the remaining gap with a plausible chain of prehuman fossils. Palaeontologists also must construct such a transitional chain connecting the same creature with modern apes. Little progress has yet been made in that direction.

At the time of 'Abdu'l-Bahá's Stanford address, evolutionists felt confident that palaeontology would quickly redraw the family trees of man and ape, showing just where and how the two lines were joined. Today, after more than eighty years of intense research, their goal remains as elusive and tantalizing as ever. The longer the search continues, the easier it becomes to believe 'Abdu'l-Bahá was right – that fossil proof of such kinship will always remain out of reach. Niles Eldredge and Ian Tattersall, in *The Myths of Human Evolution*, conclude that man's search for his ancestry is probably futile. If the evidence were there, they write, 'one could confidently expect that as more hominid fossils were found the story of human evolution would become clearer. Whereas, if anything, the opposite has occurred' (quoted by James Gorman, *Discover*, January 1983, pp. 83-4).

We are, of course, free to speculate on what new findings may come to light as a result of deeper digging. Nevertheless, the correspondence to date between 'Abdu'l-Bahá's prediction and actual events is nothing less than astounding.

MECHANICAL MODELS AND THE NEW PHYSICS

During the opening decades of the twentieth century, physicists were committed to explaining all phenomena by means of mechanical models. A mechanical model is a precise picture or replica based on human sensory experience. It corresponds in a literally accurate way – not merely a figurative or poetic way – to the thing it represents.

The notion that all reality could be brought under the umbrella of mechanical models was central to 'classical' physics (sometimes called Newtonian, after Isaac Newton). Classical physics portrayed the universe as a vast, clockwork machine, all parts of which were in principle completely visualizable. This plausible interpretation led physicists to regard matter as composed of particles resembling tiny marbles or grains of sand; light, heat, magnetism and similar forces as vibrations, resembling sound waves or ripples in a pond; and time and space as a fixed frame of reference – a limitless arena within which objects and forces interacted but which remained unaffected by their presence. In such a universe, every event (given enough information) must be completely predictable, for each is predetermined, in all its aspects, by the events that lead up to it.

Most scientists found a mechanistic world view difficult to reconcile with any spiritual or mystical philosophy. Machines are material; and by placing primary emphasis on the material, machine-like aspects of reality, one seems to rule out such abstract concepts as God, the soul, free will and the like. Newton, a devout Christian, would have winced had he realized how powerfully the system of thought associated with his name would promote materialism; yet that is what it did.

Bahá'ís, like other believers in the Bible, necessarily subscribe to a belief in spiritual realities that do not lend themselves to mechanical interpretation. Our present inquiry, however, concerns none of the metaphysical aspects of such a controversy but only those that are scientifically testable. Of crucial interest here is 'Abdu'l-Bahá's teaching that *even some physical processes* (including, among other things, the transmission of light) cannot be faithfully depicted by mechanical models or visualized by the human mind. By so stating, He anticipated some of the twentieth century's most startling discoveries – those that formed the basis of relativity and quantum physics. Let us examine His words more closely.

All objects of human knowledge, according to 'Abdu'l-Bahá, fall into one of two categories. They are either 'sensible realities' or 'intellectual realities' (SAQ 183). Sensible realities, as the name implies, are those we can detect with our physical senses such as sight, hearing and the like. These are the familiar objects of everyday experience – shoes, ships and sealing wax; raindrops and roses; 'stuff you can hit with a stick', as someone once explained it. (I suppose 'Abdu'l-Bahá would include under this heading things we can detect only with the aid of physical instruments such as telescopes and infrared goggles, these being extensions of our normal senses.)

An intellectual reality, on the other hand, is one that 'has no outward form and no place and is not perceptible to the senses' (SAQ 83). The term 'intellectual' in this context does not mean imaginary, nor does it refer exclusively to generalities like 'patriotism' or 'the square root of pi'. As 'Abdu'l-Bahá explains it, the expression includes such intangibles as the human soul and its qualities – realities that exist and produce concrete effects in the world but which are abstract in that they occupy no space and have no specific physical location:

> . . . if you examine the human body, you will not find a special spot or locality for the spirit, for it never had a place; it is immaterial. It has a connection with the body like that of the sun with this mirror. The sun is not within the mirror, but it has a connection with the mirror . . . the mind has no place, but it is connected with the brain . . . In the same way, love has no place, but it is connected with the heart; so the Kingdom has no place, but is connected with man (SAQ 242).

Lacking form, volume and position, an intellectual reality cannot be pictured, nor can it be detected by any physical senses or instruments. 'In explaining these intellectual realities,' says 'Abdu'l-Bahá, 'one is obliged to express them by sensible figures' which have inward rather than outward significance:

> So the symbol of knowledge is light, and of ignorance, darkness; but reflect, is knowledge sensible light, or ignorance sensible darkness? No, they are merely symbols. These are only intellectual states . . . but when we seek for explanations in the external world, we are obliged to give them sensible form . . . These expressions are metaphors, allegories, mystic explanations in the world of signification (SAQ 84-5).

'Abdu'l-Bahá was not content to state this idea simply as a

nebulous spiritual precept. Instead, as noted above, He boldly applied it to the physical world in a scientifically testable way. Let us turn now to these scientific implications of His teaching.

The Missing Ether

PROPHECY 29: *The nonexistence of a mechanical ether (the supposed light-carrying medium posited by classical physics) and its redefinition as an abstract reality.*

ABSTRACT: *Physicists of the nineteenth and early twentieth centuries believed in an undetectable substance called ether – one that supposedly pervaded all space, defining its extent and acting as a medium for light and other electromagnetic waveforms. 'Abdu'l-Bahá challenged this concept, denying that ether has any objective physical existence. It should be regarded – He said – rather as an intellectual abstraction. This position was later vindicated by Einstein as a key insight of his theory of relativity. The crude, mechanical ether of yesteryear is replaced in modern theory by a quasi-mathematical framework physicists call the 'fabric' of the space-time continuum. Although most scientists (with notable exceptions such as Jeans and Eddington) decline to use the old-fashioned name, this radically redefined ether is an entity whose characteristics precisely match those affirmed by 'Abdu'l-Bahá.*

BACKGROUND: By classifying all things real as either sensible or intellectual in character, 'Abdu'l-Bahá posed a curious problem for turn-of-the-century physics: Where in this scheme was one to place ether, the hypothetical vehicle for the propagation of light? Ether, as conceived by classical physicists, did not fit comfortably within either of 'Abdu'l-Bahá's contrasting categories.

During the latter part of the 1800s evidence had mounted steadily that light (once regarded as a stream of particles) was actually a wave or vibration. It seemed self-evident, however, that waves must have something to wave in and that vibration cannot exist without something to vibrate. Yet light, as well as heat, radio waves and other forms of radiant energy, seemed to pass freely through the vacuum of empty space. Scientists explained this anomaly by suggesting that all space must be suffused with an invisible, intangible, all-pervasive medium serving to transmit the waves. To the physicists of that era, this mysterious substance – the ether – was as real as the radiation it carried.

Ether was not a 'sensible reality' since it could not, even in principle, be detected by any conceivable sensory equipment. Nor was it understood by physicists as an 'intellectual reality' in 'Abdu'l-Bahá's sense of the term: It was an objective physical substance; it had extension and volume (since each cubic foot of space contained one cubic foot of ether) as well as location (for that cube of ether always remained in the same absolute position); and it functioned in a strictly mechanical way. Waves of light moved through the ether exactly as sound waves moved through air, so that the process could be accurately diagrammed even if the ether itself was unseen.

'Abdu'l-Bahá indicated that this conception was wrong. In explaining the distinction between the two types of reality, He left no doubt as to where ether belonged: 'Even ethereal matter, the forces of which are said in physics to be heat, light, electricity and magnetism, is an intellectual reality . . .' (SAQ 83). He emphasized that it was 'not material', had 'no outward form and no place', and was describable only by symbols and metaphors no more to be taken literally than those referring to any other abstract phenomenon (SAQ 83-4).

From the standpoint of classical physics, this was rank heresy. Although 'Abdu'l-Bahá was using conventional terminology, He was redefining it so radically as to imply that the crude, mechanical ether postulated by physicists did not exist. Light, in His view, was indeed propagated by a medium; but it was a subtle, conceptual medium – a placeless abstraction more like a mathematical progression or a logical relationship than a transparent fluid.

A crack had appeared in the ether hypothesis as early as 1887, when A. A. Michelson and Edward Morley, trying to detect relative differences in the speed of light caused by the earth's motion through the ether, failed to find any. This result caused consternation among physicists but they explained it away – and rescued their belief in ether – by invoking the 'Lorentz contraction'. This idea, developed by Hendrik Lorentz, meant that the earth itself, along with all measuring devices on it, shrank in the direction of its own motion, by an amount just enough to mask the lightspeed differential.

The Lorentz contraction turned out to be real enough but it failed in the long run to salvage the idea of a mechanical ether. When Albert Einstein published his special theory of relativity in 1905, he retained the contraction, showing it to be a result of the relative nature of space and time. However, he dispensed with a mechanical ether, demonstrating that it was both meaningless and unnecessary. Space and time for him were not things but mere relationships among things and events, their measurements varying according to the observer's velocity and frame of reference. If absolute Newtonian space did not exist, then neither could any magical substance that supposedly filled such a space and defined its dimensions.

Nor was an ether required to explain the transmission of light waves, for in Einstein's view at this point, there were no such waves. He advanced a new, more sophisticated theory of light that restored its particle nature, showing that light consisted of lumps of energy called 'quanta' or 'photons'. Despite the wavelike phenomena associated with light, these massless particles supposedly moved through space like ordinary matter, needing no intervening medium.

Since 'Abdu'l-Bahá and Einstein (both of whom agreed in rejecting a physical ether) made their statements on light during the same general period, one may fairly ask whether the Bahá'í leader was simply reacting to news of Einstein's discovery. The answer, so far as I can discover, must be a cautious 'no'. 'Abdu'l-Bahá's remark about ether occurs in a talk on spiritual symbolism contained in *Some Answered Questions*. These talks, as noted previously, were delivered from 1904 through early 1906. Although individual talks are undated, and their chronological order is not always clear (since the compiler regrouped them according to subject), the talk in question contains internal evidence that it was delivered towards the beginning or middle of this period.* Einstein's first relativity paper ('On the Electrodynamics of Moving Bodies') was published in the German *Annals of Physics* in September 1905 – towards the end, that is, of the same period. Einstein at that time was not a professional scientist but a 'technical expert, third class' for the Swiss patent office in Bern. A low-level bureaucrat who knew no scientists, he himself was entirely unknown both to the scientific community and the public. Although he rose to prominence rather quickly, as such things go, he did not do so overnight. Max Born, one of Europe's top physicists, first learned of Einstein's theory at a physics conference in 1907 (a year after the last of the talks in *Some Answered Questions* was delivered). Except for a certain Professor Loria, who brought up his name, neither Born nor any of the other

---

*In this talk 'Abdu'l-Bahá explains the role of symbolism in religious discourse, calling it 'a subject that is essential for the comprehension of the questions that we have mentioned, and of others of which we are about to speak' (SAQ 83). A large number of the talks throughout the rest of the book seem to take for granted an understanding of the introductory material 'Abdu'l-Bahá presents here. It therefore appears that this talk probably came early in the series and that the compiler's decision to place it near the front of the book fairly approximates its relative position.

scientists at the conference had even heard of Einstein. 'As far as the outside world was concerned,' writes his biographer, 'he remained totally unknown until 1912, when some aspects of relativity became headline news in Austria . . .' (Clark, *Einstein* 141).

It is therefore difficult to see how 'Abdu'l-Bahá, isolated from the world in His Turkish prison, entirely lacking in formal education or access to Western journals, could have scooped the European physicists to whom Einstein addressed his arguments and whose attention he was actively seeking.

Still, suppose we concede for argument's sake that 'Abdu'l-Bahá might somehow have learned of Einstein and correctly evaluated his discovery. Even after we grant this quite implausible assumption, a fact of greater importance remains: While 'Abdu'l-Bahá supported Einstein's conclusion in one respect, He challenged it in another. Both men agreed in denying the existence of a mechanical ether but Einstein went beyond this by denying that light required a medium of any kind. 'Abdu'l-Bahá, on the contrary, indicated that light did travel through a medium, though that medium had only a conceptual, non-localized form of existence. A full decade would pass before this issue would be settled.

By portraying space and time as relative relationships, Einstein in 1905 had reduced them to mere shadows of their former Newtonian selves. In 1915, however, he himself gave them new life in his general theory of relativity – a dramatically expanded version incorporating his earlier, 'special' theory as a subset. The three dimensions of space and the single dimension of time merged into a four-dimensional 'continuum' with amazing properties. Having already acquired elasticity, it now acquired shape as well, in that it becomes curved in the presence of matter – the more massive the matter, the greater the curvature. Other objects, following the most direct path through curved spacetime, tend to accelerate; we experience this acceleration as the pull of gravity. A gravitational field is thus an expression of spacetime geometry. This curvature does not propagate itself instantaneously; it ripples through the universe at precisely the speed of light – 186,282 miles per second. It became natural, in general relativity, to speak of spacetime as a 'fabric' that could warp, bend, tear, undulate, close on itself and otherwise undergo astounding contortions.

Relativity describes the large-scale structure of the universe. In 1927 an even more revolutionary theory – quantum mechanics – was developed to describe its small-scale structure, the world of subatomic particles. If the space of general relativity was remarkable, that of quantum mechanics was downright magical. The 'quantum vacuum', as it was called, was not a vacuum at all but a 'seething ocean' with a 'foamy structure', manifesting itself as the fizz and bubble of 'virtual particles' that pop up, interact briefly with normal particles, then fade back into the abyss (Ferris, *Coming of Age* 364).

Thus overhauled, the concept of space presented a weird paradox. It remained as abstract as truth or justice; one would find it neither here nor there but only in the universal equations of cosmic law. Yet it also was, somehow, as real as the planets gliding along its curved contours or the storm-tossed particles ploughing through its billowing quantum flux. Whatever it might be, it clearly was more than an empty nothingness.

Meanwhile, new research was investing light with a paradoxical character of its own. Einstein had not succeeded, after all, in reducing light to a stream of particles; light's wavelike properties refused to be banished. Niels Bohr established a new 'principle of complementarity' according to which light, in some unpicturable yet mathematically consistent way, must be construed simultaneously as *both* a wave *and* a stream of particles.

To the extent that light was a wave, it still needed a medium for its transmission. By this time, however, the concept of spacetime was complex and functional enough to do the job; there was no need to postulate a new ether, or even to revive the name. (The term 'ether', already in disrepute anyway, had acquired unsavoury connotations through the doomed efforts of a few reactionary physicists to discredit Einstein's relativity principle.) In other words, ether – redefined as an 'intellectual reality' in 'Abdu'l-Bahá's sense of the phrase – is not some undetectable fluid occupying space; it *is* space.

Light is one form of electromagnetic field; and all fields – gravitational, electromagnetic and those of the weak and strong nuclear forces – are understood generally as disturbances in the spacetime continuum. Only in the case of gravitation has this understanding so far been made mathematically explicit. However, the all-embracing goal of modern physics is to develop a 'unified field theory' that will interpret all four of these forces as variations of one underlying field. John A. Wheeler, widely regarded as the dean of American physics, argued that not only light and gravitation but matter itself would one day stand revealed as expressions of spacetime geometry. 'What else is there out of which to build a particle', he asked, 'except geometry itself?' (Misner, Thorne and Wheeler, *Gravitation* 1202).

Be that as it may, the old-fashioned, literal, mechanical ether, whose death-knell 'Abdu'l-Bahá sounded, is gone for good. Meanwhile, the 'intellectual reality' He substituted for it (and to which He applied the same familiar name) is alive and well in the mathematics of modern theory. When physicists describe the abstract 'fabric' of the relativistic continuum or the mathematical 'ocean' of quantum space, they are describing a reality which (so far as I can see) is identical to what 'Abdu'l-Bahá called ether. Whatever we call it, it is the conceptual framework that links physical events and objects and which, in some mysterious non-mechanical way, transmits light and electromagnetism.

'Abdu'l-Bahá's terminology, though perhaps unorthodox, places Him in excellent company. Martin Gardner notes in

Relativity for the Million that a number of prominent physicists have, over the years, proposed restoring the name 'ether', though not in the old sense of an immutable frame of reference. (Gardner, *Relativity for the Million* 34-5). Sir Arthur Eddington, who understood relativity theory as well as anyone,* routinely used the traditional term 'ether' exactly as 'Abdu'l-Bahá did: He transferred it, that is, to the abstract notion of spacetime invoked by today's authorities. Thus Eddington defines light as 'aetherial vibrations of varying wave-lengths' and pictures himself 'hanging from a round planet head outward into space, and with a wind of aether blowing at no one knows how many miles a second through every interstice of my body' (Eddington, *Quantum Questions* 189, 208). Sir James Jeans writes in a similar vein: 'We can now see how the ether, in which all the events of the universe take place, could reduce to a mathematical abstraction and become as abstract and as mathematical as parallels of latitude and meridians of longitude' (Jeans, *Quantum Questions* 142). 'Although the classical concept of the ether is now considered obsolete,' explains L. Pearce Williams of Cornell University, 'the concept of space in modern physics retains certain affinities with an ether: space is not conceived as something totally vacuous but as the seat of various energetic processes' (Williams, 'Ether', *The Encyclopedia Americana*, 1989, vol. X, p. 609). Physicist Charles Misner is still more explicit: 'There is a billion dollar industry – the TV industry – which does nothing except produce in empty space potentialities for electrons, were they to be inserted there, to perform some motion. A vacuum so rich in marketable potentialities cannot properly be called a void; it is really an ether' (quoted in Yourgrau and Breck, *Cosmology, History, and Theology* 95; and Ferris, *Coming of Age* 352).

---

*It is said that Eddington, upon being told that he was one of only three people who truly understood Einstein's theory, paused, then said, 'I am trying to think who the third person is.'

The Collapse of Mechanical Models

PROPHECY 30: *The breakdown of mechanical models (literal images) as a basis for understanding the physical world.*

ABSTRACT: *Classical physics had relied for centuries on mechanical models as a supposedly all-sufficient basis for understanding the physical world. (A mechanical model is an image or replica corresponding in some objective way – not merely a metaphorical way – to the thing it represents.) 'Abdu'l-Bahá stated forcefully that 'nature . . . in its essence' is utterly incompatible with mechanical models. Its deepest building blocks can no more be expressed by objective description than can such abstractions as 'love' or 'truth'. Such assertions were, at that time, even more daring and radical than 'Abdu'l-Bahá's rejection of a material ether. Yet His insights were fully validated, more than fifteen years later, by the development of quantum mechanics – the mathematical description of subatomic particles and their behaviour. The resulting collapse of mechanical models lies at the very heart of the revolution in physics which, in this century, has shaken the world, transformed every aspect of modern life, and (in the words of Sir James Jeans) made the universe appear 'more like a great thought than like a great machine'.*

BACKGROUND: The disappearance of classical ether shook the mechanistic world view but did not, at the outset, destroy it. Scientists continued for some time to believe that everything real is objective, localized and consistent with mechanical models – even those things forever beyond detection by sensory means. They placed in this category the fundamental building blocks of nature itself – namely, subatomic particles.

It was well understood, since early in this century, that things are composed of atoms which in turn are composed of smaller components called protons, neutrons and electrons. The presence of these particles could be deduced from their indirect effects but they could not be sensed or seen, even with the strongest microscope. They simply were too small – so small that any amount of light, even a single photon, would knock them helter-skelter and fail to register them correctly. For all anyone knew, these particles could in turn be further subdivided.* Yet however deeply buried they might be, and whether one pictured them as miniature billiard balls, whirling sparks, or whatnot, the assumption remained that some literal image should apply. This meant it should be possible – at least in principle – to build a large-scale replica that would correctly mimic the behaviour of the atom and all its parts. Classical physics saw nothing wrong with such mechanical yet non-sensible entities.

However, if one accepted at face value 'Abdu'l-Bahá's distinction between 'sensible' and 'intellectual' realities, a doubt arose. It seemed to rule out not only a mechanical ether but mechanical atoms as well. He had already stated that whatever could not be sensed has 'no outward existence', 'no outward form and no place'. Nor was He timid about applying this principle to the fundamental realities of the physical world. Immediately after His statement redefining ether as a conceptual abstraction, He added: 'In the same way, nature, also, in its essence is an intellectual reality and is not sensible' (SAQ 84). If we could but peer beneath the facade of sense perception (He seemed to be saying), we would find that even the physical world is built upon a foundation that is abstract, unpicturable and non-localized.

Though they did not know it then (circa 1905), physicists were about to crack that facade. During the next few years they worked feverishly to make sense of new findings that were pouring in about atomic phenomena. Their objective was to find a workable mechanical model of the atom. Something, however, was wrong. The more one focused the picture, the fuzzier it became. The mechanical interpretation became increasingly strained and convoluted until scientists, in desperation, were forced to abandon it for theories with

*This turns out to be true, at least for protons and neutrons, which are composed of still smaller units called quarks.

strange overtones of mysticism.

First came the revelation (from Einstein's special theory of relativity in 1905) that matter is really congealed energy. Energy is defined in physics as 'the capacity to do work'; beyond this, it seems meaningless to ask what energy 'really' is. On the other hand, it feels odd to heft a stone and say, 'I'm holding a lump of hardened "capacity to do work"'. What could this mean?

A second shock came with the announcement by Niels Bohr, in 1913, that subatomic particles teleport – they move, that is, by vanishing in one spot and popping up in another, without having crossed the intervening space. The distances involved are short; longer trips are accomplished by a discontinuous series of short bursts or hops. Motion on the subatomic scale is not a flowing blend but a pattern of jumps, more like a Charlie Chaplin movie than a Baryshnikov ballet. Just as the still frames of a movie create the illusion of continuity, so do the 'quantum leaps' of moving matter.* Physicists gulped, but swallowed the picture.

Even more unsettling was the fact that the exact distance, direction and timing of each jump seemed, within limits, to be quite random. The absolute predestination implied by Newtonian mechanism was a myth; the past history of a particle did not completely determine its next move. Einstein, already nervous about where particle physics seemed

---

*The quantum leap is more than a mathematical convention; were it not real, the sun could not shine. As we have seen, it is nuclear fusion that powers the sun; and fusion occurs when one proton slams into another. Yet each proton is surrounded by a seamless electrical force-field called the Coulomb barrier. If protons moved in continuous lines, they would, in most cases, bounce off the barrier; the sun would freeze and the stars would wink out. In flashing instantly from point to point, however, a fortunate proton will sometimes pop through another's shield without having touched it. These random hits occur just often enough to keep the sun ablaze. We can all – quite literally – thank our lucky stars for this 'quantum tunnelling' to which we owe our lives.

headed, lost his patience over this one. 'I find the idea quite intolerable', he wrote, 'that an electron exposed to radiation should choose *of its own free will*, not only its moment to jump off, but also its direction' (Einstein, quoted in Born, *The Born-Einstein Letters* 82; and Ferris, *Coming of Age* 290; Einstein's italics). He argued that 'hidden variables', unknown and undetectable, must be in control. However, physicist John S. Bell later found a theorem proving that such variables, if they existed, would have to be capable of affecting events instantaneously throughout the universe. Since a basic premise of Einstein's theory is that no physical signal can travel faster than light, any hidden variables would 'border on what we now call psychic phenomena' (Wolf, *Taking the Quantum Leap* 201). This seemed even stranger and less mechanical than the picture Einstein rejected.

Just as light waves sometimes behaved like particles, so matter particles sometimes behaved like waves. A single electron, for instance, could spread like a wave, passing through two slits of a screen at the same time and producing an interference pattern; yet any and all efforts to observe it would detect only a pinpoint. Its behaviour was described by the 'Schrödinger pulse', a mathematical wave function with no recognizable form in physical space. It did not resemble a water wave, a sound wave or any other familiar analogy.

The decisive break with classical mechanics came in 1927 when Werner Heisenberg unveiled his famous uncertainty principle. This concerns the position and velocity of a subatomic particle. (Velocity is a combination of speed and direction; it is the mathematical description of a particle's motion.) On a superficial level, the uncertainty principle means we cannot measure both the position and velocity of a particle at the same time. Any method we use to evaluate one will perturb the other, so that we cannot know it. Unfortunately, a number of popular works on science give the misleading impression that there is nothing more to the uncertainty principle than that; nature (they imply) is simply hiding from our clumsy methods. If this were so, the principle would never have been the shattering revelation it was.

What Heisenberg found is not simply that we cannot *know* the precise position and velocity of a particle at the same time. He found that it cannot *have* them both at the same time. The special 'matrix' mathematics governing subatomic behaviour precludes the very existence of such simultaneous variables. The more there is to know about one, the less there is to know about the other – regardless of what we actually know. The more accurately we measure a particle's position, the more fuzzy its velocity becomes; and the more accurately we measure its velocity, the more fuzzy its position becomes. This fuzziness is not only in our minds; it is a property of the particle itself.

What of an unobserved particle? According to the standard interpretation of quantum mechanics, such a particle has an infinite number of different positions and velocities (a blur of overlapping histories, so to speak), each more or less probable, but none completely real. The particle is nothing more than a ghostly potentiality, a swirl of mutually exclusive possibilities each vying for the right to exist. By choosing to observe either its position or its velocity (for we cannot do both), we make the particle more real in that respect but at the cost of making it less real in the other.

The thundering implications of the uncertainty principle have barely begun to penetrate modern thought; even many professional philosophers seem strangely deaf to its rumble. Physics, says John A. Wheeler, has 'destroyed the concept of the world as "sitting out there". The universe will never afterwards be the same' (John A. Wheeler, quoted in Wolf, *Taking the Quantum Leap* 152). Quantum mechanics portrays the world not as a collection of concrete objects, nor even as tiny bits of 'stuff' swarming through mostly empty space, but as a statistical composite of shifting probabilities. Any large-scale object is a vast collection of such quasi-abstract entities – entities which, by augmenting one another, invest the object with a semblance of position, motion and recognizable form. Each in itself, however, is entirely unpicturable, with no distinct location in space and time. Modern physics thus confirms what 'Abdu'l-Bahá taught long before: The natural universe below the reach of sense perception is, in its essence, utterly incompatible with mechanical models. We can describe it not by any literal image but only by symbols and metaphors. 'When it comes to atoms,' writes Niels Bohr, 'language can be used only as in poetry' (Bohr, quoted in Ferris, *Coming of Age* 384).

The subjective, non-local nature of the material universe is no mere philosophical teaser; it can be – and has been – tested by laboratory experiment. John Clauser, a physicist with the University of California at Berkeley, is one who has done so, using insights derived from the Bell theorem mentioned above. Summarizing his results, he writes:

> Physicists have consistently attempted to model microscopic phenomena in terms of objective entities, preferably with some definable structure . . . We have found that it is not possible to do so in a natural way, consistent with locality, without an observable change in the experimental predictions (Clauser, quoted in *Taking the Quantum Leap* 206).

It is fitting that physics – the most concrete of the so-called 'hard sciences' – was the first to confirm the metaphorical nature of physical reality affirmed by 'Abdu'l-Bahá. Since the dawn of quantum mechanics in the 1920s, virtually every major physics breakthrough has in some way reinforced this outlook. The result has been, in the words of Sir James Jeans, 'a wide measure of agreement which, on the physical side of science, approaches almost to unanimity that the stream of knowledge is heading towards a nonmechanical reality; the universe begins to look more like a great thought than like a great machine' (Jeans, *Quantum Questions* 144).

9

Prophetic Fruits:
Things to Come

Surely the Sovereign Lord does nothing without revealing
his plan to his servants the prophets (Amos 3:7 NIV).

Virtually all of the predictions we discussed in Chapters 7
and 8 concern events that might easily have served to discredit Bahá'u'lláh (and which seemed likely at the time to do
so). The fates of the most powerful sovereigns and empires
of His day; the occurrence and outcome of two bloody World
Wars; the dramatic rise – and equally dramatic fall – of
communism; specific developments in Israel and America,
in the Christian, Muslim and Bahá'í Faiths, in physics, cosmology, palaeontology and medicine – any of these might
have turned out differently in such a way as to cast doubt
upon Bahá'u'lláh's claim. Napoleon III, Sulṭán 'Abdu'l-'Azíz
or Náṣiri'd-Dín Sháh might have been spared an untimely
end. Queen Victoria might, like most of her royal contemporaries, have fallen from power. Germany might have won (or
avoided altogether) either of the great wars on which it
embarked. Communism might never have gained worldwide
importance, or, having gained such importance, it might
have gone on to gain world domination as well. Bahá'u'lláh
might have died in prison. His Faith, like every world religion before it, might have broken into sects and factions.
Nuclear power and transmutation of elements might have
proved impossible. Piltdown Man might have been established as a genuine 'missing link' as more fossil specimens
came to light. Classical physics might have successfully

fought off the challenges posed by relativity and quantum mechanics.

None of these things came to pass. Instead, the Bahá'í prophecies (most of which sounded preposterous in the beginning) were in every instance fulfilled by seemingly improbable events that clicked into place with clockwork precision.

Coincidence? Mere human foresight? Hardly. This is an imposing array of facts calling for a serious and considered explanation. God in His Word assures us that 'there is none like me, declaring the end from the beginning'. Perfect predictive power comes only from Him, through the inspiration of the Holy Spirit. Anyone who claims to reveal God's will, to speak with His voice, must vindicate such a claim by this unique token of divine authority: 'Produce your cause, saith the Lord . . . Let them bring them forth, and shew us what shall happen . . . Shew the things that are to come hereafter . . .' (Isa. 41:21-3). Does Bahá'u'lláh measure up to this biblical criterion?

In considering this evidence, we may well wonder whether Bahá'u'lláh (or those whose authority He endorsed) made any further prophecies not detailed above. If so, how did these fare? The answer is that the Báb, Bahá'u'lláh and 'Abdu'l-Bahá all did make additional predictions. Many are found in their personal correspondence and involve events in the private lives of lesser-known individuals (some of them Bahá'ís, some not). These too – in every single case with which I am familiar – have stood the test of time. However, I am in no position to undertake a comprehensive review of such prophecies, nor would space permit it. Instead I have focused on those which involve major events and figures, and of which the outcomes can be verified by any reader with access to a good library.

Also absent from the above review is any discussion of prophecies derived primarily from anecdote, hearsay or unconfirmed conversations. Such second-hand reports, however useful they may be, are not considered Bahá'í scripture and are not binding on believers. The foregoing compilation relies only on statements from the authenticated writings of the Bahá'í founders or from authorized, verbatim transcripts of their formal talks. Other Bahá'í prophecies are expressed simply as hints or clues, or – like the 'sealed' visions of the Bible – in deliberately coded language. Since these are meant to be understood, if at all, only after their fulfilment, they have no place in this discussion. Nor would it make sense to dwell here on long-range prophecies (such as the Most Great Peace) which may yet take centuries to unfold. We must decide on the basis of evidence available within our own earthly lifetimes – and such evidence we already have in abundance.

There is, however, one last category of Bahá'í prophecy that warrants attention. It consists of relatively short-range predictions involving events that even now are unfolding in the world. While none of the half-dozen or so prophecies in this category can yet claim to be completely fulfilled, all are at least partially fulfilled and new events move daily in the directions they indicate. Although His followers are long accustomed to seeing Bahá'u'lláh's predictions materialize on live news broadcasts, the experience never loses its tingling sense of immediacy. Here, then, are some on-going dramas and prophesied outcomes that Bahá'ís watch with confidence:

Unity in Freedom

Bahá'u'lláh wrote: 'After a time, all the governments on earth will change. Oppression will envelop the world. And following a universal convulsion, the sun of justice will rise from the horizon of the unseen realm' (PDC 166-17). Shortly after World War I 'Abdu'l-Bahá described the 'prevailing state of the world' as one of 'irreligion and consequent anarchy' which He said would bring in its wake a 'temporary reversion to coercive government' (BNE 247-8). The accent was on 'temporary', for He wrote elsewhere that the world must eventually achieve 'unity in freedom' (SAB 32). Stressing the connection between peace and freedom, He said: 'To cast aside centralization which promotes despotism is the exigency of the time. This will be productive of international peace' (PUP 167).

The twentieth century has indeed seen a worldwide tide of totalitarianism and coercive government on a scale unprecedented in history. Today, that tide clearly is ebbing. The collapse of colonialism, of communism and of countless other 'isms' has brought representative government and economic freedom within reach of countless peoples who once lived in virtual slavery. Bursting upon the world stage as if from nowhere, a worldwide pro-democracy movement has scored victory after victory on every continent. Floodgates of information have been opened, bringing news and knowledge to people in every corner of the globe via radio, television, computers, fax machines, copiers, the Internet and a host of other rapidly evolving technologies. The resulting freedom of thought has struck terror into the heart of every would-be dictator, for only by suppressing ideas can any government long suppress its people.

Dictatorships there still are, of course, as well as many other forms of oppression and exploitation. The tide of history, however, seems at last to have turned, making the worldwide triumph of freedom likely if not inevitable. There may yet be generations of struggle, punctuated by countless setbacks, before such a vision can become reality; but it no longer seems naive to believe in it. Small wonder the Universal House of Justice has written, 'The spirit of liberty which in recent decades has swept over the planet with such tempestuous force is a manifestation of the vibrancy of the Revelation brought by Bahá'u'lláh' (The Universal House of Justice, *Individual Rights and Freedoms* 31).

Swords into Plowshares

More than a century ago Bahá'u'lláh urged the world's rulers to hammer out a peace treaty enshrining one inviolable principle: 'Should any one among you take up arms against another, rise ye all against him, for this is naught but manifest justice' (WOB 40). This simple policy, He argued, once adopted by mutual consent, then enforced consistently and without favouritism by collective action, would abolish war.* Thus would be fulfilled the vision of Isaiah and Micah: 'they shall beat their swords into plowshares, and their spears into pruninghooks: nation shall not lift up sword against nation, neither shall they learn war any more' (Isa. 2:4).

Bahá'u'lláh predicted categorically that the world's Great Powers, driven by 'imperative necessity', would one day forge just such a peace. As noted above, He taught that this 'Lesser Peace' would be, at first, little more than a political truce – one that would in no way solve all the world's problems or halt what He called 'the corrosion of ungodliness . . . eating into the vitals of human society' (G 200). However, it would pave the way for the gradual healing and spiritualization of the world through His Revelation, leading in the fullness of time to what He called the 'Most Great Peace' – the millennial Kingdom when 'the earth shall be filled with the knowledge of the Lord, as the waters cover the sea' (Isa. 11:9).

While Bahá'ís recognize that the Most Great Peace may take centuries to achieve, they find in their sacred teachings many signs that 'the Lesser Peace cannot be too far distant . . .' (Letter of the Universal House of Justice, April 1990). 'Abdu'l-Bahá foretold that substantial progress towards world peace, including some unspecified but critically important threshold in its development, would materialize

---

*Bahá'u'lláh's peace plan, we should note, is based neither upon idealistic pacifism nor upon any naive assumption that evil men will willingly curb their sinful and militant natures. While calling for a sane measure of disarmament, it requires that each nation retain sufficient force both to defend itself and to keep internal order. Without such capability, there would be no way to enforce the plan's key provision – namely, that warlike behaviour by any one nation be met with the armed resistance of all others.

within this century: '. . .the unity of nations . . . in this century will be firmly established, causing all the peoples of the world to regard themselves as citizens of one common fatherland' (WOB 39). The dramatic ending of the Cold War, the rapid emergence of a global economy, new technologies for world travel and communication – these and many more trends have already swept away barriers to peace that only yesterday appeared insurmountable. Meanwhile, the development of ever deadlier and more horrifying doomsday weapons renders what Bahá'u'lláh called the 'imperative necessity' for peace daily more imperative.

Humanity's Ordeal

Few things worth having come easily, least of all world peace. Bahá'u'lláh makes it clear that the road to peace will be rocky and painful. We have already quoted His words to the effect that the 'sun of justice' will rise only after a 'universal convulsion' and that 'imperative necessity' will drive the world's leaders to establish peace. Many Bahá'í prophecies suggest that a key factor in the emergence of world peace will be a great calamity or catastrophe destined to shake humankind out of its apathy. Bahá'u'lláh writes:

> The world is in travail and its agitation waxeth day by day. Its face is turned towards waywardness and unbelief. Such shall be its plight that to disclose it now would not be meet and seemly. Its perversity will long continue. And when the appointed hour is come, there shall suddenly appear that which shall cause the limbs of mankind to quake. Then and only then will the Divine Standard be unfurled and the Nightingale of Paradise warble its melody (WOB 33).

Bahá'ís do not claim to know the exact nature of this apocalyptic upheaval – military, economic, environmental or something completely unexpected. It could be a continuation or intensification of the chaotic social breakdown already in evidence around us. What is certain, according to the Bahá'í writings, is that the longer Bahá'u'lláh the Divine Physician, is 'withheld from healing the ills of the world, the more severe will be the crises, and the more terrible the sufferings of the patient' (Shoghi Effendi, 21 November 1949, LOG 131). Bahá'u'lláh emphasizes that the calamity, though tragic in its immediate effects, will in the long run prove to have been both necessary and providential. According to the Bahá'í teachings:

> The flames which His Divine justice have kindled cleanse an unregenerate humanity, and fuse its discordant, its warring elements as no other agency can cleanse or fuse them. It is not only a retributory and destructive fire, but a disciplinary and creative process . . . God's purpose is none other than to usher in, in ways He alone can bring about, and the full significance of which He alone can fathom, the Great, the Golden Age of a long-divided, a long-afflicted humanity. Its present state, indeed even its immediate future, is dark, distressingly dark. Its distant future, however, is radiant, gloriously radiant – so radiant that no eye can visualize it (PDC 116).

The Destiny of America

In His Book of Laws (the Kitáb-i-Aqdas or Most Holy Book) Bahá'u'lláh confers upon the 'Rulers of America and the Presidents of the Republics therein' a mandate unlike that of any other nation: 'Bind ye the broken with the hands of justice, and crush the oppressor who flourisheth with the rod of the commandments of your Lord, the Ordainer, the All-Wise' (Kitáb-i-Aqdas para. 88). However great its many shortcomings, America has, in countless ways, already risen to carry out this divine mission. Throughout the world she has raised the banner of human rights, serving as a tireless advocate for liberty and self-government. 'Abdu'l-Bahá writes: 'The continent of America is in the eyes of the one true God the land wherein the splendours of His light shall be revealed, where the mysteries of His Faith shall be unveiled, where the righteous will abide and the free assemble' (WOB 75). Lauding the past accomplishments of its people and government, He says, 'Its future is even more promising, for its influence and illumination are far-reaching. It will lead all nations spiritually' (WOB 76).

'Abdu'l-Bahá knew that America could never fulfil such promises without first overcoming a number of grave weaknesses. We have already seen, for example, that He regarded racial prejudice as a threat to America's very survival. He held a similar view of the dangers inherent in materialism and moral decline. Commenting on these warnings and promises, Shoghi Effendi writes of America:

> Tribulations, on a scale unprecedented in its history, and calculated to purge its institutions, to purify the hearts of its people, to fuse its constituent elements, and to weld it into one entity with its sister nations in both hemispheres, are inevitable (CF 37).

> The woes and tribulations which threaten it are partly avoidable, but mostly inevitable and God-sent . . . These same fiery tribulations will not only firmly weld the American nation to its sister nations in both hemispheres, but will through their cleansing effect, purge it thoroughly of the accumulated dross which ingrained racial prejudice, rampant materialism, widespread ungodliness and moral laxity have combined, in the course of successive generations, to produce, and which have prevented her thus far from assuming the role of world spiritual leadership forecast by 'Abdu'l-Bahá's unerring pen – a role which she is bound to fulfil through travail and sorrow' (CF 126-7).

The two remaining prophecies concern the future of the Bahá'í Faith itself.

The Bahá'ís of Persia

The Faith of Bahá'u'lláh has been bitterly persecuted in His native land since its inception in 1844. Twenty thousand early believers were slain, many after appalling torture. Believers have endured systematic discrimination and sporadic violence to the present day. Hundreds of Bahá'ís were executed following Persia's Islamic revolution of 1979 and hundreds of thousands more are, at this time, denied work, education, legal marriage, pensions, freedom of assembly and other basic rights.

Bahá'u'lláh has promised that God will eventually bless Persia with a just ruler who 'will gather together the flock of God which the wolves have scattered. Such a ruler will, with joy and gladness, turn his face towards, and extend his favours unto, the people of Bahá' (Kitáb-i-Aqdas para. 91). An authoritative summary of Bahá'í prophecies states: 'The sovereign who, as foreshadowed in Bahá'u'lláh's Most Holy Book, must adorn the throne of His native land, and cast the shadow of royal protection over His long-persecuted followers, is as yet undiscovered' (GPB 411).

Growth and Opposition

Bahá'í sacred writings forecast a remarkable increase in the membership of the Faith, swelling from a trickle to a steady stream, and finally to large-scale enrolments in many countries. No one who has tracked the history of the movement can fail to see the beginnings of this process in India, Africa, South America, the Caribbean and other lands. Since 1963, when there were about 400,000 Bahá'ís worldwide, membership in the Cause has grown to nearly six million believers. If its explosive growth has gone largely unnoticed, that is only because the Bahá'í Faith has simultaneously become (as attested by the World Christian Encyclopedia and the Encyclopedia Britannica) the most widespread world religion other than Christianity. These converging trends – numerical growth and geographical diffusion – are rapidly raising it out of obscurity throughout the planet.

Bahá'ís see these victories as only the first signs of the coming mass acceptance. Their scriptures further predict that the Faith's expansion and consolidation will eventually bring strong opposition not only in Persia but in America, Europe, Asia and Africa. Despite this expectation, Bahá'ís do not court opposition or seek controversy. Wherever they live, they are law-abiding citizens, loyal to their respective governments; they strictly avoid political entanglements; and they foster cordial relations with all religions and progressive social movements. Neither in appearance nor in reality are they a threat to the well-being of others. The Faith's claims, however, are imposing, its laws and principles challenging, and its proposed reforms deep and far-reaching. One must expect these to excite misgivings and, at times, resistance.

Bahá'ís are confident that opposition will not harm the long-term prospects of their Cause. Rather, they feel that such opposition – like the persecution of early Christians – will invite closer public scrutiny, lead to a clearer understanding of the Faith's claims and purposes, and eventually dispel the apprehension that prompted resistance in the first place.

If any of these predictions sound incredible, we may well ponder the words of Arthur C. Clarke: 'Most of the things that have happened in the last fifty years have been fantastic, and it is only by assuming that they will continue to be so that we have any hope of anticipating the future' (*Profiles of the Future*, 29). Most great historical and scientific developments seem incredible or even impossible until after the fact; only in hindsight do they appear inevitable.

The dozens of explicit Bahá'í prophecies that have already been fulfilled seemed every bit as startling, when first uttered, as the handful that remain. Most of the latter are already partially fulfilled and new events bring them daily nearer to reality. 'Abdu'l-Bahá's confident assertion, uttered

almost ninety awesomely turbulent years ago, today rings
truer than ever:

> . . . all that was recorded in the Tablets to the Kings is being
> fulfilled: if from the year AD 1870 we compare the events
> that have occurred, we will find everything that has hap-
> pened has appeared as predicted; only a few remain which
> will afterward become manifested (SAQ 33-4).

10

How Knoweth this Man Letters?

And the spirit of the Lord shall rest upon him, the spirit of wisdom and understanding, the spirit of counsel and might, the spirit of knowledge and of the fear of the Lord; And shall make him of quick understanding in the fear of the Lord (Isa. 11:2-3).

O the depth of the riches both of the wisdom and knowledge of God! (Rom. 11:33).

Prophecy need not always be expressed as mere prediction – as a statement of the form 'such-and-such will happen'. When Bahá'u'lláh revealed that elements can change their chemical identities, He was explaining something that had always been true. His announcement was nevertheless prophetic in that it disclosed an as-yet-unknown reality destined someday to be made manifest. Divine revelation can show us 'things to come' not only by stating predictions but also by disclosing knowledge that is ahead of its time, by anticipating future problems and solutions or in countless other ways.

Those who reveal God's Word must be able to prophesy in this larger sense. We can easily imagine a psychic able to predict the future with pinpoint accuracy (right down to, say, stock market fluctuations), yet unable to produce anything of lasting spiritual or social value. Jesus and the inspired writers of the Bible clearly were much more than this. As a result, the Bible's influence went beyond individual salvation. It forged a new civilization, more advanced than any before, blazing its trail and lighting its path for centuries. An achievement so profound requires knowledge of the future but also related knowledge of many other kinds. God demands of all who speak in His name that they show not only 'the things that are to come hereafter' but also 'the former things, what they be, that we may consider them . . .' (Isa. 41:22-3). Truly prophetic knowledge is all-encompassing.

The Bible emphasizes a further characteristic of revealed wisdom. It is bestowed by God alone, not by any amount of training, research or experience. We read in John's Gospel:

> Now about the midst of the feast Jesus went up into the temple, and taught. And the Jews marvelled, saying, How knoweth this man letters, never having learned? (John 7:14-15).

Being one with God's Spirit, Christ was (as the Bahá'í teachings say) 'omniscient at will' (UD 449). He had no need of human schooling, for infinite knowledge was woven into His very being. Christ's family history and background were familiar to the people, who knew very well He had had no formal education. (He was, after all, a 'mere' carpenter's son.) Yet in His every encounter with the scribes and Pharisees, He bested them effortlessly. These exchanges, as recorded in the Bible, testify not only to His incomparable wisdom and insight but to the fact He towered above His learned adversaries even in their own fields of study.

Dramatic signs of this innate knowledge were visible in Christ from childhood. When He was twelve, and Joseph and Mary could not locate Him after a trip to Jerusalem, they searched frantically:

> . . . after three days they found him in the temple, sitting in the midst of the doctors, both hearing them, and asking them questions. And all that heard him were astonished at his understanding and answers (Luke 2:46-7).

The Bible thus shows that inborn, untutored knowledge is

an inherent characteristic of Christ. We may reasonably infer that His latter-day manifestation – described in the Bible as 'one like unto the Son of man' (Rev. 1:13) – should possess this same perfection. These considerations suggest several ways of probing more deeply into Bahá'u'lláh's claim. How extensive, we may ask, was His knowledge? Could it reasonably be regarded as 'prophetic' in the broader sense described above (and not merely that of making accurate predictions)? Did He undergo schooling or engage in research? Were His insights radically beyond the established standards of His day? Did He display skills or abilities that no amount of training could confer? Most important, was His knowledge of 'things to come' sufficiently comprehensive to fit Him for His stated mission – the launching of a new and higher civilization?

Such questions are of course fraught with value judgements concerning which reasonable people may well differ. Nevertheless, the facts of Bahá'u'lláh's life are sufficiently well documented that any serious inquirer can proceed with considerable confidence. For anyone seeking to assess Bahá'u'lláh's authenticity in light of the Bible, these questions can shed much additional light on the issues probed in the preceding chapters.

Bahá'u'lláh's Background

Bahá'u'lláh's native Persia was a land of rich culture and startling contrasts. It was the remnant of an ancient civilization which, at its height, had dominated most of the civilized world. In Old Testament days, Zoroastrian Persia had ruled an empire stretching from 'the inner confines of India and China to the farthermost reaches of Yemen and Ethiopia' (SDC 7). During her long and glamorous history, Persia produced kings such as Cyrus and Darius; poets such as Ḥáfiẓ, Rúmí, Sa'dí and 'Umar Khayyám; and artisans who dazzled the world with unrivalled carpets, steel blades, pottery and other handiwork. 'This fairest of lands', writes

'Abdu'l-Bahá, 'was once a lamp, streaming with the rays of Divine knowledge, of science and art, of nobility and high achievement, of wisdom and valour' (SDC 9).

By the eighteenth and nineteenth centuries, however, Persia had sunk into an appalling state of backwardness and decay. It had become, in the words of Sir Valentine Chirol, 'a country gangrened with corruption and atrophied with indifferentism' (Sir Valentine Chirol, *The Middle Eastern Question* 121, quoted in *Appreciations of the Bahá'í Faith* 21). Persia's people – rich and poor, learned and illiterate – were drowning in superstition and fanaticism. The country was a feudal autocracy whose rulers wielded iron control over a docile and apathetic populace. Its Muslim priesthood, vested with enormous political power, maintained sway over both rulers and populace by regularly whipping both into an emotional frenzy. Women were regarded as little more than livestock, foreigners and religious minorities as accursed heathen, and liberal ideas generally as satanic. Criminals were tortured to death in carnival-like public celebrations, the word 'criminal' being loosely construed to mean anyone who happened to displease the local priest or governor. Bribery was the indispensable lubricant of every transaction, public or private.

This was the environment of Bahá'u'lláh's formative years – the only one He knew prior to assuming His prophetic ministry. The suffocating effects of this benighted social atmosphere pervaded every department of life, including education. Most Persians were entirely uneducated, and even the upper classes (which included the nobility, government officials and well-to-do merchants) seldom aspired to anything beyond functional literacy. Male children of privileged families customarily received a few years of home tutoring in reading and writing, with emphasis on the Qur'án, Persian religious poetry and ornate penmanship. Despite its artistic flavour, such training was rudimentary, far greater importance being attached to marksmanship, swordplay, horseback riding and other physical skills. With rare exceptions, formal schooling was reserved for the Islamic professional clergy, whose members were accepted without question as the divinely-intended custodians of knowledge. These men, fiercely protective of their elite status, regarded both the nobility and the peasantry as inferior beings unfit for higher learning.

Being the child of a prominent government official, Bahá'u'lláh received the same sketchy tutoring as others of His high rank. By the standards of His own society He was literate but not learned. At no time did He attend school or devote Himself to scholarly pursuits. This very lack of academic grounding soon excited comment as He acquired a reputation for unusual knowledge and insight. As a young man He repeatedly astounded the divines by unravelling mysteries that had defied their collective ingenuity. On one occasion He appeared at the royal court to argue a case on behalf of His father, winning a favourable verdict. Both before and after He became known as head of the Bahá'í movement, His erudition won the respect of outstanding scholars and men of letters throughout the Middle East, including many who did not believe Him to be divinely inspired. Experts in diverse fields sought and received His help in solving problems peculiar to their own specialties; and even His enemies were wont to call Him 'the renowned Bahá'u'lláh'. His voluminous letters, addressed to persons from a wide assortment of ethnic and religious communities, show intimate familiarity with the diverse scriptural, historical and literary traditions of those people.

This preeminence which Bahá'u'lláh – an unschooled individual – gained among scholars and savants offers a striking parallel to the historical record of Christ. We find an extraordinary example in *God Passes By*, Shoghi Effendi's history of the Bahá'í Faith. Shortly after His banishment to Iraq, Bahá'u'lláh withdrew for two years into the wilderness of Kurdistan. This was almost a decade before the formal declaration in 1863 of His mission; and no one in the region, at that time, had any inkling of His identity. For a while He lived alone in a cave on a mountain called Sar-Galú. Soon, however, He happened to meet the head of an outstanding theological seminary* in nearby Sulaymáníyyih. This man, taking a liking to Bahá'u'lláh, persuaded Him to move to that town and accept a room owned by the seminary. His appearance there brought Bahá'u'lláh into contact with three leading lights of Sunní Islam – men who, despite their own immense stature, quickly became devoted admirers and freely acknowledged Him their superior. These were Shaykh 'Uthmán, leader of the Naqshbandíyyih Order, whose adherents included the sultán and his court; Shaykh 'Abdu'r-Rahmán, leader of the Qádiríyyih Order, who commanded the allegiance of at least a hundred thousand devout followers; and Shaykh Ismá'íl, head of the seminary and leader of the Khálidíyyih Order – a man so venerated that his supporters considered him co-equal with Khálid, the order's almost legendary founder. Shoghi Effendi writes:

> When Bahá'u'lláh arrived in Sulaymáníyyih none at first, owing to the strict silence and reserve He maintained, suspected Him of being possessed of any learning or wisdom. It was only accidentally, through seeing a specimen of His exquisite penmanship shown to them by one of the students who waited upon Him, that the curiosity of the learned instructors and students of that seminary was aroused, and they were impelled to approach Him and test the degree of His knowledge and the extent of His familiarity with the arts and sciences current amongst them (GPB 122).

A delegation headed by Shaykh Ismá'íl himself, and consisting of the seminary's most eminent doctors and most distinguished students, called upon Bahá'u'lláh, requesting that He expound for them the most complex themes from a celebrated but extraordinarily difficult book by the famous Andalusian mystic Shaykh Muhyi'd-Dín-i-'Arabí. 'God is My

---

*The seminary was called Takyiy-i-Mawláná Khálid.

witness', was Bahá'u'lláh's instant reply, 'that I have never seen the book you refer to. I regard, however, through the power of God . . . whatever you wish me to do as easy of accomplishment.' A series of daily interviews followed, in which Bahá'u'lláh 'was able to resolve their perplexities in so amazing a fashion that they were lost in admiration'. Not only did He clarify for them the book's obscure passages and its author's thinking, He also corrected various errors in the text, supporting His views with 'proofs and evidences that were wholly convincing to His listeners' (GPB 122-3).

As the fame of this episode spread, the region's inhabitants – scholars, mystics, princes and peasants – began to throng Bahá'u'lláh's door, plying Him with questions. He replied with 'numerous discourses and epistles' which, in Shoghi Effendi's words, 'disclosed new vistas to their eyes, resolved the perplexities that agitated their minds, unfolded the inner meaning of many hitherto obscure passages in the writings of the various commentators, poets and theologians, of which they had remained unaware, and reconciled the seemingly contradictory assertions which abounded in these dissertations, poems and treatises' (GPB 123-4). Magnetized by His love, the people of Kurdistan showered Him with esteem and affection. At no time during this period (1854-6) did Bahá'u'lláh openly announce His claim or unveil His divine station. Descendants of these overwhelmingly non-Bahá'í Arabs, a century and a half later, still wonder as to the identity of the amazing 'wise man' who tarried in their midst, and still cherish souvenirs and stories of His visit handed down by their forefathers.

Such was the impression Bahá'u'lláh made upon His most illustrious contemporaries. We cannot, of course, afford to rely blindly on their judgement, any more than we would rely blindly on those who denounced Him. Fortunately, most of Bahá'u'lláh's original writings have been preserved; a comprehensive and representative selection have been translated into English (as well as into many other languages); and more translations are appearing all the time.

Bahá'u'lláh did not restrict His writing to such stereotypically 'religious' topics as metaphysics and character development. He revealed divine principles governing law, international relations, arms control, political administration, education, group dynamics, economics, health, psychology, medicine and science, to name just a few. These writings, along with the large and growing body of scholarly literature they have evoked, make it fairly easy for any thoughtful reader to assess Bahá'u'lláh's contributions objectively. Many distinguished people, familiar with these contributions in their respective fields yet themselves not Bahá'ís, have praised His work in terms scarcely less glowing than those of His nineteenth-century admirers.

Vast erudition is not necessarily a token of divine inspiration. We do not regard men such as Aristotle, Leonardo da Vinci, Isaac Newton or Albert Einstein as bearers of revealed truth. One reason is that we can, by studying their lives, trace their gradual acquisition of knowledge through years of schooling and research. Westerners often approach the study of Bahá'u'lláh with the preconception that He can be explained in the same way – that His was a brilliant and creative mind, blossoming under the benign influence of a cosmopolitan environment, advanced education and contact with other similarly gifted individuals. His brilliance and creativity are not, of course, in doubt; but every other element of this explanation is false. Bahá'u'lláh grew to adulthood in an atmosphere of extreme prejudice, fanaticism, superstition and ignorance. The limited education He received offered nothing to counteract the pernicious influence of His early conditioning or to explain the phenomenal knowledge and vision He displayed. We may – indeed we must – say He rose above the limitations of His environment. We cannot explain Him as its product.

Recognizing this fact, we may suspect that Bahá'u'lláh was simply a self-taught prodigy. Those of us who live in the twentieth-century West tend to believe that any sufficiently motivated person can acquire an education by voracious reading. However, matters were not so simple in nineteenth-century Persia. Bahá'u'lláh was from His earliest youth a well-known, highly visible figure, at a time when it was unthinkable for a man of his station to pursue higher learning. Public libraries were unknown. Books – often hand-copied – were rare and exorbitantly expensive. Scholarly reference libraries were confined to Muslim theological universities, where they were haunted by the clergy – men who would have bristled at the thought of a 'lesser mortal' invading their sacred turf. Bahá'u'lláh might have found a way to gain access to a university library or He might (by spending a large chunk of the family fortune) have built up a useful private collection. But He could not have carried out either project, much less devoted years of His life to research and study, without attracting widespread attention. So brazen an affront to the rigid customs of Persian society would have raised eyebrows, and aroused indignation, throughout much of the country.

The fact that Bahá'u'lláh did none of these things is one of the strongest points of agreement between His supporters and His avowed enemies. When He advanced His claim to manifest the divine spirit, His adversaries – missing the point altogether – countered by stressing His entire lack of higher education. Many found it impossible to believe that God might choose as His instrument of revelation someone who had never earned a degree in theology. Bahá'u'lláh acknowledges their protests:

> Lay not aside the fear of God, O ye the learned of the world, and judge fairly the cause of this unlettered One . . . Certain ones among both commoners and nobles have objected that this wronged One is neither a member of the ecclesiastical order nor a descendant of the Prophet. Say: O ye that claim to be just! Reflect a little while, and ye shall recognize how infinitely exalted is His present state above the station ye claim He should possess. The Will of the Almighty hath decreed that out of a house wholly devoid

of all that the divines, the doctors, the sages and scholars commonly possess His Cause shall proceed and be made manifest (G 98-9).

His Tablet to the Sháh states:

> . . . the breezes of the All-Glorious were wafted over Me, and taught me the knowledge of all that hath been . . . The learning current amongst men I studied not; their schools I entered not. Ask of the city wherein I dwelt, that thou mayest be well assured that I am not of them who speak falsely (ESW 39).

Still, a fact is one thing, its interpretation quite another. There is no serious doubt that Bahá'u'lláh – like Jesus – was 'unlettered'. A sceptic may well wonder, however, whether His supposedly innate knowledge has been exaggerated. One can always construct elaborate scenarios purporting to show how Bahá'u'lláh might have acquired the necessary training in secrecy. However unwarranted or far-fetched such ideas may be, many people understandably find it easier to accept them than to entertain the idea that Christ has returned. It would therefore be helpful if we could identify specific features of Bahá'u'lláh's knowledge that cannot easily be dismissed as overblown or explained away as the result of clandestine study.

As it happens, there are several such features. One of them we have already explored in detail – namely, the occurrence in Bahá'u'lláh's writings of many daring but accurate predictions. However, there are at least three other factors which, given His situation, weigh heavily against any effort to equate His knowledge with ordinary human learning. These are 1) the farsightedness of Bahá'u'lláh's social principles, 2) His phenomenal mastery of Arabic, and 3) the speed and spontaneity with which He composed His writings. Let us examine each of these factors more closely.

Farsightedness

The characteristic I call 'farsightedness' refers to the way Bahá'u'lláh's teachings have consistently proved to be ahead of their time. A century after His ascension – a century during which the world has changed more than in all previous recorded history – His writings remain astoundingly modern in tone, outlook and substance; in fact, this modernity becomes more striking each year. The change, of course, has been not in His writings but rather in the world itself as it has developed along lines that render His teachings ever more suitable to its needs. Bahá'u'lláh did not write only about the world in which He lived. He also wrote, explicitly and with exceptional insight, about the world in which we live today – a global village entering the twenty-first century. In so doing He gave humanity its *first comprehensive inventory* of the principles now generally held to be on the cutting edge of social advancement. His proposals have set the agenda for all the great upheavals and reform struggles that have raged ever since.

Bible scholar George Townshend, an eminent Anglican clergyman who became a Bahá'í, writing together with Shoghi Effendi, describes this evolutionary process as follows:

> The humanitarian and spiritual principles enunciated decades ago in the darkest East by Bahá'u'lláh and moulded by Him into a coherent scheme are one after the other being taken by a world unconscious of their source as the marks of progressive civilization (Introduction to *The Dawn-Breakers* xxxvi).

Commenting elsewhere on the same phenomenon, he writes:

> Slowly the veil lifts from the future. Along whatever road thoughtful men look out they see before them some guiding truth, some leading principle, which Bahá'u'lláh gave long ago and which men rejected (Introduction to *God Passes By* ix).

273

This gradual (and largely unconscious) adoption of Bahá'í ideals as symbols of enlightened modernism has become the twentieth century's single most pervasive trend. Examples abound – an especially revealing one occurred in April 1963, the month when Bahá'ís celebrated the centenary of Bahá'u'lláh's formal declaration of His mission.

In that very month Pope John XXIII issued his last pastoral letter, the encyclical *Pacem in Terris* (Peace on Earth). This brilliant document – a summary of prerequisites for peace and progress in the decades ahead – evoked worldwide praise from non-Catholics and Catholics alike. It eventually earned a Nobel Peace Prize for its author. Pope John did not claim originality for any of his points. He presented them simply as a fusion and synthesis of the best in contemporary thought, weaving them into a single package in order to bring them to the forefront of public discussion. The principles were: 1) creation of a world community; 2) independent investigation of truth; 3) universal education; 4) equality of men and women; 5) abolition of prejudice; 6) recognition of the oneness of God; 7) the reconciliation of science and religion; 8) world disarmament; 9) a spiritual approach to economics; and 10) loyalty to government. Also included was a warning on the dangers of atomic energy.*

Every one of these points is a recurring theme of Bahá-'u'lláh's writings.** With the exception of His own warn-

---

*For detailed citations from *Pacem in Terris*, correlating its highlights with those of Bahá'u'lláh's writings, see Ugo Giachery, 'One God, One Truth, One People', *Bahá'í World*, vol. XV, pp. 612-19.

**There is no invariable, stock list of 'official' Bahá'í principles. Bahá'u'lláh's writings seldom contain descriptive headings; they cover thousands of topics and defy easy categorization. To indicate the spirit of His teachings, however, Bahá'í writers generally list eight to twelve thematic ideas, rewording or rearranging them slightly to suit the context. Two important Bahá'í principles are missing from *Pacem in Terris* — the essential unity of all religions and the adoption of a universal auxiliary language. Otherwise, its main points correspond
(continued...)

ing on atomic energy (circa 1890), they all are major planks of the peace programme He drafted in the late 1860s and early 1870s, and which He in that same period called to the attention of world leaders (including Pope Pius IX). Bahá-'u'lláh, unlike Pope John, gave detailed guidance on translating these matters from theory into practice. By the time the Pope announced the principles, they had already become familiar to enlightened men and women everywhere. Bahá-'u'lláh, on the other hand, announced them at a time when they were largely unknown both to leaders of thought and the public; their feasibility had not been seriously explored in any part of the world; and their interconnectedness as prerequisites of peace was unheard of.

However we interpret His modernity, it clearly betokens a knowledge far ahead of anything Bahá'u'lláh might have learned or deduced from any course of study available in His lifetime. We cannot realistically say that Bahá'u'lláh 'merely' displayed an unusual gift for extrapolating future trends from existing conditions. Modern sociologists consider it humanly impossible – even with the aid of up-to-the-minute research libraries, electronic databanks, computer simulations and the like – to project social trends more than a few years into the future. Every attempt at scientific forecasting of social changes has been a dismal failure. Even if we suppose Bahá'u'lláh might somehow have succeeded where today's science fails, such a feat would have required an extraordinary amount of raw data. The information needed for such far-reaching deductions certainly was not to be found in nineteenth-century Middle Eastern literature. Whether it was available in the West is doubtful but entirely moot: Bahá'u'lláh had no access to Western literature and no contact (save for one brief visit in the closing days of His life) with any Western scholar.

(...continued)
closely to the familiar principles listed and described in hundreds of Bahá'í publications since the Faith's beginning.

We must also remember that the nineteenth century produced many outstanding intellectuals and visionaries, studying in the best universities, working in the best libraries and sharing ideas and insights with one another. Not one of these thinkers, in the East or the West, even came close to matching Bahá'u'lláh's vision. He alone, with none of their advantages, produced the writings that have best stood the test of time – the only writings that each year become more relevant to world events rather than less, and the only ones conspicuously free of the narrow outlook, naive misconceptions and outright superstition that plagued the thought of His day. Surely these considerations challenge us to weigh seriously Bahá'u'lláh's own explanation: 'This thing is not from Me, but from One Who is Almighty and All-Knowing' (PDC 40).

Bahá'u'lláh's Use of Arabic

Bahá'u'lláh's insight into the problems and conditions of a future age undoubtedly is impressive. As evidence of inspired knowledge, however, it is admittedly circumstantial. If nothing else, we can always chalk it up to a series of fantastically lucky guesses. Can we point to some specific, highly technical body of knowledge which Bahá'u'lláh demonstrably mastered without study – a subject that normally cannot be acquired without years of training?

Such a subject is not hard to find. It is the Arabic written language. 'Abdu'l-Bahá, discussing proofs of Bahá'u'lláh's inspiration, cites His virtuosity with Arabic as a clear example of innate knowledge:

> Bahá'u'lláh had never studied Arabic; He had not had a tutor or teacher, nor had He entered a school. Nevertheless, the eloquence and elegance of His blessed expositions in Arabic, as well as His Arabic writings, caused astonishment and stupefaction to the most accomplished Arabic scholars, and all recognized and declared that He was incomparable and unequaled (SAQ 34).

This point deserves careful consideration. One of the first things a student of the Bahá'í Faith learns is that Bahá'u'lláh wrote both in Persian and in Arabic. This fact, in itself, hardly seems surprising. Millions of people are bilingual, with or without formal training. For a Westerner, there is a natural tendency to assume that Persian and Arabic are probably similar languages, widely used by Bahá'u'lláh's countrymen, from whom He might have acquired both by simple exposure. Such an assumption, however, turns out to be flawed in two key respects.

First, Persian and Arabic do not especially resemble one another. They have similar alphabets, to be sure (Persian has four extra letters), and there has been some mutual influence. This derives in part from the fact that they are spoken in adjacent countries. A more fundamental reason is that Islam, the prevailing religion of Persia, reveres as its holy book the Qur'án, which was originally revealed in Arabic. But the differences are profound and they far outweigh any cosmetic similarities. The two do not even belong to the same family of languages: Arabic is Semitic while Persian is Indo-European.

Second, Arabic is not widely used or spoken in Persia; nor was it so used or spoken in Bahá'u'lláh's lifetime. Neither the nobility nor the peasantry, as a rule, knew anything of the language. The one class for which knowledge of Arabic was considered important was the Islamic clergy, who used it in their study of the Qur'án. These Muslim divines laboured for years to master the subtleties of Arabic grammar and terminology, as well as its complex literary conventions. Most of them regarded no treatise as worthy of attention unless it was written in Arabic; and they tended to pepper their sermons and discourses with complex Arabic expressions which few if any members of their congregations could fathom.

It is certainly possible to acquire a working knowledge of conversational Arabic through association with persons who speak it. This is how all children first learn their native tongues. There is, however, a peculiarity of Arabic that takes on extreme importance in this connection. 'In Arabic', explains Phillip K. Hitti, 'distinction should be made between the written, or classical form, and the spoken, or colloquial' (Hitti, 'Arab Civilization', *Encyclopedia Americana*, vol. II, p. 152). Ordinary spoken Arabic takes the form of various local dialects or vernaculars, used in everyday commerce but rarely written. These have relatively little in common with one another. In contrast, written Arabic (also known as 'standard' or 'formal' Arabic) is the same throughout the Arabic-speaking world. It is therefore used for literary and technical communication, as well as for diplomatic correspondence. It is, however, markedly different from any of the standard dialects in its vocabulary, its grammar, its syntax and its stylistic requirements.* Simply put, written and conversational Arabic differ enough to constitute, for all practical purposes, different languages.

This radical distinction between the written and spoken word has consequences that might seem odd to an English-speaking individual. Much Arabic fiction, for instance, gives the impression of being written in two languages, the classical for narrative and a local vernacular for dialogue. (Some Arabic fiction uses the classical form throughout, producing dialogue with little resemblance to actual speech anywhere; and a few works use the vernacular only.) We are accustomed to the idea that anyone who speaks excellent English, and who knows script well enough to transcribe that English word for word, can write excellent English as well. Indeed, the best advice an English teacher can give a student is, 'Speak correctly, and write the way you speak.' But this would be terrible advice for a student of Arabic! One might learn to converse in fluent or even eloquent Arabic, and learn in addition

---

*Though rarely used in face-to-face communication, the spoken form of classical Arabic is employed on certain formal occasions and, today at least, is used increasingly on Arabic radio. (Radio was of course non-existent in Bahá'u'lláh's lifetime.)

to copy one's speech onto paper verbatim. Yet doing so would not enable anyone to write Arabic that is correct or even necessarily comprehensible. One would remain, in every way that matters, quite illiterate.

Learning to write adequately – not brilliantly, just adequately – in Arabic requires years of disciplined instruction. A. F. L. Beeston, author of *The Arabic Language Today*, states flatly that the classical Arabic used for writing and formal speech 'must be learned in school' (Beeston, 'Arabic Language', *Academic American Encyclopedia*, vol. II, p. 100). The details of the language are subtle, intricate and arbitrary. They are acquired through painstaking drill and memorization; and a structured training programme, administered by a competent instructor, is generally deemed indispensable. With this sort of grounding, one may become passably literate.

Even more difficult, by a whole order of magnitude, is the specialized literary Arabic used in Muslim religious writing. 'In this latter case,' says *Collier's Encyclopedia*, 'the knowledge of Arabic is restricted to the learned' (Della Vida, 'Arabic Language', *Collier's Encyclopedia*, vol. II, p. 393). This form presents technical challenges so imposing as to daunt any but the most accomplished experts. Native Arabic-speaking scholars, steeped from childhood in the richness and beauty of the language, intimately familiar with its culture and traditions, can and do spend lifetimes augmenting their knowledge of this seemingly infinite subject.

Bahá'u'lláh, as stated above, had no training in Arabic and no experience that might have equipped Him to deal with its complex literary formalities. However, from the earliest beginnings of His forty-year prophetic ministry, He wrote interchangeably in Persian and Arabic, proving Himself equally adept in both languages. His Arabic compositions – some in prose, others in poetry – are unrivalled whether from the standpoint of literary beauty or technical proficiency. Though He often broke with convention, preferring to originate His own distinctive styles, His command of established patterns was complete. Time and again He demonstrated His ability to work in any classical or traditional form, adhering strictly to its most rigorous requirements.

Among the many experts who marvelled at His mastery of Arabic were the learned doctors of the theological seminary in Sulaymáníyyih, who, as described above, interrogated Him during His sojourn in Kurdistan. Having received satisfying answers to their preliminary questions, they resolved to put Bahá'u'lláh's Arabic wizardry to a supreme test. 'No one among the mystics, the wise, and the learned', they said, 'has hitherto proved himself capable of writing a poem in a rhyme and meter identical with that of the longer of the two odes, entitled Qaṣídiy-i-Tá'íyyih composed by Ibn-i-Fárid [a famous Egyptian poet]. We beg you to write for us a poem in that same meter and rhyme' (GPB 123). Bahá'u'lláh at once complied by dictating, in precisely the style they had requested, no less than two thousand verses. Shoghi Effendi comments:

> Such was their reaction to this marvellous demonstration of the sagacity and genius of Bahá'u'lláh that they unanimously acknowledged every single verse of that poem to be endowed with a force, beauty and power far surpassing anything contained in either the major or minor odes composed by that celebrated poet (GPB 123).

Deeming much of the poem's subject matter premature, Bahá'u'lláh then selected 127 verses which He allowed His astonished examiners to keep. These much-loved couplets, known as the *Ode of the Dove*, are today widely circulated and studied among His Arabic-speaking followers.

Literary Arabic traditionally incorporates subtle wordplay, often involving the deliberate breaking of grammatical rules to achieve a desired effect. (The Qur'án, which Arabs regard as the ultimate stylistic model, employs this technique throughout with superb finesse.) This is harder than it may sound. Anyone who attempts it without knowing precisely what he is doing will butcher the language, producing text that is clumsy or even incomprehensible. Although Bahá-'u'lláh, in some of His works, upholds textbook standards with scrupulous consistency, in others He manipulates or disregards them at will – always enhancing the eloquence of His message by so doing. His own footnotes to the *Ode of the Dove*, for example, call attention to a couple of apparent deviations from standard grammar but argue convincingly that His usage is, in the context, entirely proper.*

Those of us who cannot read Arabic must, of course, rely for information on those who can (just as students of the Bible, unless they understand Greek or Hebrew, must obtain much of their knowledge from scholars of the original manuscripts). Accurate translation is therefore a critically important discipline. Some of Bahá'u'lláh's more intricate Arabic compositions (especially His poetry) are considered virtually impossible to translate. The *Ode of the Dove* is one of these. One may paraphrase the meaning but it is no simple task to capture, in an alien tongue, the subtle rhythms and nuances which bring that meaning vividly to life. Despite such difficulties, a large and rapidly growing body of Bahá-'u'lláh's writing, both Arabic and Persian, is available today in English. As Guardian of the Faith, Shoghi Effendi – an Oxford-trained scholar – set the standard for this on-going work. His own translations reflect a superb command of all three languages, combined with authoritative insight into the texts' meaning. Whenever possible, his English renderings

---

*Despite the clearly conscious nature of these decisions, and the scholarly precedents behind them, Bahá'u'lláh's liberties with language sometimes drew fire from Arabic purists. These same purists, ironically, censured 'Abdu'l-Bahá (who learned Arabic from Bahá-'u'lláh) for the opposite practice – that of adhering strictly to grammatical rules. Facing this impossible double standard, 'Abdu'l-Bahá exclaimed, 'What can we do? If we make mistakes, they criticize us on those grounds. If we make no mistakes, they criticize us on those grounds!' (Quoted by Marzieh Gail in a letter to the writer.)

are used (in conjunction with the Arabic and Persian originals) as the basis for translation of Bahá'í scripture into
languages other than English.

Readers sometimes ask why Bahá'í translations often
employ 'Old English' terminology – 'thee' and 'thou', 'hath'
and 'hast', and so forth. Shoghi Effendi adopted this slightly
archaic usage (which echoes the King James Version of the
Bible) in order better to suggest the exalted and highly
expressive character of Bahá'u'lláh's language. Through this
and other appropriate literary devices we obtain a glimpse
of the towering eloquence and beauty of Bahá'u'lláh's composition. Regrettably, it is a glimpse and nothing more.
According to all competent testimony, His originals are in
every instance incomparably superior to any translation.
Shoghi Effendi describes one of his own finest translations
as 'one more attempt . . . however inadequate . . . to approach what must always be regarded as the unattainable
goal – a befitting rendering of Bahá'u'lláh's matchless utterance' (Shoghi Effendi, opening note to *The Book of Certitude*).

A Torrent of Eloquence

A third token of the superhuman origin and nature of
Bahá'u'lláh's knowledge is the seemingly impossible speed
and spontaneity with which He composed His writings.
Further enumerating the 'signs' of His father's prophetic
authenticity, 'Abdu'l-Bahá writes:

> Another of His signs is the marvel of His discourse, the
> eloquence of His utterance, the rapidity with which His
> Writings were revealed . . . By thy very life! This thing is
> plain as day to whoever will regard it with the eye of justice
> (SAB 15).

This phenomenon – documented both by eyewitness accounts and by empirical evidence – is one that no amount
of education could adequately explain.

Any human mind, however great its capacity, is finite and fallible unless aided by some higher power. It follows that writing is a trial-and-error procedure for any normal author. Some writers, to be sure, are extremely prolific; a few of these are able to work long hours at high speed and produce (much of the time) relatively good work. But even for this select minority, serious writing involves certain necessities. These include preliminary thought and research, occasional hesitation and backtracking, and a certain amount of polishing and revision. Any composition a writer dashes off without these essential steps will be, at best, a 'rough draft'. Such work – however fine it may be overall – will show wide variations in quality, more or less obvious lapses in consistency and organization, and a general lack of attention to detail. The entire history of secular literature demonstrates that no ordinary human author, composing extemporaneously, can create perfectly finished work at all times and under all conditions.

But human limitations, as we said before, do not apply to the divine Logos – to the One whose very name is 'the Word'. The Gospels show that Jesus never was at a loss for words, even in difficult situations that would have left an ordinary man speechless or inarticulate. His many discourses, such as the Sermon on the Mount, apparently poured from His lips without forethought: 'For I have spoken not of myself;' He explained, 'but the Father which sent me, he gave me a commandment, what I should say, and what I should speak' (John 12:49). The same should naturally be true of Christ's latter-day reappearance, when He descends from heaven as 'one like unto the Son of man'.

In view of Bahá'u'lláh's claim to be that promised One, the manner in which He composed His writings is therefore highly significant. Most of His 'writings' are not, strictly speaking, writings at all; they were dictated by Him to one or more secretaries, who would later recopy them. Bahá'u'lláh would then verify the accuracy of the transcripts and

283

affix His seal or signature. During dictation the words would cascade from His lips in a steady stream, so rapidly as to tax the abilities of the most gifted stenographer. He seldom had any opportunity for prior reflection or rehearsal, since the bulk of His work consists of replies to letters He had not seen or heard until moments before He began to speak. During dictation He did not grope for words, lose His train of thought, or, having spoken, retract one phrase in order to substitute another.

After the secretary's notes were neatly recopied, Bahá-'u'lláh, in checking the final version, would sometimes correct a word or two that had been transcribed incorrectly. At no time, however, did He revise or polish His own actual utterances. When the workload was heavy and time short, He would sometimes dispense with the step of checking the transcript Himself. Instead, He would dictate the Tablet aloud a second time, while the secretary followed along proofreading the transcript from Bahá'u'lláh's utterances (Adib Taherzadeh, 'The Station of Bahá'u'lláh', a tape-recorded talk delivered in 1987 in Brazil).

Until the end of His life, Bahá'u'lláh poured out His writings in sessions that often lasted for hours at a time. (Within two days and nights, for example, He composed the *Book of Certitude*, one of His major works: its English translation exceeds 250 pages.) Most of these writings He produced under conditions of bitter adversity, often when He was weak from hunger, illness or exhaustion, stricken with grief, harassed by enemies or mortally endangered by their schemes. He Himself describes His words as 'a copious rain' (GPB 133) commenting, 'Such are the outpourings . . . from the clouds of Divine Bounty that within the space of an hour the equivalent of a thousand verses hath been revealed' (GPB 171).

A believer named Siyyid Asadu'lláh-i-Qumí, who was present during some of these sessions, left the following account:

I recall that as Mírzá Áqá Ján [Bahá'u'lláh's primary secretary] was recording the words of Bahá'u'lláh at the time of revelation, the shrill sound of his pen could be heard from a distance of about twenty paces . . .

Mírzá Áqá Ján had a large ink-pot the size of a small bowl. He also had available about ten to twelve pens and large sheets of paper in stacks. In those days all letters which arrived for Bahá'u'lláh were received by Mírzá Áqá Ján. He would bring these into the presence of Bahá'u'lláh and, having obtained permission, would read them. Afterwards [Bahá'u'lláh] would direct him to take up his pen and record the Tablet which was revealed in reply . . .

Such was the speed with which he used to write the revealed Word that the ink of the first word was scarcely yet dry when the whole page was finished. It seemed as if someone had dipped a lock of hair in the ink and applied it over the whole page. None of the words was written clearly and they were illegible to all except Mírzá Áqá Ján. There were occasions when even he could not decipher the words and had to seek the help of Bahá'u'lláh. When revelation had ceased, then . . . Mírzá Áqá Ján would rewrite the Tablet in his best hand and dispatch it to its destination . . . (quoted in Taherzadeh, *Revelation of Bahá'u'lláh*, vol. 1, pp. 35-6).

Nabíl-i-A'ẓam, a Bahá'í historian who accompanied Bahá-'u'lláh throughout much of His exile and imprisonment, and who chronicled both his own first-hand observations and the eyewitness accounts of others, adds the following details:

A number of secretaries were busy day and night and yet they were unable to cope with the task. Among them was Mírzá Báqir-i-Shírází . . . He alone transcribed no less than two thousand verses every day. He laboured during six or seven months. Every month the equivalent of several volumes would be transcribed by him and sent to Persia. About twenty volumes, in his fine penmanship, he left behind as a remembrance . . . (GPB 171).

Many other observers have left similar accounts. However, we need not rely entirely on their testimony to verify this phenomenon. After Bahá'u'lláh's Tablets were dispatched, the original notes of Mírzá Áqá Ján and other secretaries were generally distributed to resident Bahá'ís and visiting pilgrims as souvenirs. The early believers treasured these keepsakes and called them 'revelation writing'. Countless specimens of this stenography have since been collected at the Bahá'í World Centre in Israel. (To understand the value of these historical documents, simply suppose the disciples of Christ had taken notes as He spoke and preserved them for study by future generations of scholars.) Handwritten dictation, scribbled frantically and without pause by a secretary working under high pressure, looks much the same in any language. The 'revelation writing' therefore bears eloquent testimony to the circumstances of its origin. By comparing its almost illegible scrawl with careful Arabic or Persian penmanship, anyone – even knowing nothing of the languages themselves – can visualize the speed and continuity with which Bahá'u'lláh's secretaries worked.*

The torrential flow of Bahá'u'lláh's utterance could more easily be explained away if the resulting writings were occasionally of lacklustre quality. Such is not the case, however. The calibre of His work is not only strikingly uniform but uniformly superlative. This of course does not mean His writings are all alike; one of the very things that makes them excellent is the astounding diversity they incorporate. 'At one time,' says Bahá'u'lláh, 'We spoke in the language of the lawgiver; at another in that of the truth seeker and the mystic . . .' (GPB 217). However, all His compositions are from beginning to end highly polished, meticulously organized, lucidly presented and vibrant with spiritual power and beauty.

*For photostatic copies of 'revelation writing' see page 110 of Adib Taherzadeh's *The Revelation of Bahá'u'lláh*, vol. 1. Contrast, for example, with the neatly transcribed Arabic Tablet reproduced as the frontispiece of the same book.

There are various standards by which to judge quality in writing. Some of these – such as eloquence or beauty – will vary considerably according to individual taste. Others are not so elastic. If, for instance, an author quotes from the works of others, or even from his own works, we are entitled to ask how accurately he has done so. Bahá'u'lláh would sometimes quote liberally from scriptures of past religions, or from works by sages, mystics, historians and the like. Many of these excerpts are from obscure or little-known works to which He seemingly had no access at the time. He could not, in any event, have stopped to look them up without interrupting His pacing and His dictation. Both the original notes and eyewitness reports indicate that He always dictated these passages afresh: He did not simply instruct the secretary to look up the necessary text and insert it. (Sometimes His sources required hours or even months of research by scholars to verify.) Bahá'u'lláh's citations are always scrupulously precise. So rigorous is His use of such secondary material that we would never know (if the historical record were less clear) that we are reading extemporaneous composition.

Closing Comments

This chapter explores the broadest possible sense in which Bahá'u'lláh's knowledge (like that of Jesus) might be considered 'prophetic'. In so doing, it looks beyond the specific historical and scientific predictions detailed earlier. We have taken particular notice of facts that seem to rule out any possibility of His having acquired His insights by ordinary human means. To restate our main findings:

Bahá'u'lláh spent His crucial formative years in an atmosphere of profound superstition and prejudice, receiving only the most superficial tutoring. Despite these disadvantages, His knowledge aroused the wonder and admiration of many eminent scholars. Three especially striking features of that knowledge testify to its intuitive and seemingly superhuman character: 1) His farsightedness: Bahá'u'lláh in His writings foreshadowed all the sweeping social changes of the twentieth century, anticipating and addressing the needs of a global society not yet even dimly visualized by His most advanced contemporaries. 2) His mastery of Arabic literary writing: He demonstrated, apparently without study or training, a flawless command of this highly technical subject which normally takes many years of drill and discipline to acquire. 3) His creative speed and spontaneity: He consistently produced highly polished, superbly organized, deeply thoughtful writing, embellished with exact quotations from a wide variety of sources, at high speed in completely extemporaneous fashion.

Do such observations prove that Bahá'u'lláh spoke with divine inspiration and authority? Perhaps not in any absolute sense of the word 'prove'. In religion, as in science, proof is a matter of degree, for there is no body of evidence that cannot be explained in more than one way. Our task is to determine, in light of scripture and the promptings of the Holy Spirit, which explanation best makes sense of all the available evidence. I have tried in this chapter to sharpen the focus, to present facts which, added to the successful historical and scientific predictions described in previous chapters, simplify such a decision.

However, there is evidence yet to come. Everything we have discussed so far relates to the extent and possible source of Bahá'u'lláh's knowledge. Important though this may be, knowledge is far from the only characteristic we should expect to find in 'one like unto the Son of Man'. Our next two chapters will consider some of the other expectations which – according to the Bible – the return of Christ must satisfy.

11

He Shall Glorify Me

> He who speaks on his own authority seeks his own glory; but
> he who seeks the glory of him who sent him is true, and in
> him there is no falsehood (John 7:16-8).

Miracles, as we discussed in Chapter 6, cannot qualify as a
decisive proof of divine authority. One reason is that false
Christs can perform 'lying wonders' (II Thess. 2:9) sufficiently impressive to 'deceive the very elect' (Matt. 24:24).
Another is that miracles, even if genuine, convince only those
who actually see them (and even such witnesses may explain
them away).

For this reason we have been focusing on scriptural
credentials which – according to God's own testimony –
cannot be forged or counterfeited. The Bible teaches emphatically that no false prophet or satanic deceiver can tear
the veil from the future, showing us 'things that are to come
hereafter'. God has reserved for Himself this unique ability;
He exercises it only through His chosen mouthpiece and
representative; and He commands us to judge by this criterion all who claim to speak on His behalf.

Bahá'u'lláh, who identifies Himself as the return of that
Logos or 'quickening spirit' called Christ, clearly passes this
scriptural test. Applying God's standard as rigorously as we
wish (indeed, the more rigorously the better), we find Him
fully qualified to speak with divine authority. His power to
disclose the future is one He demonstrated time and time
again. 'No possibility is left', He writes, 'for anyone either to
turn aside or protest' (ESW 150). We may (as in Chapters 7

to 9) interpret 'things to come' in terms of specific predictions. Or we may (as in Chapter 10) construe the expression more broadly, as encompassing any knowledge that is ahead of its time, knowledge that anticipates future needs or illumines the issues of an age yet unborn. Either way, the evidence shouts aloud that Bahá'u'lláh possessed this spiritual gift which – according to the Bible – comes from God and God alone.

In theory, perhaps, these facts should be sufficient witness to Bahá'u'lláh's veracity. However, God in His mercy has given us, in the Bible, additional standards by which to discern the origin of spiritual gifts. Even knowing that successful prophecy emanates only from a heavenly source and that Bahá'u'lláh manifests this divine sign, we must deal with the fact that His success shatters a multitude of human preconceptions. It is entirely reasonable, under such circumstances, to want reassurance – some additional safeguard against trickery, some guarantee that we have overlooked no loophole through which a diabolically clever false prophet might slip.

The New Testament furnishes this extra margin of safety. Its guidance is simple: When someone backs a claim of divine authority with seemingly authentic spiritual gifts, we must investigate his attitude towards Christ. Does he teach that Jesus of Nazareth was the historical Christ – the divine Messiah who appeared as the 'Word made flesh'? Does he acknowledge Christ as the Lord and Saviour of humanity and the Son of God? In short, does he glorify Christ by testifying to the truth of His claims as revealed in the Bible? If so, then we can and must have confidence in His other proofs, because no sinister supernatural power can evince such an attitude of reverence.

Although we have considered these scriptures before, they bear repeating. Paul explains:

> Now concerning spiritual gifts, brethren, I would not have
> you ignorant . . . Wherefore I give you to understand, that

no man speaking by the Spirit of God calleth Jesus accursed: and that no man can say that Jesus is the Lord, but by the Holy Ghost (I Cor. 12:1-3).

The Apostle John writes in the same vein:

> Beloved, believe not every spirit, but try the spirits whether they are of God: because many false prophets are gone out into the world. Hereby know ye the Spirit of God: Every spirit that confesseth that Jesus Christ is come in the flesh is of God: And every spirit that confesseth not that Jesus Christ is come in the flesh is not of God: and this is that spirit of antichrist, whereof ye have heard that it should come; and even now already is it in the world (I John 4:1-3).

> . . . even now there are many antichrists . . . Who is a liar but he that denieth that Jesus is the Christ? He is antichrist, that denieth the Father and the Son. Whosoever denieth the Son, the same hath not the Father: but he that acknowledgeth the Son hath the Father also (I John 2:18-23).

Christ Himself sums up the requirement in His commentary on the Spirit of Truth: 'He shall glorify me: for he shall receive of mine, and shall shew it unto you' (John 16:14).

There are two ways to glorify Christ: by word and by deed. Bahá'u'lláh did both. Let us briefly revisit His written and spoken tributes to Christ, then explore the even more explicit testimony of His personal life.

To the words of Bahá'u'lláh we have referred extensively throughout this volume. The main points that bear repeating are that Bahá'u'lláh does forcefully uphold the Sonship, Lordship and Divinity of the historical Jesus Christ, and that He affirms and defends Christ's virgin birth, atonement, resurrection, ascension and saving grace, the necessity of His sacrifice and the unerring truth of His Gospel. Being central to Bahá'u'lláh's theology and integral to His own claim, these teachings – say the Bahá'í writings – lie at the 'bedrock' of Bahá'í belief (PDC 110). Acceptance of Christianity's divine truth is among the 'essential prerequisites of admittance into the Bahá'í fold of Jews, Zoroastrians, Hindus, Buddhists, and the followers of other ancient faiths, as well as of agnostics and even atheists' (PDC 114). Simply put, no one can be a Bahá'í without accepting Jesus of Nazareth as the Son of God and the divine Messiah revealed in Judeo-Christian scripture.

What may not be evident, from a summary such as this, is the reverence and passion with which Bahá'u'lláh declares these holy truths. In the exaltation of its language, the force of its conviction and the fervour of its love, Bahá'u'lláh's praise of Christ is – I firmly believe – unsurpassed in the world's religious literature. This spirit of devotion also comes across clearly in the words of 'Abdu'l-Bahá, who, as Bahá-'u'lláh's authorized successor, brought His teachings to the Western world. We already have quoted a number of examples; here are several more:

> Reflect how Jesus, the Spirit of God, was, notwithstanding His extreme meekness and perfect tender-heartedness, treated by His enemies. So fierce was the opposition which He, the Essence of Being and Lord of the visible and invisible, had to face, that He had nowhere to lay His head (G 57).

> When the Lord Christ was crowned with thorns, He knew that all the diadems of the world were at His feet. All earthly crowns, however brilliant, powerful and resplendent, bowed in adoration before the crown of thorns! It was from this sure and certain knowledge He spoke, when He said: 'All power is given unto Me, in Heaven and in earth' (PT 167-8).

> When the Lord Christ came He spread the light of the Holy Spirit on all around Him, and His disciples and all who received His illumination became enlightened, spiritual beings (PT 63).

Look at the Gospel of the Lord Christ and see how glorious it is! Yet even today men fail to understand its priceless beauty . . . (PT 48).

The deepest wisdom which the sages have uttered, the profoundest learning which any mind hath unfolded, the arts which the ablest hands have produced, the influence exerted by the most potent of rulers, are but manifestations of the quickening power released by His transcendent, His all-pervasive, and resplendent Spirit . . . Blessed is the man who, with a face beaming with light, hath turned towards Him (G 85-6).

He [Jesus] re-interpreted and completed the Law of Moses and fulfilled the Law of the Prophets. His word conquered the East and the West. His Kingdom is everlasting. He exalted those Jews who recognized Him. They were men and women of humble birth, but contact with Him made them great and gave them everlasting dignity (PT 56).

. . . the reality of Christ, the Spirit of Christ, the perfections of Christ all came from heaven. Consequently, by saying He was the bread which came from heaven He meant that the perfections which He showed forth were divine perfections, that the blessings within Him were heavenly gifts and bestowals, that His light was the light of reality. He said, 'If any man eat of this bread, he shall live for ever' . . . How manifest the meaning is! How evident! For the soul which acquires divine perfections and seeks heavenly illumination from the teachings of Christ will undoubtedly live eternally (PUP 450-1).

Consider those who rejected the Spirit [Jesus] when He came unto them with manifest dominion. How numerous the Pharisees who had secluded themselves in synagogues in His name, lamenting over their separation from Him, and yet when the portals of reunion were flung open and the divine Luminary shone resplendent from the Dayspring of Beauty, they disbelieved in God, the Exalted, the Mighty. They failed to attain His presence, notwithstanding that His advent had been promised them in the Book of Isaiah as well as in the Books of the Prophets and the Messengers. No one from among them turned his face towards the Dayspring of divine bounty except such as were destitute of any power amongst men. And yet, today, every man endowed with power and invested with sovereignty prideth himself on His Name . . . Take good heed and be of them that observe the warning (TB 9-10).

In one of His own prayers, Bahá'u'lláh recalls the ardour with which Christ prayed in Gethsemane as He steeled Himself to face the agony of crucifixion:

He Who was Thy Spirit (Jesus), O my God, withdrew all alone in the darkness of the night preceding His last day on earth, and falling on His face to the ground besought Thee saying: 'If it be Thy will, O my Lord, my Well-Beloved, let this cup, through Thy grace and bounty, pass from me.' By Thy beauty, O Thou Who art the Lord of all names and the Creator of the heavens! I can smell the fragrance of the words which, in His love for Thee, His lips have uttered, and can feel the glow of the fire that had inflamed His soul in its longing to behold Thy face and in its yearning after the Day-Spring of the light of Thy oneness, and the Dawning-Place of Thy transcendent unity (PM 192-3).

Bible scholar Michael Sours has recently published a book entitled *Jesus Christ in Sacred Bahá'í Literature*. Well over one hundred pages long, it is a compilation, with introductory notes, of some representative Bahá'í scriptural references praising and glorifying Christ. I see no way in which anyone, having studied this book, can fail to recognize the depth or reality of the devotion to Christ expressed in Bahá'í teachings. The extent of that devotion within the Bahá'í community itself may be judged by the fact that this book, when it appeared in 1995, became an overnight bestseller among Bahá'ís.

We must also note that Bahá'u'lláh stood up for Christ even when it was unpopular (and sometimes dangerous) to do so. As a young man, for example, He attended a large gathering of state officials and prominent citizens to hear an address by Mírzá Naẓar 'Alí Ḥakím Qazvíní, an adviser and spiritual guide of the king. Mírzá Naẓar 'Alí, a Sufi mystic, had won immense power and prestige by virtue of his position as the king's favourite. Unfortunately, he became carried away, on this occasion, by his conceit and egotism. Using himself as his example, he spoke of the 'high spiritual station' a human being supposedly can attain:

'For example,' Mírzá Naẓar 'Alí stated, 'let us say that at this very moment my servant comes and says that Jesus is standing at the door of the palace and wants permission to meet me. Because I have no further need, I do not see any desire in me for such an encounter.'

After a moment's silence, most of those listening began to nod and express agreement with this pompous declaration. Remembering Mírzá Naẓar 'Alí's preeminent position in the eyes of the king, and hoping to bask in reflected glory, the sycophants and flatterers among them began calling out, 'Yes, yes indeed!'

Bahá'u'lláh, however, would have none of it. Angered by Mírzá Naẓar 'Alí's arrogant insult to the Lord Christ, He called out, 'Sir, I have a question, if you will permit me to ask it.' Receiving permission, He continued: 'In spite of all the affection in which the shah holds you, let us say that at this moment the chief executioner should come with ten of his henchmen and announce that the shah is asking for you. Examine your inner soul carefully. Would you be anxious or would you answer him with a completely calm heart, free of all fear?'

Mírzá Naẓar 'Alí and his audience were thunderstruck. All present knew the answer; the only remaining question was whether the Sufi mystic would reply truthfully. After some hesitation, Mírzá Naẓar 'Ali admitted, 'The only fair thing to say is that I would be anxious in the extreme, and the courage to remain upright and calm would flee from me. Indeed, the very power of speech would disappear.'

'Given that this is the case,' remarked Bahá'u'lláh, 'you cannot with the same lips make your former assertion.' His implication was plain: How dare this conceited priest – abjectly fearful for his physical safety – place himself above the perfect Lamb of God, who lived to sacrifice Himself in His Father's path? How could any man so terrified of the grave profess 'no further need' of Christ's salvation? Mírzá Naẓar 'Alí was exposed as the braggart he was (Mírzá Abúl-Faḍl, *Letters and Essays: 1886-1913* 54).

To fully appreciate Bahá'u'lláh's boldness, we must remember the utter ruthlessness of Persian politics and court intrigue in the nineteenth century. Church and state were one, and an individual could easily die for some affront, real or imagined, to a well-connected priest. Though widely respected, Bahá'u'lláh was young and without official rank or position. To challenge and humiliate publicly the king's favourite cleric was to court the all-too-real possibility that the chief executioner and his men, acting on some trumped-up pretext, might soon darken Bahá'u'lláh's own door.

'Like unto the Son of Man'

This brings us to our next point. To glorify Christ, to testify to His Lordship, is not merely or even primarily a matter of speech. Christ explains that to glorify Him is to 'receive of mine, and . . . shew it unto you' (John 16:14). To 'show' what is Christ's can mean to defend His teachings and exhibit their true meaning; and of course Bahá'u'lláh does this. In a deeper sense, however, it also means to translate those teachings into action: 'Herein is my Father glorified, that ye bear much fruit' (John 15:8). (Since Christ and God are one in spirit, this principle, though expressed here in terms of the Father, logically applies to both.) As to calling Him 'Lord', Christ says: 'Not every one that saith unto me, Lord, Lord, shall enter into the kingdom of heaven; but he that doeth the will of my Father which is in heaven' (Matt. 7:21).

A necessary question, then, is whether Bahá'u'lláh in His own life exemplified Christ's counsels and actions. If He truly is the returned Christ, the 'one like unto the Son of man', then He must glorify Christ by 'showing' the world what it means to be truly Christ-like. Did Bahá'u'lláh do this?

The life of Bahá'u'lláh is extensively documented. His photograph, surrounded by a wide array of personal effects, is reverently displayed in the Archives Building at the Bahá'í World Centre in Haifa. Thousands of people met Him – believers and sceptics, rich and poor, high government officials, noted scholars and ordinary people from all walks of life. These individuals left unnumbered public records, diplomatic papers, diaries, memoirs, interviews, oral histories and anecdotes, reflecting His movements and activities on an almost daily basis.

Studying Bahá'u'lláh's life, we see clearly that the deep devotion He inspired was due to more than the force of His personality or the sublimity of His teachings. It followed, as well, from His exemplary personal life and rectitude of conduct. The common thread tying together all the diverse events of His life was this: He was forced to choose, almost every day, between His own welfare and that of others. In literally every instance He sacrificed Himself for the betterment of humanity.

Scores of incidents and anecdotes illustrate this theme; we have space here to touch only the barest highlights. Some time before the public declaration of the Báb, His Forerunner, Bahá'u'lláh had turned down the lucrative government post previously occupied by His late father, Mírzá Buzurg. Instead, He devoted His considerable fortune entirely to charitable and humanitarian work. He and His wife, Navváb, who shared His priorities, were known to the masses as the 'Father of the Poor' and the 'Mother of Consolation'. Public officials and the clergy (not yet faced with the challenge of accepting or rejecting Him as the Promised One) also held him in high esteem but warned Him that His continued generosity would soon impoverish Him.

The point became moot when Bahá'u'lláh espoused the cause of the Báb, for so bold and public a stance seemed tantamount to suicide. His reputation, however, protected Him until state-sponsored persecution boiled over in the massacres that followed the Báb's martyrdom. Even then, He could have chosen safety, for the anti-Bábí hysteria erupted while He was outside the capital, visiting friends who urged Him to seek concealment. Spurning their advice, Bahá'u'lláh headed for Ṭihrán to confront the foes of the Faith, turning Himself in along the way to a military detail sent to arrest Him. He was conducted 'on foot and in chains, with bared head and bare feet' (ESW 20) under the pitiless August sun, from the hill villages north of Ṭihrán to the city's great dungeon. Along the way He was pelted with stones and filth by the crowds. At one point an old woman, wishing to play her part in punishing the vile heretic (as authorities now were depicting Him), ran alongside, begging the soldiers to pause long enough for her to cast her stone. Bahá'u'lláh gave a revealing glimpse of His nature by telling the soldiers, 'Suffer not this woman to be disappointed. Deny her not what she regards as a meritorious act in the sight of God' (DB 607-8). He then submitted patiently to the added injury, in order to cheer her blind and hardened heart.

While Bahá'u'lláh was personally forgiving, His forbearance and compassion sprang not from weakness but from deep strength. We are reminded of the way in which 'gentle Jesus, meek and mild' cleared the temple of moneychangers who (He said) had made of His Father's house a den of thieves (Matt. 21:13). Bahá'u'lláh was lionlike in His defence of the Faith, routing His enemies in debate and brilliantly exposing their hypocrisy. Though He endured persecution when He had to do so in order to prosecute His mission, He never sought it out. Throughout His life He strenuously protested the campaign of terror waged against Him and His followers by the authorities. (In one instance, an outraged Bahá'u'lláh risked His life to rebuke the Sulṭán of Turkey for the latter's cruelty to Bahá'í women and children.)

When Bahá'u'lláh entered the dungeon of Ṭihrán – the unutterably foul 'Black Pit' – He was in His mid-thirties and in the prime of health. He left it four months later an emaciated shadow, scarred for life. He had been forced, along with a number of other religious prisoners, to wear chains so heavy that they cut through flesh to rest on His collarbone; to eat food poisoned, at one point, by His enemies; to breathe air polluted with the stench of human waste and festering wounds; and to stay in a position that made sleep virtually impossible. Each day one of the Bábís would be taken out and executed, and the others reminded that their turn might come next. Bahá'u'lláh and His fellow-prisoners fueled their courage by chanting songs of praise and glorification to God – songs that could be heard even in the palace of the sháh, some distance away.

In that dungeon, in 1852, Bahá'u'lláh learned that He was the Promised One whose imminent appearance the Báb had proclaimed. This realization came to Him in a vision comparable to that of Jesus, upon whom the Spirit of God, in the form of a dove, descended after His baptism while a voice from heaven cried: 'This is my beloved Son, in whom I am well pleased' (Matt. 3:17). That same Spirit – symbolized in this instance by a Maiden – in the same way proclaimed Bahá'u'lláh's mission. 'While engulfed in tribulations', He recalled years later,

> I heard a most wondrous, a most sweet voice, calling above My head. Turning My face, I beheld a Maiden – the embodiment of the remembrance of the name of My Lord – suspended in the air before Me. So rejoiced was she in her very soul that her countenance shone with the ornament of the good-pleasure of God, and her cheeks glowed with the brightness of the All-Merciful. Betwixt earth and heaven she was raising a call which captivated the hearts and minds of men . . . Pointing with her finger unto My head, she addressed all who are in heaven and all who are on earth, saying: 'By God! This is the Best-Beloved of the worlds, and

yet ye comprehend not. This is the Beauty of God amongst you, and the power of His sovereignty within you, could ye but understand. This is the Mystery of God and His Treasure, the Cause of God and His glory unto all who are in the kingdoms of Revelation and of creation, if ye be of them that perceive' (GPB 101-2).

Bahá'u'lláh did not, until 1863, announce His claim to be the Redeemer foretold by the Báb. However, He referred to it often, in barely veiled allusions contained in the odes, essays and letters that began to flow from His pen immediately after His release from prison. At the same time (coinciding with His initial banishment to Baghdád), He arose to regenerate the devastated Bábí community; and He succeeded, by precept and example, in transforming its members into beacons of spiritual virtue whose influence radiated far and near.

Throughout the long years of exile, persecution and imprisonment that followed, Bahá'u'lláh faced danger and hardship with heroic fortitude. Wherever He went He earned a reputation as a great humanitarian, a man of deep compassion, truthfulness and integrity. Even those who refused to accept His claims and doctrines frequently expressed admiration for His personal life; the words 'saintly' and 'Christlike' appear frequently in their descriptions. In these loving words of counsel, He sets forth the standard of which He Himself was the living embodiment:

Be generous in prosperity, and thankful in adversity. Be worthy of the trust of thy neighbour, and look upon him with a bright and friendly face. Be a treasure to the poor, an admonisher to the rich, an answerer of the cry of the needy, a preserver of the sanctity of thy pledge. Be fair in thy judgement, and guarded in thy speech. Be unjust to no man, and show all meekness to all men. Be as a lamp unto them that walk in darkness, a joy to the sorrowful, a sea for the thirsty, a haven for the distressed, an upholder and defender of the victim of oppression. Let integrity and uprightness distinguish all thine acts. Be a home for the stranger, a balm to the suffering, a tower of strength for the fugitive. Be eyes to the blind, and a guiding light unto the feet of the erring. Be an ornament to the countenance of truth, a crown to the brow of fidelity, a pillar of the temple of righteousness, a breath of life to the body of mankind, an ensign of the hosts of justice, a luminary above the horizon of virtue, a dew to the soil of the human heart, an ark on the ocean of knowledge, a sun in the heaven of bounty, a gem on the diadem of wisdom, a shining light in the firmament of thy generation, a fruit upon the tree of humility (ESW 93-4).

The seamless consistency between Bahá'u'lláh's words and actions revealed itself in countless ways. He taught His followers, for example, to obey the laws and decrees of duly constituted governments (except in certain extremely grave matters of conscience; for example, a Bahá'í may not, even to save his own life, renounce his faith).* Bahá'u'lláh Himself upheld this principle even at immense personal cost. One such occasion was when, in Adrianople, on the eve of His imprisonment in the fortress of 'Akká, a number of foreign diplomats begged Him to flee and offered Him asylum in their own countries. Spurning their advice, He submitted to the imperial edict, knowing all too well that 'Akká was worse, in many respects, than the notorious 'Black Pit' of Ṭihrán. Long afterwards, when the governor of 'Akká (who by this time had entrusted his own son to Bahá'u'lláh's family for education and moral guidance) urged Him to leave the prison and offered to take full responsibility, He still refused, pointing out that such action would be contrary to the

---

*Shoghi Effendi's secretary, in a letter written on his behalf, states the Bahá'í position as follows: 'We must obey in all cases except where a spiritual principle is involved, such as denying our Faith. For these spiritual principles we must be willing to die' (LOG 445).

sulṭán's decree. Though Bahá'u'lláh deeply loved the beauty of the countryside, and His confinement deprived Him of seeing so much as a blade of grass, He voluntarily remained a prisoner for years after the original sentence had become a dead letter. He was finally persuaded to leave only in the sunset of His life, after it had become obvious that neither the sulṭán (a new one, by this time) nor anyone else in authority objected to His doing so.

Bahá'u'lláh spent His last years in the country residence of Bahjí near 'Akká, surrounded by the scenic beauty He cherished. By this time the Bahá'í Faith had grown considerably and the body of the believers had placed substantial funds at His disposal. Even so, He maintained a lifestyle of extreme austerity, spending the money not on Himself but in promoting the Faith and helping the poor of 'Akká. So generous were Bahá'u'lláh and His family that they themselves often went without things which, in other households, would have been considered necessities. Thus He ended His career with the same solicitude for the needy that had marked its inception.

There have been Muslim and Christian ecclesiastics who denounced Bahá'u'lláh as a selfish charlatan. It would be grossly unfair, however, to imply that all clergy have shown hostility to the Bahá'í Faith and its founder. Many have paid tribute to the purity and heroism of Bahá'u'lláh's life. One such was the Rev T. K. Cheyne, a renowned Bible scholar who researched Bahá'u'lláh thoroughly and expressed his findings in *The Reconciliation of Races and Religions*:

> There was living quite lately a human being of such consummate excellence that many think it is both permissible and inevitable even to identify him mystically with the invisible Godhead . . . If there has been any prophet in recent times, it is to Bahá'u'lláh that we must go. Character is the final judge. Bahá'u'lláh was a man of the highest class – that of prophets (quoted in *Appreciations of the Bahá'í Faith* 18).

A non-Bahá'í scholar, Alfred W. Martin, delivered an excellent summation in *Comparative Religion and the Religion of the Future*. He writes that since its inception the Bahá'í Faith

> has been identified with Bahá'u'lláh, who paid the price of prolonged exile, imprisonment, bodily suffering, and mental anguish for the faith He cherished – a man of imposing personality as revealed in His writings, characterized by intense moral earnestness and profound spirituality, gifted with the selfsame power so conspicuous in the character of Jesus, the power to appreciate people ideally, that is, to see them at the level of their best and to make even the lowest types think well of themselves because of potentialities within them to which He pointed, but of which they were wholly unaware; a prophet whose greatest contribution was not any specific doctrine He proclaimed, but an informing spiritual power breathed into the world through the example of His life and thereby quickening souls into new spiritual activity (quoted in *Appreciations of the Bahá'í Faith* 22-3).

To present someone's character through selected highlights and personal impressions is unsatisfactory at best. It risks being unfair, both to the reader and to the person thus presented. There are many fact-packed volumes of biographical data on the life of Bahá'u'lláh. The vignettes I have offered are intended primarily to whet curiosity and spur independent research. Any inquirer will find at his or her disposal a wealth of well-documented material for further study.

My conviction that Bahá'u'lláh lived a life of towering, almost unheard-of goodness and nobility would not by itself cause me to regard Him as One who spoke with divine authority. It goes a long way, however, towards removing any fear that His otherworldly knowledge might be of satanic origin. Christ puts it best: 'Do men gather grapes of thorns, or figs of thistles?' Without such conviction as a catalyst, I would remain unmoved by any purely logical clues or indications such as prophecies, scientific revelations, innate knowledge and the like. One whose heart is touched by the beauty of Bahá'u'lláh's life, who feels moved by the sacrificial sufferings He bore joyfully in the path of His Divine Beloved – only such a person, I would wager, will be inclined to take seriously any other evidence of inspiration, however compelling or tantalizing it might appear.

12

The Fruit of the Spirit

> Either make the tree good, and his fruit good; or else make
> the tree corrupt, and his fruit corrupt: for the tree is known
> by his fruit (Matt. 12:33).

Both of the scriptural proofs or 'fruits' we have examined so
far – prophetic foreknowledge and glorification of Christ –
are relatively objective. They derive much of their force from
well-documented historical events, 'hard facts', 'concrete
observations' and the like. These are not easily dismissed as
mere opinion or emotional bias.

Objectivity, however, is never absolute – it is a matter of
degree. All human fact-gathering and interpretation is to
some extent subjective. There are choices to be made: what
to leave in, what to leave out, how much weight to give this
or that bit of evidence, where to position this or that piece
of the puzzle. These are value judgements concerning which
two or more equally reasonable people may sometimes differ.
However hard we try (and try we must) to 'let the facts speak
for themselves', it is, in the end, our own hearts that speak.

This is exactly as it should be. The most important truths
and realities are apprehended more with the heart than with
the head. This is particularly so when we investigate the final
'fruit' by which the Bible teaches us to test a claim such as
Bahá'u'lláh's. That fruit (result or accomplishment) is the
manifestation of spiritual attributes and divine virtues. It is
a test that is both more fundamental, and more profoundly
personal, than either of the ones we have explored so far.

This still does not mean the evidence boils down to 'just
somebody's opinion'. We are dealing, as before, with reality

– with propositions that are either true or false. To discern which, we must analyze the facts, and sift the evidence, as objectively as possible, striving prayerfully to overcome prejudice and see reality as it is. Only in this way can we begin to understand the larger picture from a level at which, it is hoped, the findings of head and heart will agree.

Divine qualities collectively are designated in the New Testament by the expression 'fruit of the Spirit'. These are defined by Paul in Ephesians as comprising 'all goodness and righteousness and truth' (Eph. 5:9). In Galatians he speaks of the same 'fruit', equating it with 'love, joy, peace, longsuffering, gentleness, goodness, faith, meekness, temperance' (Gal. 5:22-3). The epistle of James adds:

> But the wisdom that is from above is first pure, then peaceable, gentle, and easy to be entreated, full of mercy and good fruits, without partiality, and without hypocrisy. And the fruit of righteousness is sown in peace of them that make peace (James 3:17-18).

Did Bahá'u'lláh manifest this 'fruit of the Spirit' which, according to the Bible, identifies 'the wisdom that is from above'? Did He do so to an extent commensurate with what we might expect of a divine and perfect Being – 'one like unto the Son of man'? If so, then we have additional reason for regarding His other tokens of inspiration as truly divine, and not as 'lying wonders' designed to lead us astray. 'A good tree', says Christ, 'cannot bring forth evil fruit, neither can a corrupt tree bring forth good fruit' (Matt. 7:18). 'Either make the tree good, and his fruit good; or else make the tree corrupt, and his fruit corrupt: for the tree is known by his fruit' (Matt. 12:33).

This book has already discussed, in the previous chapter, the fact that Bahá'u'lláh glorified Christ by deed as well as by word – by giving to humanity a vivid example of what it means to be 'one like unto the Son of man'. I chose to discuss Bahá'u'lláh's character under that heading because Christ makes it clear that such character is integral to a life that truly glorifies Him and His Father. The same evidence, of course, applies just as logically under this heading as well; the two categories overlap. Moral purity and righteous conduct clearly are 'fruits of the Spirit' in the sense referred to above by Paul.

But there are other signs by which we can judge how fully Bahá'u'lláh manifested the 'fruit of the Spirit' – that is, divine and spiritual qualities. We can ask, for example, what effect His personal qualities had on people with whom He came into direct contact. We can ask what effect His teachings have had, and still are having, in the personal lives and organized activities of those who follow Him. Finally (and this is where the investigation becomes most intensely personal), we can prayerfully explore for ourselves His written words, in order to determine first-hand what effect they might have on us.

THE PROOF OF HIS PERSON

The Christ-figure, Bahá'u'lláh has explained, is One who fully reflects the infinite perfections of the Father. He is 'endowed with all the attributes of God, such as sovereignty, dominion, and the like . . .' (G 49). Whatever He does or says is what God would do or say, for He 'manifests' God as a flawless mirror manifests or reflects the sun. He is 'the light of the world', blazing with divine energy intense enough to transform civilization and redirect history for thousands of years. Though not God in His unknowable essence, He is God in spirit; and His earthly presence therefore is the very presence of God. What would such a presence be like? How would it feel to enter His company, to converse and interact with Him and thus obtain a glimpse of His true nature?

The Bible shows that almost all who met Christ were – despite His simplicity and humble demeanour – profoundly moved. His mere presence was riveting; it affected even indifferent or apathetic onlookers like a thunderbolt. Most

307

people felt irresistibly drawn to Him; others – like bats allergic to light – recoiled. Few, if any, reactions were neutral. We have no reason to suppose this would change should Christ reappear on earth with a new name in an outwardly different human form. It is clear from scripture that the presence of 'one like unto the Son of man' must be a rare experience indeed, unforgettable and indescribable. We may reasonably expect that He should make an overpowering impression, and have a lasting impact, on persons who encounter Him – even on those of high rank and capacity.

Since Bahá'u'lláh left this earth in 1892, we can no longer physically enter His presence and thus judge firsthand how well He satisfied these expectations. The best we can do is study the reactions of those who met Him and try to see Him through their eyes. This does not mean we should substitute their judgement for our own, nor does it bind us to accept their explanations of what they experienced. (Different witnesses, in any case, explained their experiences in different and sometimes contradictory ways.) Just the same, such a study is clearly relevant for anyone wishing to evaluate Bahá'u'lláh's claim in systematic fashion. We can say, at the very least, that if someone claims to embody that 'quickening spirit' which is Christ but ordinarily makes no unusual impression on those who meet him, that person's claim must be considered suspect. If the opposite is true, then, by the same token, that impression and the qualities which produced it must to some extent strengthen his claim.

As the previous chapter indicates, Bahá'u'lláh's life is extensively documented. The historical record includes unnumbered accounts by credible eyewitnesses who met and interacted with Him, including believers and sceptics from all walks of life. What do these records show?

His Magnetic Presence

From this array of primary source material, one fact leaps out again and again, at every turn and in every possible way.

That fact is Bahá'u'lláh's spellbinding personal magnetism. 'An atmosphere of majesty', says 'Abdu'l-Bahá, 'haloed Him as the sun at midday' (GPB 124). The almost irresistible charm of His personality thrilled His friends and confused His enemies; the latter warned inquirers to avoid Him lest they become mesmerized by His 'sorcery'. Complete strangers, knowing nothing of His station, would often bow spontaneously on the occasion of a surprise meeting. High-ranking sceptics and cynics, accustomed to dealing on an equal footing with notables of every description, would become awestruck and speechless in His presence. His loyal followers, having known Him, could not bear to be separated from Him; many abandoned lives of comfort and affluence in order to share His exile and imprisonment. His hard-boiled gaolers and custodians routinely became devoted admirers, placing their resources at His disposal and offering to help Him escape – offers He would kindly but firmly refuse.

'If you had come to this blessed place ['Akká] in the days of the manifestation of the evident Light,' says 'Abdu'l-Bahá,

> if you had attained to the court of His presence, and had witnessed His luminous beauty, you would have understood that His teachings and perfection were not in need of further evidence.
>
> Only through the honour of entering His presence, many souls became confirmed believers; they had no need of other proofs. Even those people who rejected and hated Him bitterly, when they had met Him, would testify to the grandeur of Bahá'u'lláh, saying: 'This is a magnificent man, but what a pity that He makes such a claim! Otherwise, all that He says is acceptable' (SAQ 36).

Ḥájí Mírzá Haydar-'Alí, a believer residing in 'Akká who witnessed many such encounters, comments as follows:

> Although [Bahá'u'lláh] showed much compassion and loving-kindness, and approached anyone who came to His presence with tender care and humbleness, and often used

to make humorous remarks to put them at ease, yet in spite of these, no one, whether faithful or disbelieving, learned or unlettered, wise or foolish, was able to utter ten words in His presence in the usual everyday manner. Indeed, many would find themselves to be tremulous with an impediment in their speech.

Some people asked permission to attain His presence for the sole purpose of conducting arguments and engaging in controversies. As a favour on His part, and in order to fulfil the testimony and to declare conclusively the proofs, He gave these permission to enter the court of His majesty and glory. As they entered the room, heard His voice welcoming them in, and gazed at His countenance beaming with the light of grandeur, they could not help but prostrate themselves at His door. They would then enter and sit down. When He showed them where to sit, they would find themselves unable to utter a word or put forward their questions. When they left they would bow to Him involuntarily. Some would be transformed through the influence of meeting Him and would leave with the utmost sincerity and devotion, some would depart as admirers, while others would leave His presence, ignorant and heedless, attributing their experience to pure sorcery . . . To be brief, the bounties which were vouchsafed to a person as a result of attaining His presence were indescribable and unknowable. The proof of the sun is the sun itself (quoted in Taherzadeh, *Revelation of Bahá'u'lláh*, vol. 3, pp. 248-9).

One of the most overworked and debased words in the English language is 'charisma' – a word currently applied to any performer with crowd appeal and to every politician or preacher with an engaging personality. To any thoughtful student of Bahá'u'lláh's life it will be obvious that His uncanny effect on others was of an entirely different and higher order. Much of what passes today for charisma is actually the work of 'image consultants' who teach their clients how to manipulate news media, stage publicity stunts, 'dress for success' and surround themselves with symbols of leadership and authority. Bahá'u'lláh did none of these things. He lived frugally, wore simple clothing, conducted Himself in a modest and unassuming manner and (despite His audacious claim) avoided the limelight. Such was His radiance of spirit, however, that those who felt its warmth often remarked they felt transported to Paradise.

Few if any first-hand descriptions of Bahá'u'lláh dwell on details of His physical appearance. Instead, they speak of such things as His kingly dignity, His flashing eyes and penetrating gaze, and His melodious voice that always carried a sense of calm authority. Time and again such reports mention the ineffable sense of serenity and exhilaration one felt in His presence. Perhaps the best-known pen-portrait of Bahá'u'lláh is the following account by Edward Granville Browne, the distinguished Cambridge Orientalist who met Him at 'Akká in 1890:

> Though I dimly suspected whither I was going and whom I was to behold (for no distinct intimation had been given to me), a second or two elapsed ere, with a throb of wonder and awe, I became definitely conscious that the room was not untenanted. In the corner where the divan met the wall sat a wondrous and venerable figure, crowned with a felt head-dress of the kind called *taj* by dervishes (but of unusual height and make), round the base of which was wound a small white turban. The face of him on whom I gazed I can never forget, though I cannot describe it. Those piercing eyes seemed to read one's very soul; power and authority sat on that ample brow; while the deep lines on the forehead and face implied an age which the jet-black hair and beard flowing down in indistinguishable luxuriance almost to the waist seemed to belie. No need to ask in whose presence I stood, as I bowed myself before one who is the object of a devotion and love which kings might envy and emperors sigh for in vain! (quoted in Taherzadeh, *Revelation of Bahá'u'lláh*, vol. 2, pp. 12-13).

Many specific incidents could be culled from Bahá'u'lláh's life-story to illustrate His awe-inspiring majesty and the various reactions it evoked. One extreme instance occurred when the Persian consul-general in Baghdád hired a Turkish ruffian named Riḍá to assassinate Bahá'u'lláh. Armed with a pistol, Riḍá tried twice to carry out his mission – once by approaching the Bahá'í leader in a public bath and again by lying in ambush for Him as He walked the city's streets. Both times, when actually confronting his prey, the assassin lost his nerve. On the second occasion he became so frightened and bewildered that he dropped his weapon; whereupon an amused Bahá'u'lláh instructed that the pistol be handed back to him and arranged for an escort to help the dazed man find his way home (GPB 142). Riḍá himself, in later years, circulated this story.

The electrifying impact of Bahá'u'lláh's presence is clear not only from the testimony of His followers, but – in an ironic and backhanded way – from that of Muslim and Christian clergymen seeking to discredit Him. Realizing that this phenomenon required an explanation, His detractors laboured to supply one that would not enhance the credibility of His prophetic claim. One oft-repeated theory was that visitors were carefully conditioned in advance to see Bahá-'u'lláh as a God-like being. Each pilgrim was told (so the story went) that what he would experience depended on his own spiritual capacity: If he was a material being he would see Bahá'u'lláh only as a man; but if he was sufficiently spiritual, he would see God. Only after the visitor had been aroused to a frenzy of anticipation (the story continued) would he be allowed, for a few moments, to enter the Holy Presence and gaze adoringly at the face of his Lord. The almost magical effect of such visits was thus attributed to psychological manipulation.

This superficially plausible explanation might well convince someone who had only minimal knowledge about Bahá'u'lláh; it cannot, however, stand up to serious examination. Its fictitious character is clearly exposed by the testimony of many credible and independent eyewitnesses. E. G. Browne, for example, whose soul-stirring encounter with

Bahá'u'lláh is quoted above, was aware of this cynical theory but regarded it as nonsense. He himself, as he states, only 'dimly suspected' that he was being taken to see Bahá'u'lláh, 'for no distinct intimation had been given to me'. Browne, though a sceptic in regard to Bahá'u'lláh's claims, was hardly an enemy; but reactions similar to his were commonplace even among those who initially were far less receptive. As Ḥájí Mírzá Haydar-'Alí comments:

> When a believer describes what he has experienced in the presence of Bahá'u'lláh, his impressions may be interpreted as being formed through his attitude of self-effacement and a feeling of utter nothingness in relation to Him. But to what can it be attributed when one enters into His presence as an antagonist and leaves as a believer, or comes in as an enemy but goes out as a friend, or comes to raise controversial arguments, but departs without saying anything and, due to wilful blindness, attributing this to magic? (quoted in Taherzadeh, *Revelation of Bahá'u'lláh*, vol. 3, p. 249).

The fact is, Bahá'u'lláh's Muslim opponents were painfully aware of His power to bewitch even those who were hostile or indifferent. Aside from warning inquirers to avoid His presence (and avoiding it themselves), they introduced a further explanation for these reactions by non-believers. Their idea was, quite simply, that Bahá'u'lláh and His followers administered hypnotic drugs to their contacts. Elaborate refinements were added as the story spread: the drug – purportedly an 'extract of dates' – was said to be slipped into the delicious Persian tea customarily served to guests at Bahá'u'lláh's home. For those too wise to accept the spiked tea, there supposedly was a further stratagem: The drug would be compressed into a tiny pill and, at an opportune moment, surreptitiously tossed into the visitor's open mouth. The hypno-drug theory, ludicrous though it was, was widely aired and believed in Persia for a number of decades.

Since we can no longer physically meet Bahá'u'lláh we cannot experience for ourselves the dynamic influence His luminous spirituality is said to have exerted. We are free to explain in any way we like the subjective reactions of others. But we cannot deny, as a matter of historical fact, what those reactions were; nor can we doubt that such reactions were typical not only of believers but of unbelievers – people of capacity whose impressions can in no way be ascribed to simple-minded credulity. We may well ask ourselves: What power can consistently produce so unforgettable an impact upon human consciousness, if not that 'quickening spirit' which – the Bible promises – is to be revealed at the close of the age by 'one like unto the Son of man'?

THE DIVINE WORD

The Bible also explains that 'the wisdom that is from above' is 'full of mercy and good fruits' in the sense that it brings forth the 'fruit of the Spirit' in human life. In the Old Testament, God says:

> For as the rain cometh down, and the snow from heaven, and returneth not thither, but watereth the earth, and maketh it bring forth and bud, that it may give seed to the sower, and bread to the eater: So shall my word be that goeth forth out of my mouth: it shall not return unto me void, but it shall accomplish that which I please, and it shall prosper in the thing whereto I sent it (Isa. 55:10-11).

Christ Himself says: '. . . the words that I speak unto you, they are spirit, and they are life' (John 6:63). God's Word is 'bread from heaven' that nourishes the human soul, satisfying our spiritual hunger in the only way truly possible and nurturing the growth of spiritual attributes. We can verify this divine grace through both individual and collective experience.

Personal Transformation

Bahá'u'lláh teaches that this special, utterly unique creative power of revelation is its most directly accessible proof:

> Intone, O My servant, the verses of God that have been received by thee, as intoned by them who have drawn nigh unto Him, that the sweetness of thy melody may kindle thine own soul, and attract the hearts of all men. Whoso reciteth, in the privacy of his chamber, the verses revealed by God, the scattering angels of the Almighty shall scatter abroad the fragrance of the words uttered by his mouth, and shall cause the heart of every righteous man to throb. Though he may, at first, remain unaware of its effect, yet the virtue of the grace vouchsafed unto him must needs sooner or later exercise its influence upon his soul. Thus have the mysteries of the Revelation of God been decreed by virtue of the Will of Him Who is the Source of power and wisdom (G 295).

Elsewhere He writes:

> Through the Teachings of this Day Star of Truth every man will advance and develop until he attaineth the station at which he can manifest all the potential forces with which his inmost true self hath been endowed (G 68).

Whence comes this inimitable power of the Divine Word to evoke spiritual qualities? According to Bahá'u'lláh, it flows naturally from the fact that revelation is, in a sense, those very qualities in crystallized form. The words spoken by God through His Logos are an outward expression of that inward reality which is the Holy Spirit. Internalizing them by immersing ourselves in scripture, and meditating prayerfully upon them, bathes our souls in divine light. The resulting unfoldment is akin to the germination of a seed exposed to sun, rain and life-giving soil.

Echoing the counsels of Paul, Bahá'u'lláh explains that we harden ourselves to this quickening power if we insist on reading revealed scripture in a strictly materialistic sense. The resulting superficial understanding is akin to skimming the surface of a life-giving ocean – skimming, but never diving. The vitalizing power of God's Word resides not on its surface but in its depth: 'Number me not', says a Bahá'í prayer, 'with them who read Thy words and fail to find Thy hidden gift which, as decreed by Thee, is contained therein, and which quickeneth the souls of Thy creatures and the hearts of Thy servants' (PM 83). Bahá'u'lláh refers to divine revelation as 'the Ocean Whose waters refresh, by virtue of the Will of God, the souls of men' (G 293) and He writes:

> My holy, My divinely ordained Revelation may be likened unto an ocean in whose depths are concealed innumerable pearls of great price, of surpassing lustre. It is the duty of every seeker to bestir himself and strive to attain the shores of this ocean, so that he may, in proportion to the eagerness of his search and the efforts he hath exerted, partake of such benefits as have been pre-ordained in God's irrevocable and hidden Tablets (G 326).

Of all the evidence Bahá'u'lláh offers, His own written word is the one to which we have the most immediate access. It is something we can experience directly, with no need to rely on data compiled by historians, biographers, scientists, literary scholars and the like. What does this mean, in practical terms, to an inquirer who seeks to determine whether the words of Bahá'u'lláh are divine or human in origin?

Simply this: Plunge into a thoughtful and prayerful study of His writings! Do not rely on the opinions, interpretations or commentaries of individual Bahá'ís; go directly to the source. Read Bahá'u'lláh with an open mind and an open heart; delve below the surface to determine whether His words really do contain 'hidden pearls' of meaning and implication. If they seem to do so, then explore and reflect upon those deeper meanings. This in no way implies that any seeker must start out by believing Bahá'u'lláh is who He claims to be; the goal, after all, is to find out. Nor does it mean that an uncommitted reader must necessarily agree with everything that Bahá'u'lláh says. If, at some point, one comes to believe in Bahá'u'lláh's divine authority, then logically one must also believe in His teachings – but an investigator is under no such obligation. The point is not to agree but to understand; and, in seeking that understanding, to put oneself in a position to experience spiritual transformation.

The late Dr Daniel C. Jordan, a Bahá'í psychologist and educator, analyzes this process of transformation in a fascinating paper entitled 'Becoming Your True Self'. He makes one particularly crucial point:

> Personal transformation is a fundamental reason that people are attracted to the Faith, develop conviction as to its truth, and finally become Bahá'ís. The reason is simple. People who come in contact with the Faith and feel themselves being transformed by it have an experience that is self-validating. No one can take that experience away from them and no intellectual argument can make it appear insignificant or unreal. Feeling oneself becoming the best of what one can potentially be constitutes the highest joy. It promotes a sense of self-worth, obviates the need for expressing hostility, and guarantees a compassionate social conscience – all prerequisites of world unity and peace (*Becoming Your True Self* 4).

Immersing ourselves in the 'ocean' of Bahá'u'lláh's writings is easy but not necessarily effortless. Bahá'u'lláh (as quoted above) states that the benefits one derives will be 'in proportion to the eagerness of his search and the efforts he hath exerted'. For Bahá'ís, the study of their sacred texts is a lifetime endeavour requiring, among other things, willingness to entertain new ideas and to relinquish cherished prejudices and misconceptions as their understanding grows. Shoghi Effendi writes: 'The more we read the Writings, the more truths we can find in them, the more we will see that our previous notions were erroneous' (WG 89).

One helpful approach may be to use Bahá'u'lláh's written prayers in one's personal devotions. There are several translated volumes of such prayers, covering every imaginable need and topic – prayers for insight, for spiritual development, for aid and assistance, for praise and thanksgiving, for special occasions, for friends and family, and for innumerable other purposes. (Bahá'ís can and do pray in their own words but they believe that the prayers of Bahá'u'lláh, being divinely revealed, have a special potency that no human speech can match.) Or one may prefer simply to meditate on the writings. Bahá'u'lláh Himself states that 'One hour's reflection is preferable to seventy years of pious worship' (KI 138).

One may choose a specific theme – life after death, world peace, the nature of God, or any other subject in which one takes an interest – and explore what Bahá'u'lláh says about it, pulling together His statements from various places in various books. Often, in this way, one will gain some sudden insight by realizing that a seemingly unrelated statement actually has a direct bearing on the problem. Or one may take a specific book by Bahá'u'lláh and study it from beginning to end – perhaps His *Book of Certitude*, in which He 'unseals' the inward meaning of age-old prophecy; or His *Hidden Words*, in which He sets forth the essentials of good character and spiritual development; or His *Seven Valleys*, in which He defines true mysticism; or His *Epistle to the Son of the Wolf*, in which He reminisces about His own life and presents a mini-anthology of His earlier writings. There are many others, including compilations of His most important letters and essays. The approach is less important than the effort, for Bahá'u'lláh promises divine assistance to anyone who sincerely tries to uncover the truth.

If Bahá'u'lláh really speaks with the Voice of God, then such an experiment, carried out open-mindedly and with reasonable patience, should enable us to sense the superhuman power and potency with which He claims His words are charged: 'Though he may, at first, remain unaware of its effect, yet the virtue of the grace vouchsafed unto him must needs sooner or later exercise its influence upon his soul.' By putting this promise to the test we gain the most direct and important evidence imaginable in our quest.

The Bahá'í Community

While personal exposure and introspection are the best ways to taste the 'fruit of the Spirit' in any purported revelation, they are not the only ways. If (as Bahá'u'lláh claims) 'the Lord of Lords is come', and if His words and teachings are truly 'bread from heaven', then there should be observable social consequences – particularly in the emerging worldwide Bahá'í community. According to Bahá'u'lláh, this community is actually an embryonic civilization destined to establish the Christ-promised Kingdom of God on earth. In that case it should display a dynamic cohesiveness, an evolutionary vigour, contrasting starkly with the social disintegration prevalent in today's world. Such a phenomenon might not be obvious to a casual observer: Arnold Toynbee remarks in *A Study of History* that the Christian Faith itself, in the Hellenizing world of the second century, loomed no larger than the Bahá'í Faith does in the Westernizing world of today (*Study of History*, VIII, 117). Still, the signs of such a development, if they exist, should be visible to anyone who consciously looks for them.

Those signs abound. The relative newness and smallness of the Bahá'í Faith render all the more amazing two of its most striking characteristics: its human diversity and its geographical spread.

As to its diversity, the various races, tribes, nationalities, and religious and ethnic backgrounds represented within the Bahá'í community number in the thousands, while the community's continuing expansion leaves all official statistics obsolete long before they can be published. The list of the breakdown of ethnic groups to which Bahá'ís belong runs to many pages of fine print; when we scan those pages we usually find every human subgroup we have ever heard of, plus countless others we have not.

Marcus Bach, former professor of comparative religion at the University of Iowa, verified this diversity in his travels:

> Wherever I have gone to research the faith called Bahá'í, I have been astonished at what I have found . . . I am continually intrigued by the Bahá'í people . . . representing the basic cultural and ethnic groups around the world and embracing obscure and little-known localities in far-flung lands where even Christianity has barely gone . . . I have met them in the most unexpected places, in a war-torn village in southeast Asia, in African cities, in industrial Mexico, in the executive branches of big industry in Írán, in schools and colleges on foreign campuses, in American cities and villages, wherever people dream of the age-old concept of the brotherhood of man and the fatherhood of God . . . the Bahá'ís are there (Bach, *Strangers* 75-6).

As Bach suggests, the Bahá'í commitment to diversity goes far beyond membership statistics; it transforms the personal lives of its adherents. Long before the civil rights movement in the American South, or the dismantling of apartheid in South Africa, Bahá'í communities in those places were actively practising racial integration and intermarriage. The Faith has brought together Brahmins and untouchables in caste-conscious India, Protestants and Catholics in strife-torn Northern Ireland, Jews and Arabs in the Middle East. Robert Semple, a member of the Management Committee of the Presbyterian Church, is among many to make such comments as these:

> . . . nor can one wonder at the rapid growth in Christian Countries of the new Bahá'í World Faith, which is also gaining many adherents among the people of Asia and Africa; for that Faith has as its motive power a burning belief in the Fatherhood of God, the brotherhood of men, of all creeds and races, and, here is the point, like the early

Christian Church, it practises what it preaches (quoted in Evans and Gail, 'The Voice from Inner Space', *World Order*, Summer 1967, p. 40).

Closely linked to this diversity is the astonishing geographical distribution of the international Bahá'í community. As mentioned previously, the *Encyclopedia Britannica*, in its 1988 Yearbook and subsequent annual editions, published a table of comparative statistics for each of the important world religions. While the Bahá'í Faith was among the smaller of these numerically, the *Britannica* ranked it as second only to Christianity in the number of countries where it has a 'significant following'.

Numerical size is of course less important, at this early stage in the evolution of the community, than its long-term growth. It is estimated that the ranks of Bahá'u'lláh's followers grew from about 400,000 in 1963 to 3.5 million by 1985, then to 5 million by 1991. Up-to-date figures are well-nigh impossible to come by, but there is every indication that this rapid expansion is continuing and even accelerating. The *World Christian Encyclopedia*, perhaps the best-respected authority on such matters, ranks the Bahá'í Faith among the world's fastest-growing religions.

One might expect that a far-flung, rapidly expanding and richly diverse community would quickly divide itself into rival factions, as virtually every other movement – religious or secular – has done under similar circumstances. Yet the Bahá'í Faith, for well over a century, has remained unified both administratively and spiritually. This seamless cohesion – noted with admiration by many independent observers – is all the more remarkable considering that the Faith strongly promotes individual initiative, freedom of expression and independent investigation of truth.

A particularly heartening sign of the Bahá'í community's cohesive vitality is its shared sense of history. Bahá'í historian Douglas Martin expresses the Faith's pride in a legacy which includes, among other things, twenty thousand early martyrs:

Apart from its lively interest in the spiritual giants of earlier Revelations it has its own archetypal heroes and saints (for whom its children are named) whose lives provide moral example and whose spiritual achievements have already begun to evoke the first halting response of Bahá'í artists, writers and musicians. Today, all around the world, an entire generation of Japanese, Italian, Bolivian, Ugandan, Canadian and Persian children are being educated in this common tradition (Martin, 'Bahá'u'lláh's Model for World Fellowship', *World Order*, Fall 1976, pp. 16-7).

Together they are learning, for instance, the story of the mother of Ashraf, a young Persian Bahá'í. The mother was seated in a room with Ashraf's teenage wife when the two women heard an approaching mob chanting anti-Bahá'í hate slogans. Before either could react, someone in the crowd hurled into the room the severed head of Ashraf; whereupon the young bride fainted. The mother, however, calmly washed the blood from her son's head, then threw it back to the crowd with words now cherished by Bahá'ís everywhere: 'What we have given to God we do not take back!'

Still another remarkable feature of Bahá'í community life is its effectiveness as a catalyst for harmonious social change. Bahá'í groups and individuals, working at the grassroots level in thousands of localities throughout the planet, are translating Bahá'u'lláh's universal ideals into practical programmes of social and economic development. Their achievements have won, and are increasingly winning, not only the admiration but the active support of public and private agencies with which they coordinate their humanitarian efforts.

Combined with its astonishing diversity and its geographical spread, these characteristics – rapid growth, administrative and spiritual unity, a shared sense of history and a demonstrated commitment to social change – invest the Bahá'í community with a pulsating evolutionary vigour that one must experience to understand. Having experienced it, we are free to explain it in any way we like; what we cannot do is ignore it or deny its reality.

The springboard for this discussion was Bahá'u'lláh's teaching that the revealed Word of God is its own proof by virtue of its inimitable qualities – one of these being the power to bring into being a new civilization. We have therefore surveyed various facts that support the Faith's vision of itself as the nucleus and prototype of a burgeoning divine Kingdom. There is, of course, no mathematically rigorous way to interpret such signs; sociology is anything but an exact science. Nevertheless, they testify to the awe-inspiring influence that Bahá'u'lláh's words have already exerted, and continue to exert, in the lives of an ever-swelling portion of humanity. Shoghi Effendi sums up the situation:

> The Faith of Bahá'u'lláh has assimilated, by virtue of its creative, its regulative and ennobling energies, the varied races, nationalities, creeds and classes that have sought its shadow, and have pledged unswerving fealty to its cause. It has changed the hearts of its adherents, burned away their prejudices, stilled their passions, exalted their conceptions, ennobled their motives, coordinated their efforts, and transformed their outlook. While preserving their patriotism and safeguarding their lesser loyalties, it has made them lovers of mankind . . . While maintaining intact their belief in the Divine origin of their respective religions, it has enabled them to visualize the underlying purpose of these religions, to discover their merits, to recognize their sequence, their interdependence, their wholeness and unity . . .
>
> . . . this world-enfolding System, this many-hued and firmly-knit Fraternity, infus[es] into every man and woman it has won to its cause a faith, a hope, and a vigour that a wayward generation has long lost, and is powerless to recover. They who preside over the immediate destinies of this troubled world, they who are responsible for its chaotic

state, its fears, its doubts, its miseries will do well, in their bewilderment, to fix their gaze and ponder in their hearts upon the evidences of this saving grace of the Almighty that lies within their reach – a grace that can ease their burden, resolve their perplexities, and illuminate their path (WOB 197-201).

13

The Valley of Decision

Multitudes, multitudes in the valley of decision: for the day
of the Lord is near in the valley of decision (Joel 3:14).

Decide, then, for Me or against Me (Bahá'u'lláh, PDC 45).

This book details many striking parallels between Christ and
Bahá'u'lláh. None is more striking than the way in which
their claims leave no middle ground. We must decide.

As C. S. Lewis points out in *Mere Christianity* (and as we
discussed in Chapter 6), we cannot rationally dismiss Christ
as 'merely a great moral teacher'. Christ never meant to leave
us that option. He claimed to be a divine and perfect Being
– all-powerful, all-knowing, sinless, infallible – entitled by His
station to the complete devotion and unconditional obedience of everyone on earth. No one can make such claims
simply by virtue of being a great teacher or a wise human
being. Unless he happens to be speaking the truth, anyone
saying such things is either a raving lunatic or a scheming
liar. He may be (as Lewis puts it) 'the Devil of Hell', but he
is not a great moral teacher – unless he also is, in reality, who
and what he claims to be. In any case, we must decide.

If this reasoning is sound (as I believe it is), then does it
not apply just as strongly to Bahá'u'lláh? We can accept Him
or denounce Him; but we cannot, if we wish to be reasonable, admire Him as 'simply a great moral teacher' while
brushing off His claims. He deliberately did not leave us any
middle ground. We must decide.

In the case of Christ, we can easily make this decision by studying His life, His words and His accomplishments, including their effect among His followers and on the great Christian community He inspired. We need only apply the standard He Himself set forth: 'By their fruits ye shall know them.' If we do this, earnestly seeking the truth, we find abundant evidence that Christ was neither insane nor deceptive. From the known facts of His life and ministry we can systematically rule out every reasonable explanation for His behaviour except the one He Himself offered – that He really was the embodied Spirit of God, the divine Word, the 'only begotten of the Father'. This in a nutshell is the case for Christianity.

Again, if this reasoning is sound (and so it seems to me), then does it not apply with at least equal force to Bahá'u'lláh? By studying the 'fruits' of His life, and seeking therein an understanding for His motives and His accomplishments, we can eliminate any plausible possibility that He might have been either a deluded madman or a calculating conniver. It then becomes difficult to think of any logical alternative except that He was indeed who and what He claimed. This inference is strengthened a thousand-fold by many clear indications that He did, in fact, possess more-than-human knowledge and abilities.

We will never be able to excuse ourselves by saying we were unable to find out. Christ assures us that 'if any man's will is to do [God's] will, he shall know whether the teaching is from God or whether I am speaking on my own authority' (John 7:16 RSV). This divine principle applies as surely to Christ's second advent as it did two thousand years ago. God is always ready to redeem His sacred promise: 'Ask, and it shall be given you; seek, and ye shall find; knock, and it shall be opened unto you . . .' (Matt. 7:7). 'Then ye shall call upon me, and ye shall go and pray unto me, and I will hearken unto you. And ye shall seek me, and find me, when ye shall search for me with all your heart' (Jer. 29:12-13). '. . . by their fruits ye shall know them' (Matt. 7:20) – not 'may know them', but 'shall know them'. If we seek, prayerfully and with all our hearts, for wisdom in the banquet of 'fruits' God has spread before us, then we will be able, in Bahá'u'lláh's words, to 'ascertain whether or not such a light hath appeared' (G 103).

Keeping these promises in mind, let us review briefly the evidence which this book brings to bear on the validity of Bahá'u'lláh's claims.

The Case for Bahá'u'lláh

Christ's promise of His latter-day return – coming 'down from heaven' with 'power and great glory', seen by 'every eye' – has for nearly two thousand years been interpreted in rigidly materialistic fashion. This is so despite manifold signs that this was never Christ's intention. Among these signs:

a) Christ Himself repeatedly denounces materialistic interpretation of scripture and prophecy.

b) He and His disciples insist that He already did, in a spiritual sense, fulfil these very same conditions in His first advent.

c) The Bible proclaims that the prophecies concerning His Second Coming are 'sealed' by God so as not to be generally understood until after their fulfilment, when they are 'unsealed' by 'one like unto the Son of Man'.

d) Christ promises that in the day of His return, both He and His followers will bear a 'new name' – a name known to and recognized by only those who 'receive' it.

e) He frequently states that His latter-day arrival will be like that of a 'thief' in the 'night'.

f) He emphatically warns His waiting servants that they must 'watch' for this thief-like return so 'that when he cometh and knocketh, they may open unto him immediately'.

Bahá'u'lláh claims to be the fulfilment of these prophecies. He writes: 'Jesus, the Spirit of God . . . hath once more, in my person, been made manifest unto you' (G 101). 'He who is the Lord of Lords is come overshadowed with clouds, and the decree hath been fulfilled by God, the Almighty, the Unrestrained . . . He, verily, hath again come down from Heaven even as He came down from it the first time' (PDC 31). The Second Coming, according to Bahá'u'lláh, refers not to the return of the physical body, nor to that of the human personality or individual soul but rather to the reappearance of that same 'spirit and power' that made Jesus of Nazareth the Christ, or Anointed One. Bahá'u'lláh claims to be the return of Christ in the same sense that John the Baptist – according to Christ Himself – was the return of Elijah; the rebirth of the same 'quickening spirit' that made Christ one with God; a new embodiment of that same pre-existent 'Word' that was 'with God' and that 'was God' from eternity; the same Divine Sun – the earthly 'image of the invisible' – shining once more in a new human mirror.

Bahá'u'lláh does not ask us to follow Him blindly. He asks only that we examine His 'clear evidence' with an open mind and an open heart, weighing it in the uncompromising balance of the Bible. The purpose of this book has been to identify the biblical standards and apply them to Bahá'u'lláh.

The Bible gives three criteria by which it commands us to evaluate anyone claiming to speak with divine authority. According to the Bible, no one – no human imposter, no satanic deceiver – can pass these tests unless He truly does speak the word of God through the power of the Holy Spirit. The tests are:

1) He must, through inspired knowledge, disclose 'things to come' (since only God can both see and shape the future).
2) He must glorify Christ, testifying to His Lordship as the Son of God and acknowledging Him in word and deed as the divine Messiah 'come in the flesh'.
3) He must manifest the 'fruit of the Spirit' in the form of divine virtues, exemplifying these in His own life and causing them to flourish among those who follow Him.

These proofs depend, in each case, not primarily on words or claims but rather on outcomes and accomplishments. The biblical standard is based upon results. Christ draws our attention to this point by encapsulating all the various scriptural criteria in one memorable phrase: 'By their fruits ye shall know them.'

What, then, are some of the 'fruits' of Bahá'u'lláh?

The writings of Bahá'u'lláh (along with those of the Báb and 'Abdu'l-Bahá, which bear the stamp of His authority) are liberally sprinkled with prophecies. These prophecies are detailed and specific; they name names and give locations; most refer to an identifiable time frame of limited duration. They cover, according to Bahá'u'lláh Himself, 'most of the things which have come to pass on this earth' (ESW 148) in such wise that 'No possibility is left for anyone either to turn aside or protest' (ESW 150). Most of them ran counter to the conventional wisdom of the time. All were published well in advance of the events to which they refer, giving sceptics every opportunity to show that Bahá'u'lláh was capable of making mistakes. Yet not one prophecy proved to be in error. The great majority have been spectacularly fulfilled, sometimes at the last possible moment and against seemingly insuperable odds. The fulfilment of the few remaining others seems to be materializing before our eyes.

Prophecies of a historical nature taken from the Bahá'í sacred writings include: the unexpected defeat and downfall of Napoleon III, emperor of France; the defeat of Germany in two bloody wars, resulting in the 'lamentations of Berlin'; the conspicuous success and stability of Queen Victoria's reign; the dismissal of 'Álí Páshá, prime minister of Turkey; the subsequent overthrow and assassination of his chief, Sultán 'Abdu'l-'Azíz; the dismantling of the Ottoman Empire and the extinction of the 'outward splendour' of its capital, Constantinople; the fate of Persia's Náṣiri'd-Dín Sháh as an 'object lesson for the world'; the restrictions imposed upon the Persian monarchy by that country's Constitutional Revolution; the precipitous decline in the fortunes and prestige of monarchy throughout the world; the steady erosion of political and social power wielded by ecclesiastical institutions; the extinction of the Caliphate, which held a position in Sunní Islam similar to that of the Papacy in Roman Catholicism; the spread of communism – the 'Movement of the Left' – and its rise to world power; the subsequent collapse of that same movement as a direct result of its obsession with forced economic equality; the rise of Israel as a Jewish homeland; the violent persecution of Jews on the European continent, culminating in the Nazi holocaust; America's violent racial struggles which, as foretold, threatened the country's survival by polarizing it during the tensest moments of the Cold War; Bahá'u'lláh's own release from the prison of 'Akká and the pitching of His tent on Mount Carmel; the seizure and desecration of Bahá'u'lláh's Baghdád House – a Bahá'í Holy Shrine – by Muslim fanatics; and the complete collapse of every attempt to create sects and factions within the Bahá'í Faith.

Bahá'í prophecies which anticipated scientific discoveries include: the explosive acceleration of scientific and technological progress; the discovery of atomic weaponry capable of poisoning the entire atmosphere of the earth; the transmutation of elements, a long-sought technology now known to be responsible for nuclear power and which, as foreseen by Bahá'u'lláh, has therefore brought humanity to the brink of catastrophe; the discovery that complex chemical elements evolve in nature from simpler ones; the recognition that planets are an inevitable consequence of normal star-formation; space travel 'with the rapidity of rising lightning', reaching out not only to other planets but 'from the globe of the earth to the globe of the sun'; the realization that certain forms of cancer are communicable; the failure of all efforts to identify a 'missing link' or common ancestor between man and ape; the collapse in physics of the theory of a mechanical ether and its replacement by an intellectual abstraction ('spacetime'); and the breakdown of mechanical models as a basis for understanding the physical world.

Whereas the prophecies mentioned above have already been fulfilled, others seem to involve on-going developments still taking place in the world today. These foretell, among other things, that a worldwide tide of oppression will be followed by a renaissance of liberty, leading ultimately to 'unity in freedom'; that a system of collective security will emerge in which all nations, driven by 'imperative necessity', will resist aggression by any recalcitrant member; that these and other trends will lead ultimately to 'the unity of nations – a unity which in this century will be firmly established, causing all the peoples of the world to regard themselves as citizens of one common fatherland'; that a 'universal convulsion' will chasten and awaken humanity as a prelude to world peace; that America will play a leading role in the forging of that peace; and that the Bahá'í Faith, emerging from obscurity, will overcome repression in various places to become a pattern and prototype for the society of the future.

His seeming ability to peer into the future was not the only sign of Bahá'u'lláh's other-worldly knowledge. He spent His entire life in an atmosphere dominated by nineteenth-century Islamic fundamentalism, first in Persia, then as a prisoner of the Turks. He received only the most perfunctory tutoring, never went to school, never studied Western literature, indeed never experienced any outward influence that might plausibly have broadened His horizons or countered any of the deleterious effects of His early conditioning. Yet there is the startling modernity of His writing – a modernity which becomes more, rather than less, apparent every year as His social prescriptions become increasingly relevant to world events, and which has evoked praise and appreciation from a host of independent observers. It was Bahá'u'lláh who gave to the world its first comprehensive inventory of the spiritual and humanitarian principles that today constitute the essence of leading-edge thought. It was Bahá'u'lláh who, long before such a concept had occurred to even His most advanced contemporaries, first described the world in detail as a global village and perceptively analyzed the problems it would face. He wrote with high eloquence and technical virtuosity not only in His native Persian, but in Arabic – a language He never had any opportunity to study, yet which, according to scholars, cannot be mastered without years of arduous formal training. He composed His writings, in both languages, without premeditation, hesitation or revision, dictating for hours at a time with such speed as to tax the most skilled stenographers. These spontaneous outpourings consistently display the very qualities one would expect of revelation: highly polished style, lucid organization and exceptional literary force. At the same time they exclude the lapses and inconsistencies typical of human extemporaneous rambling.

Bahá'u'lláh glorified Christ not only by His words and teachings, but – more importantly – by showing the world what it truly means to walk in Christ's footsteps. When necessary, He risked His own life in order publicly to defend Christ's honour. His personality and character were what one would logically expect of 'one like unto the Son of Man'. His spirituality was by all accounts so radiant, so majestic and magnetic as to lift Him high above the rank and file of humanity. Even hardened sceptics and high-ranking officials, upon meeting Him, would bow spontaneously. Would-be debaters would find themselves speechless and humble in His presence. His enemies in the clergy warned curiosity-seekers to avoid Him lest they fall under His spell; they circulated absurd theories to account for His soul-stirring impact on credible witnesses. Bahá'u'lláh's character was as outstanding and unusual as His force of personality. His lifelong conduct was marked by courage, a passion for justice, self-sacrificing love for humanity and airtight symmetry of word and deed.

Beyond such considerations as these, Bahá'u'lláh claims (and millions of His followers believe) that His very words throb with a spiritual power no human author can duplicate. According to the Bible, such power – power to nourish the soul, to satisfy its hunger, to mediate its growth and unfoldment – is a unique identifying characteristic of that 'bread of life' which is the Word of God. Bahá'u'lláh invites seekers to immerse themselves in the ocean of His words, and, by seeking out the 'hidden pearls' of meaning those words contain, to experience for themselves the creative and transforming influence of this power. This personal experiment enables any inquirer to evaluate, through the promptings of his or her own heart, whether Bahá'u'lláh's writings are of divine or merely human origin. One can further test such a power by observing its apparent effects in the emergence of the Bahá'í worldwide community.

These are some of the findings which emerge from my own systematic probing of Bahá'u'lláh's claim. No one needs to take my word for any of these statements. The evidence is open to any seeker who chooses to examine it. Let us suppose, therefore, that others repeat this investigation and verify these findings. How may we then explain them?

To me, the only straightforward, logically compelling, spiritually satisfying and scripturally sound explanation for these facts is the one offered by Bahá'u'lláh Himself: He spoke and acted with divine authority through the inspiration of the Holy Spirit. Accepting such a conclusion means accepting, by extension, the most startling element of His claim – specifically, that He is the spiritual return of Christ 'in the glory of the Father', fulfilling the biblical prophecies of the Second Coming. This is a claim of awesome magnitude, one not to be accepted blindly or lightly. However, after many years of study and reflection, I find nothing in the Bible to contradict Bahá'u'lláh's claim, and everything to confirm it.

Building the Kingdom

Suppose these things are true. Where does this leave us?

Our generation of believers is facing a crisis unparalleled in Christian history – a crisis consisting of both a challenge and an opportunity. The challenge is that of fulfilling, with

a never-before-felt sense of urgency and purpose, our beloved Master's admonition: 'Seek ye first the Kingdom of
God.' Our opportunity is to build 'on earth as it is in heaven'
that very Kingdom, hastening thereby the day when Satan
will be overthrown and bound, when every knee will bow
before Christ, when the Prince of Peace will be enthroned
in every heart, when 'the earth shall be filled with the knowledge of the Lord, as the waters cover the sea'. What believing
heart, contemplating these Bible promises, can fail to beat
faster? Who, considering the tragedy and devastation now
convulsing our world, can fail to see the need? Which of us
would not give our very lives to advance that victory by even
a single day?

A hundred generations of missionaries have preached the
gospel of Christ to all nations for a witness. Through heroic,
self-sacrificing effort, they have laid in the world a firm
foundation for Christ's millennial reign. Their work, however, remains incomplete. To this day, the world at large
does not know Christ as it ought, acknowledging Him as its
Lord and Saviour. Bahá'u'lláh says this must change – that
it will change – and that His God-sent Revelation is the
divinely ordained instrument through which this change will
finally come about. Through the recognition of Bahá'u'lláh's
claims, and through acceptance of His inspired Message, the
world will at long last turn to Christ and embrace salvation.

This glorious consummation is, according to Bahá'u'lláh,
foreordained by God from the foundation of the world. How
soon it will arrive, however, depends in large measure upon
each one of us. As the return of the pre-existent 'Word made
flesh', Bahá'u'lláh has published Christ's own blueprint for
the divine Kingdom, along with detailed instructions for
building its institutions and implementing its principles.
Most of the task is God's alone: His invisible hand is at work
in the world, demolishing obstacles, shaping events – some
in plain view, many more behind the scenes – to facilitate the
coming transformation. But He has given us our part to play
in this process: Bahá'u'lláh states that those who 'cleave to

His Cause' and 'become the instruments for its promotion
. . . have been endued with the Divine Elixir that can, alone,
transmute into purest gold the dross of the world, and have
been empowered to administer the infallible remedy for all
the ills that afflict the children of men' (G 183). Elsewhere
He says:

> Wert thou to consider this world, and realize how fleeting
> are the things that pertain unto it, thou wouldst choose to
> tread no path except the path of service to the Cause of thy
> Lord . . . O people! The Day, promised unto you in all the
> scriptures, is now come. Fear ye God, and withhold not
> yourselves from recognizing the One Who is the Object of
> your creation. Hasten ye unto Him. Better is this for you
> than the world and all that is therein. Would that ye could
> perceive it! (G 314).

Has the Bahá'í Faith proved to be an effective witness for
Christ? The evidence assures us that it has. Millions of
people – Jews, Hindus, Buddhists, agnostics and even atheists – who never before accepted Christ have come to know
and love Him through the teachings of Bahá'u'lláh. They
now appreciate His station, enjoy a personal relationship
with His spirit, and respond to His voice from whatever
quarter it speaks. They are translating that knowledge and
love into programmes of social and economic development,
into mighty institutions of learning and administration, into
social reform and spiritual enlightenment. Recognizing in
every human face the image of the Heavenly Father, they are
remodelling the earth itself into the likeness of heaven.

Countless Christians have taken leading roles in this
march to victory. Their swelling ranks include some of the
most devoted and dedicated servants of the Gospel, as well
as leading lights of their respective churches. Many (like the
illustrious George Townshend, Archdeacon of Clonfert) were
scholars of scripture, exceptionally well versed in the Bible,
and led by their studies to recognize the reappearance of

Christ in this day. Whatever their past attainments, all testify that they have, through Bahá'u'lláh, achieved a closer walk with Christ, a clearer and deeper understanding of His station, and renewed zest for carrying out His divine Will.

Christ's teaching as revealed in the Bible emphasized personal salvation. It envisioned the spiritualization of the individual. Only indirectly – through this leaven of personal transformation – was that message designed to impact society. Mighty though this impact has been, the reality is that Christ's followers are 'called out of the world', living in it but never of it. The secular nature of society has for centuries been a powerful impediment to the living of a truly God-centred life.

Christ's latter-day gospel, as enshrined in the Revelation of Bahá'u'lláh, introduces a new theme, a concept we might call 'collective salvation'. Our personal relationship with God is as important as ever; but it takes on a new dimension. Society, as an organism in its own right, must now be reborn, resurrected, reshaped in accordance with the newly revealed laws of God. This spiritualization of society will in time produce a world civilization that encourages and facilitates personal spirituality instead of obstructing it. Social and cultural norms, law, education, entertainment, business practices, public policy – all these are to be renewed and restructured, producing an environment that enhances and intensifies each individual's spiritual growth. Instead of a one-way process, where society is illumined through the individual, the process must become two-way; that is, society and the individual must illuminate each other. This is – according to the Bahá'í teachings – the 'fundamental distinction' (PDC 119) between the message of Jesus and that of Bahá'u'lláh. In the words of Bahá'u'lláh Himself:

> Verily, [Jesus] said: 'Come ye after Me, and I will make you to become fishers of men.' In this day, however, We say: 'Come ye after Me, that We may make you to become the quickeners of mankind' (PDC 120).

If 'the Lord of Lords is come', then it is no longer enough – if it ever was – to be concerned solely or even primarily with our own salvation. Such an attitude would be a betrayal of everything Christ teaches in the Bible. There He instructs His followers to seek first God's Kingdom, to spread the gospel of the Kingdom, to pray for the coming of the Kingdom 'on earth as it is in heaven'. Now – Bahá'u'lláh tells us – that very Kingdom is here. Ours is the challenge and the opportunity to erect its structure, brick by brick.

To recognize Bahá'u'lláh – to know Him as the true return of that 'quickening spirit' called Christ – is to possess immense power: 'He that summoneth men in My name', writes Bahá'u'lláh, 'is, verily, of Me, and he will show forth that which is beyond the power of all that are on earth' (PDC 102). Knowledge is power; and with great power comes great responsibility.

This brings us back to the point with which this chapter opened: We must decide. If there is even a possibility, however remote, that Bahá'u'lláh is who He claims to be, then ours is the duty to find out, and to act upon our findings. This issue is of more than life-or-death importance – to us, and to the countless other souls who, here and hereafter, will be influenced by our decision.

It is good to know a thing intellectually; but this is not enough. It is better still to know a thing intuitively; but this, too, is not enough. Even after we understand all the rational and scriptural proofs; even after we feel, deep within ourselves, that they ring true, we may still be plagued at times by those shadowy doubts and fears Bahá'u'lláh calls the 'whisperings of Satan'. There is only one way to reach the deepest level of insight and confidence, to banish every trace of uncertainty – and that is to act on what we know.

How may we best translate our knowledge into action?

This question – like the question of Bahá'u'lláh's authenticity – is highly personal. No doubt there are many potentially satisfying answers, and each person must discover the one that best suits himself or herself. According to Bahá-'u'lláh, however, God's first choice is that we 'cleave to His [Bahá'u'lláh's] Cause' and 'become the instruments for its promotion' (G 183). Anyone who, having acknowledged Bahá'u'lláh's claim, feels moved to identify formally with the Bahá'í Faith is lovingly invited to do so. (See Appendix B, 'Becoming a Bahá'í'.)

Once the facts are all in, and the evidence is all sifted, still we must 'choose to do God's will', prayerfully determined to follow Him wherever He leads. That choice will boil down, in the last analysis, to these words of Christ: '. . . the sheep follow [the shepherd]; for they know his voice' (John 10:4). Do we hear Christ's own voice in the voice of Bahá'u'lláh? That is something each human being must discover for himself or herself. But we will never hear, unless we listen; never see, unless we look; never know, unless we consider.

Any Christian pondering these choices is invited to study Bahá'u'lláh's *Most Holy Tablet*, His famous letter addressed to the heart of each and every believer in Christ. I can do no better than close with the following excerpts:

> O followers of the Son! Have ye shut out yourselves from Me by reason of My Name? Wherefore ponder ye not in your hearts? Day and night ye have been calling upon your Lord, the Omnipotent, but when He came from the heaven of eternity in His great glory, ye turned aside from Him and remained sunk in heedlessness.
>
> Consider those who rejected the Spirit [Jesus] when He came unto them with manifest dominion . . . They failed to attain His presence, notwithstanding that His advent had been promised them in the Book of Isaiah as well as in the Books of the Prophets and the Messengers. No one from among them turned his face towards the Dayspring of divine bounty except such as were destitute of any power amongst men. And yet, today, every man endowed with power and invested with sovereignty prideth himself on His Name . . . Take good heed and be of them that observe the warning.

... We, verily, have come for your sakes, and have borne the misfortunes of the world for your salvation. Flee ye the One Who hath sacrificed His life that ye may be quickened? Fear God, O followers of the Spirit, and walk not in the footsteps of every divine that hath gone far astray. Do ye imagine that He seeketh His own interests, when He hath, at all times, been threatened by the swords of the enemies; or that He seeketh the vanities of the world, after He hath been imprisoned in the most desolate of cities? Be fair in your judgement and follow not the footsteps of the unjust.

Open the doors of your hearts. He Who is the Spirit [Jesus] verily standeth before them. Wherefore banish ye Him Who hath purposed to draw you nigh unto a Resplendent Spot? ... We, in truth, have opened unto you the gates of the Kingdom. Will ye bar the doors of your houses in My face? This indeed is naught but a grievous error. He, verily, hath again come down from heaven, even as He came down from it the first time. Beware lest ye dispute that which He proclaimeth, even as the people before you disputed His utterances. Thus instructeth you the True One, could ye but perceive it.

... This is the Word which the Son concealed, when to those around Him He said: 'Ye cannot bear it now.' And when the appointed time was fulfilled and the Hour had struck, the Word shone forth above the horizon of the Will of God. Beware, O followers of the Son, that ye cast it not behind your backs. Take ye fast hold of it. Better is this for you than all that ye possess. Verily He is nigh unto them that do good. The Hour which We had concealed from the knowledge of the peoples of the earth and of the favoured angels hath come to pass ... He hath testified of Me, and I do testify of Him. Indeed, He hath purposed no one other than Me. Unto this beareth witness every fair-minded and understanding soul.

Though beset with countless afflictions, We summon the people unto God, the Lord of names ... My body hath endured imprisonment that ye may be released from the bondage of self. Set your faces then towards His countenance and follow not the footsteps of every hostile oppressor. Verily, He hath consented to be sorely abased that ye may attain unto glory, and yet, ye are disporting yourselves in the vale of heedlessness. He, in truth, liveth in the most desolate of abodes for your sakes, whilst ye dwell in your palaces.

. . . He is come in the sheltering shadow of Testimony, invested with conclusive proof and evidence, and those who truly believe in Him regard His presence as the embodiment of the Kingdom of God. Blessed is the man who turneth towards Him, and woe betide such as deny or doubt Him.

Announce thou unto the priests: Lo! He Who is the Ruler is come. Step out from behind the veil in the name of thy Lord, He Who layeth low the necks of all men. Proclaim then unto all mankind the glad-tidings of this mighty, this glorious Revelation. Verily, He Who is the Spirit of Truth is come to guide you unto all truth. He speaketh not as prompted by His own self, but as bidden by Him Who is the All-Knowing, the All-Wise.

Say, this is the One Who hath glorified the Son and hath exalted His Cause. Cast away, O peoples of the earth, that which ye have and take fast hold of that which ye are bidden by the All-Powerful, He Who is the Bearer of the Trust of God. Purge ye your ears and set your hearts towards Him that ye may hearken to the most wondrous Call which hath been raised from Sinai, the habitation of your Lord, the Most Glorious. It will, in truth, draw you nigh unto the Spot wherein ye will perceive the splendour of the light of His countenance which shineth above this luminous Horizon.

O concourse of priests! Leave the bells, and come forth, then, from your churches. It behoveth you, in this day, to proclaim aloud the Most Great Name among the nations. Prefer ye to be silent, whilst every stone and every tree shouteth aloud: 'The Lord is come in His great glory!'? Well is it with the man who hasteneth unto Him. Verily, he is numbered among them whose names will be eternally recorded and who will be mentioned by the Concourse on High. Thus hath it been decreed by the Spirit in this wondrous Tablet. He that summoneth men in My name is, verily, of Me, and he will show forth that which is beyond the power of all that are on earth . . . Well is it with the slumberer who is stirred by the Breeze of God and ariseth from amongst the dead, directing his steps towards the Way of the Lord. Verily, such a man is regarded, in the sight of God, the True One, as a jewel amongst men and is reckoned with the blissful.

. . . In the East the light of His Revelation hath broken; in the West have appeared the signs of His dominion. Ponder this in your hearts, O people, and be not of those who have turned a deaf ear to the admonitions of Him Who is the Almighty, the All-Praised. Let the Breeze of God awaken you. Verily, it hath wafted over the world. Well is it with him that hath discovered the fragrance thereof and been accounted among the well-assured.

O concourse of bishops! Ye are the stars of the heaven of My knowledge. My mercy desireth not that ye should fall upon the earth. My justice, however, declareth: 'This is that which the Son hath decreed.' And whatsoever hath proceeded out of His blameless, His truth-speaking, trustworthy mouth, can never be altered. The bells, verily, peal out My Name, and lament over Me, but My spirit rejoiceth with evident gladness . . . We have summoned all created things to attain the presence of thy Lord, the King of all names. Blessed is the man that hath set his face towards God, the Lord of the Day of Reckoning.

. . . Bethlehem is astir with the Breeze of God. We hear her voice saying: 'O most generous Lord! Where is Thy great glory established? The sweet savours of Thy presence have quickened me, after I had melted in my separation from Thee. Praised be Thou in that Thou hast raised the veils, and come with power in evident glory.' We called unto her from behind the Tabernacle of Majesty and Grandeur: 'O Bethlehem! This Light hath risen in the orient, and travelled towards the occident, until it reached thee in the evening of its life. Tell Me then: Do the sons recognize the Father, and acknowledge Him, or do they deny Him, even as the people aforetime denied Him [Jesus]?' Whereupon she cried out saying: 'Thou art, in truth, the All-Knowing, the Best-Informed.' Verily, We behold all created things moved to bear witness unto Us. Some know Us and bear witness, while the majority bear witness, yet know Us not.

. . . Blessed the slumberer who is awakened by My Breeze. Blessed the lifeless one who is quickened through My reviving breaths. Blessed the eye that is solaced by gazing at My beauty . . . Blessed the insatiate soul who casteth away his selfish desires for love of Me and taketh his place at the banquet table which I have sent down from the heaven of divine bounty for My chosen ones . . . Blessed the ear that hath heard and the tongue that hath borne witness and the eye that hath seen and recognized the Lord Himself, in His great glory and majesty, invested with grandeur and dominion . . . Blessed is the man who hath detached himself from all else but Me, hath soared in the atmosphere of My love, hath gained admittance into My Kingdom, gazed upon My realms of glory, quaffed the living waters of My bounty, hath drunk his fill from the heavenly river of My loving providence, acquainted himself with My Cause, apprehended that which I concealed within the treasury of My Words, and hath shone forth from the horizon of divine knowledge engaged in My praise and glorification. Verily, he is of Me. Upon him rest My mercy, My loving-kindness, My bounty and My glory (TB 9-21).

Appendix A

Frequently Asked Questions

The focus of this book is specifically on Bible evidence by which we can understand and evaluate Bahá'u'lláh's claim. It is not intended as a general treatise on His teachings. There are, however, important secondary questions not treated in the main text which are bound to be of interest to any Christian. These include the Bahá'í views of Satan, the nature of evil, the reality of heaven and hell, baptism and communion, and the relationship of the Bahá'í Faith to religions other than Christianity.

These issues are addressed in this appendix. Further information may be obtained from Bahá'í literature listed in the bibliography.

What does the Bahá'í Faith teach about Satan and the nature of evil?

Concerning Satan, there are two distinct issues: 1) Do Bahá'ís believe in Satan? 2) If so, who or what is he? The answer to the first question is straightforward: Yes, the Bahá'í Faith categorically affirms the reality of Satan. The second question, concerning his identity and nature, is more complex. A Christian friend, having heard that Bahá'ís interpret figuratively many of the Bible accounts of Satan, wrote to me as follows:

> Throughout the Bible Satan is referred to as a being. Christ spoke to Satan as to a person. It is taught that Satan

tempted Christ in the wilderness. In the book of Job, Satan is quoted. He stood before God and accused Job. We are warned in the New Testament that 'your adversary the devil, as a roaring lion, walketh about, seeking whom he may devour' (I Peter 5:8). This all seems to say that there is a malevolent being which was created by God and yet has rebelled. He seeks to be like the Most High. He stands in juxtaposition to Him. This is not written in the flowery language of symbolism, but rather is plain and vivid . . . I see too many such personal representations to cast it lightly aside. What are your thoughts?

To my friend I sent the following explanation:

You are clearly correct about the way in which Satan is portrayed in the Bible. He is portrayed precisely the same way throughout Bahá'í sacred scripture. Bahá'u'lláh writes, for example: 'Watch over yourselves, for the Evil One is lying in wait, ready to entrap you. Gird yourselves against his wicked devices, and, led by the light of the name of the All-Seeing God, make your escape from the darkness that surroundeth you' (G 94). He refers elsewhere to certain enemies of God as 'abject manifestations of the Prince of Darkness' (KI 122). The Báb wrote to the Shah of Persia: 'The things which have, from the first day till now, befallen Me at the hand of thy people are but the work of Satan' (SWB 25). Elsewhere: 'O ye the servants of the Merciful One! Enter ye, one and all, through this Gate and follow not the steps of the Evil One, for he prompteth you to walk in the ways of impiety and wickedness; he is, in truth, your declared enemy' (SWB 56-7). There are countless similar passages from the Báb, Bahá'u'lláh and 'Abdu'l-Bahá; and I can no more cast them 'lightly aside' than can you. No matter how we interpret these references, we are dealing here with something that is both real and extremely dangerous.

'Abdu'l-Bahá comments as follows:

The reality underlying this question is that the evil spirit, Satan or whatever is interpreted as evil, refers to the lower nature in man. This baser nature is symbolized in various ways. In man there are two expressions: One is the expression of nature; the other the expression of the spiritual realm (PUP 294-5).

Elsewhere He defines this 'baser nature' as 'the insistent self, the evil promptings of the human heart' (SAB 256). Shoghi Effendi, Guardian of the Bahá'í Faith, describes the lower self as 'the ego, the dark, animalistic heritage each one of us has, the lower nature that can develop into a monster of selfishness, brutality, lust and so on. It is this self we must struggle against . . .' (LOG 113).

When we balance all these admonitions and explanations, it becomes clear that there is no basis for the charge sometimes levelled against the Bahá'í Faith by its critics, namely, that 'Bahá'ís don't believe in the Devil'. Of course we do: There is a Satan; he is alive and kicking inside each and every human being. Nor would it be accurate even to deny that Satan is a personality or conscious entity. The human self (whether operating in high or low gear) is a conscious personal entity of the utmost subtlety, brilliance and ingenuity. We are our own worst enemy. Once I thought about these issues I began to notice, for example, with what perverse cleverness I place temptation in my own path, then concoct one slick rationalization after another as to why I should succumb. Or how I can struggle for decades to cultivate humility, perhaps finally taking a single halting step in that direction; whereupon my satanic lower self, waiting gleefully for that moment, claps me on the back, puts its arm around my shoulder, and says, 'My, my! Aren't we doing great! Bet all those other slobs wish they were as humble as we are' – thus yanking me back down into the infernal pit. This Satan character is an absolute @#$%^&*!

Another facet of this problem is the nature of evil. The Bahá'í teachings explain that evil is a negative condition rather than a positive existence. Evil, in other words, is the absence of good just as darkness is the absence of light, or a vacuum is the absence of air. The mistaken inference is sometimes made that evil, being a kind of spiritual void, is 'mere non-existence' or nothingness and therefore need not be worried about. This is illogical. Shoghi Effendi explains: 'We know absence of light is darkness, but no one would assert darkness was not a fact. It exists even though it is only the absence of something else. So evil exists too, and we cannot close our eyes to it . . .' (LOG 513). Darkness may be a nothingness but it can feel downright tangible when it engulfs us; and it can lead us over the edge of an abyss. The abyss itself is a nothingness – an absence of solid ground – but it can swallow and destroy us. A vacuum, or even a low-pressure area, has only negative existence; yet it can conjure up a tornado capable of striking with the force of an atomic bomb.

Given this perspective, I personally do not believe that Satan is in every sense a purely internal phenomenon. Bahá-'u'lláh writes:

> Indeed the actions of man himself breed a profusion of satanic power. For were men to abide by and observe the divine teachings, every trace of evil would be banished from the face of the earth. However, the widespread differences that exist among mankind and the prevalence of sedition, contention, conflict and the like are the primary factors which provoke the appearance of the satanic spirit. Yet the Holy Spirit hath ever shunned such matters. A world in which naught can be perceived save strife, quarrels and corruption is bound to become the seat of the throne, the very metropolis, of Satan (TB 176-7).

Note how He says that 'a profusion of satanic power' results from 'factors which provoke the appearance of the satanic spirit'. I have given much thought to this passage, and other related ones, in the Bahá'í writings and the Bible. From such scriptures I infer that the evil actions and interactions of human beings – actions dictated by the 'Satan of self' – give rise to evil forces that are *in some sense* external to ourselves. By driving out the Holy Spirit (which Bahá'u'lláh says 'hath ever shunned such matters') we create in the world around us a spiritual vacuum or negativity, a kind of undertow tending to drag down our spirits just as the ocean's pull can drag down our bodies. This negativity fuels and strengthens the animal instinct within ourselves. I suspect that this same force, once set in motion, can trigger wars, natural disasters, ecological crises and many similar catastrophes. (Shoghi Effendi reportedly told the late Marzieh Gail, a prominent Bahá'í writer and translator, that a particularly diabolical arch-villain had left a spiritual 'pool of evil' on the island where he spent his final years; and that this residue was responsible for the succession of disasters that had since befallen that country.) We sow the wind; we reap the whirl-wind.

I would therefore say that Satan, as presented both in the Bahá'í teachings and in the Bible, really has two distinct meanings: In one sense, he represents the dark, rebellious lower nature that each one of us has; and in another, he symbolizes the destructive spiritual forces we unleash in the world by yielding to the demon within.

Now the natural question is why, if this is true, do both the Bible and the Bahá'í teachings most often portray Satan as a single individual distinct from ourselves? Because – at least this is my opinion – we must think and behave *as if* we are fighting an external adversary. The practical conse-quences of the Bahá'í view are identical to those of the traditional Christian view: We battle 'against principalities, against powers . . . against spiritual wickedness in high places' (Eph. 6:12). These play tricks on our minds, ply us with temptation, appear as angels of light and roam the earth seeking whom to devour. Even if (as I believe) such forces – internal and external – ultimately arise from within our-selves, they are more easily resisted if we think of them in terms of Satan.

Our intellectual understanding of this issue is far less crucial than whether we are motivated to struggle and thereby rise above ourselves. Since the Bahá'í concept of Satan is somewhat abstract and multi-faceted, one doubts that it could easily have been explained, two thousand years ago, to literal-minded Hebrews who wrestled with even the simplest spiritual ideas. Christ and the Bible writers, in my opinion, never bothered to interpret the symbolism because they knew the reaction of most readers would be, 'Oh, good, there's really no Devil, so I have nothing to worry about.' They therefore left the underlying reality as something to be disclosed in a future age, when humanity could deal with its implications in a more mature way.

Although He never explicitly defines Satan, there are instances where Christ clearly employs the term just as it is used in Bahá'í scripture. One is His famous rebuke to Peter: 'Get behind Me, Satan . . . for you are not on the side of God, but of men' (Matt. 16:23 RSV). Here He explicitly calls Peter 'Satan'. This makes sense only if He is using the name figuratively as referring to Peter's own lower nature. Another example is the passage in which Christ alludes to His future betrayal by Judas Iscariot: 'Have not I chosen you twelve, and one of you is a devil?' (John 6:70). Not 'serves the devil'; not 'is possessed by the devil' – but '*is* a devil'. Judas was a devil in that he had surrendered to the innate tendency of the human ego to rebel against God.

Symbolism, in the Bahá'í view, is not always or necessarily evidenced by 'flowery' language. Many Bible parables, for example, are stated as if they were historical fact. (Indeed, some may have been, though that is not their point.) Bahá'ís believe that Satan's temptation of Christ is a figurative account of the struggle Christ waged within Himself as the full truth of His station and mission burst upon His unfolding human consciousness. The Christ-figure, as Christians and Bahá'ís agree, is both fully human and fully divine. The human nature within Him was certainly aware of the omnipotence He wielded as the embodiment of the Spirit of God, and of the fact that He could have chosen to use His power for personal gain. So even Christ had to wrestle the 'Satan of self'. This same struggle, in another form, is apparent in His prayer at Gethsemane, when He acknowledges that He, personally, prefers not to undergo the agony of crucifixion: 'nevertheless not as I will, but as thou wilt' (Matt. 26:39).

I would view in similar light the other Bible accounts of Satan, Lucifer or whatever alias he happens to be using on any given day. (This 'being', whoever he is, seems to show up everywhere, wearing an astounding array of clever disguises!) Although Job, for instance, may well have been a real person, we have no real reason to think that the purpose of his story as recorded in the Bible was principally biographical. He is being used there as the protagonist of a parable, a story designed to make a spiritual point. In the same vein, Bahá'ís believe that although Adam was indeed a historical figure, the Genesis account of Adam (where Satan first appears) is written in spiritual language designed to convey deep metaphysical and spiritual realities. (For a detailed exposition of some of these meanings see *Some Answered Questions* and other Bahá'í texts.)

What do Bahá'ís believe about an afterlife? What are Heaven and Hell?

Bahá'ís do not believe in reincarnation. Bahá'u'lláh teaches that the human soul comes into being at the moment of conception, and that, having done so, it is immortal. He writes:

> Know thou of a truth that the soul, after its separation from the body, will continue to progress until it attaineth the presence of God, in a state and condition which neither the revolution of ages and centuries, nor the changes and chances of this world, can alter. It will endure as long as the Kingdom of God, His sovereignty, His dominion and power

will endure . . . Blessed is the soul which, at the hour of its separation from the body, is sanctified from the vain imaginings of the peoples of the world. Such a soul liveth and moveth in accordance with the will of its Creator, and entereth the all-highest Paradise . . . The nature of the soul after death can never be described, nor is it meet and permissible to reveal its whole character to the eyes of men. The Prophets and Messengers of God have been sent down for the sole purpose of guiding mankind to the straight path of truth. The purpose underlying their revelation hath been to educate all men, that they may, at the hour of death, ascend, in the utmost purity and sanctity and with absolute detachment, to the throne of the Most High . . . The world beyond is as different from this world as this world is different from that of the child while still in the womb of its mother (G 155-7).

The Bahá'í teachings further state:

The mysteries of which man is heedless in the earthly world, those will he discover in the heavenly world, and there will he be informed of the secrets of truth; how much more will he recognize or discover persons with whom he has been associated . . .

. . . The difference and distinction will naturally become realized between all men after their departure from this mortal world. But this distinction is not in respect to place, but in respect to the soul and conscience. For the Kingdom of God is sanctified from time and place; it is another world and another universe . . . And know thou for a certainty that in the divine worlds, the spiritual beloved ones will recognize each other, and will seek union with each other, but a spiritual union. Likewise, a love that one may have entertained for any one will not be forgotten in the world of the Kingdom. Likewise, thou wilt thou forget there the life that thou hadst in the material world (TAB 205-6).

The purpose of this life is to acquire the spiritual capacities we will need in the next – qualities without which we will be unable to grow, develop and progress towards God as we otherwise might. Christ says, 'Behold, the kingdom of God is within you' (Luke 17:21). It is in this sense (and not a physical or geographical sense) that Heaven and Hell are realities. Heaven is nearness to God; Hell is remoteness from God. Bahá'u'lláh writes:

> Whoso hath recognized the Day Spring of Divine guidance and entered His holy court hath drawn nigh unto God and attained His Presence, a Presence which is the real Paradise, and of which the loftiest mansions of heaven are but a symbol . . . Whoso hath failed to recognize Him will have condemned himself to the misery of remoteness, a remoteness which is naught but utter nothingness and the essence of the nethermost fire. Such will be his fate, though to outward seeming he may occupy the earth's loftiest seats and be established upon its most exalted throne (G 70-1).

> As to Paradise: It is a reality and there can be no doubt about it, and now in this world it is realized through love of Me and My good-pleasure. Whosoever attaineth unto it God will aid him in this world below, and after death He will enable him to gain admittance into Paradise whose vastness is as that of heaven and earth . . . Likewise apprehend thou the nature of hell-fire and be of them that truly believe. For every act performed there shall be a recompense according to the estimate of God, and unto this the very ordinances and prohibitions prescribed by the Almighty amply bear witness (TB 189).

> It is clear and evident that all men shall, after their physical death, estimate the worth of their deeds, and realize all that their hands have wrought. I swear by the Day Star that shineth above the horizon of Divine power! They that are the followers of the one true God shall, the moment they depart out of this life, experience such joy and gladness as would be impossible to describe, while they that live in error shall be seized with such fear and trembling, and shall be filled with such consternation, as nothing can exceed. Well

is it with him that hath quaffed the choice and incorruptible wine of faith through the gracious favour and the manifold bounties of Him Who is the Lord of all Faiths . . . (G 171).

As these words imply, our faith and conduct in this life have consequences that remain with us eternally. It is all too easy to make choices we may rue until the end of time. Nevertheless, Bahá'ís do not believe in a sadistic Creator who abandons any of His children to endless torture, physical or spiritual. The principle which applies here is that stated in Hebrews 12:6: 'whom the Lord loveth he chasteneth'. The purpose of discipline – even stern discipline – is to awaken the soul so that, through painful experience, it can see its error and mend its ways. Neither God nor the wayward soul could ever benefit from the infliction of infinite agony excluding any hope of ultimate reprieve. The Bahá'í teachings state:

> It is even possible that the condition of those who have died in sin and unbelief may become changed; that is to say, they may become the object of pardon through the bounty of God, not through His justice – for bounty is giving without desert, and justice is giving what is deserved. As we have power to pray for these souls here, so likewise we shall possess the same power in the other world, which is the Kingdom of God. Are not all the people in that world the creatures of God? Therefore, in that world also they can make progress (SAQ 232).

How may we reconcile such a view with the Bible's cryptic references to 'everlasting fire' (Matt. 18:8) and 'eternal damnation' (Mark 3:29)? Much confusion, perhaps, grows out of our tendency to think of eternity in terms of earthly duration. Bahá'u'lláh teaches that the spiritual realm of God is one in which chronological time, as it affects our life here, has no meaning. Even on this physical plane we often find in spiritual joy or deprivation a timeless quality, in light of which such distinctions as 'temporary' or 'permanent' seem rather artificial. Who knows what it may be like to feel the same emotions in a state wherein our sense of time, as we once knew it, will have vanished, while our other perceptions are vastly intensified? Might we not experience eternity in a single moment, or vice versa?

What is certain is that we now have opportunities for service and spiritual growth that will never recur, here or hereafter. If we neglect them, our remorse – once we realize their importance – may well burn within us throughout all the worlds of God. The reality of damnation is this sense of irretrievable loss. Its prospect should provide ample incentive to take seriously the counsel of Bahá'u'lláh: 'Free thyself from the fetters of this world, and loose thy soul from the prison of self. Seize thy chance, for it will come to thee no more' (PHW 40).

How do Bahá'ís view baptism and communion?

The physical rituals we associate with baptism and communion have been discontinued by Bahá'u'lláh. However, their inner reality – the spiritual meaning by virtue of which they are considered holy sacraments – is preserved and indeed amplified in the Bahá'í Faith. The effect is not to abolish either sacrament but to shift emphasis from its outward expression to its inward spirit.

We must emphasize that these shifts do not reflect 'man-made' changes introduced into religion by human whim. Emanating as they do from commandments of Bahá'u'lláh, they are, in the Bahá'í view, ordained by God alone. Such changes in outward expression find clear parallels in the history of Christianity. The Jewish rituals of circumcision and animal sacrifice (though clearly based in the Law of God) were transformed, on Christ's authority, into spiritual equivalents no longer primarily dependent on physical behaviour. St Paul thus explains: 'For we are the true circumcision, who worship God in spirit' (Phil. 3:3 RSV). '. . . real circumcision is a matter of the heart, spiritual and not literal' (Rom. 2:29 RSV). The shedding of animal blood was superseded by the atoning sacrifice of Christ Himself. Thus both practices, while outwardly discontinued, were in reality extended and reinterpreted in such a way as to emphasize their true meaning.

The Bible itself anticipates a similar shift in emphasis regarding communion. St Paul writes: 'For as often as ye eat this bread, and drink this cup, ye do shew the Lord's death *till he come* (I Cor. 11:26; emphasis added). If, as Bahá'ís believe, 'the Lord of Lords is come' to reveal 'all truth' and 'make all things new', then it is reasonable to expect that the reality of this sacrament should be clothed in a new form befitting Christ's return. Such an expression is the Bahá'í Feast. Held every nineteen days, this spiritual celebration features prayers and devotional readings, community consultation and sharing of refreshments in an atmosphere of fellowship.

Regarding baptism, the Bahá'í teachings explain:

> The principle of baptism is purification by repentance. John admonished and exhorted the people, and caused them to repent; then he baptized them. Therefore, it is apparent that this baptism is a symbol of repentance from all sin: its meaning is expressed in these words: 'O God! as my body has become purified and cleansed from physical impurities, in the same way purify and sanctify my spirit from the impurities of the world of nature, which are not worthy of the Threshold of Thy Unity!' Repentance is the return from disobedience to obedience. Man, after remoteness and deprivation from God, repents and undergoes purification . . .
>
> As Christ desired that this institution of John should be used at that time by all, He Himself conformed to it in order to awaken the people and to complete the law of the former religion . . .
>
> Christ was not in need of baptism; but as at that time it was an acceptable and praiseworthy action, and a sign of the

glad tidings of the Kingdom, therefore, He confirmed it. However, afterward He said the true baptism is not with material water, but it must be with spirit and with water [John 3:5]. In this case water does not signify material water, for elsewhere it is explicitly said baptism is with spirit and with fire [Matt. 3:11], from which it is clear that the reference is not to material fire and material water, for baptism with fire is impossible.

Therefore, the spirit is the bounty of God, the water is knowledge and life, and the fire is the love of God. For material water does not purify the heart of man; no, it cleanses his body. But the heavenly water and spirit, which are knowledge and life, make the human heart good and pure; the heart which receives a portion of the bounty of the Spirit becomes sanctified, good and pure . . .

Man cannot free himself from the rage of the carnal passions except by the help of the Holy Spirit. That is why He says baptism with the spirit, with water and with fire is necessary, and that it is essential – that is to say, the spirit of divine bounty, the water of knowledge and life, and the fire of the love of God. Man must be baptized with this spirit, this water and this fire so as to become filled with the eternal bounty. Otherwise, what is the use of baptizing with material water? No, this baptism with water was a symbol of repentance, and of seeking forgiveness of sins.

But in the cycle of Bahá'u'lláh there is no longer need of this symbol; for its reality, which is to be baptized with the spirit and love of God, is understood and established (SAQ 91-2).

Admittance into the Bahá'í community requires only a declaration of faith in Bahá'u'lláh as the Voice of God for this age and in the divinely ordained laws and institutions He has established. This declaration may be either public or private and is essentially a matter of conscience. Depending on the country, such expression of belief may be accompanied by some administrative formality such as the filling out of a registration card. The real 'baptism of fire', however, takes place in the heart when the believer makes a decisive commitment to Bahá'u'lláh and His Cause.

What is the attitude of the Bahá'í Faith towards religions other than Christianity?

Bahá'u'lláh teaches that the eternal Logos – that 'quickening spirit' called Christ – has spoken in and through the Founders of all the world's great religions. Not only has the Word appeared as Jesus and as Bahá'u'lláh, but also as Abraham, Moses, Muḥammad and others. Bahá'u'lláh writes:

> There can be no doubt whatever that the peoples of the world, of whatever race or religion, derive their inspiration from one heavenly Source, and are the subjects of one God. The difference between the ordinances under which they abide should be attributed to the varying requirements and exigencies of the age in which they were revealed. All of them, except a few which are the outcome of human perversity, were ordained of God, and are a reflection of His Will and Purpose. Arise and, armed with the power of faith, shatter to pieces the gods of your vain imaginings, the sowers of dissension amongst you. Cleave unto that which draweth you together and uniteth you. This, verily, is the most exalted Word which the Mother Book hath sent down and revealed unto you (G 217-18).

To grasp what Bahá'u'lláh is saying we must keep in mind His teaching that there is only one Christ (in the sense that there is only one all-embracing 'Lord who is the Spirit' – II Cor. 3:18 RSV). Although this one Christ has made His divine presence manifest in various human temples – Moses, Jesus, Bahá'u'lláh and so forth – He remains 'the same yesterday, and to day, and for ever' (Heb. 13:8). The various human embodiments of the Logos may differ outwardly, each possessing a separate body and an individual human soul, but inwardly they are one Spirit. All are Mirrors reflecting the same Sun, that pre-existent 'Word of God' which was 'with God' and which 'was God' from eternity.

This teaching resolves the paradox which, across the centuries, has confused and divided adherents of different religions: Each sacred Founder of a major world faith has claimed to be the 'only way' to God. Their followers, viewing them as distinct individuals, have regarded these Founders as competitors. In reality, says Bahá'u'lláh, there is no competition because each is indeed the 'only way'. Each speaks as the voice of God through the indwelling reality of the Holy Spirit. Though the same Voice may emanate from various loud-speakers, the Speaker is ever one and the same.

This Bahá'í concept of the 'oneness of religion' is much more fully spelled out in the teachings of Bahá'u'lláh than in the Bible. It is a subtle and challenging principle, one of those 'many things' of which Jesus said 'I have yet many things to say unto you, but ye cannot bear them now. Howbeit when he, the Spirit of Truth, is come, he will guide you into all truth . . .' (John 16:12-13). Nevertheless, Bahá'u'lláh's teaching in no way contradicts the Bible; rather, it is implied and supported by numerous scriptures. Christ, for example, is described in the Old Testament as that Ruler 'whose goings forth have been from of old, from everlasting' (Micah 5:2). These 'goings forth', in the Bahá'í view, include the successive visitations through which the recurring Christ figure has brought to humankind an ever-unfolding vision of God's will and purpose. St Paul explains that 'the grace of God that bringeth salvation hath appeared to all men' (Titus 2:11), while the Apostle John assures us that the 'true Light' of Christ 'lighteth every man that cometh into the world' (John 1:9). Calling Himself the 'good shepherd' and Christians His 'sheep', Jesus Himself states that He has 'other sheep . . . not of this fold' (the 'fold' or enclosure being an apparent reference to Christianity):

> I am the good shepherd, and know my sheep, and am known of mine . . . And other sheep I have, which are not of this fold: them also I must bring, and they shall hear my voice; and there shall be one fold, and one shepherd (John 10:14-16).

Bahá'ís typically interpret the 'one fold, and one shepherd' as a prophecy of Christ's return, when the major religions of the world (Judaism, Christianity, Islam, Hinduism, Buddhism and Zoroastrianism) finally recognize their underlying harmony and accept one another's divine origin.

Is the oneness of religion, as conceived by Bahá'ís, really reasonable? Some would argue that a study of comparative religion discloses irreconcilable contradictions between the world's historic faiths so that their teachings cannot all be 'of God'. Others contend that Moses, Buddha, Muḥammad and other religious figures show wide variations in greatness and character, and cannot, therefore, be identified with Christ's 'quickening spirit' of sinless perfection. How might Bahá'ís respond to such objections?

Let us first consider the supposed conflicts between the teachings of different world faiths, then discuss the personal qualifications of their Founders.

Regarding contradictory teachings, Bahá'ís are well aware of the differences in belief and practice among Christians, Hindus, Buddhists, Muslims and others. (How could we not know this, since vast numbers of people from all these persuasions meet and mingle beneath the banner of Bahá-'u'lláh?) The harmony to which Bahá'u'lláh draws our attention has nothing to do with current popular notions or with technical dogmas articulated by theologians. He is simply affirming an underlying unity of meaning and purpose in the *original teachings* of the inspired Revealers of God's Word. As centuries and millennia roll by, however, the mists of time make it increasingly difficult to discern the real intent of these Founders. Profound changes in language, culture and habits of thought intervene. Misunderstandings gradually crystallize around revealed precepts which may, even at the outset, have been grasped only dimly if at all. This process gains momentum from our all-too-human tendency to complicate simple truths and argue about them. Complex webs of doctrine, serving the political interests of priestly hierarchies, and often bearing little or no resemblance to anything ever said by the Holy Manifestation, sooner or later enshroud His fundamental principles. Most so-called conflicts between religious systems derive from human ideas about revelation, not from revelation itself. A major reason – not the only reason, but an important one – for the 'goings forth' of the Christ Spirit has been to clear away such debris periodically, restoring the pristine purity of revealed truth.

There is, for instance, a widespread notion that Christianity teaches belief in a single God, Hinduism in many 'gods' and Buddhism in no God at all. How can these three world religions all be divinely inspired if they cannot even agree on something so fundamental? This objection dissolves on close examination. Hinduism is an extremely ancient faith, so old that the very name and existence of its Founder are in dispute, and there are few if any reliable records of what He taught. Many scholars, however (including the great Hindu philosopher Rammahan Roy), have argued convincingly that Hindu scriptures (the Vedas) uphold the oneness of God and that Hinduism, though corrupted over the centuries, was originally monotheistic. Buddha appeared within a Hindu society that had already become obsessed with multiple and increasingly anthropomorphic deities. Perhaps wishing to reverse this unwholesome trend, He deemphasized the personal aspects of divinity, instead portraying the Creator as an unknowable Absolute Reality – the ultimate goal of all existence. Indeed, Buddha discouraged speculation about such metaphysical questions, focusing attention more on ethics and spiritual development. To those of us raised in Judeo-Christian tradition, accustomed as we are to thinking of God as an all-loving Father, such an abstract portrayal may indeed appear as a denial of divinity. The Bible itself shows, however, that both perceptions of God are true – and both incomplete, for God's reality transcends all human comprehension.

Some Christians argue that the New Testament concept of salvation by grace is unique to Christianity – that all other religions believe in salvation primarily through human striving. This distinction seems quite artificial. Some doctrine of divine grace, with a corollary insistence on the inadequacy of unaided human effort, exists in the sacred teachings of every world religion I have studied (specifically including Bahá'í, Christianity, Judaism, Islam, Hinduism and Buddhism). While I am no expert on comparative religion, it seems clear to me that this is a point not of division but of unity, any alleged discrepancies being purely semantic.

A clear example of how two religious systems can both be divine in origin, yet hold seemingly irreconcilable beliefs, is afforded by comparing Judaism with Christianity. Jews typically reject such Christian doctrines as the Trinity and the Incarnation, and many Jews doubt the existence of a soul or an afterlife. Yet Christians and Jews both base their faith on divinely revealed scripture. Even within each of these faiths there are vast and often irreconcilable conflicts concerning the nature of God, the soul, salvation and other essentials. None of these controversies disprove the truth of the Old and New Testaments. They do show, however, why we must exercise great caution before concluding that another religion is intrinsically incompatible with our own.

Religions do differ profoundly in such non-essential areas as dietary laws, penal codes, sacramental rituals, marriage and divorce regulations and similar social matters. These external differences, as Bahá'u'lláh says, 'should be attributed to the varying requirements and exigencies of the age in which they were revealed' (G 217). We must not confuse such secondary features with timeless principles of spirit like the Golden Rule, love of God and of one's neighbour, and the necessity of prayer, meditation, ethical behaviour, preparation for death and other matters. It is on this deep and basic level that religion is truly one. Such essentials do not change from age to age; it is only their outward expression and implementation which God, through the 'goings forth' of the Logos, from time to time adapts to the changing needs of His children.

Superficial differences aside, students of comparative religion almost always are struck by the uncanny parallels among various world faiths. These parallels range from ethical prescriptions and philosophical insights to such seemingly arbitrary details as end-time prophecy. Every Founder of a world faith has predicted a 'time of the end' when He Himself (or 'one like unto the Son of man') would return to establish justice and righteousness on earth, bringing together all humanity under one banner. These millennial expectations represent the highest hope of each religious community. It is because He represents the simultaneous fulfilment of all these aspirations that Bahá'u'lláh is qualified to raise the banner beneath which all religions can gather in unity.

If we grant an underlying oneness in the teachings of the world's major faiths, what of the lives and characters of their Founders? Christians historically have regarded Jesus as superior to all other religious figures (just as devotees of other faiths have adopted similar attitudes towards their own sacred teachers). Does it make sense to regard the Lord Christ as manifest not only in Jesus of Nazareth but in other Revelators as well?

For many Christians, this question is especially acute with regard to Moses and Muḥammad. It is often said that Moses – however great He may have been as an inspired Prophet – was a murderer and a sinner who, for His disobedience to God's command, was deservedly punished by being barred from the Promised Land. Moreover, the proposition that Jesus was greater than Moses is affirmed both in the New Testament and (as we shall see) in the Bahá'í teachings. The contrast between Christ and Muḥammad may seem even more stark. In Western societies Muḥammad is often thought of as a villain; while the Muslim holy book, the Qur'án, is sometimes viewed as an attack on everything Christians hold sacred.

Given such perceptions, Christians may naturally take offense at any suggestion that Christ, Moses and Muḥammad all manifest one perfect Spirit of divinity. However, there is much more to the story. Bahá'ís believe that the popular view of Moses as a wrongdoer arises from misunderstanding of certain Bible verses – a misunderstanding easily cleared up by careful study of the relevant texts. The widely circulated charges against Muḥammad are simply false, conflicting as they do with well-substantiated historical facts. Although a detailed exploration of all these issues is beyond the scope of this volume, let us look at the main outlines, starting with Moses.

Moses

The charge that Moses was a murderer derives from Exodus 2:11-12, in which He, having 'spied an Egyptian smiting an Hebrew', slays the Egyptian and hides the body. The word translated in the King James Version as 'smiting' is important because, in the original Hebrew, it connotes killing or slaughter. It suggests that the Egyptian was brutally beating to death a Hebrew slave, one who (like black slaves in the pre-Civil War American South) had no legal standing or recourse. At great personal cost, Moses came to the slave's defence and saved his life in the only way possible: by killing the attacker. No doubt this made Moses guilty of murder under Egyptian law – but the law thus violated was that of Pharaoh, not of God. From the standpoint of divine law and morality, Moses was innocent of any wrong. His act was one of courage and compassion.

More difficult to explain is an apparent rebuke addressed by God to Moses for an incident involving the 'water of Meribah'. It was for this supposed transgression that Moses and Aaron were denied entry into the Promised Land. God attributes this punishment to the fact that 'ye rebelled against my word at the water of Meribah' (Num. 20:24), explaining elsewhere that 'ye trespassed against me among the children of Israel at the waters of Meribah-Kadesh, in the wilderness of Zin; because ye sanctified me not in the midst of the children of Israel' (Deut. 32:51). How can we reconcile these verses with the Bahá'í belief that Moses (as a human mirror for the Divine Christ) was free from sin?

In *Some Answered Questions* 'Abdu'l-Bahá explains that God is here addressing Moses not as an individual but in His capacity as the representative of His people. Though outwardly directed at Moses, the rebuke is really intended for the children of Israel. Just as a king stands for his country, giving and receiving communications in the name of his people and making agreements on their behalf, so does a Divine Messenger:

> In the same way, every Prophet is the expression of the whole of the people. So the promise and speech of God addressed to Him is addressed to all. Generally the speech of reproach and rebuke is rather too severe for the people and would be heartbreaking to them. So the Perfect Wisdom makes use of this form of address, as is clearly shown in the Bible itself . . . (SAQ 167).

The Old Testament accounts of the episode in question bear out 'Abdu'l-Bahá's statement. Exodus 17 relates that the children of Israel, desperate for water in the desert, 'murmured against Moses' and 'tempted the Lord, saying, Is the Lord among us, or not?' God instructed Moses to strike the rock in Horeb with His rod, promising that water would gush forth:

> So Moses did this in the sight of the elders of Israel. And he called the place Massah [literally, testing] and Meribah [literally, quarrelling] because the Israelites quarrelled and because they tested the Lord . . . (Ex. 17:6-7 NIV).

Here Moses is completely obedient; it is the people who rebel by quarrelling and testing God. The incident is repeated at Kadesh, where Moses is commanded to 'Take the rod . . . and speak ye unto the rock before their eyes; and it shall give forth his water . . . And Moses took the rod from before the Lord, as he commanded him.' Denouncing the Israelites as 'ye rebels', Moses 'lifted up his hand, and with his rod he smote the rock twice, and the water came out abundantly . . .' (Num. 20:8-11). Some commentators suggest that Moses transgressed when He 'smote' the rock instead of speaking to it. However, the fact that Moses, wielding the rod 'as [God] commanded him', actually obtained water, suggests that God intended for Moses to 'speak' to the rock through the rod by striking it. Moses' own statement that the 'rebels' in this instance were the people is confirmed in verse 13: 'This is the water of Meribah, because the children of Israel strove with the Lord . . .'

It is on this occasion (verse 12) that God announces His intention to punish Moses and Aaron for the rebellion: 'Because ye believed me not, to sanctify me in the eyes of the children of Israel, therefore ye shall not bring this congregation into the land which I have given them.' In and of itself, this passage leaves the impression that Moses was at fault. Later, however, recalling how fervently He sought permission to enter the Promised Land, Moses explains the reality: 'The Lord was wroth with me *for your sakes*, and would not hear me . . .' (Deut. 3:26; emphasis added). It was on account of His followers' sins – not His own – that Moses suffered. As the surrogate for His people, He took upon Himself the burden of their guilt, thus suffering punishment in their place and shielding them from the wrath of God.

Viewed in this light, Moses' actions not only are blameless but distinctly Christlike. His role is this drama provides a clear precedent for the Christian doctrine of vicarious atonement. It anticipates and prefigures the self-sacrifice of Jesus Christ for the sins of all humanity.

The obedience of Moses as a completely faithful servant is strongly affirmed by God when His siblings, Miriam and Aaron, criticize Him 'because of the Ethiopian woman he had married' (Num. 12:1). (Current prejudices against interracial marriage are obviously nothing new.) Not only does the Lord defend Moses' conduct as proper, He severely punishes the critics – especially Miriam – saying:

> Hear now my words: If there be a prophet among you, I the Lord will make myself known unto him in a vision, and will speak unto him in a dream. My servant Moses is not so, who is *faithful in all my house*. With him will I speak mouth to mouth, even apparently, and not in dark speeches; and the similitude of the Lord shall he behold: wherefore then were ye not afraid to speak against my servant Moses? (Num. 12:6-8; emphasis added).

This passage shows that Moses is far greater than, and qualitatively different from, any 'mere' prophet such as Isaiah, Jeremiah, Daniel and the like. Though He (like Jesus) is sometimes referred to in the Bible as a prophet, Moses belongs to a higher category altogether. From a Bahá'í perspective, the difference resides in His having been a Mirror in which could be seen the radiance of the divine Christ Spirit. He was thus a direct Revealer of God's word and nature, occupying a station to which no ordinary human being can aspire.

Bahá'u'lláh's teaching emphatically does not mean that all Manifestations of the Logos are equal or identical in all respects. The Bible clearly explains the sense in which Jesus was greater than Moses:

> . . . consider the Apostle and High Priest of our profession, Christ Jesus; Who was faithful to him that appointed him, as also Moses was faithful in all his house. For this man was counted worthy of more glory than Moses, inasmuch as he who hath builded the house hath more honour than the house . . . And Moses verily was faithful in all his house, as a servant, for a testimony of those things which were to be spoken after; But Christ as a son over his own house; whose house are we, if we hold fast the confidence and the rejoicing of the hope firm unto the end (Heb. 3:1-6).

Bahá'í teachings echo this insight:

> Consider how one and the same light has reflected itself in the different mirrors or manifestations of it . . . For instance, the Sun of Reality revealed itself in the Mosaic mirror. The people who were sincere accepted and believed in it. When the same Sun shone from the Messianic mirror, the Jews who were not lovers of the Sun and who were fettered by their adoration of the mirror of Moses did not perceive the lights and effulgences of the Sun of Reality resplendent in Jesus; therefore, they were deprived of its bestowals. *Yet the Sun of Reality, the Word of God, shone from the Messianic mirror through the wonderful channel of Jesus Christ more fully and more wonderfully* (PUP 115; emphasis added).

Bahá'u'lláh does make it clear that the admitted difference in greatness between Moses and Jesus (as between any other 'goings forth' of the One Eternal Christ) is a difference of function, not of inherent capacity. Whatever human guise He adopts, the Lord Christ is the same yesterday, today and forever. He may, however, reveal more or less of His glory depending on the needs and capacities of the people to whom He comes. He may do more or less, depending on the time and circumstances of His mission. Otherwise, these human temples of the Divine Presence are one:

> They only differ in the intensity of their revelation and the comparative potency of their light . . . That a certain attribute of God hath not been outwardly manifested by these Essences of Detachment doth in no wise imply that they Who are the Day Springs of God's attributes and the Treasuries of His holy names doth not actually possess it (WOB 115).

Muḥammad

The Arabs of the early seventh century were nomadic tribesmen, tending meagre flocks and herds in the semi-desert regions of the Arabian Peninsula. Steeped in idolatry, they were prone to violence, cruelty, feuding, drinking, gambling and prostitution. Women, typically living as virtual slaves in poorly treated harems of enormous size, were held in such contempt that unwanted infant girls were buried alive. Islam quickly revolutionized these conditions. Idolatry was replaced by strict monotheism; drinking, gambling and prostitution were abolished; polygamy was greatly curtailed and the status of women immensely elevated; tribal warfare gave way to spiritual brotherhood. As a result the Arabs, within a mere one hundred years, became masters of an empire vaster than that of Rome at its peak. As Western Europe sank into the Dark Ages, Islam adorned its cities with paved and lighted streets, built flourishing universities and libraries, introduced soap, algebra, Arabic numerals, table etiquette and many other useful innovations, and (during its centuries in Spain) indirectly triggered Europe's Renaissance.

These and countless other achievements testify to the beneficent influence of one man, Muḥammad, who, as the Founder of Islam, is ironically among the most maligned individuals in history. Most of us have heard that He was a bloodthirsty conqueror who 'converted' people to Islam at swordpoint; that He was a lecherous sex fiend with hundreds or perhaps thousands of young wives and concubines; that He oppressed Christians and fostered religious intolerance; that His legacy was one of hatred and fanaticism. There is not a grain of truth in any of these charges. Concerning such allegations, 'Abdu'l-Bahá says:

> Americans and Europeans have heard a number of stories about the Prophet which they have thought to be true, although the narrators were either ignorant or antagonistic: most of them were clergy; others were ignorant Muslims who repeated unfounded traditions about Muḥammad which they ignorantly believed to be to His praise.

Thus some benighted Muslims made His polygamy the pivot of their praises and held it to be a wonder, regarding it as a miracle; and European historians, for the most part, rely on the tales of these ignorant people.

For example, a foolish man said to a clergyman that the true proof of greatness is bravery and the shedding of blood, and that in one day on the field of battle a follower of Muḥammad had cut off the heads of one hundred men! This misled the clergyman to infer that killing is considered the way to prove one's faith to Muḥammad, while this is merely imaginary (SAQ 18).

Muḥammad, a merchant by trade, was born in 570 AD. Like Jesus and Bahá'u'lláh, He received no formal schooling (though the holy book He revealed, the Qur'án, is recognized by all impartial scholars as one of the world's great literary works, and is revered by millions as divine revelation). At about age forty He announced to the scornful townspeople of Mecca that He had received a mandate from God. For thirteen years He and a handful of followers patiently endured violent persecution, turning the other cheek just as Jesus would have done. His enemies, in 622 AD, finally forced Him to flee from Mecca to the rival city of Medina, where – to their consternation – He was welcomed and elevated to the rank of chief. Enraged by Muḥammad's opposition to their idol-worship, the clans and tribes of Arabia marched on Medina intending to destroy it.

It was under these circumstances that Muḥammad became, for a short time, a kind of general, not unlike Moses, Joshua and other biblical heroes. He organized military expeditions not for conquest, or even in His own defence, but to save an innocent populace that would otherwise have been slaughtered on His account. 'Abdu'l-Bahá says:

> Look at it with justice. If Christ Himself had been placed in such circumstances . . . culminating in flight from His native land – if in spite of this these lawless tribes continued to pursue Him, to slaughter the men, to pillage their prop-

erty, and to capture their women and children – what would have been Christ's conduct with regard to them? If this oppression had fallen only upon Himself, He would have forgiven them . . . but if He had seen that these cruel and bloodthirsty murderers wished to kill, to pillage and to injure all these oppressed ones, and to take captive the women and children, it is certain that He would have protected them and would have resisted the tyrants . . . To free these tribes from their bloodthirstiness was the greatest kindness, and to coerce and restrain them was a true mercy (SAQ 20-1).

Through brilliant leadership, and against long odds, Muḥammad prevailed, then consolidated His victory by welding the rival clans into a great Arab nation. This enabled Him to introduce desperately needed reforms, including (among many others) legal measures to enhance the status of women. Polygamy, on a vast scale, was a deeply entrenched institution before Muḥammad appeared. Not only did He greatly curtail this practice, He paved the way for its eventual phasing out. He encouraged His male followers to take no more than one wife each but allowed up to four, on strict condition that all be treated with equal justice (Q 4:3). By simultaneously emphasizing that such justice is, in a practical sense, well-nigh impossible (Q 4:128), He clearly envisioned a future in which plurality of wives could be explicitly abolished.

Muḥammad Himself was celibate until the age of twenty-six, when He married a beautiful forty-two-year-old widow named Khadíjih. Defying custom, they lived together in strict monogamy until she died, twenty-three years later. Their relationship is considered one of the great love stories of all time. In the nine years following Khadíjih's death, Muḥammad married a number of widows left destitute when their husbands (usually followers of Islam, though sometimes its enemies) died in battle. Some were middle-aged, with children by former marriages, in an age when the only options available to most women were marriage, prostitution or starvation. Muḥammad also agreed to marry two daughters of desert chiefs who sought, through family ties, to forge political alliances.

While the exact number (probably twelve or thirteen) of His later marriages is uncertain, it is clear that these were dictated usually by charity and occasionally by statesmanship. Had the motive been lust, as His enemies have insinuated, Muḥammad could freely have taken any number of beautiful young wives – a thousand virgins, had He wished. Such a policy was not only possible for, but fully expected of, any ruler of His era. (Parvíz, a contemporary king of Persia, had twelve thousand wives.) The humanitarian impulse behind Muḥammad's multiple marriages is clear in any case, but particularly when we contrast His actions with the social conventions of His world.

The widespread belief that Muḥammad opposed Christianity and Christians could not be more false. The Qur'án testifies throughout to the truth of the Bible as the Word of God and Jesus Christ as the embodied 'Spirit of God'. Muḥammad discouraged use of the expression 'Son of God' because it implied, to the coarse and literal-minded Arabs, a purely biological kinship deriving from sex. He wished to emphasize (as does the Bible) that God is Spirit. Nevertheless, the Qur'án strongly upholds belief in the virgin birth. Muḥammad also denounced as false any interpretation of the Trinity that compromises the concept of the oneness of God, such interpretations being bound to reinforce the already polytheistic outlook of an idolatrous culture. Yet a spiritual understanding of the Trinity, such as we find in the letters of St Paul and the teachings of Bahá'u'lláh, is entirely consistent with the Qur'án. (See Chapter 3 of this volume.) Muḥammad once said that the Jews had failed to crucify the 'real Jesus' – a statement sometimes misconstrued to mean that an imposter was nailed to the cross in His place. His obvious meaning, however, was that in crucifying Christ's body his foes were unable to harm the true reality of His immortal spirit. These and a few other teachings are hailed by some as 'proof' that the Bible and the Qur'án are in conflict. A close look at the context and intent will expose, in every case, the hollowness of such misconceptions.

Muḥammad declared that all Christians living within His domains were under His personal protection, and that any Muslim violating their rights would answer to Him. To this pronouncement He gave legal teeth through a charter, guaranteeing and spelling out their rights in perpetuity. Thus Christians were free to worship as they chose; free to build and maintain churches (which Muslims, in the event such churches were damaged or destroyed, were to help them rebuild); free to marry Muslims without converting to Islam; and free – in return for a small annual tax – from two requirements binding on Muslims: military service and the 'poor-rate', a charitable levy.

Contrary to popular Western stereotypes (which, it must be said, are reinforced by the practice of some modern militant regimes professing to be 'Islamic'), Muḥammad's teaching permits warfare only in self-defence and under well-defined conditions. The Qur'án commands: 'Fight in the way of God against those who attack you, but begin not hostilities, for God loveth not the transgressors' (Q 2:186). Forced conversion to Islam is strictly forbidden: 'Let there be no compulsion in religion' (Q 2:257). 'What! wilt thou compel men to become believers? No soul can believe but by the permission of God . . .' (Q 10:99-100). As a result of these counsels, Christians and other minorities flourished for centuries under Muslim rule, at times when religious freedom and tolerance were unheard-of in most of Europe.*

---

*Bahá'ís, who often suffer dire persecution today in Muslim lands, know all too well that some who honour Muḥammad forget to honour His teachings. However, it would be no more fair to blame Muḥammad for their present-day excesses than it would be to blame Christ for atrocities committed in His name by Crusaders or the Inquisition.

'Abdu'l-Bahá sums up the situation clearly:

> This is the truth: we are not bigoted and do not wish to defend [Muḥammad], but we are just, and we say what is just . . . During the Middle Ages, while Europe was in the lowest depths of barbarism, the Arab peoples were superior to the other nations of the earth in learning, in the arts, mathematics, civilization, government and other sciences. The Enlightener and Educator of these Arab tribes, and the Founder of the civilization and perfections of humanity among these different races, was an illiterate Man, Muḥammad. Was this illustrious Man a thorough Educator or not? A just judgement is necessary (SAQ 20, 24).

Conclusion

It is characteristic of young children that they ask lots of questions – questions that are persistent, probing, often original and sometimes startlingly insightful. My mother, Charmian Matthews, believed that this is one of the qualities to which Jesus referred when He said that only by becoming like little children can we enter the kingdom of Heaven (Matt. 18:3). An inquisitive outlook is, in any case, strongly enjoined in scripture: 'Ask, and it shall be given you; seek, and ye shall find; knock, and it shall be opened unto you' (Matt. 7:7). 'It is the glory of God to conceal a thing: but the honour of kings is to search out a matter' (Prov. 25:2).

The questions and answers offered in this volume merely hint at the boundless riches to be found in the treasury of Bahá'u'lláh's Revelation. No book such as this can possibly raise, much less resolve, every question one might reasonably ask, whether from a Christian perspective or any other. In my experience, however, Bahá'u'lláh's teachings provide sound and satisfying answers even in cases where a particular question may, on the surface, appear unanswerable.

Having said this, I would like to repeat the invitation extended at the beginning of this book: I am eager to learn about the reader's reaction. Anyone with questions or comments about any Bahá'í-related subject is invited to correspond with me in care of the publisher. If – as may well happen – I am unable to answer a given question, I will do my best to find someone who can. Please write to me at the address given on page *x* of this book.

The great Dr Benjamin Jowett, Master of Balliol College, Oxford, once said: 'The Bahá'í Faith is the greatest light to come into the world since the time of Christ. You must watch it and never let it out of your sight.' Bahá'u'lláh asks only that we 'ascertain whether or not such a light hath appeared', then – if we find it so – follow that light. I can conceive no greater privilege than that of assisting another soul in that investigation.

The words of Christ reach us across the centuries:

. . . behold, I have set before thee an open door, and no man can shut it: for thou hast a little strength, and hast kept my word, and hast not denied my name.

. . . Him that overcometh I will make a pillar in the temple of my God, and he shall go no more out: and I will write upon him the name of my God, and the name of the city of my God, which is new Jerusalem, which cometh down out of heaven from my God: and I will write upon him my new name.

He that hath an ear, let him hear what the Spirit saith unto the churches (Rev. 3:8-13).

Appendix B

Becoming a Bahá'í

Bahá'ís are forbidden to proselytize or pressure other into accepting their beliefs. The only reason one should become a Bahá'í is because his or her heart has been touched by Bahá'u'lláh, the Glory of God. There can be no other valid reason.

Some respond quickly, others take longer, still others may never recognize Bahá'u'lláh's station at all. It is up to each individual to investigate the Cause of Bahá'u'lláh for himself or herself.

But if you can truthfully say . . .

☐ *I believe in Bahá'u'lláh as the Messenger of God for this age;*

☐ *I hereby affirm my wholehearted readiness to obey His laws and teachings; and*

☐ *I accept the authority of the institutions He has established;*

then please turn the page, fill out the attached form and present it to any member or institution of the Bahá'í community. If you are in touch with Bahá'ís in your area, give it to one of them or ask what to do with it. If not, and if you cannot find a local telephone listing for the Bahá'í Faith, then please mail or fax the form to one of the addresses listed on the next page.

National Spiritual Assembly of the
  Bahá'ís of the United States
536 Sheridan Road
Wilmette, IL 60091
UNITED STATES OF AMERICA
Tel: 1 (708) 869-9039
Fax: 1 (708) 869-0247

National Spiritual Assembly
  of the Bahá'ís of Canada
7200 Leslie Street
Thornhill
Ont L3T 6L8
CANADA
Tel: 1 (905) 889-8168
Fax: 1 (905) 889-8184

National Spiritual Assembly
  of the Bahá'ís of Australia
P.O. Box 285
Mona Vale
NSW 2103
AUSTRALIA
Tel: 61 (2) 9913-2771
Fax: 61 (2) 9970-7275

National Spiritual Assembly of the
  Bahá'ís of the United Kingdom
27 Rutland Gate
London SW7 1PD
ENGLAND
Tel: 44 (171) 584-2566
Fax: 44 (171) 584-9402

National Spiritual Assembly of the
  Bahá'ís of the Netherlands
Riouwstraal 27
2585 GB The Hague
NETHERLANDS
Tel: 31 (70) 355-4017
Fax: 31 (70) 350-6161

National Spiritual Assembly
  of the Bahá'ís of Alaska
13501 Brayton Drive
Anchorage
ALASKA 99516
Tel: 1 (907) 345-3740
Fax: 1 (907) 345-3739

National Spiritual Assembly of the
  Bahá'ís of the Hawaiian Islands
3264 Allan Place
Honolulu
HAWAII 96817
Tel: 1 (808) 595-3314
Fax: 1 (808) 595-4468

National Spiritual Assembly of the
  Bahá'ís of the Republic of Ireland
24 Burlington Road
Dublin 4
REPUBLIC OF IRELAND
Tel: 353 (1) 668-3150
Fax: 353 (1) 668-9632

National Spiritual Assembly of
  the Bahá'ís of New Zealand
P.O. Box 21-551
Henderson
Auckland 8
NEW ZEALAND
Tel: 64 (9) 837-4866
Fax: 64 (9) 837-4898

National Spiritual Assembly of
  the Bahá'ís of South Africa
P.O. Box 2142
Houghton 2041
SOUTH AFRICA
Tel: 27 (11) 487-2077
Fax: 27 (11) 487-1809

National Spiritual Assembly
  of the Bahá'ís of Germany
Eppsteiner Strasse 89
D-65719 Hofheim
GERMANY
Tel: 49 (6192) 99290
Fax: 49 (6232) 49384

National Spiritual Assembly
  of the Bahá'ís of Switzerland
Dufourstrasse 13
CH-3005 Bern
SWITZERLAND
Tel: 41 (31) 352-1020
Fax: 41 (31) 352-4716

National Spiritual Assembly
  of the Bahá'ís of Kenya
P.O. Box 47562
Nairobi
KENYA
Tel: 254 (2) 725-447
Fax: 254 (2) 726-728

National Spiritual Assembly
  of the Bahá'ís of France
45 rue Pergolese
F-75116 Paris
FRANCE
Tel: 33 (1) 4500-9026
Fax: 33 (1) 4500-0579

National Spiritual Assembly
  of the Bahá'ís of Grenada
P.O. Box 323
GRENADA
West Indies
Tel: 1 (809) 440-1863
Fax: 1 (809) 444-4647

Bahá'í Registration   (please print)

Title (Mr., Mrs., Ms., etc.) _____   Full Name — please do not use nicknames _____

Birth Date:
(if under 21)

____ / ____ / ____
Day   Month   Year

Full Address
of Residence: _____

_____   ZIP or Locality Code _____

Telephone Numbers:

Full Mailing
Address: _____   Home: _____

_____   ZIP or Locality Code _____   Work: _____

I believe in Bahá'u'lláh as the Messenger of God for this Age, and I hereby affirm my wholehearted readiness to obey His laws and teachings and to accept the authority of the institutions He has established.

Signature _____   Date _____

Bibliography

The Kings James Version of the Bible has been used throughout, except where otherwise indicated in the text.

'Abdu'l-Bahá. *Japan Will Turn Ablaze!* Japan: Bahá'í Publishing Trust, 1974.

— *Paris Talks*. London: Bahá'í Publishing Trust, 1979.

— *The Promulgation of Universal Peace*. Wilmette, Ill.: Bahá'í Publishing Trust, 1982.

— *The Secret of Divine Civilization*. Wilmette, Ill.: Bahá'í Publishing Trust, 1990.

— *Selections from the Writings of 'Abdu'l-Bahá*. Haifa: Bahá'í World Centre, 1978.

— *Some Answered Questions*. Wilmette, Ill.: Bahá'í Publishing Trust, 1990.

— *Tablets of Abdul-Baha Abbas*. New York: Bahá'í Publishing Committee. 3 vols. 1930.

Abúl-Faḍl, Mírzá. *Letters and Essays: 1886-1913*. trans. Juan R.I. Cole. Los Angeles: Kalimat Press, 1985.

Appreciations of the Bahá'í Faith, Wilmette, Ill.: Bahá'í Publishing Committee, 1947.

The Báb, *Selections from the Writings of the Báb*. Haifa: Bahá'í World Centre, 1976.

Bach, Marcus. *Strangers at the Door*. Nashville: Abingdon Press, 1971.

Bahá'í World, The. vol. 13, 1954-63. Haifa: The Universal House of Justice, 1970.

Bahá'í World Faith. Wilmette, Ill.: Bahá'í Publishing Trust, 1976.

Bahá'u'lláh. *Epistle to the Son of the Wolf*. Wilmette, Ill.: Bahá'í Publishing Trust, 1988.

— *Gleanings from the Writings of Bahá'u'lláh*. Wilmette, Ill.: Bahá'í Publishing Trust, 1983.

— *The Hidden Words*. Wilmette, Ill.: Bahá'í Publishing Trust, 1990.

— *The Kitáb-i-Aqdas, The Most Holy Book*. Haifa: Bahá'í World Centre, 1992.

— *Kitáb-i-Íqán*. Wilmette, Ill.: Bahá'í Publishing Trust, 1989.

— *Prayers and Meditations*. Wilmette, Ill.: Bahá'í Publishing Trust, 1987.

— *Proclamation of Bahá'u'lláh to the Kings and Leaders of the World*. Haifa: Bahá'í World Centre, 1967.

— *Tablets of Bahá'u'lláh revealed after the Kitáb-i-Aqdas*. Wilmette, Ill.: Bahá'í Publishing Trust, 1988.

Balyuzi, H. M. *'Abdu'l-Bahá*. Oxford: George Ronald, 1971.

Beeston, A.F.L., 'Arabic Language', *Academic American Encyclopedia*. vol. II, 1989.

Blomfield, Lady [Sara Louise]. *The Chosen Highway*. Wilmette, Ill.: Bahá'í Publishing Trust, 1967.

Born, Max. *The Born-Einstein Letters*. New York: Walker, 1971.

Britannica Book of the Year (1988).

Cheyne, T.K. *The Reconciliation of Races and Religions*. London: Adam and Charles Black, 1914.

Clark, Ronald W. *Einstein – The Life and Times*. New York: Avon Books, 1972.

Clarke, Arthur C. *Profiles of the Future*. London: Victor Gollancz Ltd., 1982.

Cooper, L. *An Introduction to the Meaning and Structure of Physics*. New York: Harper & Row, 1968.

Cotran, Ramzi S., Kumar, Vinay and Robbins, Stanley L. *Robbins Pathologic Basis of Disease*. Philadelphia: WB Saunders Company – Harcourt Brace Jovanovich, Inc. 1989.

Della Vida, G.L. 'Arabic Language', *Collier's Encyclopedia*. vol. II, 1990.

Dulbecco, Renato and Ginsberg, Harold S. *Virology*. Philadelphia: J. B. Lippincott Company, 1988.

Diary of Juliet Thompson, The. Los Angeles: Kalimát Press, 1983.

Esslemont, John E. *Bahá'u'lláh and the New Era*. London: Bahá'í Publishing Trust, 1974.

Evans, Winston and Gail, Marzieh. 'The Voice from Inner Space', *World Order*, Summer 1967.

Ferris, Timothy. *Coming of Age in the Milky Way*. New York: Anchor Books, 1989.

Gamow, George. *The Birth and Death of the Sun*. New York: Viking Press, 1946.

Gardner, Martin. *Relativity for the Million*. New York: The Macmillan Company, 1962.

Hawking, Stephen W. *A Brief History of Time*. New York: Bantam Books, 1988.

Hitti, Phillip K. 'Arab Civilization', *Encyclopedia Americana*. vol. II, 1990.

Holy Bible (King James Version, New International Version, New English Bible, Revised Standard Version).

Jordan, Daniel C. *Becoming Your True Self*. Wilmette, Ill.: Bahá'í Publishing Trust, 1968.

The Koran. trans. J. M. Rodwell. London: Dent, 1963.

Lights of Guidance: A Bahá'í Reference File. Compiled by Helen Hornby. New Delhi: Bahá'í Publishing Trust, 2nd edn. 1988.

Lovejoy, C. Owen. 'Evolution of Human Walking', *Scientific American*, November 1988.

Misner, Charles W.; Thorne, Kip S. and Wheeler, John A. *Gravitation*. San Francisco: Freeman, 1973.

Motlagh, Hushidar. *I Shall Come Again*. Mount Pleasant, Mich.: Global Perspective, 1992.

Morrison, Gayle. *To Move the World*. Wilmette, Ill.: Bahá'í Publishing Trust, 1982.

Nabíl, *The Dawn-Breakers*. Wilmette, Ill.: Bahá'í Publishing Trust, 1962.

Robbins, Stanley L. and Kumar, Vinay. *Basic Pathology*. Philadelphia: WB Saunders Company – Harcourt Brace Jovanovich, Inc. 1987.

Shoghi Effendi. *The Advent of Divine Justice*. Wilmette, Ill.: Bahá'í Publishing Trust, 1990.

— *Citadel of Faith: Messages to America 1947-1957*. Wilmette, Ill.: Bahá'í Publishing Trust, 1965.

— *God Passes By*. Wilmette, Ill.: Bahá'í Publishing Trust, rev. edn. 1974.

— *The Promised Day is Come*. Wilmette, Ill.: Bahá'í Publishing Trust, rev. edn. 1980.

— *The Unfolding Destiny of the British Bahá'í Community: The Messages of the Guardian of the Bahá'í Faith to the Bahá'ís of the British Isles*. London: Bahá'í Publishing Trust, 1981.

— *The World Order of Bahá'u'lláh*. Wilmette, Ill.: Bahá'í Publishing Trust, 1955.

Sours, Michael. *Jesus Christ in Sacred Bahá'í Literature*. Oxford: Oneworld Publications Ltd., 1995.

— *Preparing for a Bahá'í/Christian Dialogue: Volume I: Understanding Biblical Evidence*. Oxford: Oneworld Publications Ltd., 1990.

— *Preparing for a Bahá'í/Christian Dialogue: Volume 2: Understanding Christian Beliefs*. Oxford: Oneworld Publications Ltd., 1990.

— *The Prophecies of Jesus*. Oxford: Oneworld Publications Ltd., 1991.

Star of the West. Rpt in 8 vols. Oxford: George Ronald, 1984.

Taherzadeh, Adib. *The Revelation of Bahá'u'lláh*. Oxford: George Ronald, vol. 2, 1977; vol. 3, 1983.

Toynbee, Arnold. *A Study of History*, VIII. London: Oxford University Press, 1954.

The Universal House of Justice. *Individual Rights and Freedoms in the World Order*. Wilmette, Ill.: Bahá'í Publishing Trust, 1989.

— *Messages from the Universal House of Justice, 1968-1973*. Wilmette, Ill.: Bahá'í Publishing Trust, 1976.

— *Wellspring of Guidance*. Wilmette, Ill.: Bahá'í Publishing Trust, 1969.

White, Ellen G. *The Great Controversy*. Mountain View, Calif.: Pacific Press, 1971.

Wilber, Ken, ed. *Quantum Questions: Mystical Writings of the World's Greatest Physicists*. Boulder & London: Shambhala, 1984.

Williams, L. Pearce. 'Ether', *The Encyclopedia Americana*, 1989, vol. X, p. 609.

Wolf, Fred Alan. *Taking the Quantum Leap*. New York: Harper & Rowe, 1981. Perennial Library edn. 1989.

Yourgrau, Wolfgang and Breck, Allen D., eds., *Cosmology, History, and Theology*, (New York: Plenum Press, 1977.

List of Abbreviations

The following abbreviations are used in the text. Please refer to the Bibliography for full details.

AB	*'Abdu'l-Bahá* (Balyuzi)
ADJ	*The Advent of Divine Justice*
BNE	*Bahá'u'lláh and the New Era*
BWF	*Bahá'í World Faith*
CF	*Citadel of Faith*
CH	*The Chosen Highway*
DB	*The Dawn-Breakers*
ESW	*Epistle to the Son of the Wolf*
G	*Gleanings from the Writings of Bahá'u'lláh*
GPB	*God Passes By*
KI	*Kitáb-i-Íqán (Book of Certitude)*
LOG	*Lights of Guidance*
MUHJ	*Messages from the Universal House of Justice 1968-1973*
NEB	*New English Bible*
NIV	*New International Version Bible*
PB	*The Proclamation of Bahá'u'lláh*
PDC	*The Promised Day is Come*
PHW	*Persian Hidden Words*
PM	*Prayers and Meditations*
PT	*Paris Talks*
PUP	*The Promulgation of Universal Peace*
Q	*The Qur'án*
RSV	*Revised Standard Version Bible*
SAB	*Selections from the Writings of 'Abdu'l-Bahá*
SAQ	*Some Answered Questions*
SDC	*The Secret of Divine Civilization*
SWB	*Selections from the Writings of the Báb*
TAB	*Tablets of 'Abdu'l-Bahá*
TB	*Tablets of Bahá'u'lláh*
UD	*The Unfolding Destiny of the British Bahá'í Community*

WG   *Wellspring of Guidance*
WOB   *The World Order of Bahá'u'lláh*

The following abbreviations are used for books of the Bible.

Chron	Chronicles
Col	Colossians
Cor	Corinthians
Dan	Daniel
Deut	Deuteronomy
Eph	Ephesians
Ex	Exodus
Eze	Ezekiel
Gal	Galatians
Heb	Hebrews
Isa	Isaiah
Jer	Jeremiah
Mal	Malachi
Matt	Matthew
Num	Numbers
Phil	Philippians
Prov	Proverbs
Rev	Revelation
Rom	Romans
Thess	Thessalonians
Tim	Timothy
Zech	Zechariah

Index

182, 199, 211, 251, 252, 255,
257, 263, 290-6, 299, 312,
319, 325, 328, 334, 335,
337-42, 352, 354, 356, 361,
363-6
Lord of Hosts, 99, 101, 113
Lorentz, Hendrik, 239
Lovejoy, C. Owen, 232
Lucifer, 349
Lucy, 232, 233

Manifestations, 69, 71, 293, 344,
365, 366
Martin, Alfred W., 303
Martin, J. Douglas, 321
Marx, Karl, 188
Marxism, 190
Master, 4, 50, 77, 277, 373
materialism, 28, 235, 258
maturity, 122, 128, 207
mechanical model, 234, 245, 246
Messenger, 114, 363
Messiah, 4, 5, 7, 8, 10, 11, 13-15,
18, 23, 27, 80, 83, 100, 105-9,
114, 131, 138, 139, 141, 143,
147, 156, 290, 292, 328
Michelson, A. A., 207, 239
Mihdí, Mírzá, 118
Milky Way, 221, 381
Miller, William, 110
miracles, 84, 134-7, 289
mirror, 54, 55, 61-7, 78-82, 98,
203, 236, 307, 328, 363, 365,
366
Naẓar 'Alí, Mírzá, 295, 296
Misner, Charles, 244
missing link, 231-3
models, 54, 62, 64, 128, 216,
218, 222-4, 230, 234, 245,
246, 250, 280, 322
moderation, 207, 208
modernity, 275, 331
monarchy, 114, 158, 177,

179-81, 183, 329, 330
Morley, Edward, 239
Moses, 32, 42, 135, 138, 186,
293, 356, 358, 361-6, 368
Most Great Peace, 161, 253, 255
Mount Carmel, 28, 115, 119,
158, 195-7, 330
Muẓaffari'd-Dín Sháh, 177
Muḥammad VI, 173, 184
Muḥammad-'Alí, 177, 201
Muḥammad-'Alí Sháh, 177
Muḥammad, 114, 173, 177, 184,
201, 356, 358, 361, 362,
366-71
mullás, 178

Nabíl, 285, 382
Náṣiri'd-Dín Sháh, 158, 174-8,
195, 196, 251
Napoleon, 158, 161, 162, 166,
251, 329
nationalism, 185, 187, 189
nature, 49, 50, 54, 55, 57-61, 64,
70, 74, 75, 79, 80, 82, 86, 124,
145, 159, 174, 204, 209, 214,
227, 230, 231, 239, 245, 246,
248, 250, 256, 281, 282, 298,
307, 318, 329, 330, 336, 343,
345, 347, 348, 350, 351, 354,
360, 365
Navváb, 297
Nazis, 158, 190, 191, 330
Neanderthal man, 231
neutron flux, 219
New Testament, 6, 17, 42, 44, 48,
49, 54, 64, 70, 75, 80, 99, 128,
290, 306, 344, 359, 361
Newton, Isaac, 234, 270
Nicaragua, 188
Nicolas, A. L. M., 85
Nightingale of Paradise, 256

Old Testament, 4, 12, 13, 15, 18,

The Challenge of Bahá'u'lláh

Gary L. Matthews

In the 19th century Bahá'u'lláh prophesied the 'lamentations of Berlin', the downfall of Germany in two world wars; He warned against the development of nuclear weapons; He foresaw the day when space travel would be possible . . .

Who was Bahá'u'lláh? He claimed to be the Messenger of God for this age. He said His teachings held the key to a peaceful and united world. Is this true? How can we test the validity of this claim?

Gary L. Matthews suggests a number of possible ways. Such a person should:

- be able correctly to describe future events

- be able to understand scientific facts not yet discovered in His time

- possess skills not acquired in any school

- display a deep grasp of spiritual and social problems beyond the experience of His most learned contemporaries

- live a life in accord with His teachings

Matthews examines the prophecies, predictions, life and character of Bahá'u'lláh – and comes to an astounding conclusion.

Softcover: (-360-7)

Christ and Bahá'u'lláh

George Townshend

A profound and challenging book written with clarity and reverence by a dignitary of the Church of Ireland who resigned his orders to proclaim the truth that Christ has come again to an unheeding world.

For centuries this return has been a central theme of Christian hope and is associated with the establishment of the Kingdom of God on earth. Could it not be that the confusion and stress, the oppression and darkness of our day – a day which has witnessed the return of the Jews to the Holy Land – are the very signs and portents Christ gave to His followers?

The author of this book certainly believes it is so. He addresses particularly the Christians of the West, who, he says, are called first to the service of Christ at His return. He declares unequivocally that the great World Redeemer of the Bible – the Lord of Hosts, the Spirit of Truth of the New Testament – is no other than Bahá'u'lláh, Founder of the Bahá'í Faith in the 19th century.

This is a book that no Christian should miss. It might be true.

Softcover: (-005-5)

The Heart of the Gospel

George Townshend

Too long out of print – now back in softcover!

'World-history at its core and in its essence', wrote George Townshend, 'is the story of the spiritual evolution of mankind . . . The Bible makes the tracing of this evolution its own special subject.'

The Heart of the Gospel unfolds this vast perspective. It is the fruit of the author's long study of comparative religion. Using only the text of the Bible, the author provides a new reading of Scripture which is compelling and timely.

The Heart of the Gospel is a guide-book for those who seek a universal view of religion and of the contemporary world.

Softcover: (-020-9)

GR

The Bahá'í Religion
A Short Introduction to its History and Teachings

Peter Smith

Here is a straightforward, factual account of the rise of the latest of the world's universal religions. A sociologist of religion examines the tenets of the Bahá'í Faith and the beliefs and practices of the Bahá'ís. Subjects covered include:

- the emergence and development of the Bahá'í Faith
- religious doctrines
- social doctrines
- morality and spirituality
- community life
- Bahá'í administration

Includes a lengthy appendix of materials selected from the Bahá'í scriptures and from the writings of Shoghi Effendi, a chronology of Bahá'í history, and charts outlining the administrative organization of the religion.

Softcover: (-277-5)

GR